W9-CLI-791

THE COMPLETE WORKS OF ROBERT BROWNING, VOLUME VII

Portrait of Robert Browning by Samuel Lawrence, 1866.

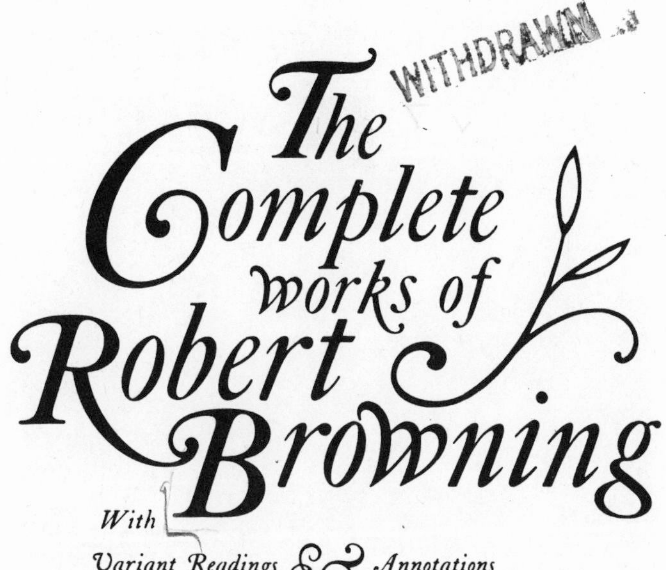

EDITORIAL BOARD

JACK W. HERRING *General Editor*

ROMA A. KING, JR.

PARK HONAN

A. N. KINCAID

ALLAN C. DOOLEY *Executive Editor*

Volume VII

OHIO UNIVERSITY PRESS
ATHENS, OHIO
BAYLOR UNIVERSITY
WACO, TEXAS
1985

Members of the Editorial Staff who have assisted in the preparation of Volume VII:

John Berkey
Ashby Bland Crowder, Jr.
Susan Crowl
Nathaniel Hart

Library of Congress Catalog Card Number: 68-18389
ISBN 0-8214-0230-7

Printed in the United States of America

CONTENTS

Preface

I contents

This edition of the works of Robert Browning is intended to be complete. It will comprise at least fourteen volumes and will contain:

1. The entire contents of the first editions of Browning's works, arranged in their chronological order of publication. (The poems included in *Dramatic Lyrics, Dramatic Romances and Lyrics,* and *Men and Women,* for example, appear in the order of their first publication rather than in the order in which Browning rearranged them for later publication.)
2. All prefaces and dedications which Browning is known to have written for his own works and for those of Elizabeth Barrett Browning.
3. The two prose essays that Browning is known to have published: the review of a book on Tasso, generally referred to as the "Essay on Chatterton," and the preface for a collection of letters supposed to have been written by Percy Bysshe Shelley, generally referred to as the "Essay on Shelley."
4. The front matter and the table of contents of each of the collected editions (1849, 1863, 1865, 1868, 1888-1889) which Browning himself saw through the press.
5. Poems published during Browning's lifetime but not collected by him.
6. Poems not published during Browning's lifetime which have come to light since his death.
7. John Forster's *Thomas Wentworth, Earl of Strafford,* to which Browning contributed significantly, though the precise extent of his contribution has not been determined.
8. Variants appearing in primary and secondary materials as defined in Section II below.
9. Textual emendations.
10. Informational and explanatory notes for each work.

II primary and secondary materials

Aside from a handful of uncollected short works, all of Browning's works but *Asolando* (1889) went through two or more editions during his lifetime. Except for *Pauline* (1833), *Strafford* (1837), and *Sordello* (1840), all the works published before 1849 were revised and corrected for the 1849 collection. *Strafford* and *Sordello* were revised and corrected for the collection of 1863, as were all the other works in that edition. Though no further poems were added in the collection of 1865, all the works were once again corrected and revised. The 1868 collection added a revised *Pauline* and *Dramatis Personae* (1864) to the other works, which were themselves again revised and corrected. The printing of the last edition of the *Poetical Works* over which Browning exercised control began in 1888, and the first eight volumes are dated thus on their title-pages. Volumes 9 through 16 of this first impression are dated 1889, and we have designated them 1889a to distinguish them from the second impression of all 16 volumes, which was begun and completed in 1889. Some of the earlier volumes of the first impression sold out almost immediately, and in preparation for a second impression, Browning revised and corrected the first ten volumes before he left for Italy in late August, 1889. The second impression, in which all sixteen volumes bear the date 1889 on their title-pages, consisted of a revised and corrected second impression of volumes 1-10, plus a second impression of volumes 11-16 altered by Browning in one instance. This impression we term 1889 (see section III below).

Existing manuscripts and editions are classified as either primary or secondary material. The primary materials include the following:

1. The manuscript of a work when such is known to exist.

2. Proof sheets, when known to exist, that contain authorial corrections and revisions.

3. The first and subsequent editions of a work that preserve evidence of Browning's intentions and were under his control.

4. The collected editions over which Browning exercised control:

1849—*Poems*. Two Volumes. London: Chapman and Hall.

1863—*The Poetical Works*. Three Volumes. London: Chapman and Hall.

1865—*The Poetical Works*. Three Volumes. London: Chapman and Hall.

1868—*The Poetical Works*. Six Volumes. London: Smith, Elder and Company. Reissued in stereotype impressions with varying title pages.

1888-1889—*The Poetical Works*. Sixteen Volumes. London: Smith, Elder and Company. Exists in numerous stereotype impressions, of which two are primary material:

1888-1889a—The first impression, in which volumes 1-8 are dated 1888 and volumes 9-16 are dated 1889.

1889—The corrected second impression of volumes 1-10 and a second impression of volumes 11-16 altered by Browning only as stated in section III below; all dated 1889 on the title pages.

5. The corrections in Browning's hand in the Dykes Campbell copy of 1888-1889a, and the manuscript list of corrections to that impression in the Brown University Library (see section III below).

Other materials (including some in the poet's handwriting) that affected the text are secondary. Examples are: the copy of the first edition of *Pauline* which contains annotations by Browning and John Stuart Mill; the copies of the first edition of *Paracelsus* which contain corrections in Browning's hand; a very early manuscript of *A Blot in the 'Scutcheon* which Browning presented to William Macready, but not the one from which the first edition was printed; informal lists of corrections that Browning included in letters to friends, such as the corrections to *Men and Women* he sent to D. G. Rossetti; Elizabeth Barrett's suggestions for revisions in *A Soul's Tragedy* and certain poems in *Dramatic Romances and Lyrics*; and the edition of *Strafford* by Emily Hickey for which Browning made suggestions.

The text and variant readings of this edition derive from collation of primary materials as defined above. Secondary materials are occasionally discussed in the notes and sometimes play a part when emendation is required.

III COPY-TEXT

The copy-text for this edition is Browning's final text: the first ten volumes of 1889 and the last six volumes of 1888-1889a, as described above. For this choice we offer the following explanation.

Manuscripts used as printer's copy for twenty of Browning's thirty-four book publications are known to exist; others may yet become available. These manuscripts, or, in their absence, the first editions of the works, might be considered as the most desirable copy-text. And this would be the case for an author who exercised little control over his text after the manuscript or first edition stage, or whose text clearly became corrupted in a succession of editions. To preserve the intention of such an author, one would have to choose an early text and emend it as evidence and judgment demanded.

With Browning, however, the situation is different, and our copy-text choice results from that difference. Throughout his life Browning continually revised his poetry. He did more than correct printer's errors and clarify previously intended meanings; his texts themselves remained fluid, subject to continuous alteration. As the manuscript which he submitted to his publisher was no doubt already a product of revision, so each subsequent edition under his control reflects the results of an ongoing process of creating, revising, and correcting. If we were to choose the manuscript (where extant) or first edition as copy-text, preserving Browning's intention would require extensive emendation to capture the additions, revisions, and alterations which Browning demonstrably made in later editions. By selecting Browning's final corrected text as our copy-text, emending it only to eliminate errors and the consequences of changing house-styling, we present his works in the form closest to that which he intended after years of revision and polishing.

But this is true only if Browning in fact exercised extensive control over the printing of his various editions. That he intended and attempted to do so is apparent in his comments and his practice. In 1855, demanding accuracy from the printers, he pointed out to his publisher Chapman, "I attach importance to the mere stops . . ." (DeVane and Knickerbocker, p. 83). There is evidence of his desire to control the details of his text as early as 1835, in the case of *Paracelsus*. The *Paracelsus* manuscript, now in the Forster and Dyce collection in the Victoria and Albert Museum Library, demonstrates a highly unconventional system of punctuation. Of particular note is Browning's unrestrained use of dashes, often in strings of two or three, instead of more precise or orthodox punctuation marks. It appears that this was done for its rhetorical effect. One sheet of Part 1 of the manuscript and all but the first and last sheets of Part 3 have had punctuation revised in pencil by someone other than Browning, perhaps J. Riggs, whose name appears three times in the margins of Part 3. In addition to these revisions, there are analogous punctuation revisions (in both pencil and ink) which appear to be in Browning's hand, and a few verbal alterations obviously in the poet's script.

A collation of the first edition (1835) with the manuscript reveals that a major restyling of punctuation was carried out before *Paracelsus* was published. However, the revisions incorporated into the first edition by no means slavishly follow the example set by the pencilled revisions of Parts 1 and 3 of the manuscript. Apparently the surviving manuscript was not used as printer's copy for the first edition. Browning may have submitted a second manuscript, or he may have revised extensively in proof. The printers may have carried out the revisions to punctuation, with or without the poet's point by point involvement. With the present evidence, we cannot be conclusive about the extent of Browning's control over the first edition of *Paracelsus*. It can be stated, however, in the light of the incompleteness of the pencilled revisions and the frequent lack of correspondence between the pencilled revisions and the lines as printed in 1835, that Browning himself may have been responsible for the punctuation of the first edition of *Paracelsus*. Certainly he was responsible for the frequent instances in the first and subsequent editions where the punctuation defies conventional rules, as in the following examples:

> What though
> It be so?—if indeed the strong desire
> Eclipse the aim in me?—if splendour break
> (Part I, ll. 329-331)

> I surely loved them—that last night, at least,
> When we . . . gone! gone! the better: I am saved
> (Part II, ll. 132-133)

> Of the body, even,)—what God is, what we are,
> (Part V, l. 642, 1849 reading)

The manuscripts of *Colombe's Birthday* (1844) and *Christmas-Eve and Easter-Day* (1850) were followed very carefully in the printing of the first editions. There are slight indications of minor house-styling, such as the spellings *colour* and *honour* for the manuscripts' *color* and *honor*. But the unorthodox punctuation, used to indicate elocutionary and rhetorical subtleties as well as syntactical relationships, is carried over almost unaltered from the manuscripts to the first editions. Similar evidence of Browning's painstaking attention to the smallest details in the printing of his poems can be seen in the manuscript and proof sheets of *The Ring and the Book* (1868-69). These materials reveal an interesting and significant pattern. It appears that Browning wrote swiftly, giving primary attention to wording and less to punctuation, being satisfied to use dashes to indicate almost any break in thought, syntax, or rhythm. Later, in the proof sheets for Books 1-6 of the poem and in the manuscript itself for Books 7-12, he changed the dashes to more specific and purposeful punctuation marks. The revised punctuation is what was printed, for the most part, in the first edition of *The Ring and the Book*; what further revisions there are conform to Browning's practice, though hardly to standard rules. Clearly Browning was in control of nearly every aspect of the published form of his works, even to the "mere stops."

Of still greater importance in our choice of copy-text is the substantial evidence that Browning took similar care with his collected editions. Though he characterized his changes for later editions as trivial and few in number, collations reveal thousands of revisions and corrections in each successive text. *Paracelsus*, for example, was extensively revised for the 1849 *Poems*; it was again reworked for the *Poetical Works* of 1863. *Sordello*, omitted in 1849, reappeared in 1863 with 181 new lines and short marginal glosses; Browning admitted only that it was "corrected *throughout*" (DeVane and Knickerbocker, p. 157). The poems of *Men and Women* (1855) were altered in numerous small but meaningful ways for both the 1863 and 1865 editions of the *Poetical Works* (See Allan C. Dooley, "The Textual Significance of Robert Browning's 1865 *Poetical Works*," *PBSA* 71 [1977], 212-18). Professor Michael Hancher, editor of Browning's correspondence with his publisher, George Smith, has cited evidence of the poet's close supervision of the 1868 collected edition ("Browning and the *Poetical Works* of 1888-1889," *Browning Newsletter*, Spring, 1971, 25-27). Mrs. Orr, writing of the same period in Browning's life, reports his resentment of those who garbled his text by misplacing his stops (*Life*, pp. 357-58).

There is plentiful and irrefutable evidence that Browning controlled, in the same meticulous way, the text of his last collected edition, that which we term 1888-1889. Hancher has summarized the relevant information:

> The evidence is clear that Browning undertook the 1888-1889 edition of his *Poetical Works* intent on controlling even the smallest minutiae of the text. Though he at one time considered supplying biographical and explanatory notes to the poems, he finally decided against such a scheme, concluding, in his letter to Smith of 12 November 1887, "I am correcting them carefully, and *that* must suffice." On 13 January 1888, he wrote, regarding the six-volume edition of his collected works published in 1868 which was to serve as the printer's copy for the final edition: "I have thoroughly corrected the six volumes of the Works, and can let you have them at once." . . . Browning evidently kept a sharp eye on the production of all sixteen of the volumes, including those later volumes. . . . Browning returned proof for Volume 3 on 6 May 1888, commenting, "I have had, as usual, to congratulate myself on the scrupulous accuracy of the Printers"; on 31 December he returned proofs of Volume 11, "corrected carefully"; and he returned "the corrected Proofs of Vol. XV" on 1 May 1889.

Throughout his long career, then, Browning continuously revised and corrected his works. Furthermore, his publishers took care to follow his directions exactly, accepting his changes and incorporating them into each successive edition. This is not to say that no one else had any effect whatsoever on Browning's text: Elizabeth Barrett made suggestions for revisions to *A Soul's Tragedy* and *Dramatic Romances and Lyrics*. Browning accepted some suggestions and rejected others, and those which he accepted we regard as his own. Mrs. Orr reports that Browning sent proof sheets to Joseph Milsand, a friend in France, for corrections (*Life*, p. 265), and that Browning accepted suggestions from friends and readers for the corrections of errors in his printed works. In some of the editions, there are slight evidences of minor house-styling in capitalization and the indication of quotations. But the evidence of Browning's own careful attention to revisions and corrections in both his manuscripts and proof sheets assures us that other persons played only a very minor role in the development of his text. We conclude that the vast majority of the alterations in the texts listed above as Primary Materials are Browning's own, and that only Browning's final corrected text, the result of years of careful work by the poet himself, reflects his full intentions.

The first impression of Browning's final collected edition (i.e., 1888-1889a) is not in and of itself the poet's final corrected text. By the spring of 1889 some of the early volumes of the first impression were already sold out, and by mid-August it was evident that a new one would be required. About this time James Dykes Campbell, Honorary Secretary of the London Browning Society, was informed by Browning that he was making further corrections to be incorporated into the new impression. According to Dykes Campbell, Browning had corrected the first ten volumes and offered to transcribe the corrections into Dykes Campbell's copy of 1888-1889a before leaving for Italy. The volumes altered in Browning's hand are now in the British Library and contain on the flyleaf of Volume 1 Dykes Campbell's note explaining precisely what happened. Of course, Dykes Campbell's copy was not the one used by the printer for the second impression. Nevertheless, these changes are indisputably Browning's and are those which, according to his own statement, he proposed to make in the new impression. This set of corrections carries, therefore, great authority.

Equally authoritative is a second set of corrections, also in Browning's hand, for part of 1888-1889a. In the poet's possession at the time of his death, this handwritten list was included in lot 179 of Sotheby, Wilkinson, and Hodge's auction of Browning materials in 1913; it is today located in the Brown University Library. The list contains corrections only for Volumes 4-10 of 1888-1889a. We know that Browning, on 26 July 1889, had completed and sent to Smith "the corrections for Vol. III in readiness for whenever you need them." By the latter part of August, according to Dykes Campbell, the poet had finished corrections for Volumes 1-10. Browning left for Italy on 29 August. The condition of the Brown University list does not indicate that it was ever used by the printer. Thus we surmise that the Brown list (completing the corrections through volume 10) may be the poet's copy of another list sent to his publisher. Whatever the case, the actual documents used by the printers—a set of marked volumes or handwritten lists—are not known to exist. A possible exception is a marked copy of *Red Cotton Night-Cap Country* (now in the Berg Collection of the New York Public Library) which seems to have been used by printers. Further materials used in preparing Browning's final edition may yet appear.

The matter is complicated further because neither set of corrections of 1888-1889a corresponds exactly to each other nor to the 1889 second impression. Each set contains corrections the other omits, and in a few cases the sets present alternative corrections of the same error. Our study of the Dykes Campbell copy of 1888-1889a reveals fifteen discrepancies between its corrections and the 1889 second impression. The Brown University list, which contains far fewer corrections, varies from the second impression in thirteen instances. Though neither of these sets of corrections was used by the printers, both are authoritative; we consider them legitimate textual variants, and record them as such. The lists are, of course, useful when emendation of the copy-text is required.

The value of the Dykes Campbell copy of 1888-1889a and the Brown University list is not that they render Browning's text perfect. The corrections to 1888-1889a must have existed in at least one other, still more authoritative form: the documents which Browning sent to his publisher. That this is so is indicated by the presence of required corrections in the second impression which neither the Dykes Campbell copy nor the Brown University list calls for. The significance of the existing sets of corrections is that they clearly indicate two important points: Browning's direct and active interest in the preparation of a corrected second impression of his final collected edition; and, given the high degree of correspondence between the two sets of corrections and the affected lines of the second impression, the concern of the printers to follow the poet's directives.

The second impression of 1888-1889 incorporated most of Browning's corrections to the first ten volumes of the first impression. There is no evidence whatever that any corrections beyond those which Browning sent to his publisher in the summer of 1889 were ever made. We choose, therefore, the 1889 corrected second impression of volumes 1-10 as copy-text for the works in those volumes. Corrections to the first impression were achieved by cutting the affected letters of punctuation out of the stereotype plates and pressing or soldering in the correct pieces of type. The corrected plates were then used for many copies, without changing the date on the title pages (except, of course, in volumes 17 [*Asolando*] and 18 [*New Poems*], added to the set by the publishers in 1894 and 1914 respectively). External evidence from publishers' catalogues and the advertisements bound into some volumes of 1889 indicate that copies of this impression were produced as late as 1913, although the dates on the title pages of volumes 1-16 remained 1889. Extensive plate deterioration is characteristic of the later copies, and use of the Hinman collator on early and late examples of 1889 reveals that the inserted corrections were somewhat fragile, some of them having decayed or disappeared entirely as the plates aged. (See Allan C. Dooley, "Browning's *Poetical Works* of 1888-1889," *SBHC* 7:1 [1978], 43-69.)

We do not use as copy-text volumes 11-16 of 1889, because there is no present evidence indicating that Browning exercised substantial control over this part of the second impression of 1888-1889. We do know that he made one correction, which he requested in a letter to Smith quoted by Hancher:

I have just had pointed out to [me] that an error, I supposed corrected, still is to be found in the 13th Volume—(Aristophanes' Apology) page 143, line 9, where the word should be Opora—without an i. I should like it altered, if that may be possible.

This correction was indeed made in the second impression. Our collations of copies of volumes 11-16 of 1889a and 1889 show no other intentional changes. The later copies do show, however, extensive type batter, numerous scratches, and irregular inking. Therefore our copy-text for the works in the last six volumes of 1888-1889 is volumes 11-16 of 1888-1889a.

IV VARIANTS

In this edition we record, with a very few exceptions discussed below, all variants from the copy-text appearing in the manuscripts and in the editions under Browning's control. Our purpose in doing this is two-fold.

1. We enable the reader to reconstruct the text of a work as it stood at the various stages of its development.

2. We provide the materials necessary to an understanding of how Browning's growth and development as an artist are reflected in his successive revisions to his works.

As a consequence of this policy our variant listings inevitably contain some variants that were not created by Browning; printer's errors and readings that may result from house-styling will appear occasionally. But the evidence that Browning assumed responsibility for what was printed, and that he considered and used unorthodox punctuation as part of his meaning, is so persuasive that we must record even the smallest and oddest variants. The following examples, characteristic of Browning's revisions, illustrate the point:

Pauline, l. 700:
  1833: I am prepared—I have made life my own—
  1868: I am prepared: I have made life my own.
"Evelyn Hope," l. 41:
  1855: I have lived, I shall say, so much since then,
  1865: I have lived (I shall say) so much since then,
"Bishop Blougram's Apology," l. 267:
  1855: That's the first cabin-comfort I secure—
  1865: That's the first-cabin comfort I secure:
The Ring and the Book, Book 11 ("Guido"), l. 1064:
  1869: What if you give up boys' and girls' fools'-play
  1872: What if you give up boy and girl fools'-play
  1889a: What if you give up boy-and-girl-fools' play

We have concluded that Browning himself is nearly always responsible for such changes. But even if he only accepted these changes (rather than originating them), their effect on syntax, rhythm, and meaning is so significant that they must be recorded in our variant listings.

The only variants we do not record are those which strongly appear to result from systematic house-styling. For example, Browning nowhere indicated that he wished to use typography to influence meaning, and our inference is that any changes in line-spacing, depth of paragraph indentation, and the like, were the responsibility of the printers of the various editions, not the poet himself. House-styling was also very probably the cause of certain variants in the apparatus of Browning's plays, including variants in stage directions which involve a change only in manner of statement, such as *Enter Hampden* instead of *Hampden enters*; variants in the printing of stage directions, such as *Aside* instead of *aside*, or [*Aside*.] instead of [*Aside*], or [*Strafford*.] instead of [*Strafford*]; variants in character designations, such as *Lady Carlisle* instead of *Car* or *Carlisle*. Browning also accepted current convention for indicating quotations (see section V below). Neither do we list changes in type face (except when used for emphasis), nor the presence or absence of a period at the end of the title of a work.

V ALTERATIONS TO THE COPY-TEXT

We have rearranged the sequence of works in the copy-text, so that they appear in the order of their first publication. This process involves the restoration to the original order of the poems included in *Dramatic Lyrics, Dramatic Romances and Lyrics*, and *Men and Women*. We realize, of course, that Browning himself was responsible for the rearrangement of these poems in the various collected editions; in his prefatory note for the 1888-1889 edition, however, he indicates that he desired a chronological presentation:

> The poems that follow are again, as before, printed in chronological order; but only so far as proves compatible with the prescribed size of each volume, which necessitates an occasional change in the distribution of its contents.

We would like both to indicate Browning's stated intentions about the placement of his poems and to present the poems in the order which suggests Browning's development as a poet. We have chosen, therefore, to present the poems in order of their first publication, with an indication in the notes as to their respective subsequent placement. We also include the tables of contents of the editions listed as Primary Materials above.

We have regularized or modernized the copy-text in the following minor ways:

1. We do not place a period at the end of the title of a work, though the copy-text does.

2. In some of Browning's editions, including the copy-text, the first word of each work is printed in capital letters. We have used the modern practice of capitalizing only the first letter.

3. The inconsistent use of both an ampersand and the word *and* has been regularized to the use of *and.*

4. We have eliminated the space between the two parts of a contraction; thus the copy-text's *it 's* is printed as *it's,* for example.

5. We uniformly place periods and commas within closing quotation marks.

6. We have employed throughout the modern practice of indicating quoted passages with quotation marks only at the beginning and end of the quotation. Throughout Browning's career, no matter which publisher or printer was handling his works, this matter was treated very inconsistently. In some of the poet's manuscripts and in most of his first editions, quotations are indicated by quotation marks only at the beginning and end. In the collected editions of 1863 and 1865, issued by Chapman and Hall, some quoted passages have quotation marks at the beginning of each line of the quotation, while others follow modern practice. In Smith, Elder's collected editions of 1868 and 1888-1889, quotation marks appear at the beginning of each line of a quotation. We have regularized and modernized what seems a matter of house-styling in both copy-text and variants.

The remaining way in which the copy-text is altered is emendation. Our policy is to emend the copy-text to eliminate apparent errors of either Browning or his printers. It is evident that Browning did make errors and overlook mistakes, as shown by the following example from "One Word More," the last poem in *Men and Women*. Stanza sixteen of the copy-text opens with the following lines:

> What, there's nothing in the moon noteworthy?
> Nay: for if that moon could love a mortal,
> Use, to charm him (so to fit a fancy,
> All her magic ('tis the old sweet mythos)
> She . . .

Clearly the end punctuation in the third line is incorrect. A study of the various texts is illuminating. Following are the readings of the line in each of the editions for which Browning was responsible:

MS:	fancy)	1855:	fancy)	1865:	fancy)	1888:	fancy
P:	fancy)	1863:	fancy)	1868:	fancy)	1889:	fancy,

The omission of one parenthesis in 1888 was almost certainly a printer's error. Browning, in the Dykes Campbell copy corrections to 1888-1889a, missed or ignored the error. However, in the Brown University list of corrections, he indicated that *fancy* should be followed by a comma. This is the way the line appears in the corrected second impression of Volume 4, but the correction at best satisfies the demands of syntax only partially. Browning might have written the line:

> Use, to charm him, so to fit a fancy,

or, to maintain parallelism between the third and fourth lines:

> Use, to charm him (so to fit a fancy),

or he might simply have restored the earlier reading. Oversights of this nature demand emendation, and our choice would be to restore the punctuation of the manuscript through 1868. All of our emendations will be based, as far as possible, on the historical collation of the passage involved, the grammatical demands of the passage in context, and the poet's treatment of other similar passages. Fortunately, the multiple editions of most of the works provide the editor with ample textual evidence to make an informed and useful emendation.

All emendations to the copy-text are listed at the beginning of the Editorial Notes for each work. The variant listings for the copy-text also incorporate the emendations, which are preceded and followed there by the symbol indicating an editor's note.

VI APPARATUS

1. *Variants.* In presenting the variants from the copy-text, we list at the bottom of each page readings from the known manuscripts, proof sheets of the editions when we have located them, and the first and subsequent editions.

A variant is generally preceded and followed by a pickup and a drop word (example a). No note terminates with a punctuation mark unless the punctuation mark comes at the end of the line; if a variant drops or adds a punctuation mark, the next word is added (example b). If the normal pickup word has appeared previously in the same line, the note begins with the word preceding it. If the normal drop word appears subsequently in the line, the next word is added (example c). If a capitalized pickup word occurs within the line, it is accompanied by the preceding word (example d). No pickup or drop words, however, are used for any variant consisting of an internal change, for example a hyphen in a compounded word, an apostrophe, a tense change or a spelling change (example e). A change in capitalization within a line of poetry will be preceded by a pickup word, for which, within an entry containing other variants, the <> is suitable (example f). No drop word is used when the variant comes at the end of a line (example g). Examples from *Sordello* (all from Book 1 except c [2] which is from Book 4):

a. 611| *1840:*but that appeared *1863:*but this appeared

b. variant at end of line: 109| *1840:*intrigue:" *1863:* intrigue.
variant within line: 82| *1840:*forests like *1863:*forests, like

c. 132| *1840:*too sleeps; but 1863:too sleeps: but 77| *1840:*that night by *1863:*that, night by night, *1888:*by night

d. 295| *1840:*at Padua to repulse the *1863:*at Padua who repulsed the

e. 284| *1840:*are *1863:*were
344| *1840:*dying-day, *1863:*dying day,

f. capitalization change with no other variants: 741| *1840:* retaining Will, *1863:*retaining will,
with other variants: 843| *1840:*Was <> Him back! Why *1863:* Is <> back!" Why *1865:*him

g. 427| *1840:*dregs; *1863:*dregs.

Each recorded variant will be assumed to be incorporated in the next edition if there is no indication otherwise. This rule applies even in cases where the change occurs between 1888-1889a, although it means that the variant note duplicates the copy-text. A variant listing, then, traces the history of a line and brings it forward to the point where it matches the copy-text.

In Browning's plays, all character designations which happen to occur in variant listings are standardized to the copy-text reading. In listing variants in the plays, we ignore character designations unless the designation comes within a numbered line. In such a case, the variant is treated as any other word, and can be used as a pickup or drop word. When a character designation is used as a pickup word, however, the rule excluding capitalized pickup words (except at the beginning of a line) does not apply, and we do not revert to the next earliest uncapitalized pickup word.

2. *Line numbers.* Poetic lines are numbered in the traditional manner by considering one complete poetic line as one unit of counting. In prose passages the unit of counting is the type lines of this edition.

3. *Table of signs in variant listings.* We have avoided all symbols and signs used by Browning himself. The following is a table of the signs needed to read the variant notes:

§ . . . §	Editor's note
<>	Words omitted
/	Line break
/ / , / / / , . . .	Line break plus one or more lines without internal variants

4. *Annotations*. In general principle, we have annotated proper names, phrases that function as proper names, and words or groups of words the full meaning of which requires factual, historical, or literary background. Thus we have attempted to hold interpretation to a minimum, although we realize that the act of selection itself is to some extent interpretative.

Notes, particularly on historical figures and events, tend to fullness and even to the tangential and unessential. As a result, some of the information provided may seem unnecessary to the scholar. On the other hand, it is not possible to assume that all who use this edition are fully equipped to assimilate unaided all of Browning's copious literary, historical, and mythological allusions. Thus we have directed our efforts toward a diverse audience.

Tables

1. *Manuscripts*. We have located manuscripts for the following of Browning's works; the list is chronological.

Paracelsus
Forster and Dyce Collection,
Victoria and Albert Museum, London

Colombe's Birthday
New York Public Library

Christmas-Eve and Easter-Day
Forster and Dyce Collection,
Victoria and Albert Museum, London

"Love Among the Ruins"
Lowell Collection,
Houghton Library, Harvard University

"The Twins"
Pierpont Morgan Library, New York

"One Word More"
Pierpont Morgan Library, New York

Dramatis Personae
Pierpont Morgan Library, New York

The Ring and the Book
British Library, London

Balaustion's Adventure
Balliol College Library, Oxford

Prince Hohenstiel-Schwangau
Balliol College Library, Oxford

Fifine at the Fair
Balliol College Library, Oxford

Red Cotton Night-Cap Country
Balliol College Library, Oxford
Aristophanes' Apology
Balliol College Library, Oxford
The Inn Album
Balliol College Library, Oxford
Of Pacchiarotto, and How He Worked in Distemper
Balliol College Library, Oxford
The Agamemnon of Aeschylus
Balliol College Library, Oxford
La Saisaiz and The Two Poets of Croisic
Balliol College Library, Oxford
Dramatic Idylls
Balliol College Library, Oxford
Dramatic Idylls, Second Series
Balliol College Library, Oxford
Jocoseria
Balliol College Library, Oxford
Ferishtah's Fancies
Balliol College Library, Oxford
Parleyings With Certain People of Importance in Their Day
Balliol College Library, Oxford
Asolando
Pierpont Morgan Library, New York

We have been unable to locate manuscripts for the following works, and request that persons with information about any of them communicate with us.

Pauline
Strafford
Sordello
Pippa Passes
King Victor and King Charles
"Essay on Chatterton"
Dramatic Lyrics
The Return of the Druses
A Blot in the 'Scutcheon
Dramatic Romances and Lyrics
Luria
A Soul's Tragedy
"Essay on Shelley"
Men and Women

2. *Editions referred to in Volume VII.* The following editions have been used in preparing the text and variants presented in this volume. The dates given below are used as symbols in the variant listings at the bottom of each page.

1868 *The Ring and the Book.* Volumes 1 and 2.
Two Volumes. London: Smith, Elder and Company.

1869	*The Ring and the Book*. Volumes 3 and 4. Two Volumes, London: Smith, Elder and Company.
1872	*The Ring and the Book*. Four Volumes. London: Smith, Elder and Company.
1888	*The Poetical Works*. Volumes 1-8. London: Smith, Elder and Company.
1889a	*The Poetical Works*. Volumes 9-16. London: Smith, Elder and Company.
1889	*The Poetical Works*. Sixteen Volumes. London: Smith, Elder and Company. (second impression of 1888-1889a)

3. *Short titles and abbreviations*. The following short forms of reference have been used in notes for this edition:

Altick	*The Ring and the Book*, ed. Richard D. Altick. Baltimore: Penguin Books, 1971.
B	Browning
BrU	Browning's list of corrections located at Brown University
Cook	A.K. Cook. *A Commentary upon Browning's "The Ring and the Book."* Hamden, Connecticut: Archon Books, 1966 (first pub. 1920).
Corrigan	*Curious Annals: New Documents Relating to Browning's Roman Murder Story*, ed. and tr. Beatrice Corrigan. Toronto: University of Toronto Press, 1956.
DC	Browning's corrections in James Dykes Campbell's copy of 1888-1889a
DeVane, *Hbk.*	William Clyde DeVane. *A Browning Handbook*. New York: Appleton-Century Crofts, 1955.
DeVane and Knickerbocker	*New Letters of Robert Browning*, ed. William Clyde DeVane and Kenneth L. Knickerbocker. New Haven: Yale University Press, 1950.
EBB	Elizabeth Barrett Browning
Gest	*The Old Yellow Book*, ed. and tr. John Marshall Gest. Philadelphia: University of Pennsylvania Press, 1927.
Griffin and Minchin	W. H. Griffin and H. C. Minchin. *The Life of Robert Browning*. New York: Macmillan, 1910.

Heydon and Kelley	*Elizabeth Barrett Browning's Letters to Mrs. David Ogilvy*, ed. Peter N. Heydon and Philip Kelley. London: Murray, 1974.
Hodell	*The Old Yellow Book*, in facsimile, ed. and tr. Charles W. Hodell. Washington: The Carnegie Institution, 1908.
Hood, *Ltrs.*	*Letters of Robert Browning Collected by T. J. Wise*, ed. Thurman L. Hood. New Haven: Yale University Press, 1933.
Irvine and Honan	William Irvine and Park Honan. *The Book, the Ring, and the Poet*. New York: McGraw-Hill, 1974.
Landis and Freeman	*Letters of the Brownings to George Barrett*, ed. Paul Landis and Ronald E. Freeman. Urbana: University of Illinois Press, 1958.
Letters of EBB	*The Letters of Elizabeth Barrett Browning*, ed. F.G. Kenyon. 2 vols. New York: Macmillan, 1897.
New Poems	*New Poems by Robert Browning and Elizabeth Barrett Browning*, ed. F.G. Kenyon. New York: Macmillan, 1915.
Orr, *Hbk.*	Mrs. Sutherland Orr. *Handbook to the Works of Robert Browning*. New Edition. Revised and in Part Rewritten by F.G. Kenyon. New York: McMillan, 1915.
Orr, *Life*	Mrs. Sutherland Orr. *Life and Letters of Robert Browning*. Second Edition. London: Smith, Elder, 1891.
OYB	Browning's source for *The Ring and the Book*, in its original format.
OYB, Everyman	*The Old Yellow Book*, ed. and tr. Charles W. Hodell. New York: E. P. Dutton (Everyman's Library), 1911.
P-C	*The Complete Works of Robert Browning*, ed. Charlotte Porter and Helen A. Clarke. New York: Thomas Y. Crowell, 1898.
RB-EBB, ed. Kintner	*The Letters of Robert Browning and Elizabeth Barrett Barrett*, 1845-1846, ed. Elvan Kintner. 2 vols. Cambridge, Mass.: The Belknap Press of Harvard University Press, 1969.
Treves	Sir Frederick Treves. *The Country of The Ring*

and the Book. London: Cassell and Company, 1913.

Vasari — Giorgio Vasari. *Lives of the Painters, Sculptors and Architects*, ed. and tr. A. B. Hinds. Intro. by William Gaunt. 4 vols. London: Dent (Everyman's Library), 1963.

Citations and quotations from the Bible refer to the King James Version.

Citations and quotations from Shakespeare refer to *The Riverside Shakespeare*, ed. G. B. Evans, et. al. Boston: Houghton Mifflin, 1974.

Acknowledgments

For providing money and services which have made it possible for us to assemble the vast materials required for the preparation of this edition, the following institutions have our especial appreciation: the Ohio University Press, the Ohio University Library, the Ohio University English Department; Baylor University and the Armstrong Browning Library of Baylor University; the American Council of Learned Societies; the Kent State University Library and its Bibliographical and Textual Center, the Kent State University Research Council, the Kent State University English Department.

We also thank the following for making available to us materials under their care: the Armstrong Browning Library; the Balliol College Library, Oxford; the Beinecke Rare Book and Manuscript Library, Yale University, and its director Mr. H. W. Liebert; the British Library; the John Hay Library, Brown University; the Houghton Library, Harvard University; the Henry E. Huntington Library; the Department of Special Collections, Kent State University, and its director Mr. Dean H. Keller; Mr. E. V. Quinn; Mr. Philip Kelley; Mr. John Murray; the Library of the Victoria and Albert Museum.

We are also grateful to Professor Paul Murphy and Professor Bartolomeo Martello for their invaluable assistance in translation of Latin and Italian sources and passages.

The frontispiece is reproduced by permission of the Armstrong Browning Library of Baylor University. The section of the map is published by permission of the British Library.

THE RING AND THE BOOK
Books I-IV

Edited by Roma A. King, Jr.

Engraving of Italian coin (1696) showing Pope Innocent XII.
Appears 1888-89 only.

Posizione
Di tutta la Causa Criminale
Contro
Guido Franceschini Nobile
Aretino, e suoi Sicarij stati
fatti morire in Roma il dì 22.
Febb:io 1698.
Il primo con la decollazione gl'altri
quattro di Forca
Romana Homicidiorum

Disputatur an et quando Maritus
possit occidere Vxorem
Adulteram
absque incursu pœnæ Ord:riæ

Title page of The Old Yellow Book.
Illustration appears 1888-89.

THE RING AND THE BOOK

I. The Ring and the Book
II. Half-Rome
III. The Other Half-Rome
IV. Tertium Quid

THE RING AND THE BOOK

1868–9

I

THE RING AND THE BOOK

Do you see this Ring?
'Tis Rome-work, made to match
(By Castellani's imitative craft)
Etrurian circlets found, some happy morn,
After a dropping April; found alive
Spark-like 'mid unearthed slope-side figtree-roots
That roof old tombs at Chiusi: soft, you see,
Yet crisp as jewel-cutting. There's one trick,
(Craftsmen instruct me) one approved device
And but one, fits such slivers of pure gold
As this was,—such mere oozings from the mine,
Virgin as oval tawny pendent tear
At beehive-edge when ripened combs o'erflow,—
To bear the file's tooth and the hammer's tap:
Since hammer needs must widen out the round,
And file emboss it fine with lily-flowers,
Ere the stuff grow a ring-thing right to wear.
That trick is, the artificer melts up wax
With honey, so to speak; he mingles gold
With gold's alloy, and, duly tempering both,
Effects a manageable mass, then works:
But his work ended, once the thing a ring,
Oh, there's repristination! Just a spirt

---

§ MS in Department of Manuscripts of the British Library. P1868, CP1868, P1869, CP1869, P1872, ed. 1868-69, 1872, 1888, 1889. For description of MS and proofs, see Editorial Notes, "Text." §

[11]| MS:tears § altered to § tear [13]| MS:tap; *P1868:*tap: [20]| MS:works.

O' the proper fiery acid o'er its face,
And forth the alloy unfastened flies in fume;
While, self-sufficient now, the shape remains,
The rondure brave, the lilied loveliness,
Gold as it was, is, shall be evermore:
Prime nature with an added artistry—
No carat lost, and you have gained a ring.

What of it? 'Tis a figure, a symbol, say;
A thing's sign: now for the thing signified.

Do you see this square old yellow Book, I toss
I' the air, and catch again, and twirl about
By the crumpled vellum covers,—pure crude fact
Secreted from man's life when hearts beat hard,
And brains, high-blooded, ticked two centuries since?
Examine it yourselves! I found this book,
Gave a *lira* for it, eightpence English just,
(Mark the predestination!) when a Hand,
Always above my shoulder, pushed me once,
One day still fierce 'mid many a day struck calm,
Across a Square in Florence, crammed with booths,
Buzzing and blaze, noontide and market-time,
Toward Baccio's marble,—ay, the basement-ledge
O' the pedestal where sits and menaces
John of the Black Bands with the upright spear,
'Twixt palace and church,—Riccardi where they lived,
His race, and San Lorenzo where they lie.
This book,—precisely on that palace-step
Which, meant for lounging knaves o' the Medici,
Now serves re-venders to display their ware,—
'Mongst odds and ends of ravage, picture-frames

---

*P1872:*works, *1888:*works: 23| MS:Of *P1868:*O' 27| MS:evermore— *P1868:*evermore: 29| MS:a Ring. *P1868:*a ring. 29-30| MS:§ ¶ § *P1868:* § no ¶, paragraph restored; see Editorial Notes § 30| MS:say, *P1868:*say; 33| MS:In § altered to § I' 35| MS:hard *P1868:*hard, 37| MS:yourselves. I *P1868:*yourselves! I 41| MS:One a § crossed out § 42| MS:in Florence crammed *P1868:*in Florence, crammed 43| MS:market-time; *P1872:*market-time, 45| MS:Of his pedestal *P1868:*O' the pedestal 50| MS:of *P1868:*o' 52| MS:'Mongst *1888:*Mongst § emended to § 'Mongst § see Editorial Notes §

White through the worn gilt, mirror-sconces chipped,
Bronze angel-heads once knobs attached to chests,
(Handled when ancient dames chose forth brocade)
Modern chalk drawings, studies from the nude,
Samples of stone, jet, breccia, porphyry,
Polished and rough, sundry amazing busts
In baked earth, (broken, Providence be praised!)
A wreck of tapestry, proudly-purposed web
When reds and blues were indeed red and blue,
Now offered as a mat to save bare feet
(Since carpets constitute a cruel cost)
Treading the chill scagliola bedward: then
A pile of brown-etched prints, two *crazie* each,
Stopped by a conch a-top from fluttering forth
—Sowing the Square with works of one and the same
Master, the imaginative Sienese
Great in the scenic backgrounds—(name and fame
None of you know, nor does he fare the worse:)
From these . . . Oh, with a Lionard going cheap
If it should prove, as promised, that Joconde
Whereof a copy contents the Louvre!—these
I picked this book from. Five compeers in flank
Stood left and right of it as tempting more—
A dogseared Spicilegium, the fond tale
O' the Frail One of the Flower, by young Dumas,
Vulgarized Horace for the use of schools,
The Life, Death, Miracles of Saint Somebody,
Saint Somebody Else, his Miracles, Death and Life,—

56| MS:chalk-drawings *P1868:*chalk drawings 57| MS:porphyry, *P1868:*porphyry § emended to § porphyry, § see Editorial Notes § 59| MS:earth, broken <> praised! *P1868:*earth, (broken <> praised!) 64| MS:bedwards § altered to § bedward 66| MS:forth, *P1868:*forth 69| MS:backgrounds—name *P1868:*backgrounds—(name 70| MS:worse: *P1868:*worse:) 71| MS: 'Mongst these . . Oh *P1868:*From these *1888:*these . . . Oh 73| MS:the Louvre . . these *P1868:*the Louvre!—these 74| MS:from:five *P1868:*from. Five 76| MS:the famed § crossed out and replaced above by one word § fond Tale *P1868:*fond tale 77| MS:Of <> Flower by *P1868:*O' <> Flower, by 80| MS:Saint Somebody else <> Death, Life, *P1868:*Saint Somebody Else <> Death

With this, one glance at the lettered back of which,
And "Stall!" cried I: a *lira* made it mine.

Here it is, this I toss and take again;
Small-quarto size, part print part manuscript:
A book in shape but, really, pure crude fact
Secreted from man's life when hearts beat hard,
And brains, high-blooded, ticked two centuries since.
Give it me back! The thing's restorative
I' the touch and sight.

That memorable day,
(June was the month, Lorenzo named the Square)
I leaned a little and overlooked my prize
By the low railing round the fountain-source
Close to the statue, where a step descends:
While clinked the cans of copper, as stooped and rose
Thick-ankled girls who brimmed them, and made place
For marketmen glad to pitch basket down,
Dip a broad melon-leaf that holds the wet,
And whisk their faded fresh. And on I read
Presently, though my path grew perilous
Between the outspread straw-work, piles of plait
Soon to be flapping, each o'er two black eyes
And swathe of Tuscan hair, on festas fine:
Through fire-irons, tribes of tongs, shovels in sheaves,
Skeleton bedsteads, wardrobe-drawers agape,
Rows of tall slim brass lamps with dangling gear,—
And worse, cast clothes a-sweetening in the sun:
None of them took my eye from off my prize.
Still read I on, from written title-page

---

and Life,— 81| MS:And this *P1868:*With this 82-83| MS:§ line indicating new ¶ § 84| MS:manuscript, *P1868:*manuscript: 86| MS:hard *P1868:*hard, 89| MS:In the touch of it § last two words crossed out and replaced above by two words § and sight. *P1868:*I' 93| MS:descends, *P1868:*descends: 94| MS:copper as *P1868:*copper, as 95| MS:Thick-ancled <> them and *P1868:*them, and *1868:*Thick-ankled 100| MS:straw work *P1868:*straw-work 102| MS:And a swathe *P1868:*And swathe 107| MS:of these § altered to § them <> page. § word and period crossed out and replaced above by § prize. 108| MS:title-here § *-here* crossed out and replaced by § -page

To written index, on, through street and street,
At the Strozzi, at the Pillar, at the Bridge;
Till, by the time I stood at home again
In Casa Guidi by Felice Church,
Under the doorway where the black begins
With the first stone-slab of the staircase cold,
I had mastered the contents, knew the whole truth
Gathered together, bound up in this book,
Print three-fifths, written supplement the rest.
"*Romana Homicidiorum*"—nay,
Better translate—"A Roman murder-case:
Position of the entire criminal cause
Of Guido Franceschini, nobleman,
With certain Four the cutthroats in his pay,
Tried, all five, and found guilty and put to death
By heading or hanging as befitted ranks,
At Rome on February Twenty Two,
Since our salvation Sixteen Ninety Eight:
Wherein it is disputed if, and when,
Husbands may kill adulterous wives, yet 'scape
The customary forfeit."

Word for word,
So ran the title-page: murder, or else
Legitimate punishment of the other crime,
Accounted murder by mistake,—just that
And no more, in a Latin cramp enough
When the law had her eloquence to launch,
But interfilleted with Italian streaks
When testimony stooped to mother-tongue,—
That, was this old square yellow book about.

Now, as the ingot, ere the ring was forged,

110| MS:At the Strozzi <> the Bridge, *P1868:*At the Strozzi <> the Bridge; 112| MS:by Felice's § altered to § by Felice 114| MS:stone slab *P1868:*stone-slab 117| MS:rest, *P1868:*rest. 119| MS:translate—"A Roman Murder Case: *P1868:* translate—"A Roman murder-case: 123| MS:Tried all five and found *P1868:* Tried, all five, and found 128| MS:wives yet *P1868:*wives, yet 129| MS: § vertical line between *forfeit* and *Word* with marginal note indicating new ¶ § for word *P1868:*for word, 134| MS:the Law *P1868:*the law 135| MS:interfilletted with Italian § crossed out and replaced above by § vulgar § crossed out and replaced by

Lay gold, (beseech you, hold that figure fast!)
So, in this book lay absolutely truth,
Fanciless fact, the documents indeed,
Primary lawyer-pleadings for, against,
The aforesaid Five; real summed-up circumstance
Adduced in proof of these on either side,
Put forth and printed, as the practice was,
At Rome, in the Apostolic Chamber's type,
And so submitted to the eye o' the Court
Presided over by His Reverence
Rome's Governor and Criminal Judge,—the trial
Itself, to all intents, being then as now
Here in the book and nowise out of it;
Seeing, there properly was no judgment-bar,
No bringing of accuser and accused,
And whoso judged both parties, face to face
Before some court, as we conceive of courts.
There was a Hall of Justice; that came last:
For Justice had a chamber by the hall
Where she took evidence first, summed up the same,
Then sent accuser and accused alike,
In person of the advocate of each,
To weigh its worth, thereby arrange, array
The battle. 'Twas the so-styled Fisc began,
Pleaded (and since he only spoke in print
The printed voice of him lives now as then)
The public Prosecutor—"Murder's proved;
With five . . . what we call qualities of bad,
Worse, worst, and yet worse still, and still worse yet;

---

original reading § *P1868:*interfilleted 139| MS:gold (beseech *P1868:*gold, (beseech 143| MS:aforesaid Five, real *P1868:*aforesaid Five; real 146| MS:At Rome in <> type *P1868:*At Rome, in <> type, 147| MS:of *P1868:*o' 149| MS:the Trial *P1868:*the trial 152| MS:Seeing there <> Judgment-seat § *seat* crossed out and replaced above by § bar, *P1868:*Seeing, there <> judgment-bar, 154| MS:to face, *P1868:*to face 156| MS:last, *P1868:*last: 157| MS:a closet § crossed out and replaced above by § chamber *P1868:*For justice *1888:*For Justice 161| MS:weigh the evidence' worth, arrange *P1868:*weigh that evidence' *1888:*weigh its worth, thereby arrange 163| MS:Pleaded—and *P1868:* Pleaded (and 164| MS:then— *P1868:*then) 165| MS:The Public *P1868:* The public 166| MS:five . . what *1888:*five . . . what 167| MS:still, and

Crest over crest crowning the cockatrice,
That beggar hell's regalia to enrich
Count Guido Franceschini: punish him!"
Thus was the paper put before the court
In the next stage, (no noisy work at all,)
To study at ease. In due time like reply
Came from the so-styled Patron of the Poor,
Official mouthpiece of the five accused
Too poor to fee a better,—Guido's luck
Or else his fellows',—which, I hardly know,—
An outbreak as of wonder at the world,
A fury-fit of outraged innocence,
A passion of betrayed simplicity:
"Punish Count Guido? For what crime, what hint
O' the colour of a crime, inform us first!
Reward him rather! Recognize, we say,
In the deed done, a righteous judgment dealt!
All conscience and all courage,—there's our Count
Charactered in a word; and, what's more strange,
He had companionship in privilege,
Found four courageous conscientious friends:
Absolve, applaud all five, as props of law,
Sustainers of society!—perchance
A trifle over-hasty with the hand
To hold her tottering ark, had tumbled else;
But that's a splendid fault whereat we wink,
Wishing your cold correctness sparkled so!"

---

still worse yet, *P1868:*still, and still worse yet; 169| MS:beggar Hell's *P1868:* beggar hell's 171| MS:before the Court *P1868:*before the court 172| MS:stage,—no <> all,— *P1868:*stage, (no <> all,) 175| MS:the Five *P1868:*the five 177| MS:fellows', which *1888:*fellows',—which 178| MS: § crowded between lines 177-79 § 181| MS:crime, what cause § crossed out and replaced above by § hint 182| MS:Of <> inform me first! *P1868:*O' <> inform us first! 183| MS:rather; recognize, I say, *P1868:*rather! Recognize, we say, 184| MS:done a *P1868:*done, a 185| MS:there's the man *P1868:*there's our Count 187| MS:Who § crossed out and replaced above by § He 188| MS: § original line illegible; perhaps § Four more with courage and a conscience too: § altered to § Found four courageous conscientious friends— *P1868:*friends: 189| MS:Absolve, and praise the Five, laws instruments, § last six words crossed out and replaced by § applaud all Five, as props of law, *P1868:*all five 190| MS: society! perchance *P1868:*society!—perchance 191| MS:over hasty *P1868:* over-hasty 192| MS:To prop § crossed out and replaced above by one word §

Thus paper second followed paper first,
Thus did the two join issue—nay, the four,
Each pleader having an adjunct. "True, he killed
—So to speak—in a certain sort—his wife,
But laudably, since thus it happed!" quoth one:
Whereat, more witness and the case postponed.
"Thus it happed not, since thus he did the deed,
And proved himself thereby portentousest
Of cutthroats and a prodigy of crime,
As the woman that he slaughtered was a saint,
Martyr and miracle!" quoth the other to match:
Again, more witness, and the case postponed.
"A miracle, ay—of lust and impudence;
Hear my new reasons!" interposed the first:
"—Coupled with more of mine!" pursued his peer.
"Beside, the precedents, the authorities!"
From both at once a cry with an echo, that!
That was a firebrand at each fox's tail
Unleashed in a cornfield: soon spread flare enough,
As hurtled thither and there heaped themselves
From earth's four corners, all authority
And precedent for putting wives to death,
Or letting wives live, sinful as they seem.
How legislated, now, in this respect,
Solon and his Athenians? Quote the code
Of Romulus and Rome! Justinian speak!
Nor modern Baldo, Bartolo be dumb!
The Roman voice was potent, plentiful;
Cornelia de Sicariis hurried to help
Pompeia de Parricidiis; Julia de

---

hold< >ark had *P1868:*ark, had 199| MS:happed," quoth *P1868:*happed!" quoth 205| MS:miracle," quoth *P1868:*miracle!" quoth 206| MS:witness and *P1868:*witness, and 207| MS:aye *P1868:*ay 208| MS:reasons!"—interposed *P1868:*reasons!" interposed 209| MS:mine!"—pursued *P1868:*mine!" pursued 211| MS:A cry from both at once with § transposed to § From both at once a cry with 212| MS:foxes *P1868:*fox's 217| MS:live sinful *P1868:* live, sinful 218| MS:legislated, they § crossed out and replaced above by § now 220| MS:and Rome! Justinian, speak! *P1868:*and Rome!

Something-or-other jostled *Lex* this-and-that;
King Solomon confirmed Apostle Paul:
That nice decision of Dolabella, eh?
That pregnant instance of Theodoric, oh!
Down to that choice example Ælian gives
(An instance I find much insisted on)
Of the elephant who, brute-beast though he were,
Yet understood and punished on the spot
His master's naughty spouse and faithless friend;
A true tale which has edified each child,
Much more shall flourish favoured by our court!
Pages of proof this way, and that way proof,
And always—once again the case postponed.

Thus wrangled, brangled, jangled they a month,
—Only on paper, pleadings all in print,
Nor ever was, except i' the brains of men,
More noise by word of mouth than you hear now—
Till the court cut all short with "Judged, your cause.
Receive our sentence! Praise God! We pronounce
Count Guido devilish and damnable:
His wife Pompilia in thought, word and deed,
Was perfect pure, he murdered her for that:
As for the Four who helped the One, all Five—
Why, let employer and hirelings share alike
In guilt and guilt's reward, the death their due!"

So was the trial at end, do you suppose?
"Guilty you find him, death you doom him to?
Ay, were not Guido, more than needs, a priest,

Justinian speak! 225| MS:Something or other <> this and that. *P1868:*Something-or-other <> this-and-that; 231| MS:was § altered to § were 233| MS:naughty wife § crossed out and replaced above by one word § spouse <> friend— *P1868:*friend; 234| MS:true Tale *P1868:*true tale
235| MS:more shall § inserted above § <> our Judge. § crossed out and replaced by § Court! *P1868:*court! 237-38| MS:§ no ¶ § *P1868:*§ ¶ § *1888:*§ no ¶; paragraph restored; see Editorial Notes § 240| MS:in § altered to §i' 242| MS: the Court <> cause! *P1868:*the court <> cause. 243| MS:sentence. Praise God. We *P1868:*sentence! Praise God! We 249| MS:In Guilt and that § crossed out § *P1868:*In guilt 249-50| MS:§ line and marginal note indicating new ¶ §
250| MS:the Trial *P1868:*the trial 252| MS:a Priest, *P1868:*a priest,

Priest and to spare!"—this was a shot reserved;
I learn this from epistles which begin
Here where the print ends,—see the pen and ink
Of the advocate, the ready at a pinch!—
"My client boasts the clerkly privilege,
Has taken minor orders many enough,
Shows still sufficient chrism upon his pate
To neutralize a blood-stain: *presbyter,*
Primae tonsurae, subdiaconus,
Sacerdos, so he slips from underneath
Your power, the temporal, slides inside the robe
Of mother Church: to her we make appeal
By the Pope, the Church's head!"

A parlous plea,
Put in with noticeable effect, it seems;
"Since straight,"—resumes the zealous orator,
Making a friend acquainted with the facts,—
"Once the word 'clericality' let fall,
Procedure stopped and freer breath was drawn
By all considerate and responsible Rome."
Quality took the decent part, of course;
Held by the husband, who was noble too:
Or, for the matter of that, a churl would side
With too-refined susceptibility,
And honour which, tender in the extreme,
Stung to the quick, must roughly right itself
At all risks, not sit still and whine for law
As a Jew would, if you squeezed him to the wall,

253| MS:reserved, *P1868:*reserved; 254| MS:from the letters which *P1868:*from epistles which 256| MS:the Advocate <> pinch, § altered to § pinch!— *P1868:*the advocate 259| MS:his curls *P1868:*his pate 264| MS:Of Mother *P1868:*Of mother 265| MS:the Pope, the Churches Head!" § line and marginal note indicating new ¶ § *P1868:*Church's head!" 266| MS:seems, *P1868:*seems; 267| MS:zealous man of law *P1868:*zealous orator, 272| MS:course, *P1868:*course; 273| MS:too, *P1868:*too: 275| MS:too refined *P1868:*too-refined 276| MS:And § crossed out and replaced above by one word § With honour *P1868:*And honour 279| MS:would if <> wall *P1868:*would, if <>

Brisk-trotting through the Ghetto. Nay, it seems,
Even the Emperor's Envoy had his say
To say on the subject; might not see, unmoved,
Civility menaced throughout Christendom
By too harsh measure dealt her champion here.
Lastly, what made all safe, the Pope was kind,
From his youth up, reluctant to take life,
If mercy might be just and yet show grace;
Much more unlikely then, in extreme age,
To take a life the general sense bade spare.
'Twas plain that Guido would go scatheless yet.

But human promise, oh, how short of shine!
How topple down the piles of hope we rear!
How history proves . . . nay, read Herodotus!
Suddenly starting from a nap, as it were,
A dog-sleep with one shut, one open orb,
Cried the Pope's great self,—Innocent by name
And nature too, and eighty-six years old,
Antonio Pignatelli of Naples, Pope
Who had trod many lands, known many deeds,
Probed many hearts, beginning with his own,
And now was far in readiness for God,—
'Twas he who first bade leave those souls in peace,
Those Jansenists, re-nicknamed Molinists,
('Gainst whom the cry went, like a frowsy tune,

---

wall, 280| MS:seems *P1868:*seems, 282| MS:subject, might not see unmoved *P1868:*subject; might not see, unmoved, 284-90| MS:here:/ 'Twas *P1868:*here. § lines 285-89 added § 'Twas 290-91| MS: § line and marginal note indicating new ¶ § 291| MS:promise, short § crossed out and replaced above by four words § oh, how brief of § last two words crossed out, *short* reinstated § of shine turns shade! § last two words and exclamation point crossed out and replaced by § ! 291-93| MS:shine!/ How <> proves . . but § crossed out and replaced above by § nay, *P1868:*shine!/ How topple down the piles of hope we rear!/ How <> proves . . . nay 295| MS:dogs-sleep § altered to § dog-sleep <> open eye, § crossed out and replaced above by § orb, 297| MS:too and eighty six *P1868:*too, and eighty-six 299| MS:had trod § crossed out § seen § crossed out and replaced by § trod many lands, known § crossed out and replaced above by § and § crossed out and replaced by one word § known many men § written over by § deeds, 300| MS:hearts beginning *P1868:*hearts, beginning 302| MS:peace *P1868:*peace, 303| MS:Those Jansenists now nicknamed Molinists *P1868:*Those Jansenists, re-nicknamed Molinists, 304| § crowded between lines 303-4 § MS:a fetid tune *P1868:*a frowsy tune,

Tickling men's ears—the sect for a quarter of an hour
I' the teeth of the world which, clown-like, loves to chew
Be it but a straw 'twixt work and whistling-while,
Taste some vituperation, bite away,
Whether at marjoram-sprig or garlic-clove,
Aught it may sport with, spoil, and then spit forth)
"Leave them alone," bade he, "those Molinists!
Who may have other light than we perceive,
Or why is it the whole world hates them thus?"
Also he peeled off that last scandal-rag
Of Nepotism; and so observed the poor
That men would merrily say, "Halt, deaf and blind,
Who feed on fat things, leave the master's self
To gather up the fragments of his feast,
These be the nephews of Pope Innocent!—
His own meal costs but five carlines a day,
Poor-priest's allowance, for he claims no more."
—He cried of a sudden, this great good old Pope,
When they appealed in last resort to him,
"I have mastered the whole matter: I nothing doubt.
Though Guido stood forth priest from head to heel,
Instead of, as alleged, a piece of one,—
And further, were he, from the tonsured scalp

305-10| MS:§ line between lines 304-5 and marginal note *insert underneath*, followed by these lines closely written in the margin § 306| MS:In <> clown like *P1868:*I' <> clown-like 307| MS:a flower § crossed out and replaced above by one word § straw twixt <> whistling while— *P1868:*whistling-while, *1888:*'twixt 308| MS:away *P1868:*away, 310-12| MS:forth)/ Who <> perceive. *P1868:*forth)/ "Leave them alone," bade he, "those Molinists!/ Who <> perceive, 313| MS:them so?" § written over by § thus?" 314| MS:§ crowded between lines 313-15 § 315| MS:Of the Popes' Nephews: § last two words and colon crossed out and replaced above by one word and semi-colon § Nepotism; and so loved § crossed out and replaced above by § observed 316| MS:say "Halt *P1868:*say, "Halt 317| MS:on the § crossed out § <> the master § altered to § master's then § crossed out and replaced by § self 320| MS:Whose own <> costs us five *P1868:*His own <> costs but five 322| MS:this same § crossed out and replaced above by one word § great good old Pope § crossed out and replaced by illegible word which, in turn, is crossed out and *Pope* is restored § *P1868*: old Pope, 324| MS:matter: and § crossed out and replaced by § I 326| MS:one, *P1868:*one,—

To the sandaled sole of him, my son and Christ's,
Instead of touching us by finger-tip
As you assert, and pressing up so close
Only to set a blood-smutch on our robe,—
I and Christ would renounce all right in him.
Am I not Pope, and presently to die,
And busied how to render my account,
And shall I wait a day ere I decide
On doing or not doing justice here?
Cut off his head to-morrow by this time,
Hang up his four mates, two on either hand,
And end one business more!"

So said, so done—
Rather so writ, for the old Pope bade this,
I find, with his particular chirograph,
His own no such infirm hand, Friday night;
And next day, February Twenty Two,
Since our salvation Sixteen Ninety Eight,
—Not at the proper head-and-hanging-place
On bridge-foot close by Castle Angelo,
Where custom somewhat staled the spectacle,
('Twas not so well i' the way of Rome, beside,
The noble Rome, the Rome of Guido's rank)
But at the city's newer gayer end,—
The cavalcading promenading place
Beside the gate and opposite the church
Under the Pincian gardens green with Spring,
'Neath the obelisk 'twixt the fountains in the Square,

329| MS:by the finger-tip *P1868:*by finger-tip 331| MS:robe, *P1868:*robe,— 339| MS:more!" § vertical line and marginal note indicating new ¶ § So 340| MS:old Pope wrote this, *P1868:*old Pope bade this, 345| MS:Not by § crossed out and replaced above by § at 346| MS:At § crossed out and replaced above by one word § On the Bridge-foot by *P1868:*On bridge-foot close by 347| MS:the show-beside § crossed out and replaced above by § spectacle, 348-50| MS:well in the way of noble § crossed out § Rome, beside, § last word apparently added in revision, as were line 349 and parentheses enclosing lines 348-49 § / <> the City's newer, gayer *P1868:*i' <> of Rome <> / The noble Rome, the Rome of Guido's rank)/ <> city's newer gayer 354| MS:By the middle of § last two words crossed out and replaced above by five words § obelisk 'twixt the fountains in the Square, § comma apparently added in revision § Del Popolo, § last two words

Did Guido and his fellows find their fate,
All Rome for witness, and—my writer adds—
Remonstrant in its universal grief,
Since Guido had the suffrage of all Rome.

This is the bookful; thus far take the truth,
The untempered gold, the fact untampered with,
The mere ring-metal ere the ring be made!
And what has hitherto come of it? Who preserves
The memory of this Guido, and his wife
Pompilia, more than Ademollo's name,
The etcher of those prints, two *crazie* each,
Saved by a stone from snowing broad the Square
With scenic backgrounds? Was this truth of force?
Able to take its own part as truth should,
Sufficient, self-sustaining? Why, if so—
Yonder's a fire, into it goes my book,
As who shall say me nay, and what the loss?
You know the tale already: I may ask,
Rather than think to tell you, more thereof,—
Ask you not merely who were he and she,
Husband and wife, what manner of mankind,
But how you hold concerning this and that
Other yet-unnamed actor in the piece.

---

crossed out § *P1868:*'Neath the obelisk 355| MS:fellows meet § crossed out and replaced above by one word § find their death § crossed out and replaced by § fate, 356| MS:witness and *P1868:*witness, and 357| MS:Remonstrance § altered to § Remonstrant 358| MS:Since Guido passed for a wronged man in § last six words crossed out and replaced above by five words § had the suffrage of all Rome. 358-59| MS:§ line between lines and marginal note indicating new ¶ § 360| MS:gold, and § crossed out and replaced by § the 361| MS:ere the § crossed out and replaced above by § a § crossed out and original reading restored § ring be § crossed out and replaced above by § is § crossed out and original reading restored § made. *P1868:*made! 361-62| MS:§ ¶ § *1868:*§ no ¶ § 363| MS:this Guido and *P1868:*this Guido, and 364| MS:Pompilia more < > name, § crossed out and replaced above by § fame, § crossed out and original reading restored § *P1868:* Pompilia, more 365| MS:That § crossed out and replaced by one word § The < > prints two < > each *P1868:*prints, two < > each, 366| MS:snowing white § crossed out and replaced above by § broad 370| MS:goes the § crossed out and replaced by one word § my book *P1868:*book, 371| MS:what's your § crossed out and replaced by § the *P1868:*what 372| MS:ask *P1868:*ask, 373| MS:think to tell § last two words inserted above § you more *P1868:*you, more 374| MS:Ask then § crossed out and replaced above by § you 377| MS:actors < >

The young frank handsome courtly Canon, now,
The priest, declared the lover of the wife,
He who, no question, did elope with her,
For certain bring the tragedy about,
Giuseppe Caponsacchi;—his strange course
I' the matter, was it right or wrong or both?
Then the old couple, slaughtered with the wife
By the husband as accomplices in crime,
Those Comparini, Pietro and his spouse,—
What say you to the right or wrong of that,
When, at a known name whispered through the door
Of a lone villa on a Christmas night,
It opened that the joyous hearts inside
Might welcome as it were an angel-guest
Come in Christ's name to knock and enter, sup
And satisfy the loving ones he saved;
And so did welcome devils and their death?
I have been silent on that circumstance
Although the couple passed for close of kin
To wife and husband, were by some accounts
Pompilia's very parents: you know best.
Also that infant the great joy was for,
That Gaetano, the wife's two-weeks' babe,
The husband's first-born child, his son and heir,
Whose birth and being turned his night to day—
Why must the father kill the mother thus
Because she bore his son and saved himself?

Well, British Public, ye who like me not,
(God love you!) and will have your proper laugh

---

piece: *P1868:*actor <> piece. 378| MS:young bright § crossed out and replaced above by § frank 379| MS:priest declared *P1868:*priest, declared 381| MS: certain bring § crossed out and replaced above by § brought § crossed out and original reading restored § 382| MS:Giuseppe Caponsacchi,—his *P1868:*Giuseppe Caponsacchi;—his 383| MS:In the matter— § dash crossed out and replaced by comma § *P1868:*I' 384| MS:couple slaughtered *P1868:*couple, slaughtered 391| MS:angel guest *CP1868:*angel-guest 393| MS:saved, *P1868:*saved; 398| MS:parents—you *P1868:*parents: you 399| MS:infant that § crossed out § the great § inserted above line § <> for *P1868:*for, 400| MS:two-weeks *P1868:* two-weeks' 402| MS:being had turned *P1868:*being turned 404-5| MS: § line and marginal note indicting new ¶ § you *P1868:*ye 406| MS:your usual § crossed out § laugh beside § last word clearly added in revision § *P1868:*your proper

At the dark question, laugh it! I laugh first.
Truth must prevail, the proverb vows; and truth
—Here is it all i' the book at last, as first
There it was all i' the heads and hearts of Rome
Gentle and simple, never to fall nor fade
Nor be forgotten. Yet, a little while,
The passage of a century or so,
Decads thrice five, and here's time paid his tax,
Oblivion gone home with her harvesting,
And all left smooth again as scythe could shave.
Far from beginning with you London folk,
I took my book to Rome first, tried truth's power
On likely people. "Have you met such names?
Is a tradition extant of such facts?
Your law-courts stand, your records frown a-row:
What if I rove and rummage?" "—Why, you'll waste
Your pains and end as wise as you began!"
Everyone snickered: "names and facts thus old
Are newer much than Europe news we find
Down in to-day's *Diario*. Records, quotha?
Why, the French burned them, what else do the French?
The rap-and-rending nation! And it tells
Against the Church, no doubt,—another gird
At the Temporality, your Trial, of course?"

---

laugh 407| MS:question, do so. § last two words and period crossed out and replaced above by two words and exclamation point § laugh it! I 408| MS:Here's § crossed out § truth § altered to § Truth and prevalent, as § last three words and comma crossed out and replaced above by two words and dash § must prevail—the proverb runs: § crossed out and replaced by § vows; and truth § last word clearly added in revision § 409| MS:in *P1868:*i' 410| MS:in *P1868:*i'
411| MS:fall and § crossed out and replaced by § nor 412| MS:And § crossed out and replaced above by § Nor be forgotten:yet *P1868:*forgotten. Yet 415| MS: § crowded between lines 414 and 416§ gone off § crossed out and replaced above by § home 416| MS:all left § last word added below § smooth, § comma added in revision § shaven § crossed out and replaced below by one word § again as the § crossed out § scythe will play § last two words crossed out and replaced above by one word § would shave. § word and period added in revision § *P1868:*could 417| MS:folk *P1868:*folk, 419| MS:On the likely *P1868:*On likely 420| MS:Is no tradition *P1868:*Is a tradition 421| MS:a-row, *P1868:*a-row:
422| MS:rummage?" "Why *P1868:*rummage?" "—Why 423| MS:began," *P1868:*began!" 425| MS:than Europe's *P1868:*than Europe
426| MS:Down § added above line § In our § crossed out § <> *Diario*: records *P1868:*Down in <> *Diario*. Records 430| MS:the Temporalities § altered to § Temporality 431| MS:time" submitted *P1868:*time," submitted

"—Quite otherwise this time," submitted I;
"Clean for the Church and dead against the world,
The flesh and the devil, does it tell for once."
"—The rarer and the happier! All the same,
Content you with your treasure of a book,
And waive what's wanting! Take a friend's advice!
It's not the custom of the country. Mend
Your ways indeed and we may stretch a point:
Go get you manned by Manning and new-manned
By Newman and, mayhap, wise-manned to boot
By Wiseman, and we'll see or else we won't!
Thanks meantime for the story, long and strong,
A pretty piece of narrative enough,
Which scarce ought so to drop out, one would think,
From the more curious annals of our kind.
Do you tell the story, now, in off-hand style,
Straight from the book? Or simply here and there,
(The while you vault it through the loose and large)
Hang to a hint? Or is there book at all,
And don't you deal in poetry, make-believe,
And the white lies it sounds like?"

Yes and no!

From the book, yes; thence bit by bit I dug
The lingot truth, that memorable day,
Assayed and knew my piecemeal gain was gold,—
Yes; but from something else surpassing that,
Something of mine which, mixed up with the mass,
Made it bear hammer and be firm to file.
Fancy with fact is just one fact the more;
To-wit, that fancy has informed, transpierced,
Thridded and so thrown fast the facts else free,

432| MS:world *P1868:*world, 437| MS:country:mend *P1868:*country. Mend 438| MS:might § crossed out and replaced above by § may 443| MS:enough *P1868:*enough, 444| MS:ought thus have § last two words crossed out and replaced above by two words § so to dropt § altered to § drop 447| MS:there *P1868:*there, 448| MS:The <> large, *P1868:*(The <> large) 449| MS:there a book at all *P1868:*there book at all, 450| MS:make-believe, ? § question mark crossed out § 451| MS:It § crossed out and replaced above by five words § And the white lies it sounds so, come, be candid § last four words crossed out § like?" 453| MS:The entire § crossed out and replaced by one word § lingot truth, on § crossed out § 460| MS:and so thrown § last two words added above line §

As right through ring and ring runs the djereed
And binds the loose, one bar without a break.
I fused my live soul and that inert stuff,
Before attempting smithcraft, on the night
After the day when,—truth thus grasped and gained,—
The book was shut and done with and laid by
On the cream-coloured massive agate, broad
'Neath the twin cherubs in the tarnished frame
O' the mirror, tall thence to the ceiling-top.
And from the reading, and that slab I leant
My elbow on, the while I read and read,
I turned, to free myself and find the world,
And stepped out on the narrow terrace, built
Over the street and opposite the church,
And paced its lozenge-brickwork sprinkled cool;
Because Felice-church-side stretched, a-glow
Through each square window fringed for festival,
Whence came the clear voice of the cloistered ones
Chanting a chant made for midsummer nights—
I know not what particular praise of God,
It always came and went with June. Beneath
I' the street, quick shown by openings of the sky
When flame fell silently from cloud to cloud,
Richer than that gold snow Jove rained on Rhodes,
The townsmen walked by twos and threes, and talked,
Drinking the blackness in default of air—
A busy human sense beneath my feet:
While in and out the terrace-plants, and round
One branch of tall datura, waxed and waned

---

fastened so § last two words altered to § fast 461| MS:through fifty § crossed out and replaced above by two words § ring and rings § altered to § ring
463| MS:stuff *P1868:*stuff, 469| MS:Of < > cieling-top *P1868:*O' < > ceiling-top 470| MS:reading, and § crossed out and replaced above by § from *P1868:*reading, and that 473| MS:terrace built *P1868:*terrace, built
474| MS:church *P1868:*church, 475| MS:lozenge brickwork < > cool, *P1868:* lozenge-brickwork < > cool; 482| MS:In the street, quick § inserted above line § < > the sky § crossed out and replaced by § heaven *P1868:*I' < > the sky
483| MS:silently § altered to *silent* and then restored to original § 487| MS:sense between § crossed out and replaced above by one word § beneath my feet; *P1868:*feet:

The lamp-fly lured there, wanting the white flower.
Over the roof o' the lighted church I looked
A bowshot to the street's end, north away
Out of the Roman gate to the Roman road
By the river, till I felt the Apennine.
And there would lie Arezzo, the man's town,
The woman's trap and cage and torture-place,
Also the stage where the priest played his part,
A spectacle for angels,—ay, indeed,
There lay Arezzo! Farther then I fared,
Feeling my way on through the hot and dense,
Romeward, until I found the wayside inn
By Castelnuovo's few mean hut-like homes
Huddled together on the hill-foot bleak,
Bare, broken only by that tree or two
Against the sudden bloody splendour poured
Cursewise in day's departure by the sun
O'er the low house-roof of that squalid inn
Where they three, for the first time and the last,
Husband and wife and priest, met face to face.
Whence I went on again, the end was near,
Step by step, missing none and marking all,
Till Rome itself, the ghastly goal, I reached.
Why, all the while,—how could it otherwise?—
The life in me abolished the death of things,
Deep calling unto deep: as then and there
Acted itself over again once more
The tragic piece. I saw with my own eyes

490| MS:lampfly *P1868:*lamp-fly 491| MS:of *P1868:*o' 492| MS:end north *P1868:*end, north 494| MS:the Apennine, *P1868:*the Apennine. 497| MS:part *P1868:*part, 500| MS:my way § inserted above line § <> dense *P1868:*dense, 501| MS:Romewards § altered to § Romeward 505| MS:splendor *P1868:*splendour 506| MS:in his departure by the day *1888:* in day's departure by the sun 507| MS:On the low house-roofs and ignoble § crossed out and replaced above by two words § the squalid inn *P1868:*house-roof of that squalid inn *1888:*O'er the 508| MS:time as the *P1868:*time and the 512| MS:reached: *P1868:*reached. 513| MS:while, how <> otherwise, *P1868:* while,—how <> otherwise?— 514| MS:things *P1868:*things, 515| MS:unto deep, as *P1868:*unto deep: as 517| MS:piece: I *P1868:*piece. I

In Florence as I trod the terrace, breathed
The beauty and the fearfulness of night,
How it had run, this round from Rome to Rome—
Because, you are to know, they lived at Rome,
Pompilia's parents, as they thought themselves,
Two poor ignoble hearts who did their best
Part God's way, part the other way than God's,
To somehow make a shift and scramble through
The world's mud, careless if it splashed and spoiled,
Provided they might so hold high, keep clean
Their child's soul, one soul white enough for three,
And lift it to whatever star should stoop,
What possible sphere of purer life than theirs
Should come in aid of whiteness hard to save.
I saw the star stoop, that they strained to touch,
And did touch and depose their treasure on,
As Guido Franceschini took away
Pompilia to be his for evermore,
While they sang "Now let us depart in peace,
Having beheld thy glory, Guido's wife!"
I saw the star supposed, but fog o' the fen,
Gilded star-fashion by a glint from hell;
Having been heaved up, haled on its gross way,
By hands unguessed before, invisible help
From a dark brotherhood, and specially
Two obscure goblin creatures, fox-faced this,
Cat-clawed the other, called his next of kin
By Guido the main monster,—cloaked and caped,
Making as they were priests, to mock God more,—
Abate Paul, Canon Girolamo.

521| MS:Because you < > know they < > Rome *P1868:*Because, you < > know, they < > Rome, 522| MS:parents as *P1868:*parents, as 523| MS:The poor ignoble pair who *P1868:*Two poor ignoble hearts who 526| MS:This world's *P1868:*The world's 530| MS:First § crossed out and replaced above by § What 531| MS:in help § crossed out and replaced above by § aid 532| MS:stoop that *1868:*stoop, that 535| MS:forevermore *P1868:*for evermore, 536| MS:they cried "Now < > peace *P1868:*they sang "Now < > peace, 538| MS:of the fen *P1868:*o' the fen, 539| MS:hell, *P1868:*hell; 540| MS:Which had been < > way *P1868:*Having been < > way, 544| MS:called the § crossed out and replaced above by § his 545| MS:To § crossed out and replaced above by § By < > monster, cloaked and caped *P1868:*monster,—cloaked and caped, 546| MS:more, *P1868:* more,— 547| MS:Abate Paul, Canon Girolamo; *P1868:*Abate Paul, Canon

These who had rolled the starlike pest to Rome
And stationed it to suck up and absorb
The sweetness of Pompilia, rolled again
That bloated bubble, with her soul inside,
Back to Arezzo and a palace there—
Or say, a fissure in the honest earth
Whence long ago had curled the vapour first,
Blown big by nether fires to appal day:
It touched home, broke, and blasted far and wide.
I saw the cheated couple find the cheat
And guess what foul rite they were captured for,—
Too fain to follow over hill and dale
That child of theirs caught up thus in the cloud
And carried by the Prince o' the Power of the Air
Whither he would, to wilderness or sea.
I saw them, in the potency of fear,
Break somehow through the satyr-family
(For a grey mother with a monkey-mien,
Mopping and mowing, was apparent too,
As, confident of capture, all took hands
And danced about the captives in a ring)
—Saw them break through, breathe safe, at Rome again,
Saved by the selfish instinct, losing so
Their loved one left with haters. These I saw,
In recrudescency of baffled hate,
Prepare to wring the uttermost revenge
From body and soul thus left them: all was sure,
Fire laid and cauldron set, the obscene ring traced,

Girolamo. 550| MS:roll § altered to § rolled 551| MS:bubble with <> inside *P1868:*bubble, with <> inside, 552| MS:there *P1868:*there— 554| MS:vapor first *P1868:*vapour first, 556| MS:broke and blasted *P1868:* broke, and blasted 558| MS:for, *P1868:*for,— 560| MS:That heart of them § altered to § theirs caught up then § altered to § thus *P1868:*That child of 561| MS:of the power <> air *P1868:*o' the Power <> Air 562| MS:would to *P1868:*would, to 563| MS:them in the agony of fear *P1868:*them, in the potency of fear, 565| MS:monkey-mien *P1868:*monkey-mien, 566| MS:mowing was <> too) § parenthesis crossed out § *P1868:*mowing, was <> too, 568| MS:the victims § crossed out and replaced above by § captives <> ring § altered to § ring) 569| MS:—Break through and breathe safe, back at *P1868:*—Saw them break through, breathe safe, at 571| MS:saw *P1868:*saw, 572| MS:baffled rage § crossed out and replaced by § hate *P1868:*hate, 574| MS:sure: *P1868:*sure, 575| MS:traced *P1868:*traced,

The victim stripped and prostrate: what of God?
The cleaving of a cloud, a cry, a crash,
Quenched lay their cauldron, cowered i' the dust the crew,
As, in a glory of armour like Saint George,
Out again sprang the young good beauteous priest
Bearing away the lady in his arms,
Saved for a splendid minute and no more.
For, whom i' the path did that priest come upon,
He and the poor lost lady borne so brave,
—Checking the song of praise in me, had else
Swelled to the full for God's will done on earth—
Whom but a dusk misfeatured messenger,
No other than the angel of this life,
Whose care is lest men see too much at once.
He made the sign, such God glimpse must suffice,
Nor prejudice the Prince o' the Power of the Air,
Whose ministration piles us overhead
What we call, first, earth's roof and, last, heaven's floor,
Now grate o' the trap, then outlet of the cage:
So took the lady, left the priest alone,
And once more canopied the world with black.
But through the blackness I saw Rome again,
And where a solitary villa stood
In a lone garden-quarter: it was eve,
The second of the year, and oh so cold!
Ever and anon there flittered through the air
A snow-flake, and a scanty couch of snow
Crusted the grass-walk and the garden-mould.

576| MS:prostrate: where was God? *P1868:*prostrate: what of God? 578| MS:in *P1868:*i' 579| MS:As in <> George *P1868:*As, in <> George, 580| MS:young, § comma crossed out § good, § comma crossed out § potent priest *P1868:*good beauteous priest 582| MS:splendid moment § crossed out and replaced above by § minute 583| MS:in *P1868:*i' 585| MS:—Checking that § crossed out and replaced above by § the <> me had *P1868:*me, had 588| MS:life *P1868:*life, 590| MS:sign such <> suffice *P1868:*sign, such <> suffice, 591| MS:of the power <> air, *P1868:*o' the Power <> Air, 593| MS:call first earth's <> and last heaven's *P1868:*call, first, earth's <> and, last, heaven's 594| MS:grate of the *P1868:*grate o' the 596| MS:And canopied § altered to § And once more canopied <> black once more, § last three words and comma altered to § black. 599| MS:lone suburb § crossed out § <> eve *P1868:*eve, 600| MS:year and *P1868:*year, and 601| MS:there quivered § crossed out and replaced above by § flittered 603| MS:garden mould

All was grave, silent, sinister,—when, ha?
Glimmeringly did a pack of were-wolves pad
The snow, those flames were Guido's eyes in front,
And all five found and footed it, the track,
To where a threshold-streak of warmth and light
Betrayed the villa-door with life inside,
While an inch outside were those blood-bright eyes,
And black lips wrinkling o'er the flash of teeth,
And tongues that lolled—Oh God that madest man!
They parleyed in their language. Then one whined—
That was the policy and master-stroke—
Deep in his throat whispered what seemed a name—
"Open to Caponsacchi!" Guido cried:
"Gabriel!" cried Lucifer at Eden-gate.
Wide as a heart, opened the door at once,
Showing the joyous couple, and their child
The two-weeks' mother, to the wolves, the wolves
To them. Close eyes! And when the corpses lay
Stark-stretched, and those the wolves, their wolf-work done,
Were safe-embosomed by the night again,
I knew a necessary change in things;
As when the worst watch of the night gives way,
And there comes duly, to take cognizance,
The scrutinizing eye-point of some star—
And who despairs of a new daybreak now?
Lo, the first ray protruded on those five!

---

*P1868:*garden-mould. 605| MS:werewolves *P1868:*were-wolves
606| MS:snow, and § crossed out § those flames § inserted above § 607| MS:five footed it and found the track *P1868:*five found and footed it, the track,
608| MS:where the threshold streak *P1868:*where a threshold-streak
610| MS:eyes *P1868:*eyes, 611| MS:teeth *P1868:*teeth, 612| MS:lolled . . Oh *P1868:*lolled—Oh 616| MS:§ crowded between lines 615-17, clearly added in revision § cried— *P1868:*cried: 618| MS:heart opened *P1868:*heart, opened
619| MS:couple and *P1868:*couple, and 620| MS:mother to *P1868:*mother, to
621| MS:when these corpses *P1868:*when the corpses 622| MS:wolfwork *P1868:*wolf-work 623| MS:safe, embosomed *P1868:*safe-embosomed
624| MS:things *P1868:*things; 625| MS:way *P1868:*way, 626| MS:duly to <> cognisance *P1868:*duly, to <> cognisance *1888:*cognizance

It reached them, and each felon writhed transfixed.
Awhile they palpitated on the spear
Motionless over Tophet; stand or fall?
"I say, the spear should fall—should stand, I say!"
Cried the world come to judgment, granting grace
Or dealing doom according to world's wont,
Those world's-bystanders grouped on Rome's cross-road
At prick and summons of the primal curse
Which bids man love as well as make a lie.
There prattled they, discoursed the right and wrong,
Turned wrong to right, proved wolves sheep and sheep wolves,
So that you scarce distinguished fell from fleece;
Till out spoke a great guardian of the fold,
Stood up, put forth his hand that held the crook,
And motioned that the arrested point decline:
Horribly off, the wriggling dead-weight reeled,
Rushed to the bottom and lay ruined there.
Though still at the pit's mouth, despite the smoke
O' the burning, tarriers turned again to talk
And trim the balance, and detect at least
A touch of wolf in what showed whitest sheep,
A cross of sheep redeeming the whole wolf,—
Vex truth a little longer:—less and less,
Because years came and went, and more and more
Brought new lies with them to be loved in turn.
Till all at once the memory of the thing,—
The fact that, wolves or sheep, such creatures were,—
Which hitherto, however men supposed,
Had somehow plain and pillar-like prevailed
I' the midst of them, indisputably fact,

630| MS:them and *P1868:*them, and 633| MS:say the <> say" *P1868:*say, the <> say!" 635| MS:to its § crossed out and replaced above by § their wont, *P1868:*to world's wont, 636| MS:grouped at § crossed out and replaced above by § on 639| MS:wrong *P1868:*wrong, 640| MS:wrong and right *P1868:*wrong to right 641| MS:Until § crossed out and replaced above by two words § So that <> fleece *P1868:*fleece; 644| MS:decline, *P1868:*decline: 645| MS:And horribly off the <> deadweight rolled, § crossed out and replaced above by § reeled, *P1868:*Horribly off, the <> dead-weight 646| MS:and was ruined there, *P1868:*and lay ruined there. 648| MS:Of *P1868:*O' 652| MS:Vexed § altered to § Vex <> longer—less and less *P1868:*longer:—less and less, 654| MS:turn, *P1868:*turn. 659| MS:In <> indisputably truth § crossed out and

Granite, time's tooth should grate against, not graze,—
Why, this proved sandstone, friable, fast to fly
And give its grain away at wish o' the wind.
Ever and ever more diminutive,
Base gone, shaft lost, only entablature,
Dwindled into no bigger than a book,
Lay of the column; and that little, left
By the roadside 'mid the ordure, shards and weeds.
Until I haply, wandering that lone way,
Kickd it up, turned it over, and recognized,
For all the crumblement, this abacus,
This square old yellow book,—could calculate
By this the lost proportions of the style.

This was it from, my fancy with those facts,
I used to tell the tale, turned gay to grave,
But lacked a listener seldom; such alloy,
Such substance of me interfused the gold
Which, wrought into a shapely ring therewith,
Hammered and filed, fingered and favoured, last
Lay ready for the renovating wash
O' the water. "How much of the tale was true?"
I disappeared; the book grew all in all;
The lawyers' pleadings swelled back to their size,—
Doubled in two, the crease upon them yet,
For more commodity of carriage, see!—

---

replaced by § true, *P1868:*I' <> indisputably fact, 660| MS:Granite time's *P1868:*Granite, time's 661| MS:Why this was § crossed out and replaced above by § proved <> friable, fugitive, § crossed out and replaced by § fast to fly, *P1868:*Why, this <> fly 662| MS:That gives <> away to the wish of the wind, *P1868:*And give <> away at wish o' the wind. 664| MS:entablature *P1868:*entablature, 666| MS:column, and <> little left *P1868:*column; and <> little, left 667| MS:mid *P1868:*'mid 668| MS:that way, *1868:*that lone way, 669| MS:over and *P1868:*over, and 671| MS:book, could *P1868:*book,—could 672-73| MS:§ line and marginal note indicating new ¶ § 674| MS:tell a tale turned <> grave *P1868:*tell the tale, turned <> grave, 676| MS:And § crossed out and replaced above by § Such <> gold, *P1868:*gold 677| MS:wrought into a shapely ring § last four words inserted above § thereby, § altered to § therewith, 680| MS:Of *P1868:*O' 681| MS:disappeared: the <> all, *P1868:*disappeared; the <> all; 682| MS:pleading's *P1868:*pleadings 684| MS:see— *P1868:*

And these are letters, veritable sheets
That brought posthaste the news to Florence, writ
At Rome the day Count Guido died, we find,
To stay the craving of a client there,
Who bound the same and so produced my book.
Lovers of dead truth, did ye fare the worse?
Lovers of live truth, found ye false my tale?

Well, now; there's nothing in nor out o' the world
Good except truth: yet this, the something else,
What's this then, which proves good yet seems untrue?
This that I mixed with truth, motions of mine
That quickened, made the inertness malleolable
O' the gold was not mine,—what's your name for this?
Are means to the end, themselves in part the end?
Is fiction which makes fact alive, fact too?
The somehow may be thishow.
                                        I find first
Writ down for very A B C of fact,
"In the beginning God made heaven and earth;"
From which, no matter with what lisp, I spell
And speak you out a consequence—that man,
Man,—as befits the made, the inferior thing,—
Purposed, since made, to grow, not make in turn,
Yet forced to try and make, else fail to grow,—
Formed to rise, reach at, if not grasp and gain
The good beyond him,—which attempt is growth,—
Repeats God's process in man's due degree,
Attaining man's proportionate result,—

---

see!— 686| MS:brought posthaste § inserted above § <> Florence writ *P1868:* to Florence, writ 687| MS:died, you know, *P1868:*died, we find, 690| MS: Lover <> truth, didst thou fare *P1868:*Lovers <> truth, did ye fare 691| MS: Lover <> truth, find it § last two words crossed out § in my tale 'twas found. *P1868:* Lovers <> truth, found ye false my tale? 692| MS:out the *P1868:*out o' the 694| MS:then which *P1868:*then, which 696| MS:quickened and make § altered to § made *P1868:*quickened, made 697| MS:Of *P1868:*O' 698| MS:Are the means <> end in *P1868:*Are means <> end, themselves in 701| MS: very A. B. C. of *1888:*very A B C of 702| MS:made Heaven and Earth." *P1868:*made heaven and earth;" 704| MS:that man, *P1868:*that man, 710| MS:Repeats § two words *the* (possibly) *work*—crossed out and replaced above by § God's 711| MS:Attains thus man's <> result, *P1868:*Attaining man's <> result,—

Creates, no, but resuscitates, perhaps.
Inalienable, the arch-prerogative
Which turns thought, act—conceives, expresses too!
No less, man, bounded, yearning to be free,
May so project his surplusage of soul
In search of body, so add self to self
By owning what lay ownerless before,—
So find, so fill full, so appropriate forms—
That, although nothing which had never life
Shall get life from him, be, not having been,
Yet, something dead may get to live again,
Something with too much life or not enough,
Which, either way imperfect, ended once:
An end whereat man's impulse intervenes,
Makes new beginning, starts the dead alive,
Completes the incomplete and saves the thing.
Man's breath were vain to light a virgin wick,—
Half-burned-out, all but quite-quenched wicks o' the lamp
Stationed for temple-service on this earth,
These indeed let him breathe on and relume!
For such man's feat is, in the due degree,
—Mimic creation, galvanism for life,
But still a glory portioned in the scale.
Why did the mage say,—feeling as we are wont
For truth, and stopping midway short of truth,
And resting on a lie,—"I raise a ghost"?
"Because," he taught adepts, "man makes not man.
Yet by a special gift, an art of arts,
More insight and more outsight and much more
Will to use both of these than boast my mates,
I can detach from me, commission forth
Half of my soul; which in its pilgrimage

712| MS:no, may § crossed out and replaced above by § but 713| MS:Inalienable the *P1868:*Inalienable, the 714| MS:too: *P1868:*too! 718| MS:ownerless till then,— *P1868:*ownerless before,— 724| MS:once; *P1868:*once:
728| MS:light the virgin *P1868:*light a virgin 729| MS:of *P1868:*o'
730| MS:earth; *P1868:*earth, 731| MS:relume, *P1868:*relume!
732| MS:For here man's *P1868:*For such man's 737| MS:ghost?" *P1872:*ghost"?
738| MS:"Because" he <> adepts "man <> man; *P1868:*"Because," he <> adepts, "man <> man. 739| MS:gift, the § crossed out and replaced above by § an
740| MS:outsight than § crossed out § 743| MS:soul, which *P1868:*soul; which

O'er old unwandered waste ways of the world,
May chance upon some fragment of a whole,
Rag of flesh, scrap of bone in dim disuse,
Smoking flax that fed fire once: prompt therein
I enter, spark-like, put old powers to play,
Push lines out to the limit, lead forth last
(By a moonrise through a ruin of a crypt)
What shall be mistily seen, murmuringly heard,
Mistakenly felt: then write my name with Faust's!"
Oh, Faust, why Faust? Was not Elisha once?—
Who bade them lay his staff on a corpse-face.
There was no voice, no hearing: he went in
Therefore, and shut the door upon them twain,
And prayed unto the Lord: and he went up
And lay upon the corpse, dead on the couch,
And put his mouth upon its mouth, his eyes
Upon its eyes, his hands upon its hands,
And stretched him on the flesh; the flesh waxed warm:
And he returned, walked to and fro the house,
And went up, stretched him on the flesh again,
And the eyes opened. 'Tis a credible feat
With the right man and way.
                                        Enough of me!
The Book! I turn its medicinable leaves
In London now till, as in Florence erst,
A spirit laughs and leaps through every limb,
And lights my eye, and lifts me by the hair,

744| MS:O'er old § inserted above line § waste § crossed out § unwandered over § crossed out and replaced above by § waste 747| MS:A § crossed out § smoking § altered to § Smoking flax that once fed fire—§ last four words altered to § that fed fire once—prompt § inserted above § *P1868*:once: prompt 749| MS:lead at § crossed out and replaced above by § forth 750| MS:ruin in § altered to § of a vault) § last word and parenthesis crossed out and replaced by § crypt) 752| MS:Mistakenly touched § crossed out and replaced above by § felt 753| MS:once? § question mark crossed out and replaced by comma § *P1868*:once?— 754| MS:corpse-face? *P1868:*corpse-face. 756| MS:§ line clearly added in revision § 761| MS:on the flesh, the <> warm; *P1868*:on the flesh; the <> warm: 762| MS:house *P1868*:house, 767| MS:in Florence first § crossed out and replaced above by § erst, 769| MS:And § inserted in margin § <> eye, and § inserted above line § <> the very

Letting me have my will again with these
—How title I the dead alive once more?

Count Guido Franceschini the Aretine,
Descended of an ancient house, though poor,
A beak-nosed bushy-bearded black-haired lord,
Lean, pallid, low of stature yet robust,
Fifty years old,—having four years ago
Married Pompilia Comparini, young,
Good, beautiful, at Rome, where she was born,
And brought her to Arezzo, where they lived
Unhappy lives, whatever curse the cause,—
This husband, taking four accomplices,
Followed this wife to Rome, where she was fled
From their Arezzo to find peace again,
In convoy, eight months earlier, of a priest,
Aretine also, of still nobler birth,
Giuseppe Caponsacchi,—caught her there
Quiet in a villa on a Christmas night,
With only Pietro and Violante by,
Both her putative parents; killed the three,
Aged, they, seventy each, and she, seventeen,
And, two weeks since, the mother of his babe
First-born and heir to what the style was worth
O' the Guido who determined, dared and did
This deed just as he purposed point by point.
Then, bent upon escape, but hotly pressed,
And captured with his co-mates that same night,
He, brought to trial, stood on this defence—
Injury to his honour caused the act;
And since his wife was false, (as manifest
By flight from home in such companionship,)

---

§ crossed out § hair, 774| MS:beak-nosed, bushy-bearded, black-haired *P1868:* beak-nosed bushy-beared black-haired 782| MS:Followed that wife to Rome where *P1868*:Followed this wife to Rome, where 783| MS:again *P1868*:again, 784| MS:priest *P1868*:priest, 786| MS:Giuseppe Caponsacchi,—and caught *1888*:Giuseppe Caponsacchi,—caught 789| MS:killed all three, *P1868*:killed the three, 790| MS:seventeen *P1868*:seventeen, 792| MS:First born *P1868*: First-born 793| MS:Of *P1868*:O' 795| MS:escape but *P1868*:escape, but 797| MS:defence, *P1868*:defence— 799| MS:That since < > false, as *P1868*: false, (as *1888*:And since 800| MS:companionship, *P1868*:companionship,)

Death, punishment deserved of the false wife
And faithless parents who abetted her
I' the flight aforesaid, wronged nor God nor man.
"Nor false she, nor yet faithless they," replied
The accuser; "cloaked and masked this murder glooms;
True was Pompilia, loyal too the pair;
Out of the man's own heart a monster curled
Which—crime coiled with connivancy at crime—
His victim's breast, he tells you, hatched and reared;
Uncoil we and stretch stark the worm of hell!"
A month the trial swayed this way and that
Ere judgment settled down on Guido's guilt;
Then was the Pope, that good Twelfth Innocent,
Appealed to: who well weighed what went before,
Affirmed the guilt and gave the guilty doom.

Let this old woe step on the stage again!
Act itself o'er anew for men to judge,
Not by the very sense and sight indeed—
(Which take at best imperfect cognizance,
Since, how heart moves brain, and how both move hand,
What mortal ever in entirety saw?)
—No dose of purer truth than man digests,
But truth with falsehood, milk that feeds him now,
Not strong meat he may get to bear some day—
To-wit, by voices we call evidence,
Uproar in the echo, live fact deadened down,
Talked over, bruited abroad, whispered away,

802-4| MS:parents, wronged nor God nor man./ "Nor *P1868*:parents who abetted her/ I' the flight aforesaid, wronged nor God nor man./ "Nor 806| MS:loyal was the pair, *P1868*:loyal too the pair; 807| MS:heart this monster curled, *1888*:heart a monster curled 808| MS:This crime coiled <> crime, *1888*:Which crime <> crime— DC,BrU: Which—crime coiled *1889*:Which—crime coiled
812| MS:guilt. *P1868*:guilt; 813| MS:good Twelfth Innocent *P1868*:good Twelfth Innocent, 814| MS:to, who *P1868*:to: who 816| MS:again, *P1868*:again! 820| MS:Since how heart *P1868*:Since, how heart

Yet helping us to all we seem to hear:
For how else know we save by worth of word?

Here are the voices presently shall sound
In due succession. First, the world's outcry
Around the rush and ripple of any fact
Fallen stonewise, plumb on the smooth face of things;
The world's guess, as it crowds the bank o' the pool,
At what were figure and substance, by their splash:
Then, by vibrations in the general mind,
At depth of deed already out of reach.
This threefold murder of the day before,—
Say, Half-Rome's feel after the vanished truth;
Honest enough, as the way is: all the same,
Harbouring in the centre of its sense
A hidden germ of failure, shy but sure,
To neutralize that honesty and leave
That feel for truth at fault, as the way is too.
Some prepossession such as starts amiss,
By but a hair's breadth at the shoulder-blade,
The arm o' the feeler, dip he ne'er so bold;
So leads arm waveringly, lets fall wide
O' the mark its finger, sent to find and fix
Truth at the bottom, that deceptive speck.
With this Half-Rome,—the source of swerving, call
Over-belief in Guido's right and wrong
Rather than in Pompilia's wrong and right:

828| MS:hear— *P1868*:hear: 830| MS:presently to sound *P1868*:presently shall sound 833| MS:things: *P1868*:things; 834| MS:of *P1868*:o'
835| MS:substance by <> splash, *P1868*:substance, by <> splash:
836| MS:And, by *1868*:Then, by 839| MS:Say, Half Rome's <> truth,— *CP1868*:Say, Half-Rome's <> truth; 840| MS:is; all *P1868*:is: all
842| MS:The hidden <> shy and sure, *P1868*:A hidden <> shy but sure,
843| MS:Shall neutralize *P1868*:Should neutralize *1888*:To neutralize
844| MS:too: *P1868*:too. 845| MS:amiss *P1868*:amiss, 846-47| MS:§ lines reversed § 847| MS:of <> so brave, *P1868*:o' *1888*:so bold; 848| MS:And so leads waveringly *1888*:So leads arm waveringly 849| MS:Of the mark his finger meant to *P1868*:O' <> find, and *1888*:mark its finger, sent to find and
851| MS:this Half Rome *CP1868*:this Half-Rome 853| MS:right, *P1868*:right:

Who shall say how, who shall say why? 'Tis there—
The instinctive theorizing whence a fact
Looks to the eye as the eye likes the look.
Gossip in a public place, a sample-speech.
Some worthy, with his previous hint to find
A husband's side the safer, and no whit
Aware he is not Æacus the while,—
How such an one supposes and states fact
To whosoever of a multitude
Will listen, and perhaps prolong thereby
The not-unpleasant flutter at the breast,
Born of a certain spectacle shut in
By the church Lorenzo opposite. So, they lounge
Midway the mouth o' the street, on Corso side,
'Twixt palace Fiano and palace Ruspoli,
Linger and listen; keeping clear o' the crowd,
Yet wishful one could lend that crowd one's eyes,
(So universal is its plague of squint)
And make hearts beat our time that flutter false:
—All for the truth's sake, mere truth, nothing else!
How Half-Rome found for Guido much excuse.

Next, from Rome's other half, the opposite feel
For truth with a like swerve, like unsuccess,—
Or if success, by no skill but more luck
This time, through siding rather with the wife,
Because a fancy-fit inclined that way,
Than with the husband. One wears drab, one pink;

854| MS:why? 'Twas § altered to § 'Tis 857| MS:sample-speech; *P1868*:sample-speech. 858| MS:worthy with *P1868*:worthy, with 860| MS:while, *P1868*:while,— 863| MS:listen and *P1868*:listen, and 864| MS:breast *P1868*:breast, 866| MS:opposite; so they *P1868*:opposite. So, they 867| MS:of *P1868*:o' 869| MS:listen, keeping <> of *P1868*:listen; keeping <> o' 871| MS:So <> squint, *P1868*:(So <> squint) 872| MS:false, *P1868*:false: 873| MS:else. *P1868*:else! 874| MS:How Half Rome *CP1868*:How Half-Rome 876-78| MS:unsuccess,— /This <> through rather siding with *P1868*:unsuccess,—/ Or if success, by no more skill but luck:/ This *1888*:/ <> no skill but more luck/ This <> through siding rather with 879| MS:Whatever § crossed out and replaced above by § However the fancy-fit *1888*:Because a fancy-fit 880| MS:drab, one, pink; *P1868*:one pink;

Who wears pink, ask him "Which shall win the race,
Of coupled runners like as egg and egg?"
"—Why, if I must choose, he with the pink scarf."
Doubtless for some such reason choice fell here.
A piece of public talk to correspond
At the next stage of the story; just a day
Let pass and new day brings the proper change.
Another sample-speech i' the market-place
O' the Barberini by the Capucins;
Where the old Triton, at his fountain-sport,
Bernini's creature plated to the paps,
Puffs up steel sleet which breaks to diamond dust,
A spray of sparkles snorted from his conch,
High over the caritellas, out o' the way
O' the motley merchandizing multitude.
Our murder has been done three days ago,
The frost is over and gone, the south wind laughs,
And, to the very tiles of each red roof
A-smoke i' the sunshine, Rome lies gold and glad:
So, listen how, to the other half of Rome,
Pompilia seemed a saint and martyr both!

Then, yet another day let come and go,
With pause prelusive still of novelty,
Hear a fresh speaker!—neither this nor that
Half-Rome aforesaid; something bred of both:
One and one breed the inevitable three.
Such is the personage harangues you next;
The elaborated product, *tertium quid:*
Rome's first commotion in subsidence gives

881| MS:him, "which <> race *P1868*:him "Which <> race, 882| MS:Of the coupled *P1868*:Of coupled 886| MS:Story, just *P1868*:story; just 887| MS:bring <> change; *P1868*:change. *1888*:brings 888-890| MS:in the market place/ Where *P1868*:i' the market-place/ O' the Barberini by the Capucins;/ Where 893| MS:conch *P1868*:conch, 894| MS:of *P1868*:o' 895| MS:Of *P1868*:O' 899| MS:Asmoke in *P1868*:A-smoke i' 900| MS:how to <> Rome *P1868*:how, to <> Rome, 901| MS:both. *P1868*: both! 904| MS:speaker, neither *P1868*:speaker!—neither 905| MS:both; *P1868*:both: 907| MS:next, *P1868*:next; 908| MS:*quid.* *P1868*:*quid:*

The curd o' the cream, flower o' the wheat, as it were,
And finer sense o' the city. Is this plain?
You get a reasoned statement of the case,
Eventual verdict of the curious few
Who care to sift a business to the bran
Nor coarsely bolt it like the simpler sort.
Here, after ignorance, instruction speaks;
Here, clarity of candour, history's soul,
The critical mind, in short: no gossip-guess.
What the superior social section thinks,
In person of some man of quality
Who,—breathing musk from lace-work and brocade,
His solitaire amid the flow of frill,
Powdered peruke on nose, and bag at back,
And cane dependent from the ruffled wrist,—
Harangues in silvery and selectest phrase
'Neath waxlight in a glorified saloon
Where mirrors multiply the girandole:
Courting the approbation of no mob,
But Eminence This and All-Illustrious That
Who take snuff softly, range in well-bred ring,
Card-table-quitters for observance' sake,
Around the argument, the rational word—
Still, spite its weight and worth, a sample-speech.
How Quality dissertated on the case.

So much for Rome and rumour; smoke comes first:
Once let smoke rise untroubled, we descry
Clearlier what tongues of flame may spire and spit
To eye and ear, each with appropriate tinge

910| MS:of <> of *P1868:*o' <> o' 911| MS:of *P1868:*o' 916| MS:speaks, *P1868:*speaks; 917| MS:candour, story's soul, *P1868:*candour, history's soul, 918| MS:gossip's-guess. *P1868:*gossip-guess. 919| MS:thinks *P1868:*thinks, 928| MS:mob *P1868:*mob, 934| MS:quality disertated *P1868:*dissertated *P1872:* How Quality 935| MS:rumor:smoke <> first— *P1868:*rumour; smoke <> first: 936| MS:Once the smoke risen *1888:*Once let smoke rise 937| MS:Clearlier the tongues of flame that spire *P1868:*Clearlier what tongues of flame may spire

According to its food, or pure or foul.
The actors, no mere rumours of the act,
Intervene. First you hear Count Guido's voice,
In a small chamber that adjoins the court,
Where Governor and Judges, summoned thence,
Tommati, Venturini and the rest,
Find the accused ripe for declaring truth.
Soft-cushioned sits he; yet shifts seat, shirks touch,
As, with a twitchy brow and wincing lip
And cheek that changes to all kinds of white,
He proffers his defence, in tones subdued
Near to mock-mildness now, so mournful seems
The obtuser sense truth fails to satisfy;
Now, moved, from pathos at the wrong endured,
To passion; for the natural man is roused
At fools who first do wrong then pour the blame
Of their wrong-doing, Satan-like, on Job.
Also his tongue at times is hard to curb;
Incisive, nigh satiric bites the phrase,
Rough-raw, yet somehow claiming privilege
—It is so hard for shrewdness to admit
Folly means no harm when she calls black white!
—Eruption momentary at the most,
Modified forthwith by a fall o' the fire,
Sage acquiescence; for the world's the world,
And, what it errs in, Judges rectify:
He feels he has a fist, then folds his arms
Crosswise and makes his mind up to be meek.
And never once does he detach his eye

939| MS:food, pure or impure. *1888:*food, or pure or foul. 941| MS:voice *P1868:*voice, 946| MS:he, yet *P1868:*he; yet 947| MS:As with *P1868:*As, with 949| MS:defence in *P1868:*defence, in 951| MS:satisfy, *P1868:* satisfy; 952| MS:moved from <> endured *P1868:*moved, from <> endured, 953| MS:passion, for *P1868:*passion; for 954| MS:wrong, then *1888:*wrong then 956| MS:curb, *P1868:*curb; 962| MS:of *P1868:*o'
963| MS:Meek § crossed out and replaced above by § Sage acquiescence, for *P1868:*acquiescence; for 964| MS:in, judges *P1868:*in, Judges

From those ranged there to slay him or to save,
But does his best man's-service for himself,
Despite,—what twitches brow and makes lip wince,—
His limbs' late taste of what was called the Cord,
Or Vigil-torture more facetiously.
Even so; they were wont to tease the truth
Out of loth witness (toying, trifling time)
By torture: 'twas a trick, a vice of the age,
Here, there and everywhere, what would you have?
Religion used to tell Humanity
She gave him warrant or denied him course.
And since the course was much to his own mind,
Of pinching flesh and pulling bone from bone
To unhusk truth a-hiding in its hulls,
Nor whisper of a warning stopped the way,
He, in their joint behalf, the burly slave,
Bestirred him, mauled and maimed all recusants,
While, prim in place, Religion overlooked;
And so had done till doomsday, never a sign
Nor sound of interference from her mouth,
But that at last the burly slave wiped brow,
Let eye give notice as if soul were there,
Muttered "'Tis a vile trick, foolish more than vile,
Should have been counted sin; I make it so:
At any rate no more of it for me—
Nay, for I break the torture-engine thus!"
Then did Religion start up, stare amain,

968| MS:those, ranged *CP1868:*those ranged 970| MS:For all § both words crossed out and replaced above by § Despite 971| MS:limbs *P1868:*limbs' 972| MS:§ line numbering skips to 1000 § 973| MS:teaze *P1868:*tease 974| MS:loath witness toying < > time, *P1868:*witness (toying < > time) *1888:*loth 975| MS:age *P1868:*age, 978| MS:denied him way § crossed out and replaced by § course; *P1868:*course. 979| MS:since this way § last two words crossed out and replaced above by § the course 981| MS:To have out § last two words crossed out and replaced above by one word § unhusk truth close § crossed out and replaced above by § a- < > in her hulls, *P1868:*in its hulls, 983| MS:slave *P1868:*slave, 984| MS:him, racked § crossed out and replaced above by § mauled 985| MS:While prim in place Religion overlooked, *P1868:*While, prim in place, Religion overlooked; 989| MS:eye wink somewhat § last two words crossed out and replaced above by § give notice 990| MS:Said " 'Tis *P1868:*Muttered " 'Tis

Look round for help and see none, smile and say
"What, broken is the rack? Well done of thee!
Did I forget to abrogate its use?
Be the mistake in common with us both!
—One more fault our blind age shall answer for,
Down in my book denounced though it must be
Somewhere. Henceforth find truth by milder means!"
Ah but, Religion, did we wait for thee
To ope the book, that serves to sit upon,
And pick such place out, we should wait indeed!
That is all history: and what is not now,
Was then, defendants found it to their cost.
How Guido, after being tortured, spoke.

Also hear Caponsacchi who comes next,
Man and priest—could you comprehend the coil!—
In days when that was rife which now is rare.
How, mingling each its multifarious wires,
Now heaven, now earth, now heaven and earth at once,
Had plucked at and perplexed their puppet here,
Played off the young frank personable priest;
Sworn fast and tonsured plain heaven's celibate,
And yet earth's clear-accepted servitor,
A courtly spiritual Cupid, squire of dames
By law of love and mandate of the mode.
The Church's own, or why parade her seal,
Wherefore that chrism and consecrative work?
Yet verily the world's, or why go badged
A prince of sonneteers and lutanists,
Show colour of each vanity in vogue

999| MS:blind Age must § crossed out and replaced above by § shall *P1868:*blind age 1001| MS:milder mode § crossed out and replaced above by § means!" 1002| MS:Ah, but Religion did *P1868:*Ah but, Religion, did 1006| MS:then, and Guido § last two words crossed out and replaced above by one word § defendants < > to his § crossed out and replaced above by § their 1009| MS:coil *P1868:*coil!— 1010| MS:rare; *P1868:*rare. 1014| MS:young, § comma crossed out § frank, § comma crossed out § < > priest *P1868:*priest; 1015| MS:plain Heaven's *P1868:*plain heaven's 1016| MS:yet Earth's *P1868:*yet earth's 1019| MS:The Churches *P1868:*The Church's 1020| MS:consecration *1868:*consecrative 1021| MS:the World's *P1868:*the world's 1022| MS:A lord of *P1868:*A prince of

Borne with decorum due on blameless breast?
All that is changed now, as he tells the court
How he had played the part excepted at;
Tells it, moreover, now the second time:
Since, for his cause of scandal, his own share
I' the flight from home and husband of the wife,
He has been censured, punished in a sort
By relegation,—exile, we should say,
To a short distance for a little time,—
Whence he is summoned on a sudden now,
Informed that she, he thought to save, is lost,
And, in a breath, bidden re-tell his tale,
Since the first telling somehow missed effect,
And then advise in the matter. There stands he,
While the same grim black-panelled chamber blinks
As though rubbed shiny with the sins of Rome
Told the same oak for ages—wave-washed wall
Against which sets a sea of wickedness.
There, where you yesterday heard Guido speak,
Speaks Caponsacchi; and there face him too
Tommati, Venturini and the rest
Who, eight months earlier, scarce repressed the smile,
Forewent the wink; waived recognition so
Of peccadillos incident to youth,
Especially youth high-born; for youth means love,
Vows can't change nature, priests are only men,
And love likes stratagem and subterfuge
Which age, that once was youth, should recognize,
May blame, but needs not press too hard upon.

1025| MS:now as <> Court *P1868:*now, as <> court 1026| MS:at, *P1868:*at; 1027| MS:time, *P1868:*time: 1029| MS:In *P1868:*I' 1037| MS:matter. There he § crossed out § stands he *P1868:*he, 1038| MS:black-panneled *P1868:* black-panelled 1041| MS:Whereto had set a *P1868:*has *1888:*Against which sets a 1043| MS:Speaks Caponsacchi, and *P1868:*Speaks Caponsacchi; and 1045| MS:smile *P1868:*smile, 1046| MS:wink, waived *P1868:*wink; waived 1050| MS:love needs stratagem *P1868:*subterfuge: *P1872:*love likes stratagem *1888:* subterfuge 1051| MS:Which Age <> Youth, will recognize, *P1868:*age <> youth, should recognize, 1052| MS:Must blame but <> hard against. *P1868:*May

Here sit the old Judges then, but with no grace
Of reverend carriage, magisterial port:
For why? The accused of eight months since,—the same
Who cut the conscious figure of a fool,
Changed countenance, dropped bashful gaze to ground,
While hesitating for an answer then,—
Now is grown judge himself, terrifies now
This, now the other culprit called a judge,
Whose turn it is to stammer and look strange,
As he speaks rapidly, angrily, speech that smites:
And they keep silence, bear blow after blow,
Because the seeming-solitary man,
Speaking for God, may have an audience too,
Invisible, no discreet judge provokes.
How the priest Caponsacchi said his say.

Then a soul sighs its lowest and its last
After the loud ones,—so much breath remains
Unused by the four-days'-dying; for she lived
Thus long, miraculously long, 'twas thought,
Just that Pompilia might defend herself.
How, while the hireling and the alien stoop,
Comfort, yet question,—since the time is brief,
And folk, allowably inquisitive,
Encircle the low pallet where she lies
In the good house that helps the poor to die,—
Pompilia tells the story of her life.
For friend and lover,—leech and man of law
Do service; busy helpful ministrants

---

blame, but *1888:*hard upon. 1054| MS:Of lordly § crossed out and replaced above by § reverend <> port— *P1868:*port. 1059| MS:himself, menaces now *P1868:*himself, terrifies now 1062| MS:angrily, words that smite. *P1868:*angrily, speech that smites: 1064| MS:man *P1868:*man, 1065| MS:for God might § crossed out and replaced by § may *P1868:*for God, may 1067| MS:priest Caponsacchi says § crossed out and replaced by § said 1070| MS:four days' dying *P1868:*four-days'-dying 1074| MS:questions, šince <> brief *P1868:*question, —since <> brief, 1075| MS:folk allowably *P1868:*folk, allowably 1078| MS:§ line clearly added in revision § 1080| MS:service, busy, helpful

As varied in their calling as their mind,
Temper and age: and yet from all of these,
About the white bed under the arched roof,
Is somehow, as it were, evolved a one,—
Small separate sympathies combined and large,
Nothings that were, grown something very much:
As if the bystanders gave each his straw,
All he had, though a trifle in itself,
Which, plaited all together, made a Cross
Fit to die looking on and praying with,
Just as well as if ivory or gold.
So, to the common kindliness she speaks,
There being scarce more privacy at the last
For mind than body: but she is used to bear,
And only unused to the brotherly look.
How she endeavoured to explain her life.

Then, since a Trial ensued, a touch o' the same
To sober us, flustered with frothy talk,
And teach our common sense its helplessness.
For why deal simply with divining-rod,
Scrape where we fancy secret sources flow,
And ignore law, the recognized machine,
Elaborate display of pipe and wheel
Framed to unchoke, pump up and pour apace
Truth till a flowery foam shall wash the world?
The patent truth-extracting process,—ha?

---

*P1868:*service; busy helpful 1082| MS:these *P1868:*these, 1083| MS:roof *P1868:*roof, 1086| MS:much, *P1868:*much: 1087| MS:the standers by gave *P1868:*the bystanders gave 1089| MS:altogether < > a cross— § dash crossed out § *P1868:*all together < > Cross 1090| MS:with *P1868:*with, 1092| MS:So to *P1868:*So, to 1094| MS:body, but < > bear *P1868:*body: but < > bear, 1097| MS:of *P1868:*o' 1101| MS:secret truth may § last two words crossed out and replaced above by § sources 1102| MS:ignore Law *P1868:*ignore law 1104| MS:unchoak *1888:*unchoke 1105| MS:Truth in a *1888:*Truth till a

Let us make that grave mystery turn one wheel,
Give you a single grind of law at least!
One orator, of two on either side,
Shall teach us the puissance of the tongue
—That is, o' the pen which simulated tongue
On paper and saved all except the sound
Which never was. Law's speech beside law's thought?
That were too stunning, too immense an odds:
That point of vantage law lets nobly pass.
One lawyer shall admit us to behold
The manner of the making out a case,
First fashion of a speech; the chick in egg,
The masterpiece law's bosom incubates.
How Don Giacinto of the Arcangeli,
Called Procurator of the Poor at Rome,
Now advocate for Guido and his mates,—
The jolly learned man of middle age,
Cheek and jowl all in laps with fat and law,
Mirthful as mighty, yet, as great hearts use,
Despite the name and fame that tempt our flesh,
Constant to that devotion of the hearth,
Still captive in those dear domestic ties!—
How he,—having a cause to triumph with,
All kind of interests to keep intact,
More than one efficacious personage
To tranquillize, conciliate and secure,
And above all, public anxiety
To quiet, show its Guido in good hands,—

1107| MS:make all that mystery *1888:*make that grave mystery 1109| MS:orator of <> side *P1868:*orator, of <> side, 1111| MS:of <> simulates the tongue *P1868:*o' <> simulated tongue 1112| MS:saves *P1868:* saved 1113| MS:was: law's *P1868:*was. Law's 1114| MS:stunning, and § crossed out and replaced above by § too 1115| MS:vantage Law let *P1868:* vantage law *1888:*lets 1118| MS:speech, the *P1868:*speech; the 1119| MS:A masterpiece *P1868:*And masterpiece *1888:*The masterpiece 1121| MS:The § altered to § Hight Procurator <> Rome *P1868:*Called Procurator <> Rome, 1122| MS:And advocate <> mates, *P1868:*Now advocate <> mates,— 1125| MS:as potent, yet *P1868:*as mighty, yet 1128| MS:A captive <> ties,— *P1868:*Still captive <> ties!— 1129| MS:he, having *P1868:* he,—having 1130| MS:kinds *P1868:*kind 1134| MS:quiet and show

Also, as if such burdens were too light,
A certain family-feast to claim his care,
The birthday-banquet for the only son—
Paternity at smiling strife with law—
How he brings both to buckle in one bond;
And, thick at throat, with waterish under-eye,
Turns to his task and settles in his seat
And puts his utmost means in practice now:
Wheezes out law-phrase, whiffles Latin forth,
And, just as though roast lamb would never be,
Makes logic levigate the big crime small:
Rubs palm on palm, rakes foot with itchy foot,
Conceives and inchoates the argument,
Sprinkling each flower appropriate to the time,
—Ovidian quip or Ciceronian crank,
A-bubble in the larynx while he laughs,
As he had fritters deep down frying there.
How he turns, twists, and tries the oily thing
Shall be—first speech for Guido 'gainst the Fisc.

Then with a skip as it were from heel to head,
Leaving yourselves fill up the middle bulk
O' the Trial, reconstruct its shape august,
From such exordium clap we to the close;
Give you, if we dare wing to such a height,
The absolute glory in some full-grown speech
On the other side, some finished butterfly,
Some breathing diamond-flake with leaf-gold fans,

---

*P1868:*quiet, show 1137| MS:birthday banquet *P1868:*birthday-banquet 1139| MS:bond, *P1868:*bond; 1140| MS:throat with <> undereye, *P1868:* throat, with <> under-eye, *1888:*§ line indented; emended to remove indentation; see Editorial Notes § 1141| MS:in his chair *P1868:*in his seat 1142| MS:means to practice now, *P1868:*now: *1888:*means in practice 1143| MS:out law and whiffles latin *P1868:*whiffles Latin *1888:*out law-phrase, whiffles 1145| MS:the crime away. *P1868:*the big crime small: 1150| MS:laughs *P1868:*laughs, 1152| MS:he does turn, twist, try *P1868:*he turns, twists, and tries 1153| MS:be—First Speech <> against *P1868:*be—first speech <> 'gainst 1153-54| MS:§ ¶ § *P1868:*§ no ¶; paragraph restored; see Editorial Notes § 1155| MS:middle man *P1868:*middle bulk 1156| MS:Of *P1868:*O' 1157| MS:close, *P1868:*close; 1160| MS:butterfly *P1868:* butterfly, 1161| MS:And breathing <> vans, *P1868:*Some breathing <> fans,

That takes the air, no trace of worm it was,
Or cabbage-bed it had production from.
Giovambattista o' the Bottini, Fisc,
Pompilia's patron by the chance of the hour,
To-morrow her persecutor,—composite, he,
As becomes who must meet such various calls—
Odds of age joined in him with ends of youth.
A man of ready smile and facile tear,
Improvised hopes, despairs at nod and beck,
And language—ah, the gift of eloquence!
Language that goes, goes, easy as a glove,
O'er good and evil, smoothens both to one.
Rashness helps caution with him, fires the straw,
In free enthusiastic careless fit,
On the first proper pinnacle of rock
Which offers, as reward for all that zeal,
To lure some bark to founder and bring gain:
While calm sits Caution, rapt with heavenward eye,
A true confessor's gaze, amid the glare
Beaconing to the breaker, death and hell.
"Well done, thou good and faithful!" she approves:
"Hadst thou let slip a faggot to the beach,
The crew might surely spy thy precipice
And save their boat; the simple and the slow
Might so, forsooth, forestall the wrecker's fee!
Let the next crew be wise and hail in time!"

1164| MS:Giovambatista of *P1868:*Giovambattista o' 1166| MS:composite he, *P1868:*composite, he, *1888:*§ line indented; emended to remove indentation; see Editorial Notes § 1168| MS:youth, *P1868:*youth. 1172| MS:that goes as easy as a glove *1888:*that goes, goes, easy as a glove, 1173| MS:smoothens them to *P1868:*smoothens both to 1174| MS:straw *P1868:*straw, 1175| MS:fit *P1868:*fit, 1177| MS:Which happens, as *1888:*Which offers, as 1178| MS:bark to split § crossed out and replaced above by § founder and bring the § crossed out § gain, *P1868:*gain: 1179| MS:sits caution *P1868:*sits Caution 1180| MS:gaze amid *P1868:*glare, *1888:*gaze, amid the glare 1181| MS:While beaconing *P1868:*Beaconing 1182| MS:faithful!" law approves *P1868:*faithful!" she approves: *1888:*faithful " she § emended to § faithful!" she § see Editorial Notes § 1183| MS:beach *P1868:*beach, 1184| MS:crew had surely spied *1888:*crew might surely spy 1185| MS:saved < > boat, the simple mariners § crossed out and replaced above by three words § and the slow, *P1868:*boat; the *1888:*save < > slow 1186| MS:Who should have prompt forestalled < > fee.

Just so compounded is the outside man,
Blue juvenile pure eye and pippin cheek,
And brow all prematurely soiled and seamed
With sudden age, bright devastated hair.
Ah, but you miss the very tones o' the voice,
The scrannel pipe that screams in heights of head,
As, in his modest studio, all alone,
The tall wight stands a-tiptoe, strives and strains,
Both eyes shut, like the cockerel that would crow,
Tries to his own self amorously o'er
What never will be uttered else than so—
Since to the four walls, Forum and Mars' Hill,
Speaks out the poesy which, penned, turns prose.
Clavecinist debarred his instrument,
He yet thrums—shirking neither turn nor trill,
With desperate finger on dumb table-edge—
The sovereign rondo, shall conclude his *Suite*,
Charm an imaginary audience there,
From old Corelli to young Haendel, both
I' the flesh at Rome, ere he perforce go print
The cold black score, mere music for the mind—
The last speech against Guido and his gang,
With special end to prove Pompilia pure.
How the Fisc vindicates Pompilia's fame.

Then comes the all but end, the ultimate

---

*P1868:*fee: *1888:*Might so, forsooth, forestall < > fee! 1188| MS:was *P1868:*is 1189| MS:His juvenile *P1868:*Blue juvenile 1191| MS:With sudden § inserted above § age, and devastated *P1868:*age, bright devastated 1192| MS:of this man, *P1868:*o' the voice, 1193| MS:scrannel voice that *P1868:*scrannel pipe that 1194| MS:As in < > studio all alone *P1868:*As, in < > studio, all alone, 1195| MS:a tiptoe < > strains *P1868:* a-tiptoe < > strains, 1195-97| MS:strains,/ Tries *P1868:*strains,/ Both eyes shut, like the cockerel that would crow,/ Tries 1198-1209| MS:so—/ The *P1868:*§ adds lines 1199-1208 § 1199| *P1868:*To the < > walls, for Forum *1888:*Since to the < > walls, Forum 1212| MS:end, the § crossed out and replaced above by § and ultimate *1868:*end, the ultimate

Judgment save yours. Pope Innocent the Twelfth,
Simple, sagacious, mild yet resolute,
With prudence, probity and—what beside
From the other world he feels impress at times,
Having attained to fourscore years and six,—
How, when the court found Guido and the rest
Guilty, but law supplied a subterfuge
And passed the final sentence to the Pope,
He, bringing his intelligence to bear
This last time on what ball behoves him drop
In the urn, or white or black, does drop a black,
Send five souls more to just precede his own,
Stand him in stead and witness, if need were,
How he is wont to do God's work on earth.
The manner of his sitting out the dim
Droop of a sombre February day
In the plain closet where he does such work,
With, from all Peter's treasury, one stool,
One table and one lathen crucifix.
There sits the Pope, his thoughts for company;
Grave but not sad,—nay, something like a cheer
Leaves the lips free to be benevolent,
Which, all day long, did duty firm and fast.
A cherishing there is of foot and knee,
A chafing loose-skinned large-veined hand with hand,—
What steward but knows when stewardship earns its wage,
May levy praise, anticipate the lord?
He reads, notes, lays the papers down at last,
Muses, then takes a turn about the room;
Unclasps a huge tome in an antique guise,

1213| MS:the Twelfth *P1868:*the Twelfth, 1218| MS:the Court *P1868:*the court 1223| MS:black, he drops *P1868:*black, does drop 1224| MS:Sends *P1868:*Send 1225| MS:witness if need were *P1868:*witness, if need were, 1226| MS:was *P1868:*is 1232| MS:company, *P1868:*company; 1235| MS:Which all day long did *P1868:*Which, all day long, did 1236| MS:chafe of loose-skinned *P1868:*chafing loose-skinned 1239| MS:And § crossed out and replaced above by § May levies § altered to § levy praise, anticipates § *s* crossed out § 1240| MS:reads, writes, lays *P1868:*reads, notes, lays 1241| MS:room, *P1868:*room;

Primitive print and tongue half obsolete,
That stands him in diurnal stead; opes page,
Finds place where falls the passage to be conned
According to an order long in use:
And, as he comes upon the evening's chance,
Starts somewhat, solemnizes straight his smile,
Then reads aloud that portion first to last,
And at the end lets flow his own thoughts forth
Likewise aloud, for respite and relief,
Till by the dreary relics of the west
Wan through the half-moon window, all his light,
He bows the head while the lips move in prayer,
Writes some three brief lines, signs and seals the same,
Tinkles a hand-bell, bids the obsequious Sir
Who puts foot presently o' the closet-sill
He watched outside of, bear as superscribed
That mandate to the Governor forthwith:
Then heaves abroad his cares in one good sigh,
Traverses corridor with no arm's help,
And so to sup as a clear conscience should.
The manner of the judgment of the Pope.

Then must speak Guido yet a second time,
Satan's old saw being apt here—skin for skin,
All a man hath that will he give for life.
While life was graspable and gainable,
And bird-like buzzed her wings round Guido's brow,
Not much truth stiffened out the web of words
He wove to catch her: when away she flew
And death came, death's breath rivelled up the lies,
Left bare the metal thread, the fibre fine
Of truth, i' the spinning: the true words shone last.

1244| MS:stead, opes *P1868:*stead; opes 1245| MS:be read § crossed out and replaced by § conned 1246| MS:use, *P1868:*use: 1251| MS:relief. *CP1868:*relief, 1257| MS:on *P1868:*o' 1259| MS:forthwith, *P1868:*forthwith: 1260| MS:cares with § crossed out and replaced by § in 1261| MS:help *P1868:*help, 1265| MS:for skin *P1868:*for skin, 1267| MS:gainable, free *1888:*gainable, 1268| MS:To bird-like buz her *CP1868:* buzz *1888:*And bird-like buzzed her 1273| MS:truth in < > words at § crossed out and replaced above by § come last, *P1868:*truth, i' *1888:*words shone last.

How Guido, to another purpose quite,
Speaks and despairs, the last night of his life,
In that New Prison by Castle Angelo
At the bridge foot: the same man, another voice.
On a stone bench in a close fetid cell,
Where the hot vapour of an agony,
Struck into drops on the cold wall, runs down—
Horrible worms made out of sweat and tears—
There crouch, well nigh to the knees in dungeon-straw,
Lit by the sole lamp suffered for their sake,
Two awe-struck figures, this a Cardinal,
That an Abate, both of old styled friends
O' the thing part man part monster in the midst,
So changed is Franceschini's gentle blood.
The tiger-cat screams now, that whined before,
That pried and tried and trod so gingerly,
Till in its silkiness the trap-teeth joined;
Then you know how the bristling fury foams.
They listen, this wrapped in his folds of red,
While his feet fumble for the filth below;
The other, as beseems a stouter heart,
Working his best with beads and cross to ban
The enemy that comes in like a flood
Spite of the standard set up, verily
And in no trope at all, against him there:
For at the prison-gate, just a few steps
Outside, already, in the doubtful dawn,
Thither, from this side and from that, slow sweep

1274| MS:Guido to <> quite *P1868:*Guido, to <> quite, 1277| MS:the Bridge-foot. The same man, a novel § last two words crossed out and replaced above by § another *P1868:*bridge-foot: the 1278| MS:cell *P1868:*cell, 1279| MS:Down § crossed out and replaced above by § Where <> agony *P1868:*agony,
1280| MS:wall ran down *P1868:*wall, runs down *1888:*down— 1282-83| MS: § order reversed § 1283| MS:sake *P1868:*sake, 1284| MS:awestruck *P1868:*awe-struck 1285| MS:an Abate both *P1868:*an Abate, both
1286| MS:Of the part man part monster *P1868:*part-man part-monster *1888:*O' the thing part man part monster 1287| MS:blood: *P1868:*blood.
1288| MS:now that *P1868:*now, that 1289| MS:gingerly *P1868:*gingerly,
1290| MS:join, *P1868:*join; *1888:*joined; 1293| MS:below, *P1868:*below;
1298| MS:there: *1888:*§ punctuation faulty; emended to § there: § see Editorial Notes § 1300| MS:already in *P1868:*already, in

And settle down in silence solidly,
Crow-wise, the frightful Brotherhood of Death.
Black-hatted and black-hooded huddle they,
Black rosaries a-dangling from each waist;
So take they their grim station at the door,
Torches lit, skull-and-cross-bones-banner spread,
And that gigantic Christ with open arms,
Grounded. Nor lacks there aught but that the group
Break forth, intone the lamentable psalm,
"Out of the deeps, Lord, have I cried to thee!"—
When inside, from the true profound, a sign
Shall bear intelligence that the foe is foiled,
Count Guido Franceschini has confessed,
And is absolved and reconciled with God.
Then they, intoning, may begin their march,
Make by the longest way for the People's Square,
Carry the criminal to his crime's award:
A mob to cleave, a scaffolding to reach,
Two gallows and Mannaia crowning all.
How Guido made defence a second time.

Finally, even as thus by step and step
I led you from the level of to-day
Up to the summit of so long ago,
Here, whence I point you the wide prospect round—
Let me, by like steps, slope you back to smooth,
Land you on mother-earth, no whit the worse,

1302| MS:solidly *P1868:*solidly, 1303| MS:Crow-wise the <> Death, *P1868:*Crow-wise, the <> Death. 1305| MS:from the waist. *P1868:*from each waist; 1307| MS:Torches alight and cross-bones-banner spread *P1872:*Torches lit, skull-and-cross-bones-banner spread,
1308| MS:arms *P1868:*arms, 1309| MS:Grounded: nor *P1868:*Grounded. Nor
1311| MS:to Thee!" *P1868:*thee!"— 1314| MS:And Guido *P1868:*Count Guido
1316| MS:And they, intoning may *P1868:*Then they, intoning, may
1318| MS:award— *P1868:*award: 1319| MS:a scaffolding § *ing* crossed out and replaced above by § age § crossed out and original reading restored § to climb, § crossed out and replaced above by § mount § crossed out and replaced by § reach,
1321| MS:How Guido tried defence *P1868:*How Guido made defence
1322| MS:Finally even *P1868:*Finally, even 1324| MS:Up this the *P1868:*Up to the 1325| MS:This, § added in margin § Where I have § crossed out § pointed you

To feed o' the fat o' the furrow: free to dwell,
Taste our time's better things profusely spread
For all who love the level, corn and wine,
Much cattle and the many-folded fleece.
Shall not my friends go feast again on sward,
Though cognizant of country in the clouds
Higher than wistful eagle's horny eye
Ever unclosed for, 'mid ancestral crags,
When morning broke and Spring was back once more,
And he died, heaven, save by his heart, unreached?
Yet heaven my fancy lifts to, ladder-like,—
As Jack reached, holpen of his beanstalk-rungs!

A novel country: I might make it mine
By choosing which one aspect of the year
Suited mood best, and putting solely that
On panel somewhere in the House of Fame,
Landscaping what I saved, not what I saw:
—Might fix you, whether frost in goblin-time
Startled the moon with his abrupt bright laugh,
Or, August's hair afloat in filmy fire,
She fell, arms wide, face foremost on the world,
Swooned there and so singed out the strength of things.
Thus were abolished Spring and Autumn both,
The land dwarfed to one likeness of the land,
Life cramped corpse-fashion. Rather learn and love
Each facet-flash of the revolving year!—
Red, green and blue that whirl into a white,
The variance now, the eventual unity,
Which make the miracle. See it for yourselves,
This man's act, changeable because alive!

---

the prospect *P1868:*Here, whence I point you the wide prospect 1328| MS:But fed with fat of *P1868:*To feed o' the fat o' 1329| MS:Taste § added in margin § Mid § crossed out § our 1331| MS:fleece, *P1868:*fleece. 1331-33| MS:fleece,/ Though *P1868:*fleece./ Shall not my friends go feast again on sward,/ Though 1335| MS:mid *P1868:*'mid 1336| MS:back again, *P1868:*back once more, 1337| MS:unreached, *P1868:*unreached? 1339| MS:Yet Jack *P1868:*As Jack 1342| MS:Suits my mood *P1868:*Suited mood 1343| MS:pannel *P1868:*panel 1349| MS:things: *P1868:*things. 1353| MS:year, *P1868:*year!— 1356| MS:miracle: see *P1868:*miracle. See 1357| MS:This Man's Act <>

Action now shrouds, now shows the informing thought;
Man, like a glass ball with a spark a-top,
Out of the magic fire that lurks inside,
Shows one tint at a time to take the eye:
Which, let a finger touch the silent sleep,
Shifted a hair's-breadth shoots you dark for bright,
Suffuses bright with dark, and baffles so
Your sentence absolute for shine or shade.
Once set such orbs,—white styled, black stigmatized,—
A-rolling, see them once on the other side
Your good men and your bad men every one
From Guido Franceschini to Guy Faux,
Oft would you rub your eyes and change your names.

Such, British Public, ye who like me not,
(God love you!)—whom I yet have laboured for,
Perchance more careful whoso runs may read
Than erst when all, it seemed, could read who ran,—
Perchance more careless whoso reads may praise
Than late when he who praised and read and wrote
Was apt to find himself the self-same me,—
Such labour had such issue, so I wrought
This arc, by furtherance of such alloy,
And so, by one spirt, take away its trace
Till, justifiably golden, rounds my ring.

A ring without a posy, and that ring mine?

O lyric Love, half angel and half bird
And all a wonder and a wild desire,—

---

alive; *P1868:*man's act <> alive! 1358| MS:shrouds now shows <> thought, *P1868:*shrouds, now <> thought; *1888:*shrouds, nor § emended to § now § see Editorial Notes § 1359| MS:Lies like <> a-top *P1868:*Man, like <> a-top, 1360| MS:that rolls § crossed out and replaced above by § lurks 1361| MS:The one <> time that takes *P1868:*Shows one <> time to take 1363| MS:hair's-breadth gives you *P1868:*hair's breadth shoots you 1366| MS:orbs, styled white § last two words altered to § white styled <> stigmatized, *P1868:*orbs,—white <> stigmatized,— 1368| MS:bad men, every *P1868:*bad men every one, *P1872:*one 1370| MS:and shift you *P1868:*and change your 1371| MS:you *P1868:*ye
1374| MS:Than late when *P1868:*Then erst when 1377| MS:selfsame *P1868:* self-same 1380| MS:take its trace away *P1868:*take away its trace *P1872:*spirit *1888:*spirt 1383| MS:lyric love, half-angel and half-bird *P1868:*lyric Love *1888:*

Boldest of hearts that ever braved the sun,
Took sanctuary within the holier blue,
And sang a kindred soul out to his face,—
Yet human at the red-ripe of the heart—
When the first summons from the darkling earth
Reached thee amid thy chambers, blanched their blue,
And bared them of the glory—to drop down,
To toil for man, to suffer or to die,—
This is the same voice: can thy soul know change?
Hail then, and hearken from the realms of help!
Never may I commence my song, my due
To God who best taught song by gift of thee,
Except with bent head and beseeching hand—
That still, despite the distance and the dark,
What was, again may be; some interchange
Of grace, some splendour once thy very thought,
Some benediction anciently thy smile:
—Never conclude, but raising hand and head
Thither where eyes, that cannot reach, yet yearn
For all hope, all sustainment, all reward,
Their utmost up and on,—so blessing back
In those thy realms of help, that heaven thy home,
Some whiteness which, I judge, thy face makes proud,
Some wanness where, I think, thy foot may fall!

---

half angel and half bird 1386| MS:blue *P1868:*blue, 1387| MS:out in his face, *P1868:*out to his face,— 1391| MS:down *P1868:*down, 1392| MS:toil, to § altered to § toil for man to suffer < > die for man,— § altered to § die,— *P1868:* man, to 1393| MS:voice—can *P1868:*voice:can 1394| MS:then and *P1868:* then, and 1397| MS:hand *P1868:*hand— 1399| MS:be, some *P1868:*be; some 1402| MS:conclude but *P1868:*conclude, but 1403| MS:eyes that < > reach yet strain § crossed out and replaced by § yearn *P1868:*eyes, that < > reach, yet 1405| MS:on, so *P1868:*on,—so 1408| MS:where, I guess § crossed out and replaced above by § think < > fall. *P1868:*fall!

II

HALF-ROME

What, you, Sir, come too? (Just the man I'd meet.)
Be ruled by me and have a care o' the crowd:
This way, while fresh folk go and get their gaze:
I'll tell you like a book and save your shins.
Fie, what a roaring day we've had! Whose fault?
Lorenzo in Lucina,—here's a church
To hold a crowd at need, accommodate
All comers from the Corso! If this crush
Make not its priests ashamed of what they show
For temple-room, don't prick them to draw purse
And down with bricks and mortar, eke us out
The beggarly transept with its bit of apse
Into a decent space for Christian ease,
Why, to-day's lucky pearl is cast to swine.
Listen and estimate the luck they've had!
(The right man, and I hold him.)
Sir, do you see,
They laid both bodies in the church, this morn
The first thing, on the chancel two steps up,
Behind the little marble balustrade;
Disposed them, Pietro the old murdered fool
To the right of the altar, and his wretched wife
On the other side. In trying to count stabs,
People supposed Violante showed the most,
Till somebody explained us that mistake;
His wounds had been dealt out indifferent where,
But she took all her stabbings in the face,
Since punished thus solely for honour's sake,

2| MS:of *P1868:*o' 7| MS:accomodate § altered to § accommodate
14| MS:to day's *P1868:*to-day's 15| MS:had. *P1868:*had! 16| MS:man and *P1868:*man, and 17| MS:church this *P1868:*church, this
20| MS:murdered man *P1868:*murdered fool 23| MS:People thought Violante *CP1868:*People supposed Violante 27| MS:honor's *P1868:*honour's

Honoris causâ, that's the proper term.
A delicacy there is, our gallants hold,
When you avenge your honour and only then,
That you disfigure the subject, fray the face,
Not just take life and end, in clownish guise.
It was Violante gave the first offence,
Got therefore the conspicuous punishment:
While Pietro, who helped merely, his mere death
Answered the purpose, so his face went free.
We fancied even, free as you please, that face
Showed itself still intolerably wronged;
Was wrinkled over with resentment yet,
Nor calm at all, as murdered faces use,
Once the worst ended: an indignant air
O' the head there was—'tis said the body turned
Round and away, rolled from Violante's side
Where they had laid it loving-husband-like.
If so, if corpses can be sensitive,
Why did not he roll right down altar-step,
Roll on through nave, roll fairly out of church,
Deprive Lorenzo of the spectacle,
Pay back thus the succession of affronts
Whereto this church had served as theatre?
For see: at that same altar where he lies,
To that same inch of step, was brought the babe
For blessing after baptism, and there styled
Pompilia, and a string of names beside,

---

[28]| MS:term: *P1868:*term. [30]| MS:honor *P1868:*honour [31]| MS:face *P1868:*face, [32]| MS:guise: *P1868:*guise. [33]| MS:'Twas *CP1868:*It was [34]| MS:punishment, *P1868:*punishment: [36]| MS:purpose and his *P1868:* purpose, so his [38]| MS:wronged, *P1868:*wronged; [40]| MS:all as *P1868:* all, as [42]| MS:Of *P1868:*O' [43]| MS:away from *CP1868:*away, rolled from [45]| MS:so, and corpses *P1868:*so, if corpses [46]| MS:altar-step *P1868:*altar-step, [47]| MS:Roll through <> church *P1868:*Roll on through <> church, [48]| MS:of his spectacle, *P1868:*of the spectacle, [50]| MS:Whereof § *of* crossed out and replaced above by § to [52]| MS:step was *P1868:*step, was [53]| MS:baptism and *P1868:*baptism, and [54]| MS:Pompilia and <> beside

By his bad wife, some seventeen years ago,
Who purchased her simply to palm on him,
Flatter his dotage and defraud the heirs.
Wait awhile! Also to this very step
Did this Violante, twelve years afterward,
Bring, the mock-mother, that child-cheat full-grown,
Pompilia, in pursuance of her plot,
And there brave God and man a second time
By linking a new victim to the lie.
There, having made a match unknown to him,
She, still unknown to Pietro, tied the knot
Which nothing cuts except this kind of knife;
Yes, made her daughter, as the girl was held,
Marry a man, and honest man beside,
And man of birth to boot,—clandestinely
Because of this, because of that, because
O' the devil's will to work his worst for once,—
Confident she could top her part at need
And, when her husband must be told in turn,
Ply the wife's trade, play off the sex's trick
And, alternating worry with quiet qualms,
Bravado with submissiveness, prettily fool
Her Pietro into patience: so it proved.
Ay, 'tis four years since man and wife they grew,
This Guido Franceschini and this same
Pompilia, foolishly thought, falsely declared
A Comparini and the couple's child:
Just at this altar where, beneath the piece
Of Master Guido Reni, Christ on cross,
Second to nought observable in Rome,
That couple lie now, murdered yestereve.

---

*P1868:*Pompilia, and <> beside, [58]| MS:awhile: also on § crossed out and replaced above by § to *P1868:*awhile! Also [59]| MS:did Violante *P1868:*Did this Violante [63]| MS:lie, *P1868:*lie. [64]| MS:him *P1868:*him, [66]| MS:knife— *P1868:*knife; [68]| MS:beside *P1868:*beside, [69]| MS:to-boot *P1868:*to boot [71]| MS:Of *P1868:*O' [74]| MS:sexes *P1868:*sex's [76]| MS:submissiveness, quick fool *1888:*submissiveness, prettily fool [80]| MS:falsely called *P1868:*falsely declared [81]| MS:child, *P1868:*

Even the blind can see a providence here.

From dawn till now that it is growing dusk
A multitude has flocked and filled the church,
Coming and going, coming back again,
Till to count crazed one. Rome was at the show.
People climbed up the columns, fought for spikes
O' the chapel-rail to perch themselves upon,
Jumped over and so broke the wooden work
Painted like porphyry to deceive the eye;
Serve the priests right! The organ-loft was crammed,
Women were fainting, no few fights ensued,
In short, it was a show repaid your pains:
For, though their room was scant undoubtedly,
Yet they did manage matters, to be just,
A little at this Lorenzo. Body o' me!
I saw a body exposed once . . . never mind!
Enough that here the bodies had their due.
No stinginess in wax, a row all round,
And one big taper at each head and foot.

So, people pushed their way, and took their turn,
Saw, threw their eyes up, crossed themselves, gave place
To pressure from behind, since all the world
Knew the old pair, could talk the tragedy
Over from first to last: Pompilia too,
Those who had known her—what 'twas worth to them!
Guido's acquaintance was in less request;
The Count had lounged somewhat too long in Rome,
Made himself cheap; with him were hand and glove

---

child: 87| MS:dusk, DC, BrU:dusk *1889:*dusk 88| MS:church *P1868:* church, 92| MS:Of *P1868:*O' 94| MS:eye— *P1868:*eye; 97| MS:pains, *P1868:*pains: 100| MS:of *P1868:*o' 101| MS:once . . never *P1868:*once . . . never 104| MS:And two § crossed out and replaced above by § one big tapers § *s* crossed out § 104-5| MS:§ no ¶ § *P1868:*§ ¶ § 105| MS:So people <> way and *P1868:*So, people <> way, and 111| MS:request, *P1868:*request; 112| MS:The man had <> Rome *P1868:*The Count had <> Rome, 113| MS:cheap, were him *P1868:*cheap; with him

Barbers and blear-eyed, as the ancient sings.
Also he is alive and like to be:
Had he considerately died,—aha!
I jostled Luca Cini on his staff,
Mute in the midst, the whole man one amaze,
Staring amain and crossing brow and breast.
"How now?" asked I. " 'Tis seventy years," quoth he,
"Since I first saw, holding my father's hand,
Bodies set forth: a many have I seen,
Yet all was poor to this I live and see.
Here the world's wickedness seals up the sum:
What with Molinos' doctrine and this deed,
Antichrist surely comes and doomsday's near.
May I depart in peace, I have seen my see."
"Depart then," I advised, "nor block the road
For youngsters still behindhand with such sights!"
"Why no," rejoins the venerable sire,
"I know it's horrid, hideous past belief,
Burdensome far beyond what eye can bear;
But they do promise, when Pompilia dies
I' the course o' the day,—and she can't outlive night,—
They'll bring her body also to expose
Beside the parents, one, two, three a-breast;
That were indeed a sight, which might I see,
I trust I should not last to see the like!"
Whereat I bade the senior spare his shanks,
Since doctors give her till to-night to live,
And tell us how the butchery happened. "Ah,
But you can't know!" sighs he, "I'll not despair:

114| MS:sings: *P1868:*sings. 116| MS:aha, *P1868:*aha! 119| MS:Staring and < > breast amain. *P1868:*Staring amain and < > breast. 120| MS:now?" quoth I. "Tis < > years" quoth he *P1868:*now?" asked I. < > years," quoth he, *1872:*" 'Tis 121| MS:Since *P1868:*"Since 126| MS:Antichrist's < > come and doomsday *1888:*Antichrist < > comes and doomsday's 129| MS:sights." *P1868:*sights!" 130| MS:sire *1868:*sire, 132| MS:bear, *1868:*bear; 134| MS:In < > of *P1868:*I' *CP1868:*o' 136| MS:a-breast, *P1868:*a-breast; 137| MS:sight which, might *1888:*sight, which might 139| MS:senior save his time *P1868:*senior spare his shanks, 140| MS:doctors § inserted above § give her half a week § last three words crossed out and replaced above by three words § till to night to live *P1868:*to-night *1888:*live, 141| MS:happened:"Ah, *P1868:*happened. "Ah, 142| MS:know" sighs he "I'll *P1868:*know!" sighs he, "I'll 143| MS:Besides < > things *P1868:*Beside < > things—

Beside I'm useful at explaining things—
As, how the dagger laid there at the feet,
Caused the peculiar cuts; I mind its make,
Triangular i' the blade, a Genoese,
Armed with those little hook-teeth on the edge
To open in the flesh nor shut again:
I like to teach a novice: I shall stay!"
And stay he did, and stay be sure he will.

A personage came by the private door
At noon to have his look: I name no names:
Well then, His Eminence the Cardinal,
Whose servitor in honourable sort
Guido was once, the same who made the match,
(Will you have the truth?) whereof we see effect.
No sooner whisper ran he was arrived
Than up pops Curate Carlo, a brisk lad,
Who never lets a good occasion slip,
And volunteers improving the event.
We looked he'd give the history's self some help,
Treat us to how the wife's confession went
(This morning she confessed her crime, we know)
And, may-be, throw in something of the Priest—
If he's not ordered back, punished anew,
The gallant, Caponsacchi, Lucifer
I' the garden where Pompilia, Eve-like, lured
Her Adam Guido to his fault and fall.
Think you we got a sprig of speech akin
To this from Carlo, with the Cardinal there?
Too wary he was, too widely awake, I trow.

145| MS:cuts, I *P1868:*cuts; I 146| MS:in *P1868:*i'
149| MS:stay." *P1868:*stay!" 150-51| MS:§ no ¶ § *P1868:*§ ¶ §
154| MS:honorable *P1868:*honourable 156| MS:Will <> truth?,—whereof <> effect; *P1868:*(Will <> truth?) whereof <> effect.
159| MS:let *P1868:*lets 160| MS:volunteered *P1868:*volunteers
161| MS:history some *P1868:*history's self some 163| MS:crime we *P1868:* crime, we 164| MS:may be <> Priest *P1868:*the Priest— *CP1868:*may-be
167| MS:In *P1868:*I' 169| MS:speech like this § last two words crossed out and replaced above by § akin 170| MS:from Carlo with *P1868:*from Carlo, with
171| MS:Too wary, I trow, § numbering indicates last two words are to replace *he was* at end of sentence § too widely awake he was. § numbering indicates last two words are

He did the murder in a dozen words;
Then said that all such outrages crop forth
I' the course of nature when Molinos' tares
Are sown for wheat, flourish and choke the Church:
So slid on to the abominable sect
And the philosophic sin—we've heard all that,
And the Cardinal too, (who book-made on the same)
But, for the murder, left it where he found.
Oh but he's quick, the Curate, minds his game!
And, after all, we have the main o' the fact:
Case could not well be simpler,—mapped, as it were,
We follow the murder's maze from source to sea,
By the red line, past mistake: one sees indeed
Not only how all was and must have been,
But cannot other than be to the end of time.
Turn out here by the Ruspoli! Do you hold
Guido was so prodigiously to blame?
A certain cousin of yours has told you so?
Exactly! Here's a friend shall set you right,
Let him but have the handsel of your ear.

These wretched Comparini were once gay
And galliard, of the modest middle class:
Born in this quarter seventy years ago
And married young, they lived the accustomed life,
Citizens as they were of good repute:
And, childless, naturally took their ease
With only their two selves to care about
And use the wealth for: wealthy is the word,
Since Pietro was possessed of house and land—
And specially one house, when good days smiled,
In Via Vittoria, the aspectable street
Where he lived mainly; but another house

---

to replace *I trow* § *1888:*wary he 172| MS:words, *P1868:*words; 174| MS:In *P1868:*I' <> nature, when *1888:*nature when 175| MS:the Church, *P1868:*the Church: 181| MS:of *P1868:*o' 184| MS:line past *P1868:*line, past 187| MS:by The Ruspoli: so you *P1868:*by the Ruspoli! Do you 189| MS:certain friend of *P1868:*certain cousin of 193| MS:galiard *1888:*galliard 194| MS:ago, *1888:*ago 200| MS:land *P1868:*land— 201| MS:days were, *1888:*days smiled, 202| MS:In Via Vittoria, an aspectable *P1868:*In Via Vittoria, the aspectable 203| MS:mainly, and another *P1868:*mainly; but another

Of less pretension did he buy betimes,
The villa, meant for jaunts and jollity,
I' the Pauline district, to be private there—
Just what puts murder in an enemy's head.
Moreover,—here's the worm i' the core, the germ
O' the rottenness and ruin which arrived,—
He owned some usufruct, had moneys' use
Lifelong, but to determine with his life
In heirs' default: so, Pietro craved an heir,
(The story always old and always new)
Shut his fool's-eyes fast on the visible good
And wealth for certain, opened them owl-wide
On fortune's sole piece of forgetfulness,
The child that should have been and would not be.

Hence, seventeen years ago, conceive his glee
When first Violante, 'twixt a smile and blush,
With touch of agitation proper too,
Announced that, spite of her unpromising age,
The miracle would in time be manifest,
An heir's birth was to happen: and it did.
Somehow or other,—how, all in good time!
By a trick, a sleight of hand you are to hear,—
A child was born, Pompilia, for his joy,
Plaything at once and prop, a fairy-gift,
A saints' grace or, say, grant of the good God,—
A fiddle-pin's end! What imbeciles are we!
Look now: if someone could have prophesied,
"For love of you, for liking to your wife,

204| *P1872:*lees *1888:*less 205| MS:The Villa *P1868:*The villa 206| MS: In < > there, *P1868:*I' < > there— 208| MS:Moreover,—and here's < > in *P1868:*i' *1888:*Moreover,—here's 209| MS:Of *P1868:*O' 210| MS:monies' *CP1868:*moneys' 211| MS:Lifelong but *P1868:*Lifelong, but 212| MS:so Pietro *P1868:*so, Pietro 213| MS:The < > new, *P1868:*(The < > new) 214| MS:fool's eyes < > good, *P1868:*fool's-eyes < > good 215| MS:The wealth *P1868:*And wealth 216| MS:forgetfulness *P1868:*forgetfulness, 217-18| MS:§ no ¶ § *P1868:*§ ¶ § 219| MS:and a blush, *1888:*and blush, 227| MS:Plaything at once § last two words inserted above § < > fairy-gift *P1868:* fairy-gift, 228| MS:or say grant < > God, *P1868:*or, say, grant < > God,— 229| MS:fiddlepin's *P1868:*fiddle-pin's 230| MS:someone < > prophesied *P1868:*some one § emended to § someone § see Editorial Notes § < > prophesied,

I undertake to crush a snake I spy
Settling itself i' the soft of both your breasts.
Give me yon babe to strangle painlessly!
She'll soar to the safe: you'll have your crying out,
Then sleep, then wake, then sleep, then end your days
In peace and plenty, mixed with mild regret,
Thirty years hence when Christmas takes old folk"—
How had old Pietro sprung up, crossed himself,
And kicked the conjuror! Whereas you and I,
Being wise with after-wit, had clapped our hands;
Nay, added, in the old fool's interest,
"Strangle the black-eyed babe, so far so good,
But on condition you relieve the man
O' the wife and throttle him Violante too—
She is the mischief!"

We had hit the mark.
She, whose trick brought the babe into the world,
She it was, when the babe was grown a girl,
Judged a new trick should reinforce the old,
Send vigour to the lie now somewhat spent
By twelve years' service; lest Eve's rule decline
Over this Adam of hers, whose cabbage-plot
Throve dubiously since turned fools'-paradise,
Spite of a nightingale on every stump.
Pietro's estate was dwindling day by day,
While he, rapt far above such mundane care,
Crawled all-fours with his baby pick-a-back,

233-34| MS:in <> breasts,/ For that's a snake the thing you fondle so— § entire line crossed out § / Give <> painlessly, *P1868:*i' <> breasts./ Give <> painlessly!
235| MS:out *P1868:*out, 240| MS:and I *P1868:*and I,
241| MS:after-wit had <> hands *P1868:*after-wit, had <> hands;
242| MS:added in <> interest *P1868:*added, in <> interest, 245| MS:Of <> throttle his Violante *P1868:*O' <> throttle him Violante 246| MS:mischief!" We *P1868:*mischief!" § ¶ § We 250| MS:Lend vigour *P1868:*Send vigour
251| MS:service, lest *P1868:*service; lest 252| MS:hers whose *P1868:*hers, whose
254| MS:stump: *P1868:*stump. 255| MS:by day *P1868:*by day,
256| MS:care *P1868:*care, 257| MS:pickaback, *P1868:*pick-a-back,

Sat at serene cats'-cradle with his child,
Or took the measured tallness, top to toe,
Of what was grown a great girl twelve years old:
Till sudden at the door a tap discreet,
A visitor's premonitory cough,
And poverty had reached him in her rounds.

This came when he was past the working-time,
Had learned to dandle and forgot to dig,
And who must but Violante cast about,
Contrive and task that head of hers again?
She who had caught one fish, could make that catch
A bigger still, in angler's policy:
So, with an angler's mercy for the bait,
Her minnow was set wriggling on its barb
And tossed to mid-stream; which means, this grown girl
With the great eyes and bounty of black hair
And first crisp youth that tempts a jaded taste,
Was whisked i' the way of a certain man, who snapped.

Count Guido Franceschini the Aretine
Was head of an old noble house enough,
Not over-rich, you can't have everything,
But such a man as riches rub against,
Readily stick to,—one with a right to them
Born in the blood: 'twas in his very brow
Always to knit itself against the world,
Beforehand so, when that world stinted due
Service and suit: the world ducks and defers.
As such folks do, he had come up to Rome

258| MS:Sate *P1868:*Sat 260| MS:Of what § inserted above line § <> old, *P1868:*old: 261| MS:tap distinct § crossed out and replaced above by § discreet, 263| MS:And Poverty *P1868:*And poverty 263-64| MS:§ no ¶ § *P1868:*§ ¶ § 266| MS:who but his Violante must cast *P1868:*who must but Violante cast 272| MS:to the mid-stream; that is, this *1888:*to mid-stream; which means, this 273| MS:the two great *P1868:*the great 274| MS:taste *P1868:*taste, 275| MS:in <> of an old man, who *P1868:*i' <> of a certain man, who 281| MS:blood, 'twas *P1868:*blood: 'twas 282| MS:world *P1868:*world, 283| MS:So be beforehand when that stinted

To better his fortune, and, since many years,
Was friend and follower of a cardinal;
Waiting the rather thus on providence
That a shrewd younger poorer brother yet,
The Abate Paolo, a regular priest,
Had long since tried his powers and found he swam
With the deftest on the Galilean pool:
But then he was a web-foot, free o' the wave,
And no ambiguous dab-chick hatched to strut,
Humbled by any fond attempt to swim
When fiercer fowl usurped his dunghill top—
A whole priest, Paolo, no mere piece of one
Like Guido tacked thus to the Church's tail!
Guido moreover, as the head o' the house,
Claiming the main prize, not the lesser luck,
The centre lily, no mere chickweed fringe.

He waited and learned waiting, thirty years;
Got promise, missed performance—what would you have?
No petty post rewards a nobleman
For spending youth in splendid lackey-work,
And there's concurrence for each rarer prize;
When that falls, rougher hand and readier foot
Push aside Guido spite of his black looks.
The end was, Guido, when the warning showed,
The first white hair i' the glass, gave up the game,
Determined on returning to his town,
Making the best of bad incurable,
Patching the old palace up and lingering there

---

*P1872:*Beforehand so, when that world stinted 287| MS:cardinal— *P1868:*cardinal; 288| MS:on Providence *P1868:*on providence, *1888:*providence 289| MS:yet *P1868:*yet, 291| MS:his webs § crossed out and replaced above by § powers 292| MS:pool, *P1868:*pool: 293| MS:of *P1868:*o' 294| MS:dabchick <> strut *P1868:*dab-chick <> strut, 295| MS:any such attempt *P1868:*any fond attempt 296| MS:dunghill-top; *P1868:*dunghill-top— *P1872:* dunghill top— 298| MS:the Churches tail *P1868:*the Church's tail! 299| MS:of *P1868:*o' 300| MS:prize, and § crossed out § not the middle § crossed out and replaced above by § lesser 301-2| MS:§ no ¶ § *P1868:*§ ¶ § 302| MS:waiting twenty years, *CP1868:*waiting, thirty years; 305| MS:lackey's-work, *P1868:*lackey-work, 310| MS:in *P1868:*i' 313| MS:old place up

The customary life out with his kin,
Where honour helps to spice the scanty bread.

Just as he trimmed his lamp and girt his loins
To go his journey and be wise at home,
In the right mood of disappointed worth,
Who but Violante sudden spied her prey
(Where was I with that angler-simile?)
And threw her bait, Pompilia, where he sulked—
A gleam i' the gloom!

What if he gained thus much,
Wrung out this sweet drop from the bitter Past,
Bore off this rose-bud from the prickly brake
To justify such torn clothes and scratched hands,
And, after all, brought something back from Rome?
Would not a wife serve at Arezzo well
To light the dark house, lend a look of youth
To the mother's face grown meagre, left alone
And famished with the emptiness of hope,
Old Donna Beatrice? Wife you want
Would you play family-representative,
Carry you elder-brotherly, high and right
O'er what may prove the natural petulance
Of the third brother, younger, greedier still,
Girolamo, also a fledgeling priest,
Beginning life in turn with callow beak
Agape for luck, no luck had stopped and stilled.

---

*P1868:*old palace up 315| MS:honor *P1868:*honour 315-16| MS:§ no ¶ § *P1868:*§ ¶ § 318| MS:the gay mood of disappointed man, *P1868:*the right mood of disappointed worth, 321| MS:bait Pompilia where *P1868:*bait, Pompilia, where 322| MS:in the gloom! What *P1868:*i' the gloom! § ¶ § What 325| MS:hands *P1868:*hands, 326| MS:And after all brought *P1868:*And, after all, brought 327| MS:at Arezzo now *P1868:*at Arezzo well 329| MS:face long § crossed out and replaced above by § grown 334| MS:what might prove *P1868:*what may prove 336| MS:Also § in left margin § A fledgeling § inserted above § priest, too, if you please! § last four words and punctuation crossed out § Girolamo, *P1868:*Girolamo, also a<> priest, 338| MS:stilled? *P1868:*stilled.

Such were the pinks and greys about the bait
Persuaded Guido gulp down hook and all.

What constituted him so choice a catch,
You question? Past his prime and poor beside!
Ask that of any she who knows the trade.
Why first, here was a nobleman with friends,
A palace one might run to and be safe
When presently the threatened fate should fall,
A big-browed master to block door-way up,
Parley with people bent on pushing by
And praying the mild Pietro quick clear scores:
Is birth a privilege and power or no?
Also,—but judge of the result desired,
By the price paid and manner of the sale.
The Count was made woo, win and wed at once:
Asked, and was haled for answer, lest the heat
Should cool, to San Lorenzo, one blind eve,
And had Pompilia put into his arms
O' the sly there, by a hasty candle-blink,
With sanction of some priest-confederate
Properly paid to make short work and sure.

So did old Pietro's daughter change her style
For Guido Franceschini's lady-wife
Ere Guido knew it well; and why this haste
And scramble and indecent secrecy?
"Lest Pietro, all the while in ignorance,
Should get to learn, gainsay and break the match:
His peevishness had promptly put aside

340–41| MS:§ ¶ § *1888:*§ No ¶; paragraph restored; see Editorial Notes § 342| MS:beside: *P1868:*beside? *1888:*beside! 343| MS:any one who *P1868:*any she who 347| MS:With big-browed <> doorway up *P1868:*A big-browed <> door-way up, 349| MS:praying Master Pietro *P1868:*praying the mild Pietro 351| MS:Also . . but <> desired *P1868:*Also,—but <> desired, 352| MS:paid down and *P1868:*paid and 353| MS:The man was *P1868:*The Count was 355| MS:to San Lorenzo one <> eve *P1868:*to San Lorenzo, one <> eve, 356| MS:And have § crossed out and replaced above by § had 357| MS:On the sly, by <> candle's blink, *P1868:*O' the sly there, by <> candle-blink, 359–60| MS:§ no ¶ § *P1868:*§ ¶ § 363| MS:secresy? *P1868:*secrecy?

Such honour and refused the proffered boon,
Pleased to become authoritative once.
She remedied the wilful man's mistake—"
Did our discreet Violante. Rather say,
Thus did she, lest the object of her game,
Guido the gulled one, give him but a chance,
A moment's respite, time for thinking twice,
Might count the cost before he sold himself,
And try the clink of coin they paid him with.

But coin paid, bargain struck and business done,
Once the clandestine marriage over thus,
All parties made perforce the best o' the fact;
Pietro could play vast indignation off,
Be ignorant and astounded, dupe, poor soul,
Please you, of daughter, wife and son-in-law,
While Guido found himself in flagrant fault,
Must e'en do suit and service, soothe, subdue
A father not unreasonably chafed,
Bring him to terms by paying son's devoir.
Pleasant initiation!

The end, this:
Guido's broad back was saddled to bear all—
Pietro, Violante, and Pompilia too,—
Three lots cast confidently in one lap,
Three dead-weights with one arm to lift the three
Out of their limbo up to life again.
The Roman household was to strike fresh root

367| MS:honor *P1868:*honour 371| MS:game *P1868:*game, 374| MS:himself *P1868:*himself, 376| MS:'Twas pursed, the bargain struck, the business done. *P1868:*But passed, the <> done *1872:*But coin paid, bargain struck and business 378| MS:of *P1868:*o' 380| MS:dupe alike *1888:*dupe, poor soul, 381| MS:At need, § last two words inserted above § Of wife, of § crossed out § daughter and of § crossed out § *1888:*Please you, of daughter, wife and 382| MS:fault *P1868:*fault, 383| MS:Must make submission § last two words crossed out and replaced above by § e'en do suit and service 385| MS:by doing son's devoir— *P1868:*by paying son's devoir. 386| MS:initiation! The end was this— *P1868:*initiation § ¶ § The end, this: 388| MS:Pietro, Violante, and § added above § Pompilia too— *P1868:*too,— 390| MS:deadweights and one *P1868:*dead-weights with one 391| *P1868:*again: *P1872:*again.

In a new soil, graced with a novel name,
Gilt with an alien glory, Aretine
Henceforth and never Roman any more,
By treaty and engagement; thus it ran:
Pompilia's dowry for Pompilia's self
As a thing of course,—she paid her own expense;
No loss nor gain there: but the couple, you see,
They, for their part, turned over first of all
Their fortune in its rags and rottenness
To Guido, fusion and confusion, he
And his with them and theirs,—whatever rag
With coin residuary fell on floor
When Brother Paolo's energetic shake
Should do the relics justice: since 'twas thought,
Once vulnerable Pietro out of reach,
That, left at Rome as representative,
The Abate, backed by a potent patron here,
And otherwise with purple flushing him,
Might play a good game with the creditor,
Make up a moiety which, great or small,
Should go to the common stock—if anything,
Guido's, so far repayment of the cost
About to be,—and if, as looked more like,
Nothing,—why, all the nobler cost were his
Who guaranteed, for better or for worse,
To Pietro and Violante, house and home,
Kith and kin, with the pick of company
And life o' the fat o' the land while life should last.
How say you to the bargain at first blush?
Why did a middle-aged not-silly man
Show himself thus besotted all at once?

395| MS:more. *P1868:*more, 396| MS:engagement: thus *P1872:* engagement; thus 398| MS:expence, *P1868:*expense; 399| MS:the Couple *P1868:*the couple 404| MS:With a coin *1888:*With coin 405| MS:When brother *P1868:*When Brother 406| MS:thought *P1868:*thought, 408| MS:That left <> representative *P1868:*That, left <> representative, 409| MS:here *P1868:*here, 416| MS:why all *1868:*why, all 417| MS:worse *1868:*worse, 419| MS:kin with *1868:*kin, with 420| MS:on <> of *1868:*o' <> o' 422| MS:not silly *1868:*not-silly 424| MS:Quoth

Quoth Solomon, one black eye does it all.

They went to Arezzo,—Pietro and his spouse,
With just the dusk o' the day of life to spend,
Eager to use the twilight, taste a treat,
Enjoy for once with neither stay nor stint
The luxury of lord-and-lady-ship,
And realize the stuff and nonsense long
A-simmer in their noddles; vent the fume
Born there and bred, the citizen's conceit
How fares nobility while crossing earth,
What rampart or invisible body-guard
Keeps off the taint of common life from such.
They had not fed for nothing on the tales
Of grandees who give banquets worthy Jove,
Spending gold as if Plutus paid a whim,
Served with obeisances as when . . . what God?
I'm at the end of my tether; 'tis enough
You understand what they came primed to see:
While Guido who should minister the sight,
Stay all this qualmish greediness of soul
With apples and with flagons—for his part,
Was set on life diverse as pole from pole:
Lust of the flesh, lust of the eye,—what else
Was he just now awake from, sick and sage,
After the very debauch they would begin?—
Suppose such stuff and nonsense really were.
That bubble, they were bent on blowing big,
He had blown already till he burst his cheeks,
And hence found soapsuds bitter to the tongue.
He hoped now to walk softly all his days

Solomon, One *1868:*Quoth Solomon, one 425| MS:spouse *1868:*spouse, 426| MS:of *1868:*o' 430| MS:realise *1888:*realize 431| MS:noddles, vent *1868:*noddles; vent 434| MS:bodyguard *1868:*body-guard 435| MS:common things from *1868:*common life from 437| MS:grandees and their banquets *1868:*grandees who give banquets 439| MS:when . . what *1868:*when . . . what 441| MS:see *1868:*see: 448| MS:begin *1868:* begin?— 450| MS:bubble they <> big *1868:*bubble, they <> big, 451| MS:had been blowing till <> cheeks *1868:*had blown already till <> cheeks, 452| MS:hence the soapsuds bitter on his tongue. *1868:*hence found soapsuds bitter to

In soberness of spirit, if haply so,
Pinching and paring he might furnish forth
A frugal board, bare sustenance, no more,
Till times, that could not well grow worse, should mend.

Thus minded then, two parties mean to meet
And make each other happy. The first week,
And fancy strikes fact and explodes in full.
"This," shrieked the Comparini, "this the Count,
The palace, the signorial privilege,
The pomp and pageantry were promised us?
For this have we exchanged our liberty,
Our competence, our darling of a child?
To house as spectres in a sepulchre
Under this black stone-heap, the street's disgrace,
Grimmest as that is of the gruesome town,
And here pick garbage on a pewter plate
Or cough at verjuice dripped from earthenware?
Oh Via Vittoria, oh the other place
I' the Pauline, did we give you up for this?
Where's the foregone housekeeping good and gay,
The neighbourliness, the companionship,
The treat and feast when holidays came round,
The daily feast that seemed no treat at all,
Called common by the uncommon fools we were!
Even the sun that used to shine at Rome,
Where is it? Robbed and starved and frozen too,
We will have justice, justice if there be!"
Did not they shout, did not the town resound!
Guido's old lady-mother Beatrice,
Who since her husband, Count Tommaso's death,

---

the tongue. 454| MS:spirit if *1868:*spirit, if 457-58| MS:§ no ¶ § *1868:* § ¶ § 458| MS:There, minded thus, two *1868:*Thus minded then, two 460| MS:fancy meets fact *1868:*fancy strikes fact 461| MS:"This" shrieked *1868:*"This," shrieked 463| MS:And § crossed out and replaced above by § The wealth and <> was *1868:*The pomp and <> were 465| MS:child, *1868:*child? 467| MS:stone heap the *1868:*heap, the *1888:*stone-heap 472| MS:In *1868:*I' 474| MS:neighbourliness and companionship, *1868:* neighbourliness, the companionship, 475| MS:round *1868:*round, 476| MS:all *1868:*all, 480| MS:be." *1868:*be!" 482| MS:lady-mother

Had held sole sway i' the house,—the doited crone
Slow to acknowledge, curtsey and abdicate,—
Was recognized of true novercal type,
Dragon and devil. His brother Girolamo
Came next in order: priest was he? The worse!
No way of winning him to leave his mumps
And help the laugh against old ancestry
And formal habits long since out of date,
Letting his youth be patterned on the mode
Approved of where Violante laid down law.
Or did he brighten up by way of change,
Dispose himself for affability?
The malapert, too complaisant by half
To the alarmed young novice of a bride!
Let him go buzz, betake himself elsewhere
Nor singe his fly-wings in the candle-flame!

Four months' probation of this purgatory,
Dog-snap and cat-claw, curse and counterblast,
The devil's self were sick of his own din;
And Pietro, after trumpeting huge wrongs
At church and market-place, pillar and post,
Square's corner, street's end, now the palace-step
And now the wine-house bench—while, on her side,
Violante up and down was voluble
In whatsoever pair of ears would perk
From goody, gossip, cater-cousin and sib,
Curious to peep at the inside of things
And catch in the act pretentious poverty
At its wits' end to keep appearance up,

Beatrice *1868:*lady-mother Beatrice, 484| MS:in the house, the *1868:*i' the house,—the 485| MS:abdicate, *1868:*abdicate,— 486| MS:recognized, the true *1868:*recognized of true 487| MS:devil: his *1868:*devil. His 488| MS:worse: *1868:*worse! 489| MS:his sulks *1868:*his mumps 490| MS:against his ancestry *1868:*against old ancestry 491| MS:For rustic habits *1868:*And formal habits 493| MS:where the Comparini laid *1868:*where Violante laid 494| MS:change? *1868:*change, 497| MS:young beauty of the bride! *1868:*young novice of a bride! 499-500| MS:§ no ¶ § *1868:*§ ¶ § 502| MS:self had been sick <> din, *1868:*din; *P1872:*self were sick 503| MS:trumpeting of wrongs *1868:*trumpeting huge wrongs 506| MS:side *1868:*side, 509| MS:catercousin and sib *1868:*cater-cousin and sib,

Make both ends meet,—nothing the vulgar loves
Like what this couple pitched them right and left.
Then, their worst done that way, both struck tent, marched:
—Renounced their share o' the bargain, flung what dues
Guido was bound to pay, in Guido's face,
Left their hearts'-darling, treasure of the twain
And so forth, the poor inexperienced bride,
To her own devices, bade Arezzo rot,
Cursed life signorial, and sought Rome once more.

I see the comment ready on your lip,
"The better fortune, Guido's—free at least
By this defection of the foolish pair,
He could begin make profit in some sort
Of the young bride and the new quietness,
Lead his own life now, henceforth breathe unplagued."
Could he? You know the sex like Guido's self.
Learn the Violante-nature!

                                        Once in Rome,
By way of helping Guido lead such life,
Her first act to inaugurate return
Was, she got pricked in conscience: Jubilee
Gave her the hint. Our Pope, as kind as just,
Attained his eighty years, announced a boon
Should make us bless the fact, held Jubilee—

513| MS:meet:nothing *1868:*meet,—nothing 514| MS:left,— *1888:*left. 515| MS:way, struck tent and marched: *1868:*way, they struck tent, marched: *1888:* way, both struck 516| MS:of *1868:*o' 520| MS:devices, left Arezzo thus *1868:*devices, bade Arezzo rot *P1872:*rot, 521| MS:And the life *P1872:*Cursed life 522| MS:comment tremble § crossed out and replaced above by § ready 525| MS:begin make profit in § last three words inserted above § 527| MS:breathe in peace," *1868:*breathe unplagued." 529| MS:the Violante-nature. Once *1868:*the Violante-nature! § ¶ § Once 530| MS:lead his life, *1868:*lead such life, 532| MS:Was to get pricked *1868:*Was, she got pricked 533| MS:as good as *1868:*as kind as 535| MS:fact, his Jubilee— *1868:*fact, held

Short shrift, prompt pardon for the light offence,
And no rough dealing with the regular crime
So this occasion were not suffered slip—
Otherwise, sins commuted as before,
Without the least abatement in the price.
Now, who had thought it? All this while, it seems,
Our sage Violante had a sin of a sort
She must compound for now or not at all.
Now be the ready riddance! She confessed
Pompilia was a fable not a fact:
She never bore a child in her whole life.
Had this child been a changeling, that were grace
In some degree, exchange is hardly theft,
You take your stand on truth ere leap your lie:
Here was all lie, no touch of truth at all,
All the lie hers—not even Pietro guessed
He was as childless still as twelve years since.
The babe had been a find i' the filth-heap, Sir,
Catch from the kennel! There was found at Rome,
Down in the deepest of our social dregs,
A woman who professed the wanton's trade
Under the requisite thin coverture,
Communis meretrix and washer-wife:
The creature thus conditioned found by chance
Motherhood like a jewel in the muck,
And straightway either trafficked with her prize
Or listened to the tempter and let be,—
Made pact abolishing her place and part
In womankind, beast-fellowship indeed.
She sold this babe eight months before its birth
To our Violante, Pietro's honest spouse,

Jubilee— 536| *1888:*offence DC,BrU:offence, *1889:*offence, 543| MS:all: *P1872:*all, 546| MS:never had a < > life; *1868:*never bore a < > life. 547| MS:changeling, there were *1868:*changeling, that were 548| MS:theft; *1872:*theft, 551| MS:All of § crossed out and replaced above by § the 553| MS:in *1868:*i' 554| MS:kennel. There < > Rome *1868:*kennel! There < > Rome, 555| MS:of the social dregs *1868:*of our social dregs, 560| MS:muck *1868:*muck, 562| / MS:be *1868:*be,— 563| MS:A pact *1868:*Made pact 564| MS:beast fellowship indeed— *1868:*beast-fellowship *P1872:*indeed.

Well-famed and widely-instanced as that crown
To the husband, virtue in a woman's shape.
She it was, bought, paid for, passed off the thing
As very flesh and blood and child of her
Despite the flagrant fifty years,—and why?
Partly to please old Pietro, fill his cup
With wine at the late hour when lees are left,
And send him from life's feast rejoicingly,—
Partly to cheat the rightful heirs, agape,
Each uncle's cousin's brother's son of him,
For that same principal of the usufruct
It vext him he must die and leave behind.

Such was the sin had come to be confessed.
Which of the tales, the first or last, was true?
Did she so sin once, or, confessing now,
Sin for the first time? Either way you will.
One sees a reason for the cheat: one sees
A reason for a cheat in owning cheat
Where no cheat had been. What of the revenge?
What prompted the contrition all at once,
Made the avowal easy, the shame slight?
Why, prove they but Pompilia not their child,
No child, no dowry! this, supposed their child,
Had claimed what this, shown alien to their blood,
Claimed nowise: Guido's claim was through his wife,
Null then and void with hers. The biter bit,

567| MS:widely instanced *1868:*widely-instanced 569| MS:was bought and paid <> passed the *1868:*was, bought *1888:*bought, paid for, passed off the 570| MS:Off as the flesh and blood, the child *1868:*blood and child *1888:*As very flesh 575| MS:agape *1868:*agape, 578| MS:vexed *P1868:*vext 578-79| MS:§ no ¶ § *1868:*§ ¶ § 580| MS:last was true, *1868:*last, was true? 582| MS:you please § crossed out and replaced by § will. 586| MS:once *1868:*once, 589| MS:dowry; this *P1872:*dowry! this 591| MS:no wise <>

Do you see! For such repayment of the past,
One might conceive the penitential pair
Ready to bring their case before the courts,
Publish their infamy to all the world
And, arm in arm, go chuckling thence content.

Is this your view? 'Twas Guido's anyhow
And colourable: he came forward then,
Protested in his very bride's behalf
Against this lie and all it led to, least
Of all the loss o' the dowry; no! From her
And him alike he would expunge the blot,
Erase the brand of such a bestial birth,
Participate in no hideous heritage
Gathered from the gutter to be garnered up
And glorified in a palace. Peter and Paul!
But that who likes may look upon the pair
Exposed in yonder church, and show his skill
By saying which is eye and which is mouth
Thro' those stabs thick and threefold,—but for that—
A strong word on the liars and their lie
Might crave expression and obtain it, Sir!
—Though prematurely, since there's more to come,
More that will shake your confidence in things
Your cousin tells you,—may I be so bold?

This makes the first act of the farce,—anon
The sombre element comes stealing in
Till all is black or blood-red in the piece.
Guido, thus made a laughing-stock abroad,
A proverb for the market-place at home,

---

wife *1868:*no wise <> wife, 593| MS:past *1868:*past, 597-98| MS: § no ¶ § *1868:*§ ¶ § 599| MS:forward too, *1868:*forward then, 602| MS:of *1868:*o' 605| MS:Participate no *1868:*Participate in no 606| MS:Gathered in the *1868:*Gathered from the 607| MS:Glorified *1868:*And glorified 614| MS:All prematurely *1868:*—Though prematurely 615-17| MS:things./ This *1868:*things/ Your cousin tells you,—may I be so bold?/ § ¶ § This 618| MS:The sombre element comes stealing in § transposed to § Comes stealing in the sombre element *1868:*The stealing sombre element comes in *1888:*The sombre element comes stealing in 619| MS:bloodred *1868:*blood-red 620| MS:laughing

Left alone with Pompilia now, this graft
So reputable on his ancient stock,
This plague-seed set to fester his sound flesh,
What does the Count? Revenge him on his wife?
Unfasten at all risks to rid himself
The noisome lazar-badge, fall foul of fate,
And, careless whether the poor rag was 'ware
O' the part it played, or helped unwittingly,
Bid it go burn and leave his frayed flesh free?
Plainly, did Guido open both doors wide,
Spurn thence the cur-cast creature and clear scores
As man might, tempted in extreme like this?
No, birth and breeding, and compassion too
Saved her such scandal. She was young, he thought,
Not privy to the treason, punished most
I' the proclamation of it; why make her
A party to the crime she suffered by?
Then the black eyes were now her very own,
Not any more Violante's: let her live,
Lose in a new air, under a new sun,
The taint of the imputed parentage
Truly or falsely, take no more the touch
Of Pietro and his partner anyhow!
All might go well yet.

So she thought, herself,
It seems, since what was her first act and deed
When news came how these kindly ones at Rome
Had stripped her naked to amuse the world

---

stock *1868:*laughing-stock 622| MS:with this lady now *1868:*with Pompilia now 625| MS:What did the man? Revenge *1868:*the Count? Revenge *1888:*What does the 628| MS:And careless < > ware *1868:*And, careless DC, BrU:'ware *1889:*'ware 629| MS:Of < > played or *1868:*O' < > played, or 630| MS:and let his flesh alone? *1868:*and leave his frayed flesh free? 631| MS:wide *1868:*wide, 632| MS:and be free *1868:*and clear scores 635| MS:her this scandal *1868:*her such scandal 636| MS:punished too *1868:*punished most 637| MS:In < > it, why *1868:*I' < > it; why 640| MS:more Violantes *1868:*more Violante's 643| MS:Truely *1888:*Truly 644| MS:anyhow. *1868:*anyhow! 645| MS:yet. So she thought herself, *1868:*yet. § ¶ § So she thought, herself, 646| MS:since this § crossed out and replaced above by § what 647| MS:one contrived *1868:*ones at Rome 648| MS:To strip

With spots here, spots there and spots everywhere?
—For I should tell you that they noised abroad
Not merely the main scandal of her birth,
But slanders written, printed, published wide,
Pamphlets which set forth all the pleasantry
Of how the promised glory was a dream,
The power a bubble, and the wealth—why, dust.
There was a picture, painted to the life,
Of those rare doings, that superlative
Initiation in magnificence
Conferred on a poor Roman family
By favour of Arezzo and her first
And famousest, the Franceschini there.
You had the Countship holding head aloft
Bravely although bespattered, shifts and straits
In keeping out o' the way o' the wheels o' the world,
The comic of those home-contrivances
When the old lady-mother's wit was taxed
To find six clamorous mouths in food more real
Than fruit plucked off the cobwebbed family-tree,
Or acorns shed from its gilt mouldered frame—
Cold glories served up with stale fame for sauce.
What, I ask,—when the drunkenness of hate
Hiccuped return for hospitality,
Befouled the table they had feasted on,
Or say,—God knows I'll not prejudge the case,—
Grievances thus distorted, magnified,
Coloured by quarrel into calumny,—
What side did our Pompilia first espouse?
Her first deliberate measure was—she wrote,

---

her naked and amuse *1868:*Had stripped her naked to amuse [650]| MS:§ crowded between lines 649-51 § MS:For *1868:*—For [653]| MS:Pamplets *1868:*Pamphlets [654]| MS:dream *1868:*dream, [655]| MS:bubble and *P1872:*bubble, and [660]| MS:favor *1868:*favour [662]| MS:the Countship keeping head *1868:*the Countship holding head [664]| MS:of < > of < > of *1868:*o' < > o' < > o' [669]| MS:acorns let fall § last two words crossed out and replaced above by one word § shed from its mouldered *1868:*its gilt mouldered [670]| MS:with three-pauls' worth' sauce. *1888:*with stale fame for sauce. [672]| MS:hospitality *P1868:*hospitality, [673]| MS:Bespoiled the *1868:*Befouled the [675]| MS:magnified *1868:*magnified, [677]| MS:What part § crossed out and replaced above by § side [678]| MS:was to write, *1868:*was, she wrote,

Pricked by some loyal impulse, straight to Rome
And her husband's brother the Abate there,
Who, having managed to effect the match,
Might take men's censure for its ill success.
She made a clean breast also in her turn,
And qualified the couple properly,
Since whose departure, hell, she said, was heaven,
And the house, late distracted by their peals,
Quiet as Carmel where the lilies live.
Herself had oftentimes complained: but why?
All her complaints had been their prompting, tales
Trumped up, devices to this very end.
Their game had been to thwart her husband's love
And cross his will, malign his words and ways,
To reach this issue, furnish this pretence
For impudent withdrawal from their bond,—
Theft, indeed murder, since they meant no less
Whose last injunction to her simple self
Had been—what parents'-precept do you think?
That she should follow after with all speed,
Fly from her husband's house clandestinely,
Join them at Rome again, but first of all
Pick up a fresh companion in her flight,
So putting youth and beauty to fit use,—
Some gay dare-devil cloak-and-rapier spark
Capable of adventure,—helped by whom

---

*1888:*was—she 681| MS:Who having <> match *1868:*Who, having <> match, 682| MS:take the § crossed out and replaced above by § men's <> success, *1868:*success. 683| MS:And made <> turn; *1868:*She made *1888:*turn, 684| MS:She qualified <> handsomely! *1888:*And qualified <> properly, 688| MS:§ crowded between lines 687-89 § 689| MS:prompting, lies *1868:*prompting, tales 690| MS:end, *1868:*end. 694| MS:bond, *1868:*bond,— 697| MS:been . . what *1868:*been—what 699| MS:clandestinely *1868:*clandestinely, 700| MS:And join them merrily § crossed out § at <> again, first of all § last three words clearly added in revision § *1868:*Join them at <> again, but first 701| MS:Picking up as companion *1868:* Pick up a fresh companion 702| MS:Putting her youth <> use, *1868:*Putting so youth <> use, *P1872:*So putting youth <> use,— 703| MS:gay, bold gallant, cloak-and-rapier *P1868:*gay, dare-devil, cloak-and-rapier *P1872:*gay dare-

She, some fine eve when lutes were in the air,
Having put poison in the posset-cup,
Laid hands on money, jewels and the like,
And, to conceal the thing with more effect,
By way of parting benediction too,
Fired the house,—one would finish famously
I' the tumult, slip out, scurry off and away
And turn up merrily at home once more.
Fact this, and not a dream o' the devil, Sir!
And more than this, a fact none dare dispute,
Word for word, such a letter did she write,
And such the Abate read, nor simply read
But gave all Rome to ruminate upon,
In answer to such charges as, I say,
The couple sought to be beforehand with.

The cause thus carried to the courts at Rome,
Guido away, the Abate had no choice
But stand forth, take his absent brother's part,
Defend the honour of himself beside.
He made what head he might against the pair,
Maintained Pompilia's birth legitimate
And all her rights intact—hers, Guido's now:
And so far by his policy turned their flank,
(The enemy being beforehand in the place)
That,—though the courts allowed the cheat for fact,
Suffered Violante to parade her shame,
Publish her infamy to heart's content,

---

devil cloak-and-rapier 705| MS:where *1868:*were 708| MS:And to *1868:*And, to 710| MS:Fire *1868:*Fired 711| MS:In *1868:*I' 712| MS:at Rome once *1868:*at home once 713| MS:of *1868:*o' 714| MS:than that, a <> dares *1868:*than this, a <> dare 715| MS:write, *1868:*write. *1888:*write, 717| MS:give *P1868:*gave 718| MS:as I say *P1868:*as, I say, 719-20| MS:§ no ¶ § *1868:*§ ¶ § 723| MS:beside; *1868:*beside. 726| MS:intact and Guido's now— *1868:*intact—hers, Guido's now— *P1872:*now: 727| MS:his tactics turned <> flank *1868:*flank, *P1872:*his policy turned 728| MS:The <> place, *1888:*(The <> place) 729| MS:That, though the Court *1868:*That <> the courts *P1872:*That,—though 730| MS:Suffered the woman to <> shame *1868:*Suffered Violante to <> shame, 731| MS:Profess § crossed out and replaced above by § Publish <> content,— *1868:*content, 732| MS:of <> proved *1868:*o' <> proved,—

And let the tale o' the feigned birth pass for proved,—
Yet they stopped there, refused to intervene
And dispossess the innocents, befooled
By gifts o' the guilty, at guilt's new caprice.
They would not take away the dowry now
Wrongfully given at first, nor bar at all
Succession to the aforesaid usufruct,
Established on a fraud, nor play the game
Of Pietro's child and now not Pietro's child
As it might suit the gamester's purpose. Thus
Was justice ever ridiculed in Rome:
Such be the double verdicts favoured here
Which send away both parties to a suit
Nor puffed up nor cast down,—for each a crumb
Of right, for neither of them the whole loaf.
Whence, on the Comparini's part, appeal—
Counter-appeal on Guido's,—that's the game:
And so the matter stands, even to this hour,
Bandied as balls are in a tennis-court,
And so might stand, unless some heart broke first,
Till doomsday.

Leave it thus, and now revert
To the old Arezzo whence we moved to Rome.
We've had enough o' the parents, false or true,
Now for a touch o' the daughter's quality.
The start's fair henceforth, every obstacle
Out of the young wife's footpath, she's alone,
Left to walk warily now: how does she walk?
Why, once a dwelling's threshold marked and crossed

733| MS:to interpose *1868:*to intervene 734| MS:disposess < > innocent, abused *1868:*dispossess < > innocents, befooled 735| MS:of the guilty, now at guilt's caprice: *1868:*o' the guilty, at guilt's new caprice: *P1872:*caprice.
739| MS:a lie, nor *1868:*a fraud, nor 741| MS:purpose:thus *1868:*purpose. Thus
743| MS:One of the *1868:*Such be the 748| MS:game *1868:*game:
752| MS:doom's day: leave *1868:*doomsday. § ¶ § Leave 754| MS:of the parents false *1868:*o' the parents, false 755| MS:of *1868:*o' 756| MS:henceforth—every *P1872:*henceforth, every 757| MS:footpath—she's alone—*P1872:*footpath, she's alone, 758| MS:how with her? *1868:*how does she walk?
759| MS:dwelling's doorpost marked *P1872:*dwelling's threshold marked

In rubric by the enemy on his rounds
As eligible, as fit place of prey,
Baffle him henceforth, keep him out who can!
Stop up the door at the first hint of hoof,
Presently at the window taps a horn,
And Satan's by your fireside, never fear!
Pompilia, left alone now, found herself;
Found herself young too, sprightly, fair enough,
Matched with a husband old beyond his age
(Though that was something like four times her own)
Because of cares past, present and to come:
Found too the house dull and its inmates dead,
So, looked outside for light and life.

And love
Did in a trice turn up with life and light,—
The man with the aureole, sympathy made flesh,
The all-consoling Caponsacchi, Sir!
A priest—what else should the consoler be?
With goodly shoulderblade and proper leg,
A portly make and a symmetric shape,
And curls that clustered to the tonsure quite.
This was a bishop in the bud, and now
A canon full-blown so far: priest, and priest
Nowise exorbitantly overworked,
The courtly Christian, not so much Saint Paul
As a saint of Cæsar's household: there posed he
Sending his god-glance after his shot shaft,
Apollos turned Apollo, while the snake
Pompilia writhed transfixed through all her spires.
He, not a visitor at Guido's house,
Scarce an acquaintance, but in prime request

761| MS:as his place *1868:*as fit place 769| MS:Though < > own, *1868:*(Though < > own) 772| MS:So looked < > life, and lo *1868:*So, looked < > life. § ¶ §And *1888:*life. § ¶ § And love 773| MS:There in a trice turned up the life and light *1868:*trice did turn up life and light, *1888:*Did in < > turn up with life and light,— 775| MS:all-consoling Caponsacchi, sir! *1868:*all-consoling Caponsacchi, Sir! 777| MS:goodly presence and a proper *1868:*goodly shoulderblade and proper 781| MS:A Canon fullblown so far—priest, and *1868:* A canon full-blown so far: priest, and 785| MS:shaft *1868:*shaft, 788| MS:He was no visitor *1868:*He, not a visitor 789| MS:but, in *1868:*but in

With the magnates of Arezzo, was seen here,
Heard there, felt everywhere in Guido's path
If Guido's wife's path be her husband's too.
Now he threw comfits at the theatre
Into her lap,—what harm in Carnival?
Now he pressed close till his foot touched her gown,
His hand brushed hers,—how help on promenade?
And, ever on weighty business, found his steps
Incline to a certain haunt of doubtful fame
Which fronted Guido's palace by mere chance;
While—how do accidents sometimes combine!—
Pompilia chose to cloister up her charms
Just in a chamber that o'erlooked the street,
Sat there to pray, or peep thence at mankind.

This passage of arms and wits amused the town.
At last the husband lifted eyebrow,—bent
On day-book and the study how to wring
Half the due vintage from the worn-out vines
At the villa, tease a quarter the old rent
From the farmstead, tenants swore would tumble soon,—
Pricked up his ear a-singing day and night
With "ruin, ruin;"—and so surprised at last—
Why, what else but a titter? Up he jumps.
Back to mind come those scratchings at the grange,
Prints of the paw about the outhouse; rife

792| MS:path was her *1868:*path be her 794| MS:in carnival? *1868:*in Carnival? 795| MS:gown *1868:*gown, 799| MS:chance *1868:*chance; 800| MS:combine! *1868:*combine!— 802| MS:the same, *P1868:*the street, 803| MS:pray and peep *1868:*pray, or peep 803-4| MS:§ no ¶ § *1868:*§ ¶ § 807| MS:wornout *1868:*worn-out 808| MS:the Villa, teaze *1868:*the villa *1888:*tease 809| MS:the Farmstead tenants *1868:*the farmstead, tenants 811| MS:ruin, ruin"—and < > last *1868:*ruin, ruin;"—and < > last— 813| MS:came < > the gate § crossed out § grange *1868:*come < > grange, 814| MS:about the henroost § crossed out and replaced above by § outhouse,

In his head at once again are word and wink,
Mum here and *budget* there, the smell o' the fox,
The musk o' the gallant. "Friends, there's falseness here!"

The proper help of friends in such a strait
Is waggery, the world over. Laugh him free
O' the regular jealous-fit that's incident
To all old husbands that wed brisk young wives,
And he'll go duly docile all his days.
"Somebody courts your wife, Count? Where and when?
How and why? Mere horn-madness: have a care!
Your lady loves her own room, sticks to it,
Locks herself in for hours, you say yourself.
And—what, it's Caponsacchi means you harm?
The Canon? We caress him, he's the world's,
A man of such acceptance—never dream,
Though he were fifty times the fox you fear,
He'd risk his brush for your particular chick,
When the wide town's his hen-roost! Fie o' the fool!"
So they dispensed their comfort of a kind.
Guido at last cried "Something is in the air,
Under the earth, some plot against my peace.
The trouble of eclipse hangs overhead;
How it should come of that officious orb
Your Canon in my system, you must say:
I say—that from the pressure of this spring
Began the chime and interchange of bells,
Ever one whisper, and one whisper more,
And just one whisper for the silvery last,
Till all at once a-row the bronze-throats burst

---

rife *1868:*outhouse; rife 815| MS:were *1868:*are 816| MS:of *1868:*o' 817| MS:The trace § crossed out and replaced above by § musk of < > here." *1868:*o' < > here!" 817-18| MS:§ no ¶ § *1868:*§ ¶ § 818| MS:proper use of < > a case *1868:*proper help of < > a strait 819| MS:waggery the *1868:* waggery, the 820| MS:Of *1868:*O' 823| MS:courts the Countess? § last two words crossed out and replaced above by three words § your wife, Count? 829| MS:acceptance, — never fear § crossed out § dream, *1888:*acceptance— never 831| MS:He'll *1868:*He'd 832| MS:henroost, Fie on *1868:* hen-roost! Fie o' 835| MS:earth, a plot < > peace: *1868:*earth, some plot *P1872:*peace, 836| MS:eclipse is overhead, *1868:* eclipse hangs overhead, *1888:*overheard; DC, BrU:overhead; *1889:*overhead; 838| MS: system you *1868:*system, you 843| MS:once the bronze throats burst

Into a larum both significant
And sinister: stop it I must and will.
Let Caponsacchi take his hand away
From the wire!—disport himself in other paths
Than lead precisely to my palace-gate,—
Look where he likes except one window's way
Where, cheek on hand, and elbow set on sill,
Happens to lean and say her litanies
Every day and all day long, just my wife—
Or wife and Caponsacchi may fare the worse!"

Admire the man's simplicity, "I'll do this,
I'll not have that, I'll punish and prevent!"—
'Tis easy saying. But to a fray, you see,
Two parties go. The badger shows his teeth:
The fox nor lies down sheep-like nor dares fight.
Oh, the wife knew the appropriate warfare well,
The way to put suspicion to the blush!
At first hint of remonstrance, up and out
I' the face of the world, you found her: she could speak,
State her case,—Franceschini was a name,
Guido had his full share of foes and friends—
Why should not she call these to arbitrate?
She bade the Governor do governance,
Cried out on the Archbishop,—why, there now,
Take him for sample! Three successive times,
Had he to reconduct her by main-force
From where she took her station opposite
His shut door,—on the public steps thereto,
Wringing her hands, when he came out to see,
And shrieking all her wrongs forth at his foot,—
Back to the husband and the house she fled:

---

a-row § indication that *a-row* is to come between *once* and *the* § *1868:*bronze-throats 847| MS:wire! Disport *1868:*wire!—disport 848| MS:palace-gate: *1868:*palace-gate,— 850| MS:Where cheek *1868:*Where, cheek 853-54| MS:§ no ¶ § *1868:*§ ¶ § 855| MS:prevent,—" *1868:*prevent!"— 857| MS:teeth— *1868:*teeth: 858| MS:Does the fox lie down sheeplike or show fight? *1868:*The fox nor lies down sheep-like nor dares fight. 859| MS:warfare too, *1868:*warfare well, 862| MS:In *1868:*I' 868| MS:times *1868:*times, 869| MS:main force *1868:*main-force 871| MS:door on *1868:*door,—on 873| MS:foot,

Judge if that husband warmed him in the face
Of friends or frowned on foes as heretofore!
Judge if he missed the natural grin of folk,
Or lacked the customary compliment
Of cap and bells, the luckless husband's fit!

So it went on and on till—who was right?
One merry April morning, Guido woke
After the cuckoo, so late, near noonday,
With an inordinate yawning of the jaws,
Ears plugged, eyes gummed together, palate, tongue
And teeth one mud-paste made of poppy-milk;
And found his wife flown, his scritoire the worse
For a rummage,—jewelry that was, was not,
Some money there had made itself wings too,—
The door lay wide and yet the servants slept
Sound as the dead, or dosed which does as well.
In short, Pompilia, she who, candid soul,
Had not so much as spoken all her life
To the Canon, nay, so much as peeped at him
Between her fingers while she prayed in church,—
This lamb-like innocent of fifteen years
(Such she was grown to by this time of day)
Had simply put an opiate in the drink
Of the whole household overnight, and then
Got up and gone about her work secure,
Laid hand on this waif and the other stray,
Spoiled the Philistine and marched out of doors
In company of the Canon who, Lord's love,
What with his daily duty at the church,
Nightly devoir where ladies congregate,
Had something else to mind, assure yourself,
Beside Pompilia, paragon though she be,

---

*1868:*foot,— 877| MS:folk *1868:*folk, 879-80| MS:§ no ¶ § *1868:*§ ¶ § 881| MS:On merry <> morning Guido *1868:*One merry <> morning, Guido 885| MS:poppy-milk, *1868:*poppy-milk; 886| MS:scrutoire *1888:*scritoire 887| MS:not,— *1868:*not, 890| MS:well— *1868:*well. 893| MS:nay so *1868:*nay, so 894| MS:church, *1868:*church,— 899| MS:and went about *1868:*and gone about 901| MS:Philistines *1868:*Philistine 903| MS:church

Or notice if her nose were sharp or blunt!
Well, anyhow, albeit impossible,
Both of them were together jollily
Jaunting it Rome-ward, half-way there by this,
While Guido was left go and get undrugged,
Gather his wits up, groaningly give thanks
When neighbours crowded round him to condole.
"Ah," quoth a gossip, "well I mind me now,
The Count did always say he thought he felt
He feared as if this very chance might fall!
And when a man of fifty finds his corns
Ache and his joints throb, and foresees a storm,
Though neighbours laugh and say the sky is clear,
Let us henceforth believe him weatherwise!"
Then was the story told, I'll cut you short:
All neighbours knew: no mystery in the world.
The lovers left at nightfall—over night
Had Caponsacchi come to carry off
Pompilia,—not alone, a friend of his,
One Guillichini, the more conversant
With Guido's housekeeping that he was just
A cousin of Guido's and might play a prank—
(Have not you too a cousin that's a wag?)
—Lord and a Canon also,—what would you have?
Such are the red-clothed milk-swollen poppy-heads
That stand and stiffen 'mid the wheat o' the Church!—
This worthy came to aid, abet his best.
And so the house was ransacked, booty bagged,
The lady led downstairs and out of doors

---

*1868:*church, 907| MS:blunt. *1868:*blunt! 910| MS:it Romewards, halfway *1868:*it Romeward, half-way 911| MS:left to go get *1868:*left go and get 912| MS:groaningly return § crossed out § 914| MS:now *1868:*now, 916| MS:fall: *1868:*fall! 918| MS:storm *1868:*storm, 923| MS:lovers had left at nightfall—at night at least *1868:*lovers left at nightfall—over night 928-30| MS:prank,/ (Lord *1868:*prank—/ (Have not you too a cousin that's a wag?)/ —Lord 931| MS:the red-clothed § inserted above line § 932| MS:mid <> of the Church) *1868:*'mid <> o' the Church!— 933| MS:best, *1868:*best.

Guided and guarded till, the city passed,
A carriage lay convenient at the gate.
Good-bye to the friendly Canon; the loving one
Could peradventure do the rest himself.
In jumps Pompilia, after her the priest,
"Whip, driver! Money makes the mare to go,
And we've a bagful. Take the Roman road!"
So said the neighbours. This was eight hours since.

Guido heard all, swore the befitting oaths,
Shook off the relics of his poison-drench,
Got horse, was fairly started in pursuit
With never a friend to follow, found the track
Fast enough, 'twas the straight Perugia way,
Trod soon upon their very heels, too late
By a minute only at Camoscia, reached
Chiusi, Foligno, ever the fugitives
Just ahead, just out as he galloped in,
Getting the good news ever fresh and fresh,
Till, lo, at the last stage of all, last post
Before Rome,—as we say, in sight of Rome
And safety (there's impunity at Rome
For priests, you know) at—what's the little place?—
What some call Castelnuovo, some just call
The Osteria, because o' the post-house inn,
There, at the journey's all but end, it seems,
Triumph deceived them and undid them both,
Secure they might foretaste felicity
Nor fear surprisal: so, they were surprised.
There did they halt at early evening, there
Did Guido overtake them: 'twas day-break;
He came in time enough, not time too much.

937| MS:gate *1868:*gate. 938| MS:Good bye *1868:*Good-bye 940| MS:the Priest, *1868:*the priest, 941| MS:Whip *1868:*"Whip 942| MS:bagfull *1868:*bagful 945| MS:poison-drench *1868:*poison-drench, 949| MS:Was soon *1868:*Trod soon 950| MS:at Camoscia, at *P1872:*at Camoscia, reached 952| MS:in *1868:*in, 956| MS:safety—there's *1868:*safety (there's 957| MS:know—at, what's <> place, *1868:*know) at—what's <> place? *P1872:* place?— 959| MS:of <> Inn, *1868:*o' <> inn, 962| MS:Secure, they *1868:*Secure they 963| MS:so they *1868:*so, they 966| MS:enough no

Since in the courtyard stood the Canon's self
Urging the drowsy stable-grooms to haste
Harness the horses, have the journey end,
The trifling four-hours'-running, so reach Rome.
And the other runaway, the wife? Upstairs,
Still on the couch where she had spent the night,
One couch in one room, and one room for both.
So gained they six hours, so were lost thereby.

Sir, what's the sequel? Lover and beloved
Fall on their knees? No impudence serves here?
They beat their breasts and beg for easy death,
Confess this, that and the other?—anyhow
Confess there wanted not some likelihood
To the supposition so preposterous,
That, O Pompilia, thy sequestered eyes
Had noticed, straying o'er the prayerbook's edge,
More of the Canon than that black his coat,
Buckled his shoes were, broad his hat of brim:
And that, O Canon, thy religious care
Had breathed too soft a *benedicite*
To banish trouble from a lady's breast
So lonely and so lovely, nor so lean!
This you expect? Indeed, then, much you err.
Not to such ordinary end as this
Had Caponsacchi flung the cassock far,
Doffed the priest, donned the perfect cavalier.
The die was cast: over shoes over boots:
And just as she, I presently shall show,
Pompilia, soon looked Helen to the life,
Recumbent upstairs in her pink and white,
So, in the inn-yard, bold as 'twere Troy-town,

<> much: *1868:*enough, not <> much, 967| MS:There in *1868:*Since in 970| MS:four hours' running *1868:*four-hours'- running 974| *1868:*thereby, *P1872:*thereby. 975| MS:Then, what's *1868:*Sir, what's 976| MS:knees: no <> here: *1868:* knees? No <> here? 978| MS:other, anyhow— *1868:*other?—anyhow 982| MS:edge *1868:*edge, 983| MS:coat *1868:*coat, 984| MS:shoes and broad *1868:*shoes were, broad 987| MS:banish Satan from *1868:*banish trouble from 992| MS:cavalier; *P1872:*cavalier. 995| MS:Pompilia now looked *1868:*Pompilia, soon looked 997| MS:as in

There strutted Paris in correct costume,
Cloak, cap and feather, no appointment missed,
Even to a wicked-looking sword at side,
He seemed to find and feel familiar at.
Nor wanted words as ready and as big
As the part he played, the bold abashless one.
"I interposed to save your wife from death,
Yourself from shame, the true and only shame:
Ask your own conscience else!—or, failing that,
What I have done I answer, anywhere,
Here, if you will; you see I have a sword:
Or, since I have a tonsure as you taunt,
At Rome, by all means,—priests to try a priest.
Only, speak where your wife's voice can reply!"
And then he fingered at the sword again.
So, Guido called, in aid and witness both,
The Public Force. The Commissary came,
Officers also; they secured the priest;
Then, for his more confusion, mounted up
With him, a guard on either side, the stair
To the bed-room where still slept or feigned a sleep
His paramour and Guido's wife: in burst
The company and bade her wake and rise.

Her defence? This. She woke, saw, sprang upright
I' the midst and stood as terrible as truth,
Sprang to her husband's side, caught at the sword
That hung there useless,—since they held each hand
O' the lover, had disarmed him properly,—
And in a moment out flew the bright thing
Full in the face of Guido: but for help

Troy-town *1868:*as 'twere Troy-town, 998| MS:costume *1868:*costume,
1000| MS:side *1868:*side, 1001| MS:feel, familiar *1868:*feel familiar
1006| MS:else, or *1868:*else!—or 1007| MS:anywhere *1868:*anywhere,
1013| MS:So Guido *1868:*So, Guido 1019| MS:wife, in *1868:*wife:in
1021| MS:defence? This: she *1868:*defence? This. She 1022| MS:In *1868:*I'
1023| MS:her lover's side *1868:*her husband's side 1024-26| MS:useless while they held his hands,/ And *1868:*useless, since they held each hand/ O' the lover, had disarmed him properly,/ And *P1872:*useless,—since <> / <> properly,—
1026| MS:moment there flew *P1868:*moment out flew 1027| MS:of Guido,—but

O' the guards who held her back and pinioned her
With pains enough, she had finished you my tale
With a flourish of red all round it, pinked her man
Prettily; but she fought them one to six.
They stopped that,—but her tongue continued free:
She spat forth such invective at her spouse,
O'erfrothed him with such foam of murderer,
Thief, pandar—that the popular tide soon turned,
The favour of the very *sbirri*, straight
Ebbed from the husband, set toward his wife,
People cried "Hands off, pay a priest respect!"
And "persecuting fiend" and "martyred saint"
Began to lead a measure from lip to lip.

But facts are facts and flinch not; stubborn things,
And the question "Prithee, friend, how comes my purse
I' the poke of you?"—admits of no reply.
Here was a priest found out in masquerade,
A wife caught playing truant if no more;
While the Count, mortified in mien enough,
And, nose to face, an added palm in length,
Was plain writ "husband" every piece of him:
Capture once made, release could hardly be.
Beside, the prisoners both made appeal,
"Take us to Rome!"
                                        Taken to Rome they were;
The husband trooping after, piteously,
Tail between legs, no talk of triumph now—

---

*P1872:*of Guido: but 1028| MS:Of *1868:*O' 1029| MS:you the tale *P1868:*you my tale 1030| MS:pinked the man *P1868:*pinked her man 1033| MS:spouse *P1868:*spouse, 1034| MS:murderer *P1868:*murderer, 1035| MS:Thief, Pandar <> tide was changed, *P1868:*pandar <> tide soon turned, 1036| MS:The feeling of *P1868:*The favour of 1037| MS:Towards *P1868:*toward 1038| MS:pay the priest *P1868:*pay a priest 1040-41| MS:§ no ¶ § *P1868:*§ ¶ § 1043| MS:In <> admits but one reply. *P1868:*I' <> admits of no reply. 1044| MS:priest plainly in *P1868:*priest found out in 1045| MS:truant at the least *P1868:*truant if no more; 1046| MS:the man mortified *P1868:*the Count, mortified 1047| MS:And nose *P1868:*And, nose 1049| MS:Capture was made *P1868:*Capture once made 1050| MS:Beside the

No honour set firm on its feet once more
On two dead bodies of the guilty,—nay,
No dubious salve to honour's broken pate
From chance that, after all, the hurt might seem
A skin-deep matter, scratch that leaves no scar:
For Guido's first search,—ferreting, poor soul,
Here, there and everywhere in the vile place
Abandoned to him when their backs were turned,
Found,—furnishing a last and best regale,—
All the love-letters bandied 'twixt the pair
Since the first timid trembling into life
O' the love-star till its stand at fiery full.
Mad prose, mad verse, fears, hopes, triumph, despair,
Avowal, disclaimer, plans, dates, names,—was nought
Wanting to prove, if proof consoles at all,
That this had been but the fifth act o' the piece
Whereof the due proemium, months ago
These playwrights had put forth, and ever since
Matured the middle, added 'neath his nose.
He might go cross himself: the case was clear.

Therefore to Rome with the clear case; there plead
Each party its best, and leave law do each right,
Let law shine forth and show, as God in heaven,
Vice prostrate, virtue pedestalled at last,
The triumph of truth! What else shall glad our gaze
When once authority has knit the brow
And set the brain behind it to decide
Between the wolf and sheep turned litigants?

---

*P1868:*Beside, the 1054| MS:honor *P1868:*honour 1056| MS:honor's *P1868:*honour's 1057| MS:By § crossed out and replaced by § From < > all, its hurt *P1868:*all, the hurt 1058| MS:scratch instead of § last two words crossed out and replaced above by two words § that leaves no scar,— *P1868:*scar:
1063| MS:twixt *1888:*'twixt 1065| MS:Of *P1868:*O' 1066| MS:verse, hopes, fears § indication that order of last two words should be reversed §
1067| MS:names, nought *P1868:*names,—was nought 1069| MS:been the < > of *P1868:*been but the < > o' 1073-74| MS:§ no ¶ § *P1868:*§ ¶ §
1075| MS:leave the Law her rights, *P1868:*the law do right, *1888:*leave law do each right, 1076| MS:Let her shine < > show us God *P1868:*show, as God *1888:*Let law shine 1079| MS:knit his brow *P1868:*knit the brow 1081| MS:sheep

"This is indeed a business!" law shook head:
"A husband charges hard things on a wife,
The wife as hard o' the husband: whose fault here?
A wife that flies her husband's house, does wrong:
The male friend's interference looks amiss,
Lends a suspicion: but suppose the wife,
On the other hand, be jeopardized at home—
Nay, that she simply hold, ill-groundedly,
An apprehension she is jeopardized,—
And further, if the friend partake the fear,
And, in a commendable charity
Which trusteth all, trust her that she mistrusts,—
What do they but obey law—natural law?
Pretence may this be and a cloak for sin,
And circumstances that concur i' the close
Hint as much, loudly—yet scarce loud enough
To drown the answer 'strange may yet be true:'
Innocence often looks like guiltiness.
The accused declare that in thought, word and deed,
Innocent were they both from first to last
As male-babe haply laid by female-babe
At church on edge of the baptismal font
Together for a minute, perfect-pure.
Difficult to believe, yet possible,
As witness Joseph, the friend's patron-saint.
The night at the inn—there charity nigh chokes
Ere swallow what they both asseverate;
Though down the gullet faith may feel it go,
When mindful of what flight fatigued the flesh

---

now litigants? *P1868:*sheep turned litigants? 1082| MS:business" quoth the Dame: *P1868:*business" law shook head: *1888:*business!" law 1083| MS:A Husband <> on the wife, *P1868:*"A husband <> on a wife, 1084| MS:on *P1868:*o' 1090| MS:That § crossed out and replaced above by § An 1091| MS:further if <> fear *P1868:*further, if <> fear, 1092| MS:commendably *P1868:*commendable 1094| MS:obey the natural law? *1888:*obey law—natural law? 1096| MS:concur at the *P1868:*concur i' the 1098| MS:true: *P1868:*true:' 1105| MS:possible *P1868:*possible, 1106| MS:witness Joseph the *P1868:*witness Joseph, the 1107| MS:the Inn *P1868:*the inn 1108| MS:asseverate, *P1868:*asseverate; 1109| MS:go *P1868:*go,

Out of its faculty and fleshliness,
Subdued it to the soul, as saints assure:
So long a flight necessitates a fall
On the first bed, though in a lion's den,
And the first pillow, though the lion's back:
Difficult to believe, yet possible.
Last come the letters' bundled beastliness—
Authority repugns give glance to—nay,
Turns head, and almost lets her whip-lash fall;
Yet here a voice cries 'Respite!' from the clouds—
The accused, both in a tale, protest, disclaim,
Abominate the horror: 'Not my hand'
Asserts the friend—'Nor mine' chimes in the wife,
'Seeing I have no hand, nor write at all.'
Illiterate—for she goes on to ask,
What if the friend did pen now verse now prose,
Commend it to her notice now and then?
'Twas pearls to swine: she read no more than wrote,
And kept no more than read, for as they fell
She ever brushed the burr-like things away,
Or, better, burned them, quenched the fire in smoke.
As for this fardel, filth and foolishness,
She sees it now the first time: burn it too!
While for his part the friend vows ignorance
Alike of what bears his name and bears hers:
'Tis forgery, a felon's masterpiece,
And, as 'tis said the fox still finds the stench,
Home-manufacture and the husband's work.
Though he confesses, the ingenuous friend,
That certain missives, letters of a sort,
Flighty and feeble, which assigned themselves
To the wife, no less have fallen, far too oft,
In his path: wherefrom he understood just this—

1111| MS:fleshliness *P1868:*fleshliness, 1118| MS:to twice *P1868:*twice, *1888:*to—nay, 1119| MS:fall— *P1868:*fall; 1120| MS:here too there cries *P1868:*here a voice cries 1123| MS:wife *P1868:*wife, 1125| MS:§ crowded between lines 1124-26 § to say *P1868:*to ask, 1126| MS:prose *P1868:*prose, 1127| MS:then, *P1868:*then? 1129| MS:as it came § last two words crossed out § 1136| MS:'Tis forger's, § altered to § forgery, work § crossed out § 1137| MS:And, since 'tis *P1868:*And, as 'tis 1142| MS:wife no less had *P1868:*wife, no less have 1143| MS:path—wherefrom < > this *P1868:*path:wherefrom < > this—

That were they verily the lady's own,
Why, she who penned them, since he never saw
Save for one minute the mere face of her,
Since never had there been the interchange
Of word with word between them all their life,
Why, she must be the fondest of the frail,
And fit, she for the *'apage'* he flung,
Her letters for the flame they went to feed!
But, now he sees her face and hears her speech,
Much he repents him if, in fancy-freak
For a moment the minutest measurable,
He coupled her with the first flimsy word
O' the self-spun fabric some mean spider-soul
Furnished forth: stop his films and stamp on him!
Never was such a tangled knottiness,
But thus authority cuts the Gordian through,
And mark how her decision suits the need!
Here's troublesomeness, scandal on both sides,
Plenty of fault to find, no absolute crime:
Let each side own its fault and make amends!
What does a priest in cavalier's attire
Consorting publicly with vagrant wives
In quarters close as the confessional,
Though innocent of harm? 'Tis harm enough:
Let him pay it,—say, be relegate a good
Three years, to spend in some place not too far
Nor yet too near, midway 'twixt near and far,
Rome and Arezzo,—Civita we choose,
Where he may lounge away time, live at large,

1144| MS:the Lady's own, *P1868:*the lady's *1888:*own. § emended to § own, § see Editorial Notes § 1149| MS:frail *1868:*frail, 1150| MS:'apage' *P1868:'apage'* 1151| MS:feed. *1888:*feed! 1152| MS:But, since he saw her face, and heard *P1868:*But, now he sees her face and hears 1156| MS:Of *P1868:*O' 1157| MS:forth:stop his films and § last four words inserted above line § <> him. *P1868:*him! 1159| MS:thus Authority cuts it Gordian-wise— *P1868:*thus authority cuts the Gordian through, 1160| MS:the case. *P1868:*the need! 1162| MS:crime. *P1868:*crime: 1163| MS:amends. *P1868:*amends! 1166| MS:confessional *P1868:*confessional, 1168| MS:it, and be relegate a year, *P1868:*a good *1888:*it,—say, be 1169| MS:Two years *P1868:*Three years 1170| MS:twixt here and there, *P1868:*twixt near and far, *1888:*'twixt 1171| MS:and Arezzo,—Civita we'll say, *P1868:*and Arezzo,—Civita we choose,

Find out the proper function of a priest,
Nowise an exile,—that were punishment,—
But one our love thus keeps out of harm's way
Not more from the husband's anger than, mayhap
His own . . . say, indiscretion, waywardness,
And wanderings when Easter eves grow warm.
For the wife,—well, our best step to take with her,
On her own showing, were to shift her root
From the old cold shade and unhappy soil
Into a generous ground that fronts the south
Where, since her callow soul, a-shiver late,
Craved simply warmth and called mere passers-by
To the rescue, she should have her fill of shine.
Do house and husband hinder and not help?
Why then, forget both and stay here at peace,
Come into our community, enroll
Herself along with those good Convertites,
Those sinners saved, those Magdalens re-made,
Accept their ministration, well bestow
Her body and patiently possess her soul,
Until we see what better can be done.
Last for the husband: if his tale prove true,
Well is he rid of two domestic plagues—
Both wife that ailed, do whatsoever he would,
And friend of hers that undertook the cure.
See, what a double load we lift from breast!
Off he may go, return, resume old life,
Laugh at the priest here and Pompilia there

1173| MS:priest *P1868:*priest, 1174| MS:Not as an <> punishment, *P1868:*Nowise an *P1872:*punishment,— 1177| MS:own—say *P1868:*own . . . say 1179| MS:wife,—well, § inserted above line § <> her *P1868:*her, 1180| MS:showing were *P1868:*showing, were 1182| MS:south, *P1868:*south: *1888:*south 1184| MS:simply guidance, called *P1868:*simply warmth and called 1185| MS:fill thereof: *P1868:*fill of shine. 1186| MS:The house *P1868:*Do house 1187| MS:here again, *P1868:*here at peace, 1189| MS:Yourself along <> Convertites *P1868:*Herself along <> Convertites, 1191| MS:ministrations, and bestow *P1868:*ministration, well bestow 1192| MS:Your body <> possess your soul, *P1868:*Her body <> possess her soul, 1194| MS:the Husband <> tale be true *P1868:*the husband <> tale prove true, 1195| MS:of a domestic plague *P1868:*of two domestic plagues— 1196| MS:The wife <> whatsoe'er *P1868:*Both wife <> whatsoever 1198| MS:a load <> from off his breast! *P1868:* a double load <> from breast! 1200| MS:the Priest *P1868:*the priest

In limbo each and punished for their pains,
And grateful tell the inquiring neighbourhood—
In Rome, no wrong but has its remedy."
The case was closed. Now, am I fair or no
In what I utter? Do I state the facts,
Having forechosen a side? I promised you!

The Canon Caponsacchi, then, was sent
To change his garb, re-trim his tonsure, tie
The clerkly silk round, every plait correct,
Make the impressive entry on his place
Of relegation, thrill his Civita,
As Ovid, a like sufferer in the cause,
Planted a primrose-patch by Pontus: where,—
What with much culture of the sonnet-stave
And converse with the aborigines,
Soft savagery of eyes unused to roll
And hearts that all awry went pit-a-pat
And wanted setting right in charity,—
What were a couple of years to while away?
Pompilia, as enjoined, betook herself
To the aforesaid Convertites, soft sisterhood
In Via Lungara, where the light ones live,
Spin, pray, then sing like linnets o'er the flax.
"Anywhere, anyhow, out of my husband's house
Is heaven," cried she,—was therefore suited so.
But for Count Guido Franceschini, he—
The injured man thus righted—found no heaven

1202| MS:tell enquiring neighbours this— *P1868:*tell the inquiring neighbourhood—
1203| MS:remedy. *P1868:*remedy."
1205| MS:utter,—do <> the case, *P1868:* utter? Do <> the facts,
1206| MS:you. *P1868:*you!
1209| MS:silk on, every *P1868:*silk round, every
1211| MS:His relegation <> Civita *P1868:*Of relegation <> Civita,
1213| MS:Planted his primrose-patch by Pontus—where, *P1868:* Planted a primrose-patch by Pontus: where, *1888:*where,—
1214| MS:with culture *P1868:*with much culture
1216| MS:savagery with eyes <> roll, *P1868:* savagery of eyes *1888:*roll
1217| MS:pit-a-pat, *P1868:*pit-a-pat
1218| MS:§ crowded between 1217-19 § charity, *1888:*charity,—
1219| MS:wile *P1868:*while
1221| MS:aforesaid Convertites, the sisterhood *1888:*aforesaid Convertites, soft sisterhood
1225| MS:she,—and therefore *P1868:*she,—was therefore
1226| MS:And he, Count <> he *P1868:*But for Count <> he—
1227| MS:man now righted,—found *P1868:*man thus righted—

I' the house when he returned there, I engage,
Was welcomed by the city turned upside down
In a chorus of inquiry. "What, back—you?
And no wife? Left her with the Penitents?
Ah, being young and pretty, 'twere a shame
To have her whipped in public: leave the job
To the priests who understand! Such priests as yours—
(Pontifex Maximus whipped Vestals once)
Our madcap Caponsacchi: think of him!
So, he fired up, showed fight and skill of fence?
Ay, you drew also, but you did not fight!
The wiser, 'tis a word and a blow with him,
True Caponsacchi, of old Head-i'-the-Sack
That fought at Fiesole ere Florence was:
He had done enough, to firk you were too much.
And did the little lady menace you,
Make at your breast with your own harmless sword?
The spitfire! Well, thank God you're safe and sound,
Have kept the sixth commandment whether or no
The lady broke the seventh: I only wish
I were as saint-like, could contain me so.
I, the poor sinner, fear I should have left
Sir Priest no nose-tip to turn up at me!"
You, Sir, who listen but interpose no word,
Ask yourself, had you borne a baiting thus?

---

found 1228| MS:In *P1868:*I' 1230| MS:back you? *P1868:*back—you? 1234-36| MS:understand. Such Priests as yours—/ Our *P1868:*understand! Such priests as yours—/ (Pontifex Maximus whipped Vestals once)/ Our 1237| MS:So he <> fence— *P1868:*So, he <> fence? 1238| MS:fight. *P1868:*fight! 1239| MS:him *P1868:*him, 1240| MS:old Head-in-the-Sack *P1868:*old Head-i'-the-Sack 1241| MS:fought in Fiesole *P1868:*fought at Fiesole 1244| MS:at her breast with Caponsacchi's sword? *P1868:*at your breast with your own harmless sword? 1245| MS:sound *P1868:*sound, 1246| MS:And kept the eighth commandment *P1868:*Have kept the sixth commandment 1247| MS:The Lady <> the sixth: I *P1868:*The lady <> the seventh: I 1249| MS:I am a sinner, I fear *1888:*I, the poor sinner, fear 1250| MS:me." *P1868:*me!" 1252| MS:yourself had <> thus, *P1868:*yourself,

Was it enough to make a wise man mad?
Oh, but I'll have your verdict at the end!

Well, not enough, it seems: such mere hurt falls,
Frets awhile, aches long, then grows less and less,
And so gets done with. Such was not the scheme
O' the pleasant Comparini: on Guido's wound
Ever in due succession, drop by drop,
Came slow distilment from the alembic here
Set on to simmer by Canidian hate,
Corrosives keeping the man's misery raw.
First fire-drop,—when he thought to make the best
O' the bad, to wring from out the sentence passed,
Poor, pitiful, absurd although it were,
Yet what might eke him out result enough
And make it worth while to have had the right
And not the wrong i' the matter judged at Rome.
Inadequate her punishment, no less
Punished in some slight sort his wife had been;
Then, punished for adultery, what else?
On such admitted crime he thought to seize,
And institute procedure in the courts
Which cut corruption of this kind from man,

---

had <> thus? 1254-55| MS:§ no ¶ § *P1868:*§ ¶ § 1255| MS:seems: the mere *P1868:* seems:such mere 1256| MS:Frets awile, and aches long, then less and *P1868:*awhile *1888:*awhile, aches long, then grows less and 1257| MS:so is done *1888:*so gets done 1258| MS:Of the pleasant people here: on *P1868:*O' the pleasant Comparini: on 1260| MS:distilments *P1868:*distilment 1261| MS: Kept § crossed out and replaced above by § Set 1263| MS:fire-drop was,—he *P1868:* fire-drop,—when he 1264| MS:Of <> passed *P1868:*O' <> passed, 1265| MS:pitiful, inadequate § crossed out and replaced above by two words § absurd although 1267| MS:To make it worth his while he had *P1868:*And make *1888:* worth while to have had 1268| MS:in <> Rome: *P1868:*i' <> Rome. 1270| MS:been, *P1868:*been; 1272| MS:he wished § crossed out and replaced above by one word § thought to seize *P1868:*seize, 1273| MS:the Courts *P1868:* the courts 1274| MS:corruption in this *P1868:*corruption of this

Cast loose a wife proved loose and castaway:
He claimed in due form a divorce at least.

This claim was met now by a counterclaim:
Pompilia sought divorce from bed and board
Of Guido, whose outrageous cruelty,
Whose mother's malice and whose brother's hate
Were just the white o' the charge, such dreadful depths
Blackened its centre,—hints of worse than hate,
Love from that brother, by that Guido's guile,
That mother's prompting. Such reply was made,
So was the engine loaded, wound up, sprung
On Guido, who received bolt full in breast;
But no less bore up, giddily perhaps.
He had the Abate Paolo still in Rome,
Brother and friend and fighter on his side:
They rallied in a measure, met the foe
Manlike, joined battle in the public courts,
As if to shame supine law from her sloth:
And waiting her award, let beat the while
Arezzo's banter, Rome's buffoonery,
On this ear and on that ear, deaf alike,
Safe from worse outrage. Let a scorpion nip,
And never mind till he contorts his tail!
But there was sting i' the creature; thus it struck.
Guido had thought in his simplicity—
That lying declaration of remorse,
That story of the child which was no child
And motherhood no motherhood at all,
—That even this sin might have its sort of good

1276-77| MS:§ no ¶ § *P1868:*§ ¶ § 1280| MS:hate, *P1868:*hate 1281| MS:of *P1868:*o' 1282| MS:hate *P1868:*hate, 1284| MS:mother's malice: such *P1868:*mother's prompting. Such 1286| MS:On Guido who received the bolt in breast, *P1868:*On Guido, who <> breast; *1888:*received bolt full in
1288| MS:the Abate Paolo here in Rome *P1868:*the Abate Paolo still in Rome,
1291| MS:public Courts, *P1868:*public courts, 1292| MS:sloth, *P1868:*sloth:
1294| MS:buffoonery *P1868:*buffoonery, 1296| MS:nip *P1868:*nip,
1297| MS:There was a sting in <> struck: *P1868:*But there was sting i' <> struck.
1299| MS:simplicity *P1868:*simplicity— 1301| MS:child that was *P1868:*child which was 1303| MS:That <> sin had its *P1868:*—That <> sin might have its

Inasmuch as no question more could be,—
Call it false, call the story true,—no claim
Of further parentage pretended now:
The parents had abjured all right, at least,
I' the woman owned his wife: to plead right still
Were to declare the abjuration false:
He was relieved from any fear henceforth
Their hands might touch, their breath defile again
Pompilia with his name upon her yet.
Well, no: the next news was, Pompilia's health
Demanded change after full three long weeks
Spent in devotion with the Sisterhood,—
Which rendered sojourn,—so the court opined,—
Too irksome, since the convent's walls were high
And windows narrow, nor was air enough
Nor light enough, but all looked prison-like,
The last thing which had come in the court's head.
Propose a new expedient therefore,—this!
She had demanded—had obtained indeed,
By intervention of her pitying friends
Or perhaps lovers—(beauty in distress,
Beauty whose tale is the town-talk beside,
Never lacks friendship's arm about her neck)—
Obtained remission of the penalty,
Permitted transfer to some private place
Where better air, more light, new food might soothe—

1304| MS:question could be more, *1888:*question more could be,— 1305| MS:true, no *1888:*true,—no 1308| MS:In the woman still his <> plead fresh § crossed out § right now *P1868:*I' *1888:*woman owned his <> right still 1316| MS:Rendered her sojourn <> Court *P1868:*Rendering sojourn <> court *1888:*Which rendered 1317| MS:the Convent's <> high, *P1868:*the convent's <> high 1320| MS:the Court's head: *P1868:*court's head. 1321| MS:this. *P1868:*this! 1322| MS:indeed *P1868:*indeed, 1323| MS:of whatever friends *1888:*of her pitying friends 1324| MS:lover—beauty *P1868:*lovers—(beauty 1325| MS:In one whose *1888:*Beauty whose 1326| MS:neck— *P1868:*neck)— 1327| MS:—Not freedom, scarce remitted penalty, *P1868:*Not *1888:*Obtained remission of the penalty, 1328| MS:Solely the transfer *1888:*Permitted transfer 1329| MS:air and light and food might be— *P1868:*air, more light, new food *1888:*

Incarcerated (call it, all the same)
At some sure friend's house she must keep inside,
Be found in at requirement fast enough,—
Domus pro carcere, in Roman style.
You keep the house i' the main, as most men do
And all good women: but free otherwise,
Should friends arrive, to lodge them and what not?
And such a *domum*, such a dwelling-place,
Having all Rome to choose from, where chose she?
What house obtained Pompilia's preference?
Why, just the Comparini's—just, do you mark,
Theirs who renounced all part and lot in her
So long as Guido could be robbed thereby,
And only fell back on relationship
And found their daughter safe and sound again
When that might surelier stab him: yes, the pair
Who, as I told you, first had baited hook
With this poor gilded fly Pompilia-thing,
Then caught the fish, pulled Guido to the shore
And gutted him,—now found a further use
For the bait, would trail the gauze wings yet again
I' the way of what new swimmer passed their stand.
They took Pompilia to their hiding-place—
Not in the heart of Rome as formerly,
Under observance, subject to control—
But out o' the way,—or in the way, who knows?
That blind mute villa lurking by the gate
At Via Paulina, not so hard to miss
By the honest eye, easy enough to find
In twilight by marauders: where perchance

---

might soothe— 1330| MS:it all *P1868:*it, all 1332| MS:enough, *P1868:* enough,— 1333| MS:*carcere*, the Roman mode. *P1868:carcere*, in Roman style. 1334| MS:in *P1868:*i' 1335| MS:otherwise *P1868:*otherwise, 1336| MS:arrive to entertain the same. *P1868:*arrive, to lodge and entertain. *1888:* lodge them and what not? 1337| MS:*domus* *P1868:domum* *1340*| MS:you see, *P1868:*you mark, 1345| MS:So soon as that might stab *1888:*When that might surelier stab 1349| MS:him, now *P1868:*him,—now 1351| MS:In < > their creel— *P1868:*I' < > their stand. 1352| MS:hiding-place *P1868:* hiding-place— 1353| MS:formerly *P1868:*formerly, 1355| MS:of *P1868:*o' 1356| MS:blind, mute Villa *P1868:*blind mute villa 1359| MS:marauders—where

Some muffled Caponsacchi might repair,
Employ odd moments when he too tried change,
Found that a friend's abode was pleasanter
Than relegation, penance and the rest.

Come, here's the last drop does its worst to wound:
Here's Guido poisoned to the bone, you say,
Your boasted still's full strain and strength: not so!
One master-squeeze from screw shall bring to birth
The hoard i' the heart o' the toad, hell's quintessence.
He learned the true convenience of the change,
And why a convent lacks the cheerful hearts
And helpful hands which female straits require,
When, in the blind mute villa by the gate,
Pompilia—what? sang, danced, saw company?
—Gave birth, Sir, to a child, his son and heir,
Or Guido's heir and Caponsacchi's son.
I want your word now: what do you say to this?
What would say little Arezzo and great Rome,
And what did God say and the devil say
One at each ear o' the man, the husband, now
The father? Why, the overburdened mind
Broke down, what was a brain became a blaze.
In fury of the moment—(that first news
Fell on the Count among his vines, it seems,
Doing his farm-work,)—why, he summoned steward,
Called in the first four hard hands and stout hearts
From field and furrow, poured forth his appeal,
Not to Rome's law and gospel any more,

---

*P1868:*marauders—where 1361| MS:change *P1868:*change,
1364| MS:wound, *1888:*wound DC, BrU:wound: *1889:*wound:
1365| MS:say, *1888:*say DC, BrU:say, *1889:*say, 1367| MS:master squeeze <> bring its birth, *P1868:*master-squeeze <> bring to birth
1368| MS:in <> of *P1868:*i' <> o'
1370| MS:a Convent wants the *P1868:*a convent *1888:*convent lacks the
1372| MS:When in <> Villa <> gate *P1868:*When, in <> villa <> gate,
1374| MS:Gave *P1868:*—Gave 1378| MS:the Devil *P1868:*the devil
1379| MS:of *P1868:*o' 1380| MS:father. Why the *P1868:*father? Why, the
1383| MS:the man among *P1868:*the Count among 1384| MS:summoned Steward, *P1868:*summoned steward, 1387| MS:to Rome's Law <> Gospel

But this clown with a mother or a wife,
That clodpole with a sister or a son:
And, whereas law and gospel held their peace,
What wonder if the sticks and stones cried out?

All five soon somehow found themselves at Rome,
At the villa door: there was the warmth and light—
The sense of life so just an inch inside—
Some angel must have whispered "One more chance!"

He gave it: bade the others stand aside:
Knocked at the door,—"Who is it knocks?" cried one.
"I will make," surely Guido's angel urged,
"One final essay, last experiment,
Speak the word, name the name from out all names
Which, if,—as doubtless strong illusions are,
And strange disguisings whereby truth seems false,
And, since I am but man, I dare not do
God's work until assured I see with God,—
If I should bring my lips to breathe that name
And they be innocent,—nay, by one mere touch
Of innocence redeemed from utter guilt,—
That name will bar the door and bid fate pass.
I will not say 'It is a messenger,
A neighbour, even a belated man,
Much less your husband's friend, your husband's self:'
At such appeal the door is bound to ope.
But I will say"—here's rhetoric and to spare!

---

*P1868:*to Rome's law<>gospel 1388| MS:wife *P1868:*wife, 1389| MS:son, *P1868:*son: 1390| MS:whereas Law <> Gospel *P1868:*whereas law <> gospel 1391–92| MS:§ no ¶ § at Rome— *P1868:*§ ¶ § at Rome, 1393| MS:the Villa *P1868:*the villa 1395–96| MS:§ no ¶ § *P1868:*§ ¶ § 1397| MS:door—"Who *P1868:*door,—"Who 1398| MS:surely Guido must have said, *P1868:*surely Guido's angel said, *1888:*angel urged, 1399| MS:One <> essay, will experiment, *P1868:*"One <> essay, last experiment, 1402| MS:disguising whence even truth *P1868:*disguisings *1888:*disguisings whereby truth 1403| MS:And, for I am a man *1888:*And, since I am but man 1405| MS:breathe the same *P1868:*breathe that name 1406| MS:one touch *1888:*one mere touch 1408| MS:Will <> pass this time *P1868:*That name will <> pass. 1411| MS:self: *P1868:*self:'

Why, Sir, the stumbling-block is cursed and kicked,
Block though it be; the name that brought offence
Will bring offence: the burnt child dreads the fire
Although that fire feed on some taper-wick
Which never left the altar nor singed a fly:
And had a harmless man tripped you by chance,
How would you wait him, stand or step aside,
When next you heard he rolled your way? Enough.

"Giuseppe Caponsacchi!" Guido cried;
And open flew the door: enough again.
Vengeance, you know, burst, like a mountain-wave
That holds a monster in it, over the house,
And wiped its filthy four walls free at last
With a wash of hell-fire,—father, mother, wife,
Killed them all, bathed his name clean in their blood,
And, reeking so, was caught, his friends and he,
Haled hither and imprisoned yesternight
O' the day all this was.
                                        Now, Sir, tale is told,
Of how the old couple come to lie in state
Though hacked to pieces,—never, the expert say,
So thorough a study of stabbing—while the wife
(Viper-like, very difficult to slay)
Writhes still through every ring of her, poor wretch,
At the Hospital hard by—survives, we'll hope,
To somewhat purify her putrid soul

1414| MS:Why, sir < > kicked *P1868:*Why, Sir < > kicked, 1415| MS:be, the < > that brings offense *P1868:*be; the < > that brought offence 1416| MS:Is the offence < > fire, *P1868:*Will bring offence < > fire 1417| MS:on a taper-wick *1888:*on some taper-wick 1418| MS:That never < > nor did harm *P1868:*Which never < > nor singed fly: *1888:*singed a fly: 1421-22| MS:§ no ¶ § *P1868:*§ ¶ § 1422| MS:cried: *P1868:*cried; 1423| MS:open went the *P1868:*open flew the 1424| MS:mountain wave *P1868:*mountain-wave 1426| MS:free again *1872:*free at last 1427| MS:hellfire, father < > wife *P1868:*hell-fire,—father < > wife, 1430| MS:imprisoned yesterday *P1868:*imprisoned yesternight 1431| MS:The < > was. Now the whole is known, *P1868:*O' the < > was. § ¶ § Now *1888:*was. § ¶ § Now, Sir, tale is told, 1432| MS:And how *1888:*Of how 1434| MS:stabbing. While *P1868:*stabbing—while 1435| MS:Viper-like < >

By full confession, make so much amends
While time lasts; since at day's end die she must.

For Caponsacchi,—why, they'll have him here,
As hero of the adventure, who so fit
To figure in the coming Carnival?
'Twill make the fortune of whate'er saloon
Hears him recount, with helpful cheek, and eye
Hotly indignant now, now dewy-dimmed,
The incidents of flight, pursuit, surprise,
Capture, with hints of kisses all between—
While Guido, wholly unromantic spouse,
No longer fit to laugh at since the blood
Gave the broad farce an all too brutal air,
Why, he and those four luckless friends of his
May tumble in the straw this bitter day—
Laid by the heels i' the New Prison, I hear,
To bide their trial, since trial, and for the life,
Follows if but for form's sake: yes, indeed!

But with a certain issue: no dispute,
"Try him," bids law: formalities oblige:
But as to the issue,—look me in the face!—
If the law thinks to find them guilty, Sir,
Master or men—touch one hair of the five,
Then I say in the name of all that's left
Of honour in Rome, civility i' the world
Whereof Rome boasts herself the central source,—
There's an end to all hope of justice more.

---

slay, *1888:*(Viper-like < > slay) 1440| MS:lasts—since *P1868:*lasts; since 1440-41| MS:§ no ¶ § *P1868:*§ ¶ § 1441| MS:why, you'll see, they'll *P1868:*why, they'll 1442| MS:The hero of the novel, who *P1868:*of the adventure, who *1888:* As hero 1443| MS:To tell it in *1888:*To figure in 1447| MS:The moving incidents of flight, surprise, *P1868:*The incidents of flight, pursuit, surprise, 1449| MS:While Guido, the most unromantic *1888:*While Guido, wholly unromantic 1452| MS:those five luckless *P1868:*those our luckless *1888:*those four luckless 1454| MS:in *P1868:*i' 1456| MS:indeed. *P1868:*indeed! 1457| MS:dispute *P1868:*dispute, 1458| MS:bids Law: formalities have force: *P1868:*bids law: formalities oblige: 1459| MS:face,— *P1868:*face!— 1462| MS:Then § in left margin § 1463| MS:in the world, *P1868:*i' the world 1465| MS:more,

Astræa's gone indeed, let hope go too!
Who is it dares impugn the natural law,
Deny God's word "the faithless wife shall die"?
What, are we blind? How can we fail to learn
This crowd of miseries make the man a mark,
Accumulate on one devoted head
For our example?—yours and mine who read
Its lesson thus—"Henceforward let none dare
Stand, like a natural in the public way,
Letting the very urchins twitch his beard
And tweak his nose, to earn a nickname so,
Be styled male-Grissel or else modern Job!"
Had Guido, in the twinkling of an eye,
Summed up the reckoning, promptly paid himself,
That morning when he came up with the pair
At the wayside inn,—exacted his just debt
By aid of what first mattock, pitchfork, axe
Came to hand in the helpful stable-yard,
And with that axe, if providence so pleased,
Cloven each head, by some Rolando-stroke,
In one clean cut from crown to clavicle,
—Slain the priest-gallant, the wife-paramour,
Sticking, for all defence, in each skull's cleft
The rhyme and reason of the stroke thus dealt,
To-wit, those letters and last evidence
Of shame, each package in its proper place,—
Bidding, who pitied, undistend the skulls,—
I say, the world had praised the man. But no!
That were too plain, too straight, too simply just!

---

*P1868:*more. 1466| MS:too. *P1868:*too! 1467| MS:law? *P1872:*law, 1468| *P1868:*die?" *1888:*die"? 1469| MS:to see *P1868:*see, *1888:*to learn 1472| MS:example, yours *1872:*example?—yours 1474| MS:Stand like <> way *P1868:*Stand, like <> way, 1477| MS:Of the male-Grissel or the modern Job. *P1868:*modern Job!" *1888:*Be styled male-Grissel or else modern 1479| MS:himself *P1868:*himself, 1481| MS:wayside Inn *P1868:*wayside inn 1484| MS:if Providence *1868:*if providence 1485| MS:each skull § crossed out and replaced above by one word § head Rolando-stroke *P1868:*some Rolando-stroke, 1487| MS:The priest-gallant the wife his paramour, *P1868:*—Slain the priest-gallant, the wife-paramour, 1489| MS:and the reason <> dealt *P1868:*and reason <> dealt, 1490| MS:To whit *P1868:*To wit *CP1868:*To-wit 1491| MS:place, *P1868:*place,— 1492| MS:And let, who *P1868:*Bidding, who 1493| MS:man: but no— *P1868:*man. But no! 1494| MS:just— *P1868:*just!

He hesitates, calls law forsooth to help.
And law, distasteful to who calls in law
When honour is beforehand and would serve,
What wonder if law hesitate in turn,
Plead her disuse to calls o' the kind, reply
(Smiling a little) " 'Tis yourself assess
The worth of what's lost, sum of damage done.
What you touched with so light a finger-tip,
You whose concern it was to grasp the thing,
Why must law gird herself and grapple with?
Law, alien to the actor whose warm blood
Asks heat from law whose veins run lukewarm milk,—
What you dealt lightly with, shall law make out
Heinous forsooth?"
                                        Sir, what's the good of law
In a case o' the kind? None, as she all but says.
Call in law when a neighbour breaks your fence,
Cribs from your field, tampers with rent or lease,
Touches the purse or pocket,—but wooes your wife?
No: take the old way trod when men were men!
Guido preferred the new path,—for his pains,
Stuck in a quagmire, floundered worse and worse
Until he managed somehow scramble back
Into the safe sure rutted road once more,
Revenged his own wrong like a gentleman.
Once back 'mid the familiar prints, no doubt
He made too rash amends for his first fault,
Vaulted too loftily over what barred him late,
And lit i' the mire again,—the common chance,

1495| MS:hesitates—calls law at last to *P1868:*hesitates, calls law forsooth to 1496| MS:to what calls *P1868:*to who calls 1499| MS:of *P1868:*o' 1500| MS:Smiling a little "Tis *P1868:*little " 'Tis *P1872:*(Smiling a little) " 'Tis 1501| MS:done: *1872:* done. 1502| MS:touch *P1868:*touched 1503| MS:is *P1868:*was 1504| MS:herself to grapple *P1868:*herself and grapple 1506| MS:from Law < > milk. *P1868:*from law < > milk,— 1508| MS:forsooth?" § no ¶ § Why, what's *P1868:*forsooth?" § ¶ § Sir, what's 1509| MS:of *P1868:*o' 1511| MS:lease *P1868:*lease, 1512| MS:but, takes your *P1868:*but wooes your 1513| MS:way tried when < > men. *P1868:*way trod when < > men! 1514| MS:pains *P1868:*pains, 1515| MS:quagmire, sank there worse and *P1868:*quagmire, floundered worse and 1517| MS:road again, *P1868:*road once more, 1519| MS:mid *P1868:*'mid 1520| MS:fault *P1868:*fault, 1521| MS:late *P1868:*late, 1522| MS:in < > again, the

The natural over-energy: the deed
Maladroit yields three deaths instead of one,
And one life left: for where's the Canon's corpse?

All which is the worse for Guido, but, be frank—
The better for you and me and all the world,
Husbands of wives, especially in Rome.
The thing is put right, in the old place,—ay,
The rod hangs on its nail behind the door,
Fresh from the brine: a matter I commend
To the notice, during Carnival that's near,
Of a certain what's-his-name and jackanapes
Somewhat too civil of eves with lute and song
About a house here, where I keep a wife.
(You, being his cousin, may go tell him so.)

---

*P1868:*i' < > again,—the 1523| MS:over energy *P1868:*over-energy
1524| MS:one *P1868:*one, 1525-26| MS:§ ¶ § *P1868:*§ no ¶ § paragraph restored; see Editorial Notes § 1526| MS:but—be *P1868:*but, be
1527| MS:world *P1868:*world, 1530| MS:door *P1868:*door,
1532| MS:notice during < > that's close, *P1868:*notice, during < > that's near, 1535| MS:here where *P1868:*here, where

III

THE OTHER HALF-ROME

Another day that finds her living yet,
Little Pompilia, with the patient brow
And lamentable smile on those poor lips,
And, under the white hospital-array,
A flower-like body, to frighten at a bruise
You'd think, yet now, stabbed through and through again,
Alive i' the ruins. 'Tis a miracle.
It seems that, when her husband struck her first,
She prayed Madonna just that she might live
So long as to confess and be absolved;
And whether it was that, all her sad life long
Never before successful in a prayer,
This prayer rose with authority too dread,—
Or whether, because earth was hell to her,
By compensation, when the blackness broke
She got one glimpse of quiet and the cool blue,
To show her for a moment such things were,—
Or else,—as the Augustinian Brother thinks,
The friar who took confession from her lip,—
When a probationary soul that moved
From nobleness to nobleness, as she,
Over the rough way of the world, succumbs,
Bloodies its last thorn with unflinching foot,
The angels love to do their work betimes,
Staunch some wounds here nor leave so much for God.
Who knows? However it be, confessed, absolved,
She lies, with overplus of life beside
To speak and right herself from first to last,
Right the friend also, lamb-pure, lion-brave,

Title| MS:The Other Half Rome *CP1868:*The Other Half-Rome 4| MS:And under <> hospital-array *P1868:*And, under <> hospital-array, 5| MS:frighten with § crossed out and replaced above by § at 7| MS:in *P1868:*i' 10| MS:absolved: *P1868:*absolved; 11| MS:long, *P1872:*long 15| MS:compensation when *P1868:*compensation, when 18| MS:the Augustine Brother thought, *P1868:*the Augustinian Brother thinks, 19| MS:lips,— § *s* crossed out § 20| MS:moves *1888:*moved 22| MS:succumbs— *P1868:* succumbs, 23| MS:foot,— *P1868:*foot, 29| MS:lamb-pure lion-brave,

Care for the boy's concerns, to save the son
From the sire, her two-weeks' infant orphaned thus,
And—with best smile of all reserved for him—
Pardon that sire and husband from the heart.
A miracle, so tell your Molinists!

There she lies in the long white lazar-house.
Rome has besieged, these two days, never doubt,
Saint Anna's where she waits her death, to hear
Though but the chink o' the bell, turn o' the hinge
When the reluctant wicket opes at last,
Lets in, on now this and now that pretence,
Too many by half,—complain the men of art,—
For a patient in such plight. The lawyers first
Paid the due visit—justice must be done;
They took her witness, why the murder was.
Then the priests followed properly,—a soul
To shrive; 'twas Brother Celestine's own right,
The same who noises thus her gifts abroad.
But many more, who found they were old friends,
Pushed in to have their stare and take their talk
And go forth boasting of it and to boast.
Old Monna Baldi chatters like a jay,
Swears—but that, prematurely trundled out
Just as she felt the benefit begin,
The miracle was snapped up by somebody,—
Her palsied limb 'gan prick and promise life
At touch o' the bedclothes merely,—how much more
Had she but brushed the body as she tried!
Cavalier Carlo—well, there's some excuse
For him—Maratta who paints Virgins so—
He too must fee the porter and slip by

---

*P1868:*lamb-pure, lion-brave, 30| MS:boys *P1868:*boy's 34-35| MS:§ no ¶ § *1868:*§ ¶ § 36| MS:has flocked § crossed out and replaced above by § beseiged, <> two last § crossed out § 37| MS:To the place § last three words crossed out and replaced above by two words § Saint Anna's where thus § crossed out § 38| MS:of <> of *P1868:*o' <> o' 41| MS:Two <> art *P1868:*Too <> art,— 44| MS:was; *P1872:*was. 46| MS:shrive, 'twas *P1868:*shrive; 'twas 47| MS:abroad: *P1872:*abroad. 56| MS:of *P1868:*o' 58| MS:Cavalier

With pencil cut and paper squared, and straight
There was he figuring away at face:
"A lovelier face is not in Rome," cried he,
"Shaped like a peacock's egg, the pure as pearl,
That hatches you anon a snow-white chick."
Then, oh that pair of eyes, that pendent hair,
Black this and black the other! Mighty fine—
But nobody cared ask to paint the same,
Nor grew a poet over hair and eyes
Four little years ago when, ask and have,
The woman who wakes all this rapture leaned
Flower-like from out her window long enough,
As much uncomplimented as uncropped
By comers and goers in Via Vittoria: eh?
'Tis just a flower's fate: past parterre we trip,
Till peradventure someone plucks our sleeve—
"Yon blossom at the briar's end, that's the rose
Two jealous people fought for yesterday
And killed each other: see, there's undisturbed
A pretty pool at the root, of rival red!"
Then cry we "Ah, the perfect paragon!"
Then crave we "Just one keepsake-leaf for us!"

Truth lies between: there's anyhow a child
Of seventeen years, whether a flower or weed,
Ruined: who did it shall account to Christ—
Having no pity on the harmless life
And gentle face and girlish form he found,
And thus flings back. Go practise if you please

Carlo,—well *P1868:*Cavalier Carlo—well 62| MS:face— *P1872:*face: 63| MS:he *P1868:*he, 66| MS:hair *P1868:*hair, 67| MS:this, and < > other: mighty *P1868:*other! Mighty *P1872:*this and 68| MS:to draw § crossed out and replaced above by § paint 72| MS:out of window < > enough *P1868:* out her window < > enough, 76| MS:some one < > sleeve *P1868:*someone < > sleeve— 78| MS:Two rival lovers § last two words crossed out and replaced above by two words § jealous people 79| MS:other—see, still § crossed out and replaced above by § there's *P1868:*other: see 80| MS:red! *P1868:*red!" 81| MS:we, "Ah *P1872:*we "Ah 82| MS:keepsake leaf *P1868:*we, "Just < > keepsake-leaf *P1872:*we "Just 82-83| MS:§ no ¶ § *1868:*§ ¶ § 83-85| MS:child/ Ruined *P1868:*child/Of seventeen years, whether a flower or weed,/Ruined 86| MS: Who had no *P1868:*Having no 88| MS:back:go *P1872:*back. Go

With men and women: leave a child alone
For Christ's particular love's sake!—so I say.

Somebody, at the bedside, said much more,
Took on him to explain the secret cause
O' the crime: quoth he, "Such crimes are very rife,
Explode nor make us wonder now-a-days,
Seeing that Antichrist disseminates
That doctrine of the Philosophic Sin:
Molinos' sect will soon make earth too hot!"
"Nay," groaned the Augustinian, "what's there new?
Crime will not fail to flare up from men's hearts
While hearts are men's and so born criminal;
Which one fact, always old yet ever new,
Accounts for so much crime that, for my part,
Molinos may go whistle to the wind
That waits outside a certain church, you know!"

Though really it does seem as if she here,
Pompilia, living so and dying thus,
Has had undue experience how much crime
A heart can hatch. Why was she made to learn
—Not you, not I, not even Molinos' self—
What Guido Franceschini's heart could hold?
Thus saintship is effected probably;
No sparing saints the process!—which the more
Tends to the reconciling us, no saints,
To sinnership, immunity and all.

For see now: Pietro and Violante's life

90| MS:particular love's § inserted above § sake:so *P1868:*sake!—so 90-91| MS: § no ¶ § *P1868:*§ ¶ § 93| MS:Of < > he "such < > are rife, *P1868:* O' < > he, "Such < > are very rife, 94| MS:nowadays, *P1868:* now-a-days, 95| MS:Antechrist *CP1868:*Antichrist 98| MS: "Nay, brother, groaned the Augustine, "whats *P1868:*"Nay, groaned the Augustinian, "what's *CP1868:*"Nay," groaned 100| MS:While the hearts < > and born criminal, *P1868:*While hearts < > and so born criminal; 103| MS:whistle for the *P1868:*whistle to the 104| MS:know! *P1868:*know!" 104-5| MS:§ no ¶ § *P1868:*§ ¶ § 105| MS:here *P1868:*here, 109| MS: § crowded between lines 108 and 110 § Not you < > self, *P1868:*—Not you < > self— 111| MS:probably, *P1868:*probably; 114| MS:immunities *P1868:*immunity

Till seventeen years ago, all Rome might note
And quote for happy—see the signs distinct
Of happiness as we yon Triton's trump.
What could they be but happy?—balanced so,
Nor low i' the social scale nor yet too high,
Nor poor nor richer than comports with ease,
Nor bright and envied, nor obscure and scorned,
Nor so young that their pleasures fell too thick,
Nor old past catching pleasure when it fell,
Nothing above, below the just degree,
All at the mean where joy's components mix.
So again, in the couple's very souls
You saw the adequate half with half to match,
Each having and each lacking somewhat, both
Making a whole that had all and lacked nought.
The round and sound, in whose composure just
The acquiescent and recipient side
Was Pietro's, and the stirring striving one
Violante's: both in union gave the due
Quietude, enterprise, craving and content,
Which go to bodily health and peace of mind.
But, as 'tis said a body, rightly mixed,
Each element in equipoise, would last
Too long and live for ever,—accordingly
Holds a germ—sand-grain weight too much i' the scale—
Ordained to get predominance one day
And so bring all to ruin and release,—
Not otherwise a fatal germ lurked here:

118| MS:Of happiness § last two words inserted above § As we see Triton's trump. § over illegible word § *P1868:*as we yon Triton's 119| MS:happy, balanced *P1868:*happy?—balanced 120| MS:in *P1868:*i' 123| MS:thick *P1868:* thick, 126| MS:Just at the mean all joy's <> mixed. *P1868:*All at the mean where joy's <> mix. 130| MS:nought, *P1868:*nought; *P1872:*nought. 133| MS:the striving, striving *P1868:*the stirring striving 134| MS:Violantes; both *P1868:*Violante's: both 138| MS:equipoise would *P1868:*equipoise, would 139| MS:To long <> accordingly, *CP1868:*Too long <> accordingly 140| MS:in *P1868:*i' 141| MS:O'erdained <> day, *P1868:*Ordained <> day

"With mortals much must go, but something stays;
Nothing will stay of our so happy selves."
Out of the very ripeness of life's core
A worm was bred—"Our life shall leave no fruit."
Enough of bliss, they thought, could bliss bear seed,
Yield its like, propagate a bliss in turn
And keep the kind up; not supplant themselves
But put in evidence, record they were,
Show them, when done with, i' the shape of a child.
" 'Tis in a child, man and wife grow complete,
One flesh: God says so: let him do his work!"

Now, one reminder of this gnawing want,
One special prick o' the maggot at the core,
Always befell when, as the day came round,
A certain yearly sum,—our Pietro being,
As the long name runs, an usufructuary,—
Dropped in the common bag as interest
Of money, his till death, not afterward,
Failing an heir: an heir would take and take,
A child of theirs be wealthy in their place
To nobody's hurt—the stranger else seized all.
Prosperity rolled river-like and stopped,
Making their mill go; but when wheel wore out,
The wave would find a space and sweep on free
And, half-a-mile off, grind some neighbour's corn.

Adam-like, Pietro sighed and said no more:
Eve saw the apple was fair and good to taste,
So, plucked it, having asked the snake advice.
She told her husband God was merciful,

144| MS:stays, *P1868:*stays; 147| MS:fruit" *P1868:*fruit." 150| MS:up, not *P1868:*up; not 152| MS:in *P1868:*i' 154-55| MS:§ no ¶ § *P1868:*§ ¶ § 155| MS:Now one *CP1868:*Now, one 156| MS:of < > core *P1868:*o' < > core, 159| MS:runs an Usufructuary,— *1868:*runs, an usufructuary,— 161| MS:money his < > afterward— *P1868:*money, his < > afterward, 163| MS:be happy in *P1868:*be wealthy in 166| MS:go, but *P1868:*go; but 168| MS:half-a mile off, bring § crossed out and replaced above by § grind < > neighbour's § apostrophe and *s* added in revision § grist § crossed out and replaced by § corn. *P1868:*half-a-mile 168-69| MS:§ no ¶ § *1868:*§ ¶ § 171| MS:And plucked *CP1868:*So, plucked

And his and her prayer granted at the last:
Let the old mill-stone moulder,—wheel unworn,
Quartz from the quarry, shot into the stream
Adroitly, as before should go bring grist—
Their house continued to them by an heir,
Their vacant heart replenished with a child.
We have her own confession at full length
Made in the first remorse: 'twas Jubilee
Pealed in the ear o' the conscience and it woke.
She found she had offended God no doubt,
So much was plain from what had happened since,
Misfortune on misfortune; but she harmed
No one i' the world, so far as she could see.
The act had gladdened Pietro to the height,
Her spouse whom God himself must gladden so
Or not at all: thus much seems probable
From the implicit faith, or rather say
Stupid credulity of the foolish man
Who swallowed such a tale nor strained a whit
Even at his wife's far-over-fifty years
Matching his sixty-and-under. Him she blessed;
And as for doing any detriment
To the veritable heir,—why, tell her first
Who was he? Which of all the hands held up
I' the crowd, one day would gather round their gate,
Did she so wrong by intercepting thus
The ducat, spendthrift fortune thought to fling
For a scramble just to make the mob break shins?
She kept it, saved them kicks and cuffs thereby.

173| MS:And § in margin § His <> prayer was § crossed out § *P1868:*And his 176| MS:Adroitly should <> grist as before— *P1868:*Adroitly, should *1888:*Adroitly, as before should go bring grist— 181| MS:of *P1868:*o' 185| MS:No man in *P1868:*No one i' 187| MS:Her husband God *P1868:*Her husband—God *P1872:* Her spouse whom God 188| MS:all—(thus *P1872:*all: thus 190| MS:foolish soul *P1868:*foolish man 191| MS:such a cheat § crossed out and replaced above by § tale nor choked at all § last two words crossed out § a whit *P1868:*nor strained a 193| MS:his own: such fools we make ourselves) *P1868:*his sixty-and-under.) Him she blessed, *P1872:*sixty-and-under. Him <> blessed; 197| MS:In the crowd, would one day gather *P1868:*I' *P1872:*crowd, one day would gather 200| MS:shins: *P1868:*shins? 201| MS:it, and saved kicks *P1868:*it, saved them kicks

While at the least one good work had she wrought,
Good, clearly and incontestably! Her cheat—
What was it to its subject, the child's self,
But charity and religion? See the girl!
A body most like—a soul too probably—
Doomed to death, such a double death as waits
The illicit offspring of a common trull,
Sure to resent and forthwith rid herself
Of a mere interruption to sin's trade,
In the efficacious way old Tiber knows.
Was not so much proved by the ready sale
O' the child, glad transfer of this irksome chance?
Well then, she had caught up this castaway:
This fragile egg, some careless wild bird dropped,
She had picked from where it waited the foot-fall,
And put in her own breast till forth broke finch
Able to sing God praise on mornings now.
What so excessive harm was done?—she asked.

To which demand the dreadful answer comes—
For that same deed, now at Lorenzo's church,
Both agents, conscious and inconscious, lie;
While she, the deed was done to benefit,
Lies also, the most lamentable of things,
Yonder where curious people count her breaths,
Calculate how long yet the little life

203| MS:Good, § crossed out and replaced above by § Oh, clearly < > her *P1868:*Good, clearly < > Her 205| MS:girl *P1868:*girl!
206| MS:probably *P1868:*probably— 208| MS:trull *P1868:*trull,
210| MS:Of such and interruption to her trade *P1868:*Of a mere interruption to sin's trade, 213| MS:Of the child, the transfer *P1868:*O' the child, glad transfer
215| MS:egg some < > dropped *P1868:*egg, some < > dropped, 217| MS:broke this bird *P1868:*broke finch 219| MS:done, she *P1868:*done?—she
219-20| MS:§ no ¶ § *P1868:*§ ¶ § 221| MS:deed, lie § crossed out and replaced above by § now, at *P1868:*now at 225| MS:breaths *P1868:*breaths,

Unspilt may serve their turn nor spoil the show,
Give them their story, then the church its group.

Well, having gained Pompilia, the girl grew
I' the midst of Pietro here, Violante there,
Each, like a semicircle with stretched arms,
Joining the other round her preciousness—
Two walls that go about a garden-plot
Where a chance sliver, branchlet slipt from bole
Of some tongue-leaved eye-figured Eden tree,
Filched by two exiles and borne far away,
Patiently glorifies their solitude,—
Year by year mounting, grade by grade surmounts
The builded brick-work, yet is compassed still,
Still hidden happily and shielded safe,—
Else why should miracle have graced the ground?
But on the twelfth sun that brought April there
What meant that laugh? The coping-stone was reached;
Nay, above towered a light tuft of bloom
To be toyed with by butterfly or bee,
Done good to or else harm to from outside:
Pompilia's root, stalk and a branch or two
Home enclosed still, the rest would be the world's.
All which was taught our couple though obtuse,
Since walls have ears, when one day brought a priest,
Smooth-mannered soft-speeched sleek-cheeked visitor,

227-29| MS:show./ § ¶ § Well <> Pompilia, there she grew *P1868:*show,/ Give them their story, then the church its group./ § ¶ § Well <> Pompilia, the girl grew
230| MS:In *P1868:*I' 231| MS:Each like <> arms *P1868:*Each, like <> arms,
233| MS:Two § inserted in margin § Walls <> went *P1868:*Two walls <> go
234| MS:branch slipt from the bole *P1868:*branchlet slipt from bole
235| MS:eye-blossomed Eden *P1868:*eye-figured Eden 237| MS:solitude, *P1868:* solitude,— 238| MS:surmounts *1888:*surmount § emended to § surmounts § see Editorial Notes § 239| MS:brickwork yet *P1868:*brick-work, yet
241| MS:For why *P1868:*Else why *P1872:*ground *1888:*ground? 243| MS:What was that <> coping stone was reached *P1868:*What meant that <> coping-stone was reached; 244| MS:Nay, a light tuft of bloom towered above *1888:*Nay, above towered a light tuft of bloom 247| MS:root, stem and *1888:*root, stalk and
249| MS:obtuse *P1868:*obtuse, 250| MS:ears when *P1868:*ears, when
251| MS:Smooth-mannered, soft-speeched, sleek-cheeked *P1868:*Smooth-mannered

The notable Abate Paolo—known
As younger brother of a Tuscan house
Whereof the actual representative,
Count Guido, had employed his youth and age
In culture of Rome's most productive plant—
A cardinal: but years pass and change comes,
In token of which, here was our Paolo brought
To broach a weighty business. Might he speak?
Yes—to Violante somehow caught alone
While Pietro took his after-dinner doze,
And the young maiden, busily as befits,
Minded her broider-frame three chambers off.

So—giving now his great flap-hat a gloss
With flat o' the hand between-whiles, soothing now
The silk from out its creases o'er the calf,
Setting the stocking clerical again,
But never disengaging, once engaged,
The thin clear grey hold of his eyes on her—
He dissertated on that Tuscan house,
Those Franceschini,—very old they were—
Not rich however—oh, not rich, at least,
As people look to be who, low i' the scale
One way, have reason, rising all they can
By favour of the money-bag! 'tis fair—
Do all gifts go together? But don't suppose
That being not so rich means all so poor!
Say rather, well enough—i' the way, indeed,
Ha, ha, to fortune better than the best:

---

soft-speeched sleek-cheeked 254| MS:representative *CP1868:*representative, 255| MS:Count Guido had <> youth till now *CP1868:*Count Guido, had <> youth and age 256| MS:plant *P1868:*plant— 257| MS: A Cardinal *P1868:*A cardinal 261| MS:doze *P1868:*doze, 262| MS:befits *P1868:*befits, 263-64| MS:§ no ¶ § *P1868:*§ ¶ § 264| MS:great black hat *P1868:*great flap-hat 265| MS:of the hand, between-whiles *P1868:*o' the hand between-whiles 270| MS:disertated *P1868:*dissertated 271| MS:The Franceschini *P1868:*Those Franceschini 273| MS:in the scale, *P1868:*i' the scale 275| MS:money-bag:'tis *P1872:*money-bag! 'tis 277| MS:poor— *P1868:*poor! 278| MS:in *P1868:*i' 279| MS:to better fortune than the best. *P1872:*to fortune

Since if his brother's patron-friend kept faith,
Put into promised play the Cardinalate,
Their house might wear the red cloth that keeps warm,
Would but the Count have patience—there's the point!
For he was slipping into years apace,
And years make men restless—they needs must spy
Some certainty, some sort of end assured,
Some sparkle, tho' from topmost beacon-tip,
That warrants life a harbour through the haze.
In short, call him fantastic as you choose,
Guido was home-sick, yearned for the old sights
And usual faces,—fain would settle himself
And have the patron's bounty when it fell
Irrigate far rather than deluge near,
Go fertilize Arezzo, not flood Rome.
Sooth to say, 'twas the wiser wish: the Count
Proved wanting in ambition,—let us avouch,
Since truth is best,—in callousness of heart,
And winced at pin-pricks whereby honours hang
A ribbon o'er each puncture: his—no soul
Ecclesiastic (here the hat was brushed)
Humble but self-sustaining, calm and cold,
Having, as one who puts his hand to the plough,
Renounced the over-vivid family-feel—
Poor brother Guido! All too plain, he pined
Amid Rome's pomp and glare for dinginess
And that dilapidated palace-shell
Vast as a quarry and, very like, as bare—
Since to this comes old grandeur now-a-days—

---

better than the best: [280]| MS:faith *P1868:*faith, [282]| MS:Their House might get the *P1868:*Their house might wear the [283]| MS:point. *P1868:*point! [285]| MS:must see *1888:*must spy [287]| MS:Sparkle tho' only from the beacon-tip *P1868:*Sparkle, tho' from the topmost beacon-tip *P1872:*Some sparkle, tho' from topmost beacon-tip, [293]| MS:deluge here, *P1868:*deluge near, [296]| MS:Was wanting *P1868:*Proved wanting [298]| MS:Winced at those pinpricks <> hang, *P1868:*pin-pricks <> hang *P1872:*And winced at pin-pricks [304]| MS:brother Guido!—all *P1868:* brother Guido! All [305]| MS:Amid the pomp *P1868:*Amid Rome's pomp [306]| MS:delapidated *P1868:*dilapidated [307]| MS:bare *P1868:*bare— [308]| MS:nowadays— *P1868:*now-a-days—

Or that absurd wild villa in the waste
O' the hill side, breezy though, for who likes air,
Vittiano, nor unpleasant with its vines,
Outside the city and the summer heats.
And now his harping on this one tense chord
The villa and the palace, palace this
And villa the other, all day and all night
Creaked like the implacable cicala's cry
And made one's ear-drum ache: nought else would serve
But that, to light his mother's visage up
With second youth, hope, gaiety again,
He must find straightway, woo and haply win
And bear away triumphant back, some wife.
Well now, the man was rational in his way:
He, the Abate,—ought he to interpose?
Unless by straining still his tutelage
(Priesthood leaps over elder-brothership)
Across this difficulty: then let go,
Leave the poor fellow in peace! Would that be wrong?
There was no making Guido great, it seems,
Spite of himself: then happy be his dole!
Indeed, the Abate's little interest
Was somewhat nearly touched i' the case, they saw:
Since if his simple kinsman so were bent,
Began his rounds in Rome to catch a wife,
Full soon would such unworldliness surprise
The rare bird, sprinkle salt on phœnix' tail,
And so secure the nest a sparrow-hawk.
No lack of mothers here in Rome,—no dread

309| MS:wild Villa *P1868:*wild villa 310| MS:On <> though for *P1868:*O' <> though, for 312| MS:Out the city *P1868:*Outside the city 314| MS:The Villa <> Palace, Palace *P1868:*The villa <> palace, palace 315| MS:And Villa *P1868:*And villa 316| MS:Raked like *P1868:*Creaked like 317| MS:ear drum rend: nought *P1868:*ear-drum ache:nought *1888:*ear drum DC, BrU: ear-drum *1889:*ear-drum 320| MS:Hed *P1868:*He 321| MS:back some *P1868:*back, some 322| MS:way— *P1872:*way: 326| MS:Over this difficulty, then let go *P1868:*Across this difficulty: then let go, 327| MS:peace. Would *P1868:*peace! Would 330| MS:Indeed the *P1868:*Indeed, the 331| MS:in the case, you see: *P1868:*i' the case, they saw: 332| MS:so was bent, *P1868:*so were bent, 334| MS:would his unworldliness surprize *P1868:*would such unworldliness surprise 336| MS:secure his House a

Of daughters lured as larks by looking-glass!
The first name-pecking credit-scratching fowl
Would drop her unfledged cuckoo in our nest
To gather greyness there, give voice at length
And shame the brood . . . but it was long ago
When crusades were, and we sent eagles forth!
No, that at least the Abate could forestall.
He read the thought within his brother's word,
Knew what he purposed better than himself.
We want no name and fame—having our own:
No worldly aggrandizement—such we fly:
But if some wonder of a woman's-heart
Were yet untainted on this grimy earth,
Tender and true—tradition tells of such—
Prepared to pant in time and tune with ours—
If some good girl (a girl, since she must take
The new bent, live new life, adopt new modes)
Not wealthy (Guido for his rank was poor)
But with whatever dowry came to hand,—
There were the lady-love predestinate!
And somehow the Abate's guardian eye—
Scintillant, rutilant, fraternal fire,—
Roving round every way had seized the prize
—The instinct of us, we, the spiritualty!
Come, cards on table; was it true or false
That here—here in this very tenement—
Yea, Via Vittoria did a marvel hide,

---

sparrowhawk. *P1868:*secure the nest a sparrow-hawk. 338| MS:looking glass. *P1868:*looking-glass! 339| MS:name-pecking honor-scratching *P1868:*name-pecking credit-scratching 342| MS:brood . . but that was <> ago . . *P1868:*but it was <> ago *1888:*brood . . . but 343| MS:were and they § crossed out and replaced above by § it sent <> forth. *P1868:*were, and we sent <> forth! 344| MS:would *P1868:*could 346| MS:what it purposed *P1868:*what he purposed 349| MS:woman's heart *P1868:*woman's-heart 350| MS:this grimy § inserted above line § earth of ours, § last two words crossed out § *P1868:*earth, 354| MS:bent, lead § crossed out and replaced above by § live <> adopt new laws) *P1868:*adopt new modes) 355| MS:wealthy-Guido <> poor— *P1872:*wealthy (Guido <> poor) 356| MS:hand, *1872:*hand,— 357| MS:were the the lady-love *1868:*were the lady-love 358| MS:guardian-eye— *P1868:*guardian eye— 361| MS:we the *P1868:*we, the 364| MS:hide *P1868:*

Lily of a maiden, white with intact leaf
Guessed thro' the sheath that saved it from the sun?
A daughter with the mother's hands still clasped
Over her head for fillet virginal,
A wife worth Guido's house and hand and heart?
He came to see; had spoken, he could no less—
(A final cherish of the stockinged calf)
If harm were,—well, the matter was off his mind.

Then with the great air did he kiss, devout,
Violante's hand, and rise up his whole height
(A certain purple gleam about the black)
And go forth grandly,—as if the Pope came next.
And so Violante rubbed her eyes awhile,
Got up too, walked to wake her Pietro soon
And pour into his ear the mighty news
How somebody had somehow somewhere seen
Their tree-top-tuft of bloom above the wall,
And came now to apprize them the tree's self
Was no such crab-sort as should go feed swine,
But veritable gold, the Hesperian ball
Ordained for Hercules to haste and pluck,
And bear and give the Gods to banquet with—
Hercules standing ready at the door.
Whereon did Pietro rub his eyes in turn,
Look very wise, a little woeful too,
Then, periwig on head, and cane in hand,
Sally forth dignifiedly into the Square
Of Spain across Babbuino the six steps,
Toward the Boat-fountain where our idlers lounge,—
Ask, for form's sake, who Hercules might be,

---

hide, 366| MS:sun: *P1868:*sun? 369| MS:wife for Guido's *P1868:*wife worth Guido's 370-72| MS:less—. If harm was *P1868:*less—/ (A final cherish of the stockinged calf)/ If harm were 372-73| MS:§ no ¶ § *1868:*§ ¶ §
376| MS:as the *P1868:*as if the 377| MS:And Violante *P1868:*And so Violante 378| MS:her Pietro up *P1868:*her Pietro soon 379| MS:And § enclosed between parallel lines § 381| MS:tree-top tuft <> wall *P1868:*tree-top-tuft <> wall, 382| MS:apprise *1888:*apprize 383| MS:should drop its fruit, *P1868:*should feed the swine, *P1872:*should go feed swine, 389| MS:Look very § inserted above line § 390| MS:head and *P1868:*head, and 391-94| MS:the Square,/ Ask *P1868:*the Square/ Of Spain across Babbuino the six steps,/ Toward the Boat-fountain

And have congratulation from the world.

Heartily laughed the world in his fool's-face
And told him Hercules was just the heir
To the stubble once a corn-field, and brick-heap
Where used to be a dwelling-place now burned.
Guido and Franceschini; a Count,—ay:
But a cross i' the poke to bless the Countship? No!
All gone except sloth, pride, rapacity,
Humours of the imposthume incident
To rich blood that runs thin,—nursed to a head
By the rankly-salted soil—a cardinal's court
Where, parasite and picker-up of crumbs,
He had hung on long, and now, let go, said some,
Shaken off, said others,—but in any case
Tired of the trade and something worse for wear,
Was wanting to change town for country quick,
Go home again: let Pietro help him home!
The brother, Abate Paolo, shrewder mouse,
Had pricked for comfortable quarters, inched
Into the core of Rome, and fattened so;
But Guido, over-burly for rat's hole
Suited to clerical slimness, starved outside,
Must shift for himself: and so the shift was this!
What, was the snug retreat of Pietro tracked,
The little provision for his old age snuffed?
"Oh, make your girl a lady, an you list,
But have more mercy on our wit than vaunt
Your bargain as we burgesses who brag!
Why, Goodman Dullard, if a friend must speak,

---

where our idlers lounge,—/ Ask 396| MS:And heartily *P1868:*Heartily 398| MS:cornfield, and brick heap *P1868:*corn-field, and brick-heap 399| MS:be dwellingplace *P1868:*be a dwelling-place 400| MS:aye: *P1868:*ay: 401| MS:in *P1868:*i' 402| MS:rapacity— *P1868:*rapacity, 405| MS: a Cardinal's *P1868:*a cardinal's 406| MS:picker up of crumbs *P1868:*picker-up of crumbs, 408| MS:But shaken < > others,—in *1888:*Shaken < > others,—but in 409| MS:trade, and < > wear *P1868:*trade and < > wear, 410| MS:country now, *P1868:*country quick, 411| MS:him there! *P1868:*him home! 412| MS:mouse *P1868:*mouse, 413| MS:Had cared for *P1868:*Had pricked for 415| MS:over burly for the hole *P1868:*over-burly for rat's hole 419| MS:little store of pursed-up ducats § last four words crossed out and replaced above by § provision for his old age 420| MS:Oh < > lady, if you *P1868:*"Oh < > lady, an you 422| MS:burgesses count gain. *P1868:*burgesses who brag!

Would the Count, think you, stoop to you and yours
Were there the value of one penny-piece
To rattle 'twixt his palms—or likelier laugh,
Bid your Pompilia help you black his shoe?"

Home again, shaking oft the puzzled pate,
Went Pietro to announce a change indeed,
Yet point Violante where some solace lay
Of a rueful sort,—the taper, quenched so soon,
Had ended merely in a snuff, not stink—
Congratulate there was one hope the less
Not misery the more: and so an end.

The marriage thus impossible, the rest
Followed: our spokesman, Paolo, heard his fate,
Resignedly Count Guido bore the blow:
Violante wiped away the transient tear,
Renounced the playing Danae to gold dreams,
Praised much her Pietro's prompt sagaciousness,
Found neighbours' envy natural, lightly laughed
At gossips' malice, fairly wrapped herself
In her integrity three folds about,
And, letting pass a little day or two,
Threw, even over that integrity,
Another wrappage, namely one thick veil
That hid her, matron-wise, from head to foot,
And, by the hand holding a girl veiled too,
Stood, one dim end of a December day,
In Saint Lorenzo on the altar-step—
Just where she lies now and that girl will lie—
Only with fifty candles' company
Now, in the place of the poor winking one
Which saw,—doors shut and sacristan made sure,—

425| MS:penny piece *P1868:*penny-piece 426| MS:palms and let him laugh, *P1868:*palms—or likelier laugh, 427| MS:shoe? *P1868:*shoe?"
428| MS:pate *P1868:*pate, 429| MS:indeed *P1868:*indeed, 432| MS:snuff not *P1868:*snuff, not 436| MS:spokesman Paolo heard *P1868:*spokesman, Paolo, heard 439| MS:Confessed herself a § last two words crossed out and replaced above by § the playing *P1868:*Renounced the 444| MS:two *P1868:*two, 445| MS:integrity *CP1868:*integrity, 447| MS:matronwise *P1868:*matron-wise
453| MS:Now—in place *CP1868:*in the place *P1872:*Now, in

A priest—perhaps Abate Paolo—wed
Guido clandestinely, irrevocably
To his Pompilia aged thirteen years
And five months,—witness the church register,—
Pompilia, (thus become Count Guido's wife
Clandestinely, irrevocably his,)
Who all the while had borne, from first to last,
As brisk a part i' the bargain, as yon lamb,
Brought forth from basket and set out for sale,
Bears while they chaffer, wary market-man
And voluble housewife, o'er it,—each in turn
Patting the curly calm inconscious head,
With the shambles ready round the corner there,
When the talk's talked out and a bargain struck.

Transfer complete, why, Pietro was apprised.
Violante sobbed the sobs and prayed the prayers
And said the serpent tempted so she fell,
Till Pietro had to clear his brow apace
And make the best of matters: wrath at first,—
How else? pacification presently,
Why not?—could flesh withstand the impurpled one,
The very Cardinal, Paolo's patron-friend?
Who, justifiably surnamed "a hinge,"
Knew where the mollifying oil should drop
To cure the creak o' the valve,—considerate
For frailty, patient in a naughty world.
He even volunteered to supervise
The rough draught of those marriage-articles
Signed in a hurry by Pietro, since revoked:

456| MS:irrevocably, *P1868:*irrevocably 459| MS:Pompilia, thus *P1868:*Pompilia, (thus 460| MS:his, *P1868:*his,) 462| MS:in the bargain as yon lamb *P1868:*i' the bargain, as yon lamb, 463| MS:sale *P1868:*sale, 464| MS:marketman *P1868:*market-man 467| MS:there *P1868:*there, 468-69| MS:§ ¶ § *1888:*§ no ¶; paragraph restored; see Editorial Notes § 469| MS:apprised *P1868:*apprised. 471| MS:fell *P1868:*fell, 474| MS:else? but rightly pacified presently *P1868:*else? pacification presently, 475| MS:the Impurpled One, *P1868:*the impurpled one, 476| MS:patron-friend, *P1868:*patron-friend? 477| MS:justifiably declared "a hinge" *P1868:*justifiably surnamed "a hinge," 479| MS:of *P1868:*o' 480| MS:world, *P1872:*world. 482| MS:The first § crossed out and replaced above by § rough <> marriage

Trust's politic, suspicion does the harm,
There is but one way to brow-beat this world,
Dumb-founder doubt, and repay scorn in kind,—
To go on trusting, namely, till faith move
Mountains.

And faith here made the mountains move.
Why, friends whose zeal cried "Caution ere too late!"—
Bade "Pause ere jump, with both feet joined, on slough!"—
Counselled "If rashness then, now temperance!"—
Heard for their pains that Pietro had closed eyes,
Jumped and was in the middle of the mire,
Money and all, just what should sink a man.
By the mere marriage, Guido gained forthwith
Dowry, his wife's right; no rescinding there:
But Pietro, why must he needs ratify
One gift Violante gave, pay down one doit
Promised in first fool's-flurry? Grasp the bag
Lest the son's service flag,—is reason and rhyme,
Above all when the son's a son-in-law.
Words to the wind! The parents cast their lot
Into the lap o' the daughter: and the son

---

articles *P1868:*marriage-articles 484| MS:politic:suspicion <> harm. *P1868:*politic, suspicion <> harm, 485| MS:browbeat *P1868:*brow-beat 486| MS:Dumbfounder <> kind, *P1868:*Dumb-founder <> kind,— 487| MS:moved *P1868:*move 488| MS:Mountains. What faith <> move? *P1868:*Mountains. § ¶ § And faith <> move. 489| MS: late!" *P1868:*late!"— 490| MS:Bade pause <> slough *P1868:* Bade "Pause <> slough!"— 491| MS:then, more temperance now"— *P1868:*then, now temperance!"— 492| MS:eyes *P1868:*eyes, 494| MS:Casket and *P1868:*Money and 495| MS:marriage Guido *CP1868:* marriage, Guido 496| MS:right, no *P1868:*right; no 499| MS:fool's flurry? Bear § crossed out and replaced above by § Grasp the bag § crossed out and replaced by § purse *P1868:*the bag 500| MS:And keep the child § crossed out and replaced above by § son kind, quoth the rhyming saw *P1868:*Lest the son's service flag,—is reason and rhyme, 501| MS:the child's § crossed out and replaced above by § son's a son-in-law." *P1868:*son-in-law. 502| MS:Sir, he gave all; the parents *P1868:*Words to the wind! The parents 503| MS:of the daughter—

Now with a right to lie there, took what fell,
Pietro's whole having and holding, house and field,
Goods, chattels and effects, his worldly worth
Present and in perspective, all renounced
In favour of Guido. As for the usufruct—
The interest now, the principal anon,
Would Guido please to wait, at Pietro's death:
Till when, he must support the couple's charge,
Bear with them, housemates, pensionaries, pawned
To an alien for fulfilment of their pact.
Guido should at discretion deal them orts,
Bread-bounty in Arezzo the strange place,—
They who had lived deliciously and rolled
Rome's choicest comfit 'neath the tongue before.
Into this quag, "jump" bade the Cardinal!
And neck-deep in a minute there flounced they.

But they touched bottom at Arezzo: there—
Four months' experience of how craft and greed
Quickened by penury and pretentious hate
Of plain truth, brutify and bestialize,—
Four months' taste of apportioned insolence,
Cruelty graduated, dose by dose
Of ruffianism dealt out at bed and board,
And lo, the work was done, success clapped hands.
The starved, stripped, beaten brace of stupid dupes
Broke at last in their desperation loose,

---

and *P1868:*o' the daughter: and 504| MS:take <> fell. *P1868:*took <> fell,
508| MS:of Guido,—as <> usufruct *P1868:*of Guido. As <> usufruct—
510| MS:death *P1868:*death: 511| MS:when he <> Couple's charge *P1868:* when, he <> couple's charge, 513| MS:pact, *P1868:*pact.
514| MS:One who should, at <> them bread *P1868:*Guido should at <> them orts,
515| MS:Of bounty in <> place, *P1868:*Bread-bounty in <> place,—
516| MS:deliciously, and *P1868:*deliciously and 518| MS:the Cardinal: *P1868:* the Cardinal! 519| MS:there stood they. *P1868:*there flounced they.
520| MS:there *P1868:*there— 521| MS:months *P1868:*months'
523| MS:truth—brutify and bestialize. *P1868:*truth, brutify and bestialize,—
524| MS:apportioned cruelty, *P1868:*apportioned insolence, 525| MS:Insolence graduated *P1868:*Cruelty graduated 527| MS:hands; *P1868:*hands.
528| MS:stupid ones *P1868:*stupid dupes 529| MS:loose *P1868:*loose,

Fled away for their lives, and lucky so;
Found their account in casting coat afar
And bearing off a shred of skin at least:
Left Guido lord o' the prey, as the lion is,
And, careless what came after, carried their wrongs
To Rome,—I nothing doubt, with such remorse
As folly feels, since pain can make it wise,
But crime, past wisdom, which is innocence,
Needs not be plagued with till a later day.

Pietro went back to beg from door to door,
In hope that memory not quite extinct
Of cheery days and festive nights would move
Friends and acquaintance—after the natural laugh,
And tributary "Just as we foretold—"
To show some bowels, give the dregs o' the cup,
Scraps of the trencher, to their host that was,
Or let him share the mat with the mastiff, he
Who lived large and kept open house so long.
Not so Violante: ever a-head i' the march,
Quick at the bye-road and the cut-across,
She went first to the best adviser, God—
Whose finger unmistakably was felt
In all this retribution of the past.
Here was the prize of sin, luck of a lie!
But here too was what Holy Year would help,
Bound to rid sinners of sin vulgar, sin
Abnormal, sin prodigious, up to sin
Impossible and supposed for Jubilee' sake:

530| MS:lives and < > so. *P1868:*lives, and < > so; 532| MS:So bearing *P1868:* And bearing 533| MS:of the prey as *P1868:*o' the prey, as 536| MS:feels because pain makes it wise *P1868:*feels, since pain can make it wise,
537| MS:But wickedness, past growing innocent, *P1868:*But crime, past wisdom, which is innocence, 539| MS:door *CP1868:*door, 542| MS:acquaintance, after *CP1868:*acquaintance—after 544| MS:Might § crossed out and replaced above by § To show < > of the wine *P1868:*o' the cup,
548| MS:in the race, *P1868:*i' the march, 549| MS:the nigh road and *P1868:* the bye-road and 552| MS:of old crime. *P1868:*of the past. 554| MS:was the Holy Year in help, *P1868:*the Holy Year would help, *1888:*was what Holy Year

To lift the leadenest of lies, let soar
The soul unhampered by a feather-weight.
"I will" said she "go burn out this bad hole
That breeds the scorpion, baulk the plague at least
Of hope to further plague by progeny:
I will confess my fault, be punished, yes,
But pardoned too: Saint Peter pays for all."

So, with the crowd she mixed, made for the dome,
Through the great door new-broken for the nonce
Marched, muffled more than ever matron-wise,
Up the left nave to the formidable throne,
Fell into file with this the poisoner
And that the parricide, and reached in turn
The poor repugnant Penitentiary
Set at this gully-hole o' the world's discharge
To help the frightfullest of filth have vent,
And then knelt down and whispered in his ear
How she had bought Pompilia, palmed the babe
On Pietro, passed the girl off as their child
To Guido, and defrauded of his due
This one and that one,—more than she could name,
Until her solid piece of wickedness
Happened to split and spread woe far and wide:
Contritely now she brought the case for cure.

Replied the throne—"Ere God forgive the guilt,
Make man some restitution! Do your part!

---

would help, 559| MS:featherweight. *P1868:*feather-weight.
562| MS:Its hope of further creeping progeny: *1888:*Of hope to further plague by progeny: 564-67| MS:too: Saint Peter, prays for me."/ § no ¶ § So with <> for the church,/ Marched, covered over once more matronwise, *P1868:*too: Saint Peter pays for all."/ § ¶ § <> for the dome,/ Through the great door new-broken for the nonce/ Marched, muffled more than ever matron-wise, *CP1868:*So, with
568| MS:throne *P1868:*throne, 571| MS:repugnant penitentiary *P1868:*repugnant Penitentiary 572| MS:of *P1868:*o' 573| MS:To see the frightfulest <> had *P1868:*To help the frightfullest <> have 575| MS:"How *P1868:*How 579| MS:So had her single piece *P1868:*Until her solid piece
580| MS:spread her lies far *P1868:*spread woe far 581| MS:cure." *P1868:*cure.
582| MS:the priest—"Ere <> the sin, *P1868:*the throne—"Ere <> the guilt,
583| MS:restitution. Do <> part. *P1868:*restitution! Do <> part!

The owners of your husband's heritage,
Barred thence by this pretended birth and heir,—
Tell them, the bar came so, is broken so,
Theirs be the due reversion as before!
Your husband who, no partner in the guilt,
Suffers the penalty, led blindfold thus
By love of what he thought his flesh and blood
To alienate his all in her behalf,—
Tell him too such contract is null and void!
Last, he who personates your son-in-law,
Who with sealed eyes and stopped ears, tame and mute,
Took at your hand that bastard of a whore
You called your daughter and he calls his wife,—
Tell him, and bear the anger which is just!
Then, penance so performed, may pardon be!"

Who could gainsay this just and right award?
Nobody in the world: but, out o' the world,
Who knows?—might timid intervention be
From any makeshift of an angel-guide,
Substitute for celestial guardianship,
Pretending to take care of the girl's self:
"Woman, confessing crime is healthy work,
And telling truth relieves a liar like you,
But how of my quite unconsidered charge?
No thought if, while this good befalls yourself,
Aught in the way of harm may find out her?"

584| MS:heritage *P1868:*heritage, 585| MS:heir, *P1868:*heir,— 586| MS:came so, § followed by illegible smudge § broken so; *P1868:*came so, is broken so, 587| MS:before. *P1868:*before! 589| MS:penalty,—led <> thus, *P1868:*penalty, led <> thus 591| MS:behalf, *P1868:*behalf,— 592| MS:him, declare his contract null and void. *P1868:*him too such contract is null and void! 593| MS:son-in-law *P1868:*son-in-law, 595| MS:hand the bastard *P1868:*hand that bastard 596| MS:wife, *P1868:*wife,— 597| MS:bear his anger <> just. *P1868:*bear the anger <> just! 598| MS:performed, let pardon *P1868:*performed, may pardon 600| MS:of *P1868:*o' 601| MS:knows, might *P1868:*knows?—might 605| MS:"Oh yes—confessing *P1868:*"Woman, confessing 607| MS:But, what of this my unconsidered charge, *P1868:*But what of her my <> charge? *1888:*But how of my quite unconsidered 608| MS:thought of, while *1888:*thought if, while 609| MS:What in

No least thought, I assure you: truth being truth,
Tell it and shame the devil!
                                                  Said and done:
Home went Violante, disbosomed all:
And Pietro who, six months before, had borne
Word after word of such a piece of news
Like so much cold steel inched through his breast-blade,
Now at its entry gave a leap for joy,
As who—what did I say of one in a quag?—
Should catch a hand from heaven and spring thereby
Out of the mud, on ten toes stand once more.
"What? All that used to be, may be again?
My money mine again, my house, my land,
My chairs and tables, all mine evermore?
What, the girl's dowry never was the girl's,
And, unpaid yet, is never now to pay?
Then the girl's self, my pale Pompilia child
That used to be my own with her great eyes—
He who drove us forth, why should he keep her
When proved as very a pauper as himself?
Will she come back, with nothing changed at all,
And laugh 'But how you dreamed uneasily!
I saw the great drops stand here on your brow—
Did I do wrong to wake you with a kiss?'
No, indeed, darling! No, for wide awake
I see another outburst of surprise:
The lout-lord, bully-beggar, braggart-sneak,
Who not content with cutting purse, crops ear—
Assuredly it shall be salve to mine
When this great news red-letters him, the rogue!

---

*1888:*Aught in 612| MS:went Violante and disbosomed *1888:*went Violante, disbosomed 615| MS:breast bone. *P1868:*breast-blade, 616| MS:entry clapped his hands for *P1868:*entry gave a leap for 617| MS:who . . what <> quag? *P1868:*who—what <> quag?— 619| MS:mud, solidly stand *P1868:*mud, on ten toes stand 623| MS:Next, the *P1868:*What, the 625| MS:pale Pompilia thing *P1868:*pale Pompilia child 627-28| MS:§ crowded between lines 626-29 § 634| MS:another splendor of *P1868:*another outburst of 635| MS:The mock-lord *P1868:*The lout-lord 636| MS:cropt ears—§ *s* crossed out § *P1868:*crops 637| MS:I see his worship at the whipping-post! § entire line crossed out and replaced above by § Assuredly it shall be salve to mine

Ay, let him taste the teeth o' the trap, this fox,
Give us our lamb back, golden fleece and all,
Let her creep in and warm our breasts again!
Why care for the past? We three are our old selves,
And know now what the outside world is worth."
And so, he carried case before the courts;
And there Violante, blushing to the bone,
Made public declaration of her fault,
Renounced her motherhood, and prayed the law
To interpose, frustrate of its effect
Her folly, and redress the injury done.

Whereof was the disastrous consequence,
That though indisputably clear the case
(For thirteen years are not so large a lapse,
And still six witnesses survived in Rome
To prove the truth o' the tale)—yet, patent wrong
Seemed Guido's; the first cheat had chanced on him:
Here was the pity that, deciding right,
Those who began the wrong would gain the prize.
Guido pronounced the story one long lie
Lied to do robbery and take revenge:
Or say it were no lie at all but truth,
Then, it both robbed the right heirs and shamed him

639| MS:Aye <> of <> fox: *P1868:*Ay <> o' <> fox, 641| MS:again: *P1868:*again! 642| MS:What care <> selves; *P1868:*past?—we *1888:*Why care <> past? We <> selves, 643| MS:Who know <> the outside § inserted above line § wintry world *P1868:*outside world *1888:*And know 644| MS:so he carried the case <> Courts; *P1868:*so, he carried case <> courts; 645| MS:there Violante, § there follows an illegibly crossed out word § shame § crossed out § blushing to the § inserted above § 648| MS:To hinder § crossed out and replaced by § interpose, frustrate 650| MS:And this was *P1868:*Whereof was 654| MS:of *P1868:*o' 655| MS:Seemed Guido's, the <> him, *P1868:*Seemed Guido's; the <> him: 656| MS:right *P1868:*right, 657| MS:gain thereby. *P1868:*gain the good. *1888:*gain the prize. 659| MS:revenge *P1868:*revenge: 660| MS:Or, say *P1868:*Or say 661| MS:Why, it *CP1868:*Then, it

Without revenge to humanize the deed:
What had he done when first they shamed him thus?
But that were too fantastic: losels they,
And leasing this world's-wonder of a lie,
They lied to blot him though it brand themselves.

So answered Guido through the Abate's mouth.
Wherefore the court, its customary way,
Inclined to the middle course the sage affect.
They held the child to be a changeling,—good:
But, lest the husband got no good thereby,
They willed the dowry, though not hers at all,
Should yet be his, if not by right then grace—
Part-payment for the plain injustice done.
As for that other contract, Pietro's work,
Renunciation of his own estate,
That must be cancelled—give him back his gifts,
He was no party to the cheat at least!
So ran the judgment:—whence a prompt appeal
On both sides, seeing right is absolute.
Cried Pietro "Is the child no child of mine?
Why give her a child's dowry?"—"Have I right
To the dowry, why not to the rest as well?"
Cried Guido, or cried Paolo in his name:
Till law said "Reinvestigate the case!"
And so the matter pends, to this same day.

Hence new disaster—here no outlet seemed;
Whatever the fortune of the battle-field,
No path whereby the fatal man might march

662| MS:deed *P1868:*deed: 666-67| MS:§ no ¶ § mouth, *P1868:*§ ¶ § mouth. 668| MS:And so the Court *P1868:*Wherefore the court 669| MS:affect— *P1872:*affect. 673| MS:right by grace— *P1868:*right then grace— 674| MS:for a plain *P1868:*for the plain 675-77| MS:But there, that <> work,/ That <> his goods, *P1868:*But then, that <> / Renunciation of his own estate,/ That *1888:*As for that <> // <> his gifts, 678| MS:least. *P1868:*least! 679| MS:the sentence § crossed out and replaced above by § judgement: 680| MS:absolute, *P1868:*absolute. 681| MS:Cried Pietro "Is Pompilia not my child? *1888:*Cried Pietro "Is the child no child of mine? 682| MS:her my child's *1888:*her a child's 685| MS:§ crowded between lines 684-86 § So Law <> cases *P1868:*Till Law <> case!" 686| MS:pends unto this day. *P1868:*pends, unto *P1888:*pends, to this same day. 687-89| MS:disaster—that no <> seemed,—/ No

Victorious, wreath on head and spoils in hand,
And back turned full upon the baffled foe,—
Nor cranny whence, desperate and disgraced,
Stripped to the skin, he might be fain to crawl
Worm-like, and so away with his defeat
To other fortune and a novel prey.
No, he was pinned to the place there, left alone
With his immense hate and, the solitary
Subject to satisfy that hate, his wife.
"Cast her off? Turn her naked out of doors?
Easily said! But still the action pends,
Still dowry, principal and interest,
Pietro's possessions, all I bargined for,—
Any good day, be but my friends alert,
May give them me if she continue mine.
Yet, keep her? Keep the puppet of my foes—
Her voice that lisps me back their curse—her eye
They lend their leer of triumph to—her lip
I touch and taste their very filth upon?"

In short, he also took the middle course
Rome taught him—did at last excogitate
How he might keep the good and leave the bad
Twined in revenge, yet extricable,—nay
Make the very hate's eruption, very rush
Of the unpent sluice of cruelty relieve
His heart first, then go fertilize his field.

---

path *P1868:*seemed;/ Whatever the fortune of the battle-field,/ Nor path *CP1868:*// No path *1888:*disaster—here no 690| MS:Victoriously, with all his gains confirmed § last five words crossed out and replaced above by seven words § wreath on head and spoils in hand, *P1868:*Victorious, wreath 691| MS:Turning his § last two words crossed out and replaced above by one word § And back turned full § last two words inserted above § 692| MS:No cranny *P1868:*Nor cranny 694| MS:Worm like *P1868:*Worm-like 695| MS:To the other <> and the novel *CP1868:*To other *1888:*and a novel 700| MS:said when still <> pends *P1868:*said! But still <> pends, 701| MS:When dowry *P1868:*Still dowry 702| MS:§ crowded between lines 701-3 § for, *P1868:*for,— 704| MS:continues *P1868:*continue 705| MS:the darling of *P1868:*the puppet of 708| MS:I only § crossed out § touch, to § crossed out and replaced above by § and <> their very § inserted above § *P1868:*touch and 712| MS:Blent § crossed out and replaced above by § Twined 713| MS:Nay, § crossed out § make <>

What if the girl-wife, tortured with due care,
Should take, as though spontaneously, the road
It were impolitic to thrust her on?
If, goaded, she broke out in full revolt,
Followed her parents i' the face o' the world,
Branded as runaway not castaway,
Self-sentenced and self-punished in the act?
So should the loathed form and detested face
Launch themselves into hell and there be lost
While he looked o'er the brink with folded arms;
So should the heaped-up shames go shuddering back
O' the head o' the heapers, Pietro and his wife,
And bury in the breakage three at once:
While Guido, left free, no one right renounced,
Gain present, gain prospective, all the gain,
None of the wife except her rights absorbed,
Should ask law what it was law paused about—
If law were dubious still whose word to take,
The husband's—dignified and derelict,
Or the wife's—the . . . what I tell you. It should be.

Guido's first step was to take pen, indite
A letter to the Abate,—not his own,
His wife's,—she should re-write, sign, seal and send.
She liberally told the household-news,
Rejoiced her vile progenitors were gone,

---

eruption, rush *P1868:*Make < > eruption, very rush 717| MS:as if spontaneously *P1868:*as though spontaneously 719| MS:If goaded she < > in open flight, *P1868:*If, goaded, she < > in full revolt, 720| MS:in < > of the world *P1868:*i' < > o' the world, 722| MS:self punished *P1868:*self-punished 725| MS:arms. *P1868:*arms; 727| MS:On < > of the heapers Pietro < > wife *P1868:*O' < > o'the heapers, Pietro < > wife, 728| MS:the breaking three at once, *P1868:*the breakage three at once: 729| MS:free, eases § crossed out and replaced above by § no < > renounced *P1868:*renounced, 730| MS:the gain *P1868:*the gain, 731| MS:wife but all her *P1868:*wife except her 732| MS:ask Law < > was she paused *P1868:*ask law < > was law paused 733| MS:If she was dubious still which word to take *P1868:*were < > whose < > take, *CP1868:*If law were 735| MS:The wife's . . what I shall show you *P1868:*Or the wife's—the . . what I tell you *1888:*wife's—the . . . what 738| MS:wife's, she < > re-write, § there follows a word, perhaps *and*, blotted beyond legibility and replaced above by § sign seal *P1868:*wife's,—she < > sign, seal 739| MS:household news, *P1868:*household-news, 740| MS:were fled,

Revealed their malice—how they even laid
A last injunction on her, when they fled,
That she should forthwith find a paramour,
Complot with him to gather spoil enough,
Then burn the house down,—taking previous care
To poison all its inmates overnight,—
And so companioned, so provisioned too,
Follow to Rome and there join fortunes gay.
This letter, traced in pencil-characters,
Guido as easily got re-traced in ink
By his wife's pen, guided from end to end,
As if it had been just so much Chinese.
For why? That wife could broider, sing perhaps,
Pray certainly, but no more read than write
This letter "which yet write she must," he said,
"Being half courtesy and compliment,
Half sisterliness: take the thing on trust!"
She had as readily re-traced the words
Of her own death-warrant,—in some sort 'twas so.
This letter the Abate in due course
Communicated to such curious souls
In Rome as needs must pry into the cause
Of quarrel, why the Comparini fled
The Franceschini, whence the grievance grew,
What the hubbub meant: "Nay,—see the wife's own word,

---

*1888:*were gone, 741| MS:malice who had even *P1868:*malice—how they even 742| MS:This last *P1868:*A last 743| MS:paramour *P1868:*paramour, 774| MS:and thereupon § last two words crossed out and replaced above by § Accordingly join fortunes gay. *1872:*and there join 749| MS:pencil-characters *P1868:*pencil-characters, 750| MS:retraced *1888:*re-traced 751| MS:his wife, pen in hand, from *P1868:*his wife's pen guided, from *CP1868:*pen, guided from 752| MS:As it <> much Latin, Greek § crossed out § Sir, *P1868:*much Hebrew, Sir:*1888:*As if it <> much Chinese. 755| MS:letter which <> must, he said *P1868:*letter "which <> must," he *1888:*said, 756| MS:Being half kindness § crossed out and replaced above by § courtesy and half § crossed out § compliment *P1868:*"Being half <> compliment, 757| MS:sisterliness—take <> trust! *P1868:*sisterliness: take <> trust!" 764| MS:The Franchini *P1868:*The Franceschini 765| MS:the scandal meant *P1868:*the hubbub meant

Authentic answer! Tell detractors too
There's a plan formed, a programme figured here
—Pray God no after-practice put to proof,
This letter cast no light upon, one day!"

So much for what should work in Rome: back now
To Arezzo, follow up the project there,
Forward the next step with as bold a foot,
And plague Pompilia to the height, you see!
Accordingly did Guido set himself
To worry up and down, across, around,
The woman, hemmed in by her household-bars,—
Chase her about the coop of daily life,
Having first stopped each outlet thence save one
Which, like bird with a ferret in her haunt,
She needs must seize as sole way of escape
Though there was tied and twittering a decoy
To seem as if it tempted,—just the plume
O' the popinjay, not a real respite there
From tooth and claw of something in the dark,—
Giuseppe Caponsacchi.
                                        Now begins
The tenebrific passage of the tale:
How hold a light, display the cavern's gorge?
How, in this phase of the affair, show truth?
Here is the dying wife who smiles and says
"So it was,—so it was not,—how it was,
I never knew nor ever care to know—"
Till they all weep, physician, man of law,

766| MS:answer:tell *P1868:*answer! Tell 768| MS:proof,— *P1868:*proof, 769| MS:upon one day! *P1868:*upon, one day!" 770| MS:in Rome,—back *P1872:*in Rome:back 771| MS:To Arezzo, go on with the *1888:*To Arezzo, follow up the 772| MS:foot *P1868:*foot, 773| MS:you know: *P1868:*you see! 774| MS:and thereupon § last two words crossed out and replaced above by § Accordingly 775| MS:worry her § crossed out and replaced above by two words § up and <> around *P1868:*around, 776| MS:household bars, *P1868:*household-bars,— 777| MS:Chased her <> life *P1868:*life, *P1872:*Chase 779| MS:That, birdlike with *P1868:*Which, like bird with 780| MS:seize the sole *P1868:*seize as sole 781| MS:There, where was *P1868:*Though there was 783| MS:Of the popinjay—and not the respite *P1868:*not a respite *CP1868:*O' *1888:*a real respite 790| MS:how it was *P1868:*how it was, 792| MS:weep, doctor § crossed out and

Even that poor old bit of battered brass
Beaten out of all shape by the world's sins,
Common utensil of the lazar-house—
Confessor Celestino groans " 'Tis truth,
All truth and only truth: there's something here,
Some presence in the room beside us all,
Something that every lie expires before:
No question she was pure from first to last."
So far is well and helps us to believe:
But beyond, she the helpless, simple-sweet
Or silly-sooth, unskilled to break one blow
At her good fame by putting finger forth,—
How can she render service to the truth?
The bird says "So I fluttered where a springe
Caught me: the springe did not contrive itself,
That I know: who contrived it, God forgive!"
But we, who hear no voice and have dry eyes,
Must ask,—we cannot else, absolving her,—
How of the part played by that same decoy
I' the catching, caging? Was himself caught first?
We deal here with no innocent at least,
No witless victim,—he's a man of the age
And priest beside,—persuade the mocking world
Mere charity boiled over in this sort!
He whose own safety too,—(the Pope's apprised—
Good-natured with the secular offence,
The Pope looks grave on priesthood in a scrape)
Our priest's own safety therefore, may-be life,
Hangs on the issue! You will find it hard.

---

replaced above by § physician, man of law *P1868:*law, 794| MS:sins *P1868:* sins, 795| MS:The common <> Lazar-house *P1868:*Common <>lazar-house— 797| MS:something else, *1888:*something here, 798| MS:beside you all *P1868:* beside us all, 801| MS:well, and *P1868:*well and 802| MS:beyond. she is helpless *P1868:*beyond, she the helpless 804-6| MS:On her <> forth./ The *P1868:*At her <> forth,—/ How can she render service to the truth?/ The 810| MS:ask, cannot but ask, absolving her, *P1868:*ask,—we cannot else, absolving her,— 812| MS:In *P1868:*I' 814| MS:the world § crossed out and replaced above by § age 815| MS:And a priest *1888:*And priest 816| MS:this wise— *P1868:*this sort! 817-21| MS:He, whose <> too,—priests § crossed out and replaced above by parenthesis and two words § (The Pope's apprised)/ Hangs <> issue! He will *P1868:*apprised—/ Good-natured with the secular offence,/ The Pope

Guido is here to meet you with fixed foot,
Stiff like a statue—"Leave what went before!
My wife fled i' the company of a priest,
Spent two days and two nights alone with him:
Leave what came after!" He stands hard to throw.
Moreover priests are merely flesh and blood;
When we get weakness, and no guilt beside,
'Tis no such great ill-fortune: finding grey,
We gladly call that white which might be black,
Too used to the double-dye. So, if the priest
Moved by Pompilia's youth and beauty, gave
Way to the natural weakness. . . . Anyhow
Here be facts, charactery; what they spell
Determine, and thence pick what sense you may!

There was a certain young bold handsome priest
Popular in the city, far and wide
Famed, since Arezzo's but a little place,
As the best of good companions, gay and grave
At the decent minute; settled in his stall,
Or sidling, lute on lap, by lady's couch,
Ever the courtly Canon; see in him
A proper star to climb and culminate,
Have its due handbreadth of the heaven at Rome,

---

looks grave on priesthood in a scrape)/ Our priest's own safety therefore, maybe life,/ Hangs < > issue! You will *CP1868:///* < > may-be 822| MS:meet him with *P1868:*meet you with 823| MS:Stands like < > before,— *P1868:*Stiff like < > before! 824| MS:in *P1868:*i' 826| MS:after." He is hard to throw. *P1868:*after!" He *1888:*after!" He stands hard 827| MS:Moreover men are < > blood, *P1868:*Moreover priests are < > blood; 828| MS:weakness and < > beside *P1868:*weakness, and < > beside, 829| MS:We have no such ill fortune < > grey *P1868:*such great ill-fortune *CP1868:*grey, *1888:*'Tis no
831-34| MS:double-dye. Here anyhow/ Are the facts, the charactery *P1868:*double-dye. So, if the priest/ Moved by Pompilia's youth and beauty, gave/ Way to the natural weakness . . . . . Anyhow/ Here be facts, charactery *1888:*weakness . . . . Anyhow
835| MS:Determine and < > may. *P1868:*Determine, and < > may!
835-36| MS:§ ¶ § *P1868:*§ no ¶; paragraph restored; see Editorial Notes §
836| MS:young and handsome *P1868:*young bold handsome 838| MS:Famed, since § *for* written above *since* § Arezzo's *P1868:*Famed, for Arezzo's *1888:*Famed, since Arezzo's 841| *P1868:*sideling *1888:*sidling 842| MS:courtly Canon: see in such *1888:*courtly Canon; see in him 843| MS:A star shall climb apace and *1888:*A proper star to climb and 844| MS:at Rome *P1868:*at Rome,

Though meanwhile pausing on Arezzo's edge,
As modest candle does 'mid mountain fog,
To rub off redness and rusticity
Ere it sweep chastened, gain the silver-sphere!
Whether through Guido's absence or what else,
This Caponsacchi, favourite of the town,
Was yet no friend of his nor free o' the house,
Though both moved in the regular magnates' march:
Each must observe the other's tread and halt
At church, saloon, theatre, house of play.
Who could help noticing the husband's slouch,
The black of his brow—or miss the news that buzzed
Of how the little solitary wife
Wept and looked out of window all day long?
What need of minute search into such springs
As start men, set o' the move?—machinery
Old as earth, obvious as the noonday sun.
Why, take men as they come,—an instance now,—
Of all those who have simply gone to see
Pompilia on her deathbed since four days,
Half at the least are, call it how you please,
In love with her—I don't except the priests
Nor even the old confessor whose eyes run
Over at what he styles his sister's voice
Who died so early and weaned him from the world.
Well, had they viewed her ere the paleness pushed
The last o' the red o' the rose away, while yet
Some hand, adventurous 'twixt the wind and her,
Might let shy life run back and raise the flower

845| MS:edge *P1868:*edge, 846| MS:modest taper § crossed out and replaced above by § candle mid the mountain-fog *P1868:*'mid the mountain fog, *1888:*candle does 'mid mountain 847| MS:rusticity, *P1868:*rusticity 848| MS:Ere, gold thence § last two words crossed out and replaced above by two words § it sweep chastened, it § crossed out § to the silver-sphere *P1868:*chastened, gain the silver-sphere. *P1872:*silver-sphere! 849| MS:else *P1868:*else, 850| MS:favorite *P1868:*favourite 851| MS:free of *P1868:*free o' 852| MS:magnate's march— *P1868:*magnates' *P1872:*magnates' march: 860| MS:of *P1868:*o' 861| MS:sun? *P1868:*sun. 867| MS:old Confessor *P1868:*old confessor 869| MS:world; *CP1868:*world. 871| MS:of the red of *P1868:*o' the red o' 872| MS:Some sort of screen was § last four words crossed out and replaced above by two words § hand, adventurous 'twixt <> her *P1868:*her, 873| MS:To Might § above *To* §

Rich with reward up to the guardian's face,—
Would they have kept that hand employed all day
At fumbling on with prayer-book pages? No!
Men are men: why then need I say one word
More than that our mere man the Canon here
Saw, pitied, loved Pompilia?

                                        This is why;
This startling why: that Caponsacchi's self—
Whom foes and friends alike avouch, for good
Or ill, a man of truth whate'er betide,
Intrepid altogether, reckless too
How his own fame and fortune, tossed to the winds,
Suffer by any turn the adventure take,
Nay, more—not thrusting, like a badge to hide,
'Twixt shirt and skin a joy which shown is shame—
But flirting flag-like i' the face o' the world
This tell-tale kerchief, this conspicuous love
For the lady,—oh, called innocent love, I know!
Only, such scarlet fiery innocence
As most folk would try muffle up in shade,—
—'Tis strange then that this else abashless mouth
Should yet maintain, for truth's sake which is God's,
That it was not he made the first advance,
That, even ere word had passed between the two,
Pompilia penned him letters, passionate prayers,
If not love, then so simulating love
That he, no novice to the taste of thyme,
Turned from such over-luscious honey-clot

---

let the life *P1868:*Might let *1888:*let shy life 874| MS:reward up § inserted above § to the first § crossed out § 875| MS:employed the same *1888:*employed all day 878| MS:than this that our man *P1868:*this, that *1888:*than that our mere man 879| MS:loved Pompilia? § no ¶ § This is why— *P1868:*loved Pompilia? § ¶ § This is why; 880| MS:why, that <> self *CP1868:*why: that <> self— 882| MS:man to speak the truth *P1868:*man of truth 885| MS:Suffer whatever turn *P1868:*Suffer by any turn 886| MS:thrusting like a pledge to hide *P1868:*thrusting, like a badge to hide, 888| MS:flaglike in <> of *P1868:*flag-like i' <> o' 890| MS:know, *P1868*know! 891| MS:Only such *CP1868:*Only, such 892| MS:most men would *1888:*most folk would 896| MS:Than, even ere word passed *P1868:*That, even ere word had passed 899| MS:of the thyme *P1868:*of thyme, 900| MS:from the over-luscious

At end o' the flower, and would not lend his lip
Till . . . but the tale here frankly outsoars faith:
There must be falsehood somewhere. For her part,
Pompilia quietly constantly avers
She never penned a letter in her life
Nor to the Canon nor any other man,
Being incompetent to write and read:
Nor had she ever uttered word to him, nor he
To her till that same evening when they met,
She on her window-terrace, he beneath
I' the public street, as was their fateful chance,
And she adjured him in the name of God
To find out, bring to pass where, when and how
Escape with him to Rome might be contrived.
Means were found, plan laid, time fixed, she avers,
And heart assured to heart in loyalty,
All at an impulse! All extemporized
As in romance-books! Is that credible?
Well, yes: as she avers this with calm mouth
Dying, I do think "Credible!" you'd cry—
Did not the priest's voice come to break the spell.
They questioned him apart, as the custom is,
When first the matter made a noise at Rome,
And he, calm, constant then as she is now,
For truth's sake did assert and re-assert
Those letters called him to her and he came,
—Which damns the story credible otherwise.
Why should this man,—mad to devote himself,
Careless what comes of his own fame, the first,—

---

*P1868:*from such over-luscious 901| MS:of *P1868:*o' 902| MS:Till . . but *1888:*Till . . . but 903| MS:somewhere:for her part *P1868:*somewhere. For her part, 904| MS:Pompilia, quietly, constantly *P1868:*Pompilia quietly constantly 907| MS:write or read: *P1868:*write and read: 909| MS:met *P1868:*met, 911| MS:In <> street as *P1868:*I' *CP1868:*street, as 913| MS:Find out and bring *1888:*To find out, bring 914| MS:Escape with him § last two words inserted above § to <> be for her. *P1868:*be contrived. 915| MS:Means found <> laid, and time *P1868:*laid and *1888:*Means were found <> laid, time 921| MS:spell: *P1872:*spell. 922| MS:apart as *P1868:*apart, as 925| MS:reassert *1888:*re-assert 927| MS:Which *P1868:*—Which 928| MS:man mad <> himself,— *P1868:*man,—mad <> himself, 929| MS:comes to own fame the *P1868:*comes of his own *CP1868:*fame, the

Be studious thus to publish and declare
Just what the lightest nature loves to hide,
So screening lady from the byword's laugh
"First spoke the lady, last the cavalier!"
—I say,—why should the man tell truth just now
When graceful lying meets such ready shrift?
Or is there a first moment for a priest
As for a woman, when invaded shame
Must have its first and last excuse to show?
Do both contrive love's entry in the mind
Shall look, i' the manner of it, a surprise,—
That after, once the flag o' the fort hauled down,
Effrontery may sink drawbridge, open gate,
Welcome and entertain the conqueror?
Or what do you say to a touch of the devil's worst?
Can it be that the husband, he who wrote
The letter to his brother I told you of,
I' the name of her it meant to criminate,—
What if he wrote those letters to the priest?
Further the priest says, when it first befell,
This folly o' the letters, that he checked the flow,
Put them back lightly each with its reply.
Here again vexes new discrepancy:
There never reached her eye a word from him:
He did write but she could not read—could just
Burn the offence to wifehood, womanhood,

930| MS:and proclaim *P1868:*and declare 932| MS:Save a poor lady *P1868:*Nor screen a lady *1888:*So screening lady 933| MS:cavalier." *P1868:*cavalier!" 934| MS:just here *1888:*just now 935| MS:Where graceful *P1868:*When graceful 938| MS:show, *P1868:*show? 940| MS:in < > surprize, *P1868:*i' < > surprise, *1888:*surprise,— 941| MS:And after < > of *P1868:*That after < > o' 943| MS:the victor then? *P1868:*the conqueror? 944| MS:the Devil's *P1868:*the devil's 945| MS:the Husband *P1868:*the husband 946| MS:of *P1868:*of, 947| MS:In *P1868:*I' 948| MS:the Priest? *P1868:*the priest? 949| MS:The Priest < > befell *P1868:*The priest < > befell, 950| MS:of the letters, he checked *P1868:*o' the letters, that he 952| MS:again is a new *P1868:*again vexes new 953| MS:him, *P1868:*him; *1888:*him: 954| MS:read—she could *1888:*read—could just 955| MS:Burn what offended wifehood *P1872:*Burn the

So did burn: never bade him come to her,
Yet when it proved he must come, let him come,
And when he did come though uncalled,—why, spoke
Prompt by an inspiration: thus it chanced.
Will you go somewhat back to understand?

When first, pursuant to his plan, there sprang,
Like an uncaged beast, Guido's cruelty
On soul and body of his wife, she cried
To those whom law appoints resource for such,
The secular guardian,—that's the Governor,
And the Archbishop,—that's the spiritual guide,
And prayed them take the claws from out her flesh.
Now, this is ever the ill consequence
Of being noble, poor and difficult,
Ungainly, yet too great to disregard,—
This—that born peers and friends hereditary,—
Though disinclined to help from their own store
The opprobrious wight, put penny in his poke
From private purse or leave the door ajar
When he goes wistful by at dinner-time,—
Yet, if his needs conduct him where they sit
Smugly in office, judge this, bishop that,
Dispensers of the shine and shade o' the place—
And if, friend's door shut and friend's purse undrawn,

---

offence to wifehood 957-60| MS:And did <> her/ Yet when he did come all-uncalled she spoke/ <> it was./ Will *P1868:*So did <> her,/ Yet when it proved he must come, let him come,/ And when he did come though uncalled, she spoke// Will *1888:*/ <> uncalled, —why, spoke/ <> it chanced. 961| MS:sprung *P1868:*sprung, *P1872:*sprang, 962| MS:beast Guido's *P1868:*beast, Guido's 963| MS:On the weak shoulders of <> she fled *P1868:*she cried *1888:*On soul and body of 965-66| MS:§ one line altered to make two § guardian § *and* crossed out and replaced above by § —that's the Governor/ And the Archbishop,—that's *P1868:*the Governor, *1888:*guardian,—that's 968| MS:this was § crossed out and replaced above by § is 969| MS:When you are noble *P1868:*Of being noble 970| MS:disregard, *P1868:*disregard,— 971| MS:That your born <> hereditary *P1868:*That the born *1888:*This—that born <> hereditary,— 972| MS:to § followed by illegible word replaced above by § help 973| MS:opprobrious man, put *P1868:*opprobrious wight, put 974| MS:From purse of theirs or *1888:*From private purse or 978| MS:shade of *P1868:*shade o' 979| MS:if, the friend's <> and purse *1888:*if, friend's <> and friend's

Still potentates may find the office-seat
Do as good service at no cost—give help
By-the-bye, pay up traditional dues at once
Just through a feather-weight too much i' the scale,
Or finger-tip forgot at the balance-tongue,—
Why, only churls refuse, or Molinists.
Thus when, in the first roughness of surprise
At Guido's wolf-face whence the sheepskin fell,
The frightened couple, all bewilderment,
Rushed to the Governor,—who else rights wrong?
Told him their tale of wrong and craved redress—
Why, then the Governor woke up to the fact
That Guido was a friend of old, poor Count!—
So, promptly paid his tribute, promised the pair,
Wholesome chastisement should soon cure their qualms
Next time they came, wept, prated and told lies:
So stopped all prating, sent them dumb to Rome.
Well, now it was Pompilia's turn to try:
The troubles pressing on her, as I said,
Three times she rushed, maddened by misery,
To the other mighty man, sobbed out her prayer
At footstool of the Archbishop—fast the friend
Of her husband also! Oh, good friends of yore!
So, the Archbishop, not to be outdone
By the Governor, break custom more than he,
Thrice bade the foolish woman stop her tongue,
Unloosed her hands from harassing his gout,

---

purse 980| MS:The officer may <> office-hall *P1868:*The potentate may *1888:*Still potentates may <> office-seat 982| MS:By the bye, pay just as well traditional dues *P1868:*By-the-bye, pay up traditional dues at once
983-86| MS:By a feather weight in the scale, a finger-tip/ At the balance tongue,—why, only churls refuse./ Thus, when *P1868:*Just through a feather-weight too much i' the scale,/ A finger-tip forgot at the balance-tongue,—/ Why only churls refuse, or Molinists./ Thus when *1888/* Or finger-tip 987| MS:when *P1868:*whence
992| MS:old, had claims *P1868:*old, poor Count!— 993| MS:So promptly <> tribute—promised the pair *P1868:*tribute, promised the pair, *CP1868:*So, promptly
994| MS:should try cure *P1868:*should soon cure 995| MS:came and prated *1888:*came, wept, prated 996| MS:Which stopped *1888:*So stopped
997| MS:try *P1868:*try: 998| MS:say, *P1868:*said, 1000| MS:other potentate, sobbed *P1868:*other mighty man, sobbed 1001| MS:At foot of *P1868:* At footstool of 1002| MS:yore— *P1868:*yore! 1006| MS:his feet, *P1868:*his

Coached her and carried her to the Count again,
—His old friend should be master in his house,
Rule his wife and correct her faults at need!
Well, driven from post to pillar in this wise,
She, as a last resource, betook herself
To one, should be no family-friend at least,
A simple friar o' the city; confessed to him,
Then told how fierce temptation of release
By self-dealt death was busy with her soul,
And urged that he put this in words, write plain
For one who could not write, set down her prayer
That Pietro and Violante, parent-like
If somehow not her parents, should for love
Come save her, pluck from out the flame the brand
Themselves had thoughtlessly thrust in so deep
To send gay-coloured sparkles up and cheer
Their seat at the chimney-corner. The good friar
Promised as much at the moment; but, alack,
Night brings discretion: he was no one's friend,
Yet presently found he could not turn about
Nor take a step i' the case and fail to tread
On someone's toe who either was a friend,
Or a friend's friend, or friend's friend thrice-removed,
And woe to friar by whom offences come!
So, the course being plain,—with a general sigh
At matrimony the profound mistake,—
He threw reluctantly the business up,
Having his other penitents to mind.

If then, all outlets thus secured save one,
At last she took to the open, stood and stared

gout, 1008| MS:house *P1868:*house, 1009| MS:need. *P1868:*need! 1013| MS:simple priest of the city, confessed *P1868:*simple friar o' the city; confessed 1019| MS:for old love's sake *P1868:*for love 1020| MS:pluck the brand from out the flame *P1868:*pluck from out the flame the brand 1021| MS:in deep there *P1868:*in so deep 1023| MS:good priest *P1868:*good friar 1024| MS:much in the moment, but *P1868:*much at the moment; but 1026| MS:But presently *P1868:*Yet presently 1027| MS:in *P1868:*i' 1029| MS:friend, or his friend *P1868:*friend, or friend's friend 1030| MS:to him by *P1868:*to friar by 1031| MS:plain, with *P1868:*plain,—with 1034-35| MS:§ no ¶ § *P1868:*§ ¶ §

With her wan face to see where God might wait—
And there found Caponsacchi wait as well
For the precious something at perdition's edge,
He only was predestinate to save,—
And if they recognized in a critical flash
From the zenith, each the other, her need of him,
His need of . . . say, a woman to perish for,
The regular way o' the world, yet break no vow,
Do no harm save to himself,—if this were thus?
How do you say? It were improbable;
So is the legend of my patron-saint.

Anyhow, whether, as Guido states the case,
Pompilia,—like a starving wretch i' the street
Who stops and rifles the first passenger
In the great right of an excessive wrong,—
Did somehow call this stranger and he came,—
Or whether the strange sudden interview
Blazed as when star and star must needs go close
Till each hurts each and there is loss in heaven—
Whatever way in this strange world it was,—
Pompilia and Caponsacchi met, in fine,
She at her window, he i' the street beneath,
And understood each other at first look.

All was determined and performed at once.
And on a certain April evening, late
I' the month, this girl of sixteen, bride and wife
Three years and over,—she who hitherto
Had never taken twenty steps in Rome
Beyond the church, pinned to her mother's gown,
Nor, in Arezzo, knew her way through street
Except what led to the Archbishop's door,—

1038| MS:waiting *P1868:*wait 1039| MS:edge *P1868:*edge, 1040| MS:He, only, was *P1868:*He only was 1043| MS:of . . say <> for *P1868:*for, *1888:*of . . . say 1044| MS:of <> vow *P1868:*o' <> vow, 1045| MS:thus, *P1868:*thus? 1047-48| MS:§ no ¶ § *P1868:*§ ¶ § 1048| MS:Anyhow—whether,—as <> case *P1868:*whether, as <> case, *CP1868:*Anyhow, whether 1049| MS:in *P1868:*i' 1056| MS:was *P1868:*was,— 1058| MS:in *P1868:*i' 1059-60| MS:§ no ¶ § *P1868:*§ ¶ § 1062| MS:In *P1868:*I' 1065| MS:church and in her <> hand *P1868:*church, pinned to her <> gown, 1067| MS:door,

Such an one rose up in the dark, laid hand
On what came first, clothes and a trinket or two,
Belongings of her own in the old day,—
Stole from the side o' the sleeping spouse—who knows?
Sleeping perhaps, silent for certain,—slid
Ghost-like from great dark room to great dark room
In through the tapestries and out again
And onward, unembarrassed as a fate,
Descended staircase, gained last door of all,
Sent it wide open at first push of palm,
And there stood, first time, last and only time,
At liberty, alone in the open street,—
Unquestioned, unmolested found herself
At the city gate, by Caponsacchi's side,
Hope there, joy there, life and all good again,
The carriage there, the convoy there, light there
Broadening ever into blaze at Rome
And breaking small what long miles lay between;
Up she sprang, in he followed, they were safe.

The husband quotes this for incredible,
All of the story from first word to last:
Sees the priest's hand throughout upholding hers,
Traces his foot to the alcove, that night,
Whither and whence blindfold he knew the way,
Proficient in all craft and stealthiness;
And cites for proof a servant, eye that watched
And ear that opened to purse secrets up,
A woman-spy,—suborned to give and take
Letters and tokens, do the work of shame
The more adroitly that herself, who helped
Communion thus between a tainted pair,

---

*P1868:*door,— 1071| MS:of *P1868:*o' 1073| MS:great dark room, *1888:*to great dark room 1074| MS:the arrassed doors and *P1868:*the tapestries and 1075| MS:unembarassed *P1868:*unembarrassed 1076| MS:all *P1868:*all, 1077| MS:palm *P1868:*palm, 1078| MS:time last *P1868:*time, last 1081| MS:side *P1868:*side, 1084| MS:Broadening into a full blaze *1888:*Broadening ever into blaze 1086-87| MS:§ no ¶ § *P1868:*§ ¶ § 1087| MS:incredible *P1868:*incredible, 1090| MS:alcove that night *P1868:*alcove, that night, 1091| MS:way *P1868:*way, 1097| MS:herself who *P1868:*herself, who 1098| MS:a leprous pair *P1868:*a tainted pair,

Had long since been a leper thick in spot,
A common trull o' the town: she witnessed all,
Helped many meetings, partings, took her wage
And then told Guido the whole matter. Lies!
The woman's life confutes her word,—her word
Confutes itself: "Thus, thus and thus I lied."
"And thus, no question, still you lie," we say.

"Ay, but at last, e'en have it how you will,
Whatever the means, whatever the way, explodes
The consummation"—the accusers shriek:
"Here is the wife avowedly found in flight,
And the companion of her flight, a priest;
She flies her husband, he the church his spouse:
What is this?"

Wife and priest alike reply
"This is the simple thing it claims to be,
A course we took for life and honour's sake,
Very strange, very justifiable."
She says, "God put it in my head to fly,
As when the martin migrates: autumn claps
Her hands, cries 'Winter's coming, will be here,
Off with you ere the white teeth overtake!
Flee!' So I fled: this friend was the warm day,
The south wind and whatever favours flight;
I took the favour, had the help, how else?
And so we did fly rapidly all night,
All day, all night—a longer night—again,
And then another day, longest of days,

1100| MS:of *P1868:*o' 1101| MS:The many *P1868:*Helped many 1104| MS:Confutes herself § *her* crossed out and replaced above by *it* § <> lied" *P1868:*lied." 1105-6| MS:§ no ¶ § And very like thus still <> / Pompilia's word which sweeps her off in st § unfinished; entire line crossed out § / "Ay *P1868:*"And thus, no question, still § new ¶ § 1107| MS:means, however the *P1868:*means, whatever the 1108| MS:shriek *P1868:*shriek: 1109| MS:flight *P1868:*flight. *1868:*flight, 1110| MS:flight a priest, *P1868:*flight, a priest; 1111| MS:spouse, *P1868:*spouse: 1112| MS:this?" § no ¶ § Wife *P1868:*this?" § ¶ § Wife 1114| MS:honor's *P1868:*honour's 1116| MS:says "God <> fly *P1868:*says, "God <> fly, 1120| MS:day *P1868:*day, 1121| MS:wind, and <> flight *P1868:*wind and *CP1868:*flight; 1124| MS:again *P1868:*again,

And all the while, whether we fled or stopped,
I scarce know how or why, one thought filled both,
'Fly and arrive!' So long as I found strength
I talked with my companion, told him much,
Knowing that he knew more, knew me, knew God
And God's disposal of me,—but the sense
O' the blessed flight absorbed me in the main,
And speech became mere talking through a sleep,
Till at the end of that last longest night
In a red daybreak, when we reached an inn
And my companion whispered 'Next stage—Rome!'
Sudden the weak flesh fell like piled-up cards,
All the frail fabric at a finger's touch,
And prostrate the poor soul too, and I said
'But though Count Guido were a furlong off,
Just on me, I must stop and rest awhile!'
Then something like a huge white wave o' the sea
Broke o'er my brain and buried me in sleep
Blessedly, till it ebbed and left me loose,
And where was I found but on a strange bed
In a strange room like hell, roaring with noise,
Ruddy with flame, and filled with men, in front
Who but the man you call my husband? ay—
Count Guido once more between heaven and me,
For there my heaven stood, my salvation, yes—
That Caponsacchi all my heaven of help,
Helpless himself, held prisoner in the hands
Of men who looked up in my husband's face
To take the fate thence he should signify,
Just as the way was at Arezzo. Then,
Not for my sake but his who had helped me—

1126| MS:stopped *P1868:*stopped, 1129| MS:much *P1868:*much, 1132| MS:Of < > main *P1868:*O' < > main, 1133| MS:sleep *P1868:*sleep, 1141| MS:awhile.' *P1868:*awhile!' 1142| MS:a white wave of *P1868:*o' *1888:*a huge white 1144| MS:Blessedly till < > loose *P1868:*Blessedly, till < > loose, 1146| MS:noise *P1868:*noise, 1148| MS:Whom but < > husband, ay *P1868:*ay— *1888:*Who but < > husband? ay— 1149| MS:between God § crossed out and replaced above by § heaven 1150| MS:yes *P1868:*yes— 1151| MS:help *P1868:*help, 1154| MS:signify *P1868:*signify, 1155| MS:at

I sprang up, reached him with one bound, and seized
The sword o' the felon, trembling at his side,
Fit creature of a coward, unsheathed the thing
And would have pinned him through the poison-bag
To the wall and left him there to palpitate,
As you serve scorpions, but men interposed—
Disarmed me, gave his life to him again
That he might take mine and the other lives,
And he has done so. I submit myself!"
The priest says—oh, and in the main result
The facts asseverate, he truly says,
As to the very act and deed of him,
However you mistrust the mind o' the man—
The flight was just for flight's sake, no pretext
For aught except to set Pompilia free.
He says "I cite the husband's self's worst charge
In proof of my best word for both of us.
Be it conceded that so many times
We took our pleasure in his palace: then,
What need to fly at all?—or flying no less,
What need to outrage the lips sick and white
Of a woman, and bring ruin down beside,
By halting when Rome lay one stage beyond?"
So does he vindicate Pompilia's fame,
Confirm her story in all points but one—
This; that, so fleeing and so breathing forth
Her last strength in the prayer to halt awhile,
She makes confusion of the reddening white
Which was the sunset when her strength gave way,

Arezzo: then *P1868:*at Arezzo. Then, 1158| MS:of the felon trembling <> side *P1868:*o' the felon, trembling <> side, 1161| MS:palpitate *P1868:*palpitate, 1165| MS:so. I appeal to God!" *P1868:*so. I submit myself!" 1167| MS:asseverate he <> says— *P1868:*asseverate, he <> says, 1168| MS:him *P1868:*him, 1169| MS:of *P1868:*o' 1171| MS:except a flight to <> free: *P1868:*except to *P1872:*free. 1172| MS:the Husband's *P1868:*the husband's 1173| MS:for her and me: *P1868:*for both of us. 1176| MS:No need <> all,—or *P1868:*What need <> all?—or 1177| MS:No need *P1868:*What need 1178| MS:Of the women <> beside *P1868:*Of a woman <> beside, 1179| MS:when Rome was one <> beyond." *P1868:*when Rome lay one <> beyond?" 1180| MS:fame *P1868:*fame, 1181| MS:one *P1868:*one— 1182| MS:that so fleeing, and

And the next sunrise and its whitening red
Which she revived in when her husband came:
She mixes both times, morn and eve, in one,
Having lived through a blank of night 'twixt each
Though dead-asleep, unaware as a corpse,
She on the bed above; her friend below
Watched in the doorway of the inn the while,
Stood i' the red o' the morn, that she mistakes,
In act to rouse and quicken the tardy crew
And hurry out the horses, have the stage
Over, the last league, reach Rome and be safe:
When up came Guido.
                                        Guido's tale begins—
How he and his whole household, drunk to death
By some enchanted potion, poppied drugs
Plied by the wife, lay powerless in gross sleep
And left the spoilers unimpeded way,
Could not shake off their poison and pursue,
Till noontide, then made shift to get on horse
And did pursue: which means he took his time,
Pressed on no more than lingered after, step
By step, just making sure o' the fugitives,
Till at the nick of time, he saw his chance,
Seized it, came up with and surprised the pair.
How he must needs have gnawn lip and gnashed teeth,
Taking successively at tower and town,
Village and roadside, still the same report
"Yes, such a pair arrived an hour ago,

---

*P1868:*that, so fleeing and 1186| MS:sunrise terrible and red *P1868:*sunrise and its whitening red 1187| MS:came *P1868:*came: 1190| MS:dead asleep <> corpse *P1868:*dead-asleep <> corpse, 1191| MS:above, while he below *P1868:*above; her friend below 1192| MS:of the Inn, just where *P1868:*of the inn the while, 1193| MS:In that same red of the morn that she describes *P1868:*Stood i' the red o' the morn, that she mistakes, 1194| MS:to quicken and rouse § indication that *quicken* and *rouse* are to be reversed § 1196| MS:safe, *P1868:*safe: 1197| MS:came Guido,—Guido whose tale begins *P1868:*came Guido. § ¶ § Guido's tale begins— 1201| MS:left her wickedness unimpeded *P1868:*left the spoilers unimpeded 1202| MS:off the poison and pursue *P1868:*off their poison and pursue, 1204| MS:means, he <> time *P1868:*time, *P1872:*means he 1206| MS:of *P1868:*o' 1207| MS:chance *P1868:*chance, 1209| MS:have cursed and gnashed his teeth *P1868:*have gnawn lip and gnashed teeth, 1210| MS:town *P1868:*town, 1211| MS:roadside inn

Sat in the carriage just where now you stand,
While we got horses ready,—turned deaf ear
To all entreaty they would even alight;
Counted the minutes and resumed their course."
Would they indeed escape, arrive at Rome,
Leave no least loop-hole to let murder through,
But foil him of his captured infamy,
Prize of guilt proved and perfect? So it seemed.
Till, oh the happy chance, at last stage, Rome
But two short hours off, Castelnuovo reached,
The guardian angel gave reluctant place,
Satan stepped forward with alacrity,
Pompilia's flesh and blood succumbed, perforce
A halt was, and her husband had his will.
Perdue he couched, counted out hour by hour
Till he should spy in the east a signal-streak—
Night had been, morrow was, triumph would be.
Do you see the plan deliciously complete?
The rush upon the unsuspecting sleep,
The easy execution, the outcry
Over the deed "Take notice all the world!
These two dead bodies, locked still in embrace,—
The man is Caponsacchi and a priest,
The woman is my wife: they fled me late,
Thus have I found and you behold them thus,
And may judge me: do you approve or no?"

Success did seem not so improbable,
But that already Satan's laugh was heard,
His black back turned on Guido—left i' the lurch

---

still one report *P1868:*roadside, still the same report 1213| MS:Sate < > where your horse stands, *P1868:*Sat *1888:*where now you stand, 1214| MS:ready, —tarry, troth? § last two words crossed out and replaced by three words § turned deaf ear 1217| MS:indeed at § crossed out § < > Rome *P1868:*Rome, 1218| MS:Leaving no loop to let damnation through, *P1868:*Leave no least loop *1888:*least loop-hole to let murder through, 1219| MS:So foil < > infamy *P1868:*And foil < > infamy, *1888:*But foil. 1220| MS:seemed: *1888:*seemed. 1222| MS:off, Castelnuovo's inn *P1868:*off, Castelnuovo reached, 1223| MS:place *P1868:*place, 1226| MS:The halt was, and the husband's § apostrophe and *s* crossed out § *P1868:*A halt was, and her husband 1228| MS:should see in the East a signal-streak *P1868:*should spy in the east a signal-streak— 1233| MS:notice, all *P1868:*notice all 1237| MS:found, and *P1868:*found and 1238-39| MS:§ no ¶ § *P1868:* § ¶ § 1241| MS:on Guido,—left in *P1868:*on Guido—left i'

Or rather, baulked of suit and service now,
Left to improve on both by one deed more,
Burn up the better at no distant day,
Body and soul one holocaust to hell.
Anyhow, of this natural consequence
Did just the last link of the long chain snap:
For an eruption was o' the priest, alive
And alert, calm, resolute and formidable,
Not the least look of fear in that broad brow—
One not to be disposed of by surprise,
And armed moreover—who had guessed as much?
Yes, there stood he in secular costume
Complete from head to heel, with sword at side,
He seemed to know the trick of perfectly.
There was no prompt suppression of the man
As he said calmly "I have saved your wife
From death; there was no other way but this;
Of what do I defraud you except death?
Charge any wrong beyond, I answer it."
Guido, the valorous, had met his match,
Was forced to demand help instead of fight,
Bid the authorities o' the place lend aid
And make the best of a broken matter so.
They soon obeyed the summons—I suppose,
Apprised and ready, or not far to seek—
Laid hands on Caponsacchi, found in fault,
A priest yet flagrantly accoutred thus,—
Then, to make good Count Guido's further charge,
Proceeded, prisoner made lead the way,

1242-44| MS:now,/ That he burn up at <> day *P1868:*That he improve on both by one deed more,/ Burn up the better at <> day, *1888:*/ Left to improve 1247| MS:Just the <> chain must snap *P1868:*Did just the <> chain snap: 1248| MS:For his irruption was on the priest *P1868:*For his eruption *CP1868:*o' *1888:*an eruption 1249| MS:resolute, formidable, *P1868:*resolute and formidable, 1250| MS:that bold brow— *P1868:*that broad brow— 1251| MS:surprize *P1868:*surprise, 1254| MS:side *P1868:*side, 1259| MS:you save her death? *P1868:*you except death? 1260| MS:wrong but this, I *P1868:*wrong beyond, I 1261| MS:match *P1868:*match, 1262| MS:to call instead of fight *P1868:*to demand help instead of fight, 1263| MS:of *P1868:*o' 1266| MS:apprized *1888:*apprised 1267| MS:found their way § last two words crossed out and replaced by § in fault *P1868:*fault, 1268| MS:In a crowd § last three words crossed out and replaced above by two words § A priest <> thus, *P1868:*thus,—

In a crowd, upstairs to the chamber-door
Where wax-white, dead asleep, deep beyond dream,
As the priest laid her, lay Pompilia yet.

And as he mounted step and step with the crowd
How I see Guido taking heart again!
He knew his wife so well and the way of her—
How at the outbreak she would shroud her shame
In hell's heart, would it mercifully yawn—
How, failing that, her forehead to his foot,
She would crouch silent till the great doom fell,
Leave him triumphant with the crowd to see
Guilt motionless or writhing like a worm!
No! Second misadventure, this worm turned,
I told you: would have slain him on the spot
With his own weapon, but they seized her hands:
Leaving her tongue free, as it tolled the knell
Of Guido's hope so lively late. The past
Took quite another shape now. She who shrieked
"At least and for ever I am mine and God's,
Thanks to his liberating angel Death—
Never again degraded to be yours
The ignoble noble, the unmanly man,
The beast below the beast in brutishness!"—
This was the froward child, "the restif lamb
Used to be cherished in his breast," he groaned—
"Eat from his hand and drink from out his cup,
The while his fingers pushed their loving way
Through curl on curl of that soft coat—alas,
And she all silverly baaed gratitude
While meditating mischief!"—and so forth.

1272| MS:dead-asleep *P1868:*dead asleep 1273-74| MS:§ no ¶ § *P1868:*§ ¶ § 1277| MS:How in the terror she *P1868:*How at the outbreak she 1278| MS:heart would *P1868:*heart, would 1280| MS:would lie silent *P1868:*would crouch silent 1281| MS:Show his charge just with all the < > see! *P1868:*Leave him triumphant with the *1888:*see 1282| MS:worm. *CP1868:*worm? *1888:*worm! 1283| MS:turned: *P1868:*turned, 1286| MS:free—as *P1868:*free, as 1287| MS:To Guido's < > late: the Past *P1868:*Of Guido's < > late. The past 1289| MS:least and forever < > God's *P1868:*for ever < > God's, 1290| MS:to His *P1868:*to his 1291| MS:your's *P1868:*yours 1293| MS:brutishness!" *P1868:*brutishness!"— 1298| MS:alas *P1868:*alas, 1300| MS:mischief—and

He must invent another story now!
The ins and outs o' the rooms were searched: he found
Or showed for found the abominable prize—
Love-letters from his wife who cannot write,
Love-letters in reply o' the priest—thank God!—
Who can write and confront his character
With this, and prove the false thing forged throughout:
Spitting whereat, he needs must spatter whom
But Guido's self?—that forged and falsified
One letter called Pompilia's, past dispute:
Then why not these to make sure still more sure?

So was the case concluded then and there:
Guido preferred his charges in due form,
Called on the law to adjudicate, consigned
The accused ones to the Prefect of the place,
(Oh mouse-birth of that mountain-like revenge!)
And so to his own place betook himself
After the spring that failed,—the wildcat's way.
The captured parties were conveyed to Rome;
Investigation followed here i' the court—
Soon to review the fruit of its own work,
From then to now being eight months and no more.
Guido kept out of sight and safe at home:
The Abate, brother Paolo, helped most
At words when deeds were out of question, pushed

---

*P1868:*mischief!"—and 1301| MS:One must *P1868:*He must
1302| MS:of the room, *P1868:*o' the rooms 1305| MS:of the paramour *P1868:*o' *CP1868:*the priest—thank God!— 1306| MS:and so § crossed out § confronts § *s* crossed out § the characters *P1868:*confront his character 1308| MS:who *P1872:*whom 1309| MS:self, who forged *CP1868:*self?—that forged
1310| MS:dispute— *CP1868:*dispute: 1313-14| MS:charge in all due form,/ Laid the facts down and bade the letters speak,/ Called *P1868:*charges in due form,/ Called
1315| MS:the prefect <> place. *P1868:*the Prefect *1888:*place,
1316| MS:mountainlike revenge) *P1868:*mountain-like revenge!) 1317| MS:so betook him to his place again *P1868:*so to his own place betook himself
1318| MS:wild cat's *P1868:*wildcat's 1319| MS:to Rome *P1868:*to Rome;
1320| MS:in the Court *P1868:*i' the court— 1321| MS:Which now reviews the <> work— *P1868:*Soon to review the <> work, 1322| MS:months, no *P1868:*months and no 1323| MS:home— *P1868:*home: 1325| MS:words, when <> question—pushed *P1868:*words when <> question, pushed

Nearest the purple, best played deputy,
So, pleaded, Guido's representative
At the court shall soon try Guido's self,—what's more,
The court that also took—I told you, Sir—
That statement of the couple, how a cheat
Had been i' the birth of the babe, no child of theirs.
That was the prelude; this, the play's first act:
Whereof we wait what comes, crown, close of all.

Well, the result was something of a shade
On the parties thus accused,—how otherwise?
Shade, but with shine as unmistakable.
Each had a prompt defence: Pompilia first—
"Earth was made hell to me who did no harm:
I only could emerge one way from hell
By catching at the one hand held me, so
I caught at it and thereby stepped to heaven:
If that be wrong, do with me what you will!"
Then Caponsacchi with a grave grand sweep
O' the arm as though his soul warned baseness off—
"If as a man, then much more as a priest
I hold me bound to help weak innocence:
If so my worldly reputation burst,
Being the bubble it is, why, burst it may:
Blame I can bear though not blameworthiness.
But use your sense first, see if the miscreant proved,
The man who tortured thus the woman, thus
Have not both laid the trap and fixed the lure
Over the pit should bury body and soul!

1326| MS:deputy. *P1868:*deputy, 1327| MS:So Guido went by representative *P1868:*So, pleaded, Guido's representative 1328| MS:To the Court *P1868:*At the court 1329| MS:The Court <> sir— *P1868:*The court <> Sir— 1331| MS:in <> theirs— *P1868:*i' <> theirs. 1332| MS:prelude: this <> act *P1868:*prelude; this <> act: 1333| MS:crown—close *P1868:*crown, close 1333-34| MS:§ no ¶ § *P1868:*§ ¶ § 1334| MS:Well the <> shade, *P1868:*Well, the <> shade 1336| MS:Shade—but *P1868:*Shade, but 1339| MS:from thence *P1868:*from hell 1340| MS:held to me *P1868:*held me, so 1341| MS:to Heaven: *P1868:*to heaven 1342| MS:that was wrong *P1868:*that be wrong 1344| MS:Of *P1868:*O' 1345| MS:"If § added in margin § As a man, therefore § crossed out and replaced above by § then *P1868:*"If as 1349| MS: blameworthiness, *P1868:*blameworthiness. 1350| MS:miscreant here 1888: miscreant proved, 1352| MS:not thus laid *P1868:*not both laid 1353| MS:

His facts are lies: his letters are the fact—
An infiltration flavoured with himself!
As for the fancies—whether . . . what is it you say?
The lady loves me, whether I love her
In the forbidden sense of your surmise,—
If, with the midday blaze of truth above,
The unlidded eye of God awake, aware,
You needs must pry about and trace the birth
Of each stray beam of light may traverse night
To the night's sun that's Lucifer himself,
Do so, at other time, in other place,
Not now nor here! Enough that first to last
I never touched her lip nor she my hand
Nor either of us thought a thought, much less
Spoke a word which the Virgin might not hear.
Be such your question, thus I answer it."

Then the court had to make its mind up, spoke.
"It is a thorny question, yea, a tale
Hard to believe, but not impossible:
Who can be absolute for either side?
A middle course is happily open yet.
Here has a blot surprised the social blank,—
Whether through favour, feebleness or fault,
No matter, leprosy has touched our robe
And we unclean must needs be purified.

---

the grave should *P1868:*the pit should 1354| MS:letters the one fact— *P1868:* letters are the fact— 1355| MS:with his soul! *P1868:*with himself! 1356| MS:whether . . what *1888:*whether . . . what 1358| MS:surmise, *P1868:* surmise,— 1359| MS:midday sun of *P1868:*midday blaze of 1360| MS:of God himself ablaze *P1868:*of God awake, aware, 1361| MS:and track the cause *P1868:*the course *1888:*and trace the birth 1362| MS:Of some stray < > light that crosses earth *P1868:*Of each stray < > light may traverse earth, *1888:*traverse night, DC,BrU:night *1889:*night 1363| MS:sun and Lucifer himself *P1868:*himself, *1888:*sun that's Lucifer 1364| MS:place *P1868:*place, 1365| MS:here: enough *P1868:*here! Enough 1367-68| MS:Nor either of us, thought a thought, much less § last eight words inserted above § spoke a word that the *P1868:*us thought a < > / Spoke a word which the 1369| MS:That is your *P1868:*Be that your *1888:*Be such your 1369-70| MS:§ no ¶ § *P1868:*§ ¶ § *1888:*§ no ¶; paragraph restored; see Editorial Notes § 1370| MS:the Court < > spoke *P1868:*the court < > spoke. 1371| MS:question: here's a *P1868:*question, and a *1888:*question, yea, a 1372| MS:believe but *P1868:*believe, but 1374| MS:yet: *P1868:*yet. 1378| MS:And we're unclean and must be *1888:*And we unclean must

Here is a wife makes holiday from home,
A priest caught playing truant to his church,
In masquerade moreover: both allege
Enough excuse to stop our lifted scourge
Which else would heavily fall. On the other hand,
Here is a husband, ay and man of mark,
Who comes complaining here, demands redress
As if he were the pattern of desert—
The while those plaguy allegations frown,
Forbid we grant him the redress he seeks.
To all men be our moderation known!
Rewarding none while compensating each,
Hurting all round though harming nobody,
Husband, wife, priest, scot-free not one shall 'scape,
Yet priest, wife, husband, boast the unbroken head
From application of our excellent oil:
So that, whatever be the fact, in fine,
We make no miss of justice in a sort.
First, let the husband stomach as he may,
His wife shall neither be returned him, no—
Nor branded, whipped and caged, but just consigned
To a convent and the quietude she craves;
So is he rid of his domestic plague:
What better thing can happen to a man?
Next, let the priest retire—unshent, unshamed,
Unpunished as for perpetrating crime,
But relegated (not imprisoned, Sirs!)
Sent for three years to clarify his youth

---

needs be 1379| MS:And wife that runs away from *P1868:*Here is a wife makes holiday from 1380| MS:priest that plays the truant <> church *P1868:*priest caught playing truant <> church, 1387| MS:Yet there those *P1868:*The while those 1388| MS:Forbid our granting him the grace he *P1868:*Forbid we grant him the redress he 1391| MS:round yet § crossed out and replaced above by § and harming *P1868:*round though harming 1392| MS:priest, not <> scape scot-free— *P1868:*priest, scot-free not <> 'scape, 1393| MS:Yet § in margin § Priest, wife, and § crossed out § husband, show unbroken heads *P1868:*Yet priest, wife, husband, boast the unbroken head 1394| MS:oil— *P1868:*oil: 1395| MS:fact at last, *P1868:*fact, in fine, 1396| MS:It shall not miss *P1868:*It makes no miss *1888:*We make 1400| MS:craves, *P1868:*cravse; § sic § *1872:*craves; 1401| MS:plague,— *P1868:*plague: 1404| MS:§ crowded

At Civita, a rest by the way to Rome:
There let his life skim off its last of lees
Nor keep this dubious colour. Judged the cause:
All parties may retire, content, we hope."
That's Rome's way, the traditional road of law;
Whither it leads is what remains to tell.

The priest went to his relegation-place,
The wife to her convent, brother Paolo
To the arms of brother Guido with the news
And this beside—his charge was countercharged;
The Comparini, his old brace of hates,
Were breathed and vigilant and venomous now—
Had shot a second bolt where the first stuck,
And followed up the pending dowry-suit
By a procedure should release the wife
From so much of the marriage-bond as barred
Escape when Guido turned the screw too much
On his wife's flesh and blood, as husband may.
No more defence, she turned and made attack,
Claimed now divorce from bed and board, in short:
Pleaded such subtle strokes of cruelty,
Such slow sure siege laid to her body and soul,
As, proved,—and proofs seemed coming thick and fast,—
Would gain both freedom and the dowry back
Even should the first suit leave them in his grasp:
So urged the Comparini for the wife.
Guido had gained not one of the good things

---

between lines 1403-5 § 1407| MS:to Rome, *P1868:*to Rome: 1408| MS:life shake off *P1868:*life skim off 1409| MS:cause, *P1868:*cause: 1410| MS:parties to their place, § last three words crossed out and replaced above by two words § may retire, content, we hope!" *P1868:*hope." 1412| MS:to see. *P1868:*to tell. 1413| MS:The Priest *P1868:*The priest 1414| MS:her reclusion, § crossed out and replaced above by two words § convent, and Brother *P1868:*convent, brother 1416| MS:countercharged— *P1868:*countercharged; 1419| . MS:stuck *P1868:*stuck, 1422| MS:marriage bond *P1868:*marriage-bond 1424-26| MS:husbands may./ She claimed divorce *P1868:*husband may./ No more defence, she turned and made attack,/ Claimed now divorce 1427| MS:cruelty *P1868:*cruelty, 1429| MS:As proved *P1868:*As, proved 1431| MS:grasp. *P1868:*grasp: 1432| MS:So by the Comparini urged the *P1868:*So urged the

He grasped at by his creditable plan
O' the flight and following and the rest: the suit
That smouldered late was fanned to fury new,
This adjunct came to help with fiercer fire,
While he had got himself a quite new plague—
Found the world's face an universal grin
At this last best of the Hundred Merry Tales
Of how a young and spritely clerk devised
To carry off a spouse that moped too much,
And cured her of the vapours in a trice:
And how the husband, playing Vulcan's part,
Told by the Sun, started in hot pursuit
To catch the lovers, and came halting up,
Cast his net and then called the Gods to see
The convicts in their rosy impudence—
Whereat said Mercury "Would that I were Mars!"
Oh it was rare, and naughty all the same!
Brief, the wife's courage and cunning,—the priest's show
Of chivalry and adroitness,—last not least,
The husband—how he ne'er showed teeth at all,
Whose bark had promised biting; but just sneaked
Back to his kennel, tail 'twixt legs, as 'twere,—
All this was hard to gulp down and digest.
So pays the devil his liegeman, brass for gold.

But this was at Arezzo: here in Rome
Brave Paolo bore up against it all—
Battled it out, nor wanting to himself

Comparini for the 1434| MS:by this creditable *P1868:*by his creditable 1435| MS:Of *P1868:*O' 1436| MS:new— *P1868:*new, 1437| MS:fire,— *P1868:*fire, 1438| MS:plague *P1868:*plague— 1440| MS:last, best *P1868:* last best 1442| MS:much *P1868:*much, 1445| MS:the Sun did start in *P1868:*the Sun, started in 1446| MS:and so came *P1868:*and came 1449| MS:Whereat Jove said he wished that he were Mars— *P1868:*Whereat said Mercury "Would that I were Mars!" 1450| MS:rare and *P1868:*rare, and 1451| MS:Brief,—the wife's <> and courag § sic; crossed out and replaced above by § cunning, the *P1868:*Brief, the wife's <> cunning,—the 1452| MS:least *CP1868:*least, 1453| MS:husband's § apostrophe and *s* crossed out § <> never <> all,— *P1868:*ne'er <> all, 1454| MS:biting,—but *P1868:*biting; but 1455| MS:betwixt <> 'twere— *P1868:*'twixt <> 'twere,— 1457-58| MS:§ ¶ § *P1868:*§ no ¶; paragraph restored; see Editorial Notes § 1458| MS:But that was *P1868:*But this was, 1460| MS:out, not wanting *P1868:*out, nor wanting

Nor Guido nor the House whose weight he bore
Pillar-like, by no force of arm but brain.
He knew his Rome, what wheels to set to work;
Plied influential folk, pressed to the ear
Of the efficacious purple, pushed his way
To the old Pope's self,—past decency indeed,—
Praying him take the matter in his hands
Out of the regular court's incompetence.
But times are changed and nephews out of date
And favouritism unfashionable: the Pope
Said "Render Cæsar what is Cæsar's due!"
As for the Comparini's counter-plea,
He met that by a counter-plea again,
Made Guido claim divorce—with help so far
By the trial's issue: for, why punishment
However slight unless for guiltiness
However slender?—and a molehill serves
Much as a mountain of offence this way.
So was he gathering strength on every side
And growing more and more to menace—when
All of a terrible moment came the blow
That beat down Paolo's fence, ended the play
O' the foil and brought mannaia on the stage.

Five months had passed now since Pompilia's flight,
Months spent in peace among the Convert nuns.

1462| MS:Pillar-like, not by force *1888:*Pillar-like, by no force 1463| MS:work, *P1868:*wheels we set to work; *1888:*wheels to set 1466| MS:the Pope's *P1868:*the old Pope's 1468| MS:incompetence— *P1868:*incompetence; *1872:*incompetence. 1469-72| MS:For times are changed, and <> date./ As <> counter-plea *P1868:*But times are changed and <> date/ And favouritism unfashionable: the Pope/ Said "Render Caesar what is Caesar's due!"/ As *CP1868:*/// <> counter-plea, 1473| MS:counter-plea to that, *P1868:*counter-plea again, 1474| MS:divorce with *P1868:*divorce—with 1475| MS:for why *P1868:*for, why 1477| MS:slender and the slenderest serves *P1868:*slender?—and a molehill serves 1480| MS:growing verily formidable—when *P1868:*growing more and more to menace—when 1481| MS:a sudden came the crowning blow *P1868:*a terrible moment came the blow 1482| MS:the man, *P1868:*the play 1483| MS:Making endeavour useless: thus it fell. *P1868:*O' the foil and brought Mannaia on the stage. *1888:*brought mannaia 1484| MS:flight; *P1868:*flight, 1485| MS:the Convertites: *P1868:*the Convert nuns *CP1868:*nuns: *1888:*nuns.

This,—being, as it seemed, for Guido's sake
Solely, what pride might call imprisonment
And quote as something gained, to friends at home,—
This naturally was at Guido's charge:
Grudge it he might, but penitential fare,
Prayers, preachings, who but he defrayed the cost?
So, Paolo dropped, as proxy, doit by doit
Like heart's blood, till—what's here? What notice comes?
The convent's self makes application bland
That, since Pompilia's health is fast o' the wane,
She may have leave to go combine her cure
Of soul with cure of body, mend her mind
Together with her thin arms and sunk eyes
That want fresh air outside the convent-wall,
Say in a friendly house,—and which so fit
As a certain villa in the Pauline way,
That happens to hold Pietro and his wife,
The natural guardians? "Oh, and shift the care
You shift the cost, too; Pietro pays in turn,
And lightens Guido of a load! And then,
Villa or convent, two names for one thing,
Always the sojourn means imprisonment,
Domus pro carcere—nowise we relax,
Nothing abate: how answers Paolo?"
You,
What would you answer? All so smooth and fair,

1486| MS:being as it was for *P1868:*being, as it seemed, for 1487| MS:imprisonment, *P1868:*imprisonment 1488| MS:gained to *P1868:*gained, to 1489| MS:charge— *P1868:*charge: 1490| MS:fare *P1868:*fare, 1491| MS:preachings—who *P1868:*preachings, who 1492| MS:So Paolo *P1868:*So, Paolo 1493| MS:blood, when—what's <> notice this? *P1868:*blood, till—what's <> notice comes? 1494| MS:The Convent's *1888:*The convent's 1495| MS:is on the wane *P1868:*is fast o' the wane, 1496| MS:to carry on her *P1868:*to go combine her 1499| MS:Which want <> convent wall *P1868:*That want <> convent-wall, 1500| MS:and whose so *P1868:*and which so 1501| MS:certain Villa <> way *P1868:*certain villa <> way, 1502| MS:wife *P1868:*wife, 1503| MS:guardians . . oh *P1868:* guardians? "Oh 1505| MS:load: and *P1868:*load! And 1506| MS:or Convent *P1868:*or convent 1508| MS:no wise we relax *P1868:Domum pro* <> nowise we relax, *1888:Domus* 1509| MS:answers Paolo? § no ¶ § You, *P1868:* answers Paolo?" § ¶ § You, 1510| MS:answer? All's so <> fair: *P1868:*answer?

Even Paul's astuteness sniffed no harm i' the world.
He authorized the transfer, saw it made
And, two months after, reaped the fruit of the same,
Having to sit down, rack his brain and find
What phrase should serve him best to notify
Our Guido that by happy providence
A son and heir, a babe was born to him
I' the villa,—go tell sympathizing friends!
Yes, such had been Pompilia's privilege:
She, when she fled, was one month gone with child,
Known to herself or unknown, either way
Availing to explain (say men of art)
The strange and passionate precipitance
Of maiden startled into motherhood
Which changes body and soul by nature's law.
So when the she-dove breeds, strange yearnings come
For the unknown shelter by undreamed-of shores,
And there is born a blood-pulse in her heart
To fight if needs be, though with flap of wing,
For the wool-flock or the fur-tuft, though a hawk
Contest the prize,—wherefore, she knows not yet.
Anyhow, thus to Guido came the news.
"I shall have quitted Rome ere you arrive
To take the one step left,"—wrote Paolo.
Then did the winch o' the winepress of all hate,
Vanity, disappointment, grudge and greed,
Take the last turn that screws out pure revenge
With a bright bubble at the brim beside—
By an heir's birth he was assured at once

All so <> fair, 1511| MS:in *P1868:*i' 1513| MS:of the deed, *P1868:*of the same, 1514| MS:brain to find *P1868:*brain and find 1515| MS:best and notify *P1868:*best to notify 1516| MS:To Guido *P1868:*Our Guido 1518| MS:In the Villa *P1868:*I' the villa 1522| MS:explain, say <> art, *P1868:* explain (say <> art) 1524| MS:Of the maiden <> motherhood, *P1868:*Of maiden <> motherhood 1525| MS:Who changes *P1868:*Which changes 1526| MS:breeds strange *P1868:*breeds, strange 1527| MS:undreamed of shores *P1868:*undreamed-of shores, 1528| MS:blood pulse *P1868:*blood-pulse 1529| MS:be though <> wing *P1868:*be, though <> wing, 1530| MS:though the hawk *P1868:*though a hawk 1531| MS:prize,—though why she *P1868:*prize,—wherefore, she 1533| MS:have left Rome ere you can arrive *P1868:*have quitted Rome ere you arrive 1534| MS:§ crowded between 1543-45 § step open"—quoth Paolo. *P1868:*step left,"—wrote Paolo. 1535| MS:of the

O' the main prize, all the money in dispute:
Pompilia's dowry might revert to her
Or stay with him as law's caprice should point,—
But now—now—what was Pietro's shall be hers,
What was hers shall remain her own,—if hers,
Why then,—oh, not her husband's but—her heir's!
That heir being his too, all grew his at last
By this road or by that road, since they join.
Before, why, push he Pietro out o' the world,—
The current of the money stopped, you see,
Pompilia being proved no Pietro's child:
Or let it be Pompilia's life he quenched,
Again the current of the money stopped,—
Guido debarred his rights as husband soon,
So the new process threatened;—now, the chance,
Now, the resplendent minute! Clear the earth,
Cleanse the house, let the three but disappear
A child remains, depositary of all,
That Guido may enjoy his own again,
Repair all losses by a master-stroke,
Wipe out the past, all done all left undone,
Swell the good present to best evermore,
Die into new life, which let blood baptize!

So, i' the blue of a sudden sulphur-blaze,
Both why there was one step to take at Rome,
And why he should not meet with Paolo there,

---

*P1868:*o' the 1540| MS:Of *P1868:*O' 1542| MS:caprice might be,— *P1868:*might point,— *CP1868:*caprice should point,— 1543| MS:But now—see, —what <> hers *P1868:*But now—now—what <> hers, 1545| MS:husband's! but—her heir's— *P1868:*husband's but—her heir's! 1546| MS:Her heir being his,—yes, all *P1868:*That heir being his too, all 1548| MS:push but Pietro out of *P1868:*push he Pietro out o' 1550| MS:no more his child: *P1868:*no Pietro's child: 1551| MS:life you § crossed out and replaced by § was quenched, *P1868:*life he quenched, 1553| MS:soon *P1868:*soon, 1554| MS:threatened; —oh, the *P1868:*threatened;—now, the 1555| MS:Oh the *P1868:*Now, the 1557| MS:The child *P1868:*A child 1558| MS:So Guido shall enjoy <> again! *P1868:*That Guido may enjoy *1888:*again, 1559| MS:master-stroke— *P1868:*master-stroke, 1560| MS:done and left *1888:*done all left 1561| MS:Make § crossed out and replaced above by § Swell the good present into evermore, *P1868:*present to best evermore, 1562| MS:baptise! *P1868:*baptize! 1563-67| MS:So in <> sulphur-blaze/ He saw the ins and outs to the heart of hell—/

He saw—the ins and outs to the heart of hell—
And took the straight line thither swift and sure.
He rushed to Vittiano, found four sons o' the soil,
Brutes of his breeding, with one spark i' the clod
That served for a soul, the looking up to him
Or aught called Franceschini as life, death,
Heaven, hell,—lord paramount, assembled these,
Harangued, equipped, instructed, pressed each clod
With his will's imprint; then took horse, plied spur,
And so arrived, all five of them, at Rome
On Christmas-Eve, and forthwith found themselves
Installed i' the vacancy and solitude
Left them by Paolo, the considerate man
Who, good as his word, had disappeared at once
As if to leave the stage free. A whole week
Did Guido spend in study of his part,
Then played it fearless of a failure. One,
Struck the year's clock whereof the hours are days,
And off was rung o' the little wheels the chime
"Good will on earth and peace to man:" but, two,
Proceeded the same bell and, evening come,
The dreadful five felt finger-wise their way
Across the town by blind cuts and black turns
To the little lone suburban villa; knocked—
"Who may be outside?" called a well-known voice.
"A friend of Caponsacchi's bringing friends
A letter."
                That's a test, the excusers say:
Ay, and a test conclusive, I return.
What? Had that name brought touch of guilt or taste

And why there <> // And *P1868:*So, i' <> sulphur-blaze,/ And why there <> // He saw—the ins <> / And *1888:*sulphur-blaze,/ Both why 1568| MS:to the Villa, found <> of the soil *P1868:*to Vittiano, found <> o' the soil, 1569| MS: in *P1868:*i' 1570| MS:To serve for *P1868:*That served for 1573| MS: pressed the clod *P1868:*pressed each clod 1574| MS:horse with them, *P1868:* horse, plied spur, 1576| MS:On Christmas Eve *P1868:*On Christmas-Eve 1577| MS:in *P1868:*i' 1578| MS:man, *P1868:*man 1581| MS:part *P1868:* part, 1583| MS:days *P1868:*days, 1584| MS:on *P1868:*o' 1585| MS: to men:" but, two *P1868:*to man:" but, two, 1590| MS:voice, *P1868:*voice. 1591| MS:bringing you *P1868:*bringing friends 1593| MS:conclusive, I reply. *P1868:*conclusive, I return. 1594| MS:guilt and taste *P1868:*guilt or taste

Of fear with it, aught to dash the present joy
With memory of the sorrow just at end,—
She, happy in her parents' arms at length
With the new blessing of the two weeks' babe,—
How had that name's announcement moved the wife?
Or, as the other slanders circulate,
Were Caponsacchi no rare visitant
On nights and days whither safe harbour lured,
What bait had been i' the name to ope the door?
The promise of a letter? Stealthy guests
Have secret watchwords, private entrances:
The man's own self might have been found inside
And all the scheme made frustrate by a word.
No: but since Guido knew, none knew so well,
The man had never since returned to Rome
Nor seen the wife's face more than villa's front,
So, could not be at hand to warn or save,—
For that, he took this sure way to the end.

"Come in," bade poor Violante cheerfully,
Drawing the door-bolt: that death was the first,
Stabbed through and through. Pietro, close on her heels,
Set up a cry—"Let me confess myself!
Grant but confession!" Cold steel was the grant.
Then came Pompilia's turn.
                                        Then they escaped.
The noise o' the slaughter roused the neighbourhood.
They had forgotten just the one thing more

1596| MS:With the menace of <> end, *P1868:*With memory of *CP1868:*end,— 1597| MS:at last *P1868:*at length 1598| MS:babe, *CP1868:*babe,— 1599| MS:the house? *P1868:*the wife? 1600| MS:circulate,— *CP1868:*circulate, 1602| MS:Of nights and days where stealthy harbour was, *P1868:*On nights and days whither safe harbour lured, 1603| MS:in <> door, *P1868:*i' <> door? 1606| MS:The man might well have been found safe inside *P1868:*The man's own self might have been found inside 1610| MS:than the villa's *P1868:*than villa's, 1611| MS:And could <> save, *CP1868:*So, could <> save,— 1612| MS:end— *P1868:*end. 1612-13| MS:§ no ¶ § *P1868:*§ ¶ § 1613| MS:in" quoth Violante *P1868:*in," bade Violante *CP1868:*bade poor Violante 1614| MS:Drawing the § inserted above § door-bolt: her death *P1868:*door-bolt: that death 1618-20| MS: escaped./ They *P1868:*escaped./ The noise o' the slaughter roused the neighbourhood./

Which saves i' the circumstance, the ticket to-wit
Which puts post-horses at a traveller's use:
So, all on foot, desperate through the dark
Reeled they like drunkards along open road,
Accomplished a prodigious twenty miles
Homeward, and gained Baccano very near,
Stumbled at last, deaf, dumb, blind through the feat,
Into a grange and, one dead heap, slept there
Till the pursuers hard upon their trace
Reached them and took them, red from head to heel,
And brought them to the prison where they lie.
The couple were laid i' the church two days ago,
And the wife lives yet by miracle.

                                                            All is told.
You hardly need ask what Count Guido says,
Since something he must say. "I own the deed—"
(He cannot choose,—but—) "I declare the same
Just and inevitable,—since no way else
Was left me, but by this of taking life,
To save my honour which is more than life.
I exercised a husband's rights." To which
The answer is as prompt—"There was no fault
In any one o' the three to punish thus:
Neither i' the wife, who kept all faith to you,
Nor in the parents, whom yourself first duped,
Robbed and maltreated, then turned out of doors.
You wronged and they endured wrong; yours the fault.

They   1621| MS:in *P1868:*i'   1624| MS:along the open road *P1868:*along open road,   1626| MS:Arezzo-ward, reached Baccano in very deed, *P1868:* Homeward, and gained Baccano very near,   1627| MS:last, dumb, blind, dead through their feat, *P1868:*last, deaf, dumb, blind through the feat,
1628| MS:and slept there in a heap *P1868:*and, one dead heap, slept there
1630| MS:them red *P1868:*them, red   1632| MS:in *P1868:*i'   1633| MS:by a miracle. § no ¶ § All *P1868:*by miracle. § ¶ § All   1634| MS:need to ask what Guido *P1868:*need ask what Count Guido   1635| MS:say. "I avow the *P1868:*say. "I own the   1636| MS:but, he goes on to say) *P1868:*but—) "I declare the same   1638| MS:left but by this taking life away *P1868:*left me but by this of taking life *CP1868:*me, but <> life,   1640| MS:rights, no more." *P1868:*rights." To which   1642| MS:of *P1868:*o'   1643| MS:in *P1868:*i'
1644| MS:whom you first duped, then *P1868:*whom yourself first duped,
1645| MS:doors, *P1868:*doors.   1646| MS:they resented; yours *P1868:*they

Next, had endurance overpassed the mark
And turned resentment needing remedy,—
Nay, put the absurd impossible case, for once—
You were all blameless of the blame alleged
And they blameworthy where you fix all blame,
Still, why this violation of the law?
Yourself elected law should take its course,
Avenge wrong, or show vengeance not your right;
Why, only when the balance in law's hand
Trembles against you and inclines the way
O' the other party, do you make protest,
Renounce arbitrament, flying out of court,
And crying 'Honour's hurt the sword must cure'?
Aha, and so i' the middle of each suit
Trying i' the courts,—and you had three in play
With an appeal to the Pope's self beside,—
What, you may chop and change and right your wrongs
Leaving the law to lag as she thinks fit?"

That were too temptingly commodious, Count!
One would have still a remedy in reserve
Should reach the safest oldest sinner, you see!
One's honour forsooth? Does that take hurt alone
From the extreme outrage? I who have no wife,
Being yet sensitive in my degree
As Guido,—must discover hurt elsewhere

---

endured wrong; yours 1647| MS:had resentment overpassed *P1868:*had endurance overpassed 1648| MS:turned to wrong which needed remedy,— *P1868:*turned resentment needing remedy,— 1649| MS:absurd and impossible *P1868:*absurd impossible 1651| MS:they all blameworthy <> fix blame, *P1868:*they blameworthy <> fix all blame, 1654| MS:Avenge you, or <> your due; *P1868:*Avenge wrong, or <> your right; 1655| MS:And only *P1868:*Why, only 1656| MS:you,—when it inclines *P1868:*you and inclines 1657| MS:Of your wife and her parents, do *P1868:*O' the other party, do 1658| MS:Renounce the arbitrament, take the opposite course, *P1868:*Renounce arbitrament, flying out of court, 1659| MS:And cry that honour's hurt's past cure of law. *P1868:*And crying 'Honour's hurt the sword must cure?' *P1872:*cure'? 1660| MS:Ha ha, and so in *P1868:*Aha, and so i' 1661| MS:Trying in *P1868:* Trying i' 1663| MS:change, and right yourself *P1868:*change and right your wrongs 1664| MS:to do as <> fit? *P1868:*to lag as <> fit?" 1664-65| MS: § no ¶ § *P1868:*§ ¶ § 1667| MS:see: *P1868:*see! 1670| MS:Being as sensitive *P1868:*Being yet sensitive 1671| MS:discover some hurt *P1868:*discover hurt

Which, half compounded-for in days gone by,
May profitably break out now afresh,
Need cure from my own expeditious hands.
The lie that was, as it were, imputed me
When you objected to my contract's clause,—
The theft as good as, one may say, alleged,
When you, co-heir in a will, excepted, Sir,
To my administration of effects,
—Aha, do you think law disposed of these?
My honour's touched and shall deal death around!
Count, that were too commodious, I repeat!
If any law be imperative on us all,
Of all are you the enemy: out with you
From the common light and air and life of man!

1672| MS:half-compounded for *P1868:*half compounded-for 1673| MS:out all afresh, *P1868:*out now afresh, 1675| MS:imputed to me *P1868:*imputed me 1678| MS:When my coheirs excepted in a will *P1868:*When you, co-heir in a will, excepted, Sir, 1680| MS:— § added in margin § Aha <> think the law *P1868:* think law 1681| MS:death all round! *P1868:*death around! 1682| MS: repeat. *P1868:*repeat! 1683| MS:law is imperative <> all *P1868:*law be imperative <> all,

IV

TERTIUM QUID

True, Excellency—as his Highness says,
Though she's not dead yet, she's as good as stretched
Symmetrical beside the other two;
Though he's not judged yet, he's the same as judged,
So do the facts abound and superabound:
And nothing hinders that we lift the case
Out of the shade into the shine, allow
Qualified persons to pronounce at last,
Nay, edge in an authoritative word
Between this rabble's-brabble of dolts and fools
Who make up reasonless unreasoning Rome.
"Now for the Trial!" they roar: "the Trial to test
The truth, weigh husband and weigh wife alike
I' the scales of law, make one scale kick the beam!"
Law's a machine from which, to please the mob,
Truth the divinity must needs descend
And clear things at the play's fifth act—aha!
Hammer into their noddles who was who
And what was what. I tell the simpletons
"Could law be competent to such a feat
'Twere done already: what begins next week
Is end o' the Trial, last link of a chain
Whereof the first was forged three years ago
When law addressed herself to set wrong right,
And proved so slow in taking the first step
That ever some new grievance,—tort, retort,
On one or the other side,—o'ertook i' the game,

[2]| MS:yet she's *P1868:*yet, she's [3]| MS:two, *P1868:*two; [4]| MS:yet he's <> judged *P1868:*yet, he's <> judged, [5]| MS:superabound, *P1868:* superabound: [6]| MS:hinders now we *CP1868:*hinders, now we *1872:*hinders that we [10]| MS:rabble's brabble *P1868:*rabble's-brabble [14]| MS:In <> of Law *P1868:*I' <> of law [15]| MS:Law's the § crossed out and replaced above by § a [17]| MS:aha, *P1868:*aha! [22]| MS:Is the end of a trial *P1868:*Is end o' the Trial [24]| MS:right *P1868:*right, [27]| MS:one and the <> in *P1868:*

Retarded sentence, till this deed of death
Is thrown in, as it were, last bale to boat
Crammed to the edge with cargo—or passengers?
'Trecentos inseris: ohe, jam satis est!
Huc appelle!'—passengers, the word must be."
Long since, the boat was loaded to my eyes.
To hear the rabble and brabble, you'd call the case
Fused and confused past human finding out.
One calls the square round, t'other the round square—
And pardonably in that first surprise
O' the blood that fell and splashed the diagram:
But now we've used our eyes to the violent hue
Can't we look through the crimson and trace lines?
It makes a man despair of history,
Eusebius and the established fact—fig's end!
Oh, give the fools their Trial, rattle away
With the leash of lawyers, two on either side—
One barks, one bites,—Masters Arcangeli
And Spreti,—that's the husband's ultimate hope
Against the Fisc and the other kind of Fisc,
Bound to do barking for the wife: bow—wow!
Why, Excellency, we and his Highness here
Would settle the matter as sufficiently
As ever will Advocate This and Fiscal That
And Judge the Other, with even—a word and a wink—
We well know who for ultimate arbiter.
Let us beware o' the basset-table—lest
We jog the elbow of Her Eminence,
Jostle his cards,—he'll rap you out a . . . st!
By the window-seat! And here's the Marquis too!
Indulge me but a moment: if I fail
—Favoured with such an audience, understand!—

---

one or the <> i' [28]| MS:of the death *P1868:*of death [30]| MS:passengers: *P1868:*passengers? [32]| MS:be: *P1868:*be." [33]| MS:since the *P1868:*since, the [38]| MS:Of <> diagram *P1868:*O' <> diagram: [43]| MS:their trial *P1868:*their Trial [47]| MS:of Fisc *P1868:*of Fisc, [52]| MS:with even, a word in your ear, *P1868:*even—a word and a wink— [54]| MS:of *P1868:*o' [55]| MS:of His Eminence *P1868:*of Her Eminence, [56]| MS:a . . st! *1888:*a . . . st! [57]| MS:window-seat:and *P1868:*window-seat! And [59]| MS:

To set things right, why, class me with the mob
As understander of the mind of man!

The mob,—now, that's just how the error comes!
Bethink you that you have to deal with *plebs*,
The commonalty; this is an episode
In burgess-life,—why seek to aggrandize,
Idealize, denaturalize the class?
People talk just as if they had to do
With a noble pair that . . . Excellency, your ear!
Stoop to me, Highness,—listen and look yourselves!

This Pietro, this Violante, live their life
At Rome in the easy way that's far from worst
Even for their betters,—themselves love themselves,
Spend their own oil in feeding their own lamp
That their own faces may grow bright thereby.
They get to fifty and over: how's the lamp?
Full to the depth o' the wick,—moneys so much;
And also with a remnant,—so much more
Of moneys,—which there's no consuming now,
But, when the wick shall moulder out some day,
Failing fresh twist of tow to use up dregs,
Will lie a prize for the passer-by,—to-wit
Anyone that can prove himself the heir,
Seeing, the couple are wanting in a child:
Meantime their wick swims in the safe broad bowl

---

§ crowded between lines 58-60 § —Favored < > understand— *P1868:*—Favoured < > understand!— 60| MS:why class *P1868:*why, class 62| MS:now that's *P1868:*now, that's 63| MS:to do with *P1868:*to deal with 65| MS: aggrandize *P1868:*aggrandize, 66| MS:And § crossed out § idealize § altered to § Idealize 68| MS:that . . Excellency *1888:*that . . . Excellency 69| MS: Stoop with me < > yourselves. *P1868:*Stoop to me < > yourselves! 69-70| MS: § ¶ § *1888:*§ no ¶; paragraph restored; see Editorial Notes § 70| MS:This § in margin § Pietro, and § crossed out § this Violante live *P1868:*this Violante, live 74-75| MS:thereby,—/ Means plentiful for two, and more to spare. § line crossed out §/ They *P1868:*thereby./ They 76| MS:of < > monies *P1868:*o' *CP1868:*moneys 77| MS:But also *P1868:*And also 78| MS:monies < > now *P1868:*now, *CP1868:*moneys 79| MS:But when *P1868:*But, when 80| MS:Failing a fresh twist to use up the dregs, *P1868:*Failing fresh twist of tow to use up dregs, 81| MS:to-whit *P1868:*to-wit 82| MS:heir *P1868:*heir, 83| MS:Seeing the *P1868:*Seeing, the 84| MS:Meantime they both are set in *P1868:*Meantime

O' the middle rank,—not raised a beacon's height
For wind to ravage, nor dropped till lamp graze ground
Like cresset, mudlarks poke now here now there,
Going their rounds to probe the ruts i' the road
Or fish the luck o' the puddle. Pietro's soul
Was satisfied when cronies smirked, "No wine
Like Pietro's, and he drinks it every day!"
His wife's heart swelled her boddice, joyed its fill
When neighbours turned heads wistfully at church,
Sighed at the load of lace that came to pray.
Well, having got through fifty years of flare,
They burn out so, indulge so their dear selves,
That Pietro finds himself in debt at last,
As he were any lordling of us all:
And, now that dark begins to creep on day,
Creditors grow uneasy, talk aside,
Take counsel, then importune all at once.
For if the good fat rosy careless man,
Who has not laid a ducat by, decease—
Let the lamp fall, no heir at hand to catch—
Why, being childless, there's a spilth i' the street
O' the remnant, there's a scramble for the dregs
By the stranger: so, they grant him no long day
But come in a body, clamour to be paid.

What's his resource? He asks and straight obtains
The customary largess, dole dealt out
To, what we call our "poor dear shame-faced ones,"

---

their wick swims in 85| MS:Of *P1868:*O' 86| MS:For the wind <> nor swung till they graze *P1868:*For wind <> till lamp graze *1888:*nor dropped till 87| MS:As the watchman's cresset he pokes here and there *1868:*cresset, he <> there, *1888:*Like cresset, mudlarks poke now here now there, 88| MS:Going his rounds <> in *P1868:*i' *1888:*Going their rounds 89| MS:Or take the <> of *P1868:* Or fish the <> o' 90| MS:when friends exclaimed "No *P1868:*when crony smirked, "No *1888:*cronies 93| MS:When goss § crossed out § neighbours <> at mass *P1868:*at church, 95| MS:years this way, *P1868:*years of flare, 99| MS:And as the dark <> day *P1868:*And, for the <> day, *1888:*And, now that dark 100| MS:The creditors <> aside *P1868:*Creditors <> aside, 101| MS:once— *P1868:*once. 103-5| MS:decease—/ <> spilth at once *P1868:* decease—/ Let the lamp fail, no heir at hand to catch—/ <> spilth i' the street 106| MS:Of *P1868:*O' 107| MS:By strangers: so they *P1868:*By the stranger: so, they 108-9| MS:§ no ¶ § *P1868:*§ ¶ § 110-12| MS:out/ In *P1868:*out/ To,

In secret once a month to spare the shame
O' the slothful and the spendthrift,—pauper-saints
The Pope puts meat i' the mouth of, ravens they,
And providence he—just what the mob admires!
That is, instead of putting a prompt foot
On selfish worthless human slugs whose slime
Has failed to lubricate their path in life,
Why, the Pope picks the first ripe fruit that falls
And gracious puts it in the vermin's way.
Pietro could never save a dollar? Straight
He must be subsidized at our expense:
And for his wife—the harmless household sheep
One ought not to see harassed in her age—
Judge, by the way she bore adversity,
O' the patient nature you ask pity for!
How long, now, would the roughest marketman,
Handling the creatures huddled to the knife,
Harass a mutton ere she made a mouth
Or menaced biting? Yet the poor sheep here,
Violante, the old innocent burgess-wife,
In her first difficulty showed great teeth
Fit to crunch up and swallow a good round crime.
She meditates the tenure of the Trust,
Fidei commissum is the lawyer-phrase,
These funds that only want an heir to take—

---

what we call our "poor dear shame-faced ones,"/ In 113| MS:Of <> and improvident § crossed out and replaced above by two words, comma, and dash § the spendthrift,—burgesses *P1868:*O' <> spendthrift,—pauper-saints 114| MS:in <> of—ravens *P1868:*i' <> of, ravens 117| MS:On the selfish, worthless <> slug *P1868:*On selfish worthless <> slugs 118| MS:Had failed to lubricate his path *P1868:*Has failed to lubricate their path 120-22| MS:way./ <> expence *P1868:*way./ Pietro could never save a dollar? Straight/ <> expense: 124| MS:see harmed in her old days— *P1868:*see harassed in her age— 126| MS:Of <> for: . *P1868:*O' <> for! 127| MS:long, should you say, would *P1868:*long, now, would 128| MS:huddled in distress, *P1868:*huddles to the knife, 129| MS:Harrass *P1868:*Harass 131| MS:Pompilia, the *P1868:*Violante, the 133| MS:round sin. *P1868:*round crime. 134-36| MS:the Trust,/ These *P1868:*the Trust,/ *Fidei commissum* is the lawyer-phrase,/ These

Goes o'er the gamut o' the creditor's cry
By semitones from whine to snarl high up
And growl down low, one scale in sundry keys,—
Pauses with a little compunction for the face
Of Pietro frustrate of its ancient cheer,—
Never a bottle now for friend at need,—
Comes to a stop on her own frittered lace
And neighbourly condolences thereat,
Then makes her mind up, sees the thing to do:
And so, deliberate, snaps house-book clasp,
Posts off to vespers, missal beneath arm,
Passes the proper San Lorenzo by,
Dives down a little lane to the left, is lost
In a labyrinth of dwellings best unnamed,
Selects a certain blind one, black at base,
Blinking at top,—the sign of we know what,—
One candle in a casement set to wink
Streetward, do service to no shrine inside,—
Mounts thither by the filthy flight of stairs,
Holding the cord by the wall, to the tip-top,
Gropes for the door i' the dark, ajar of course,
Raps, opens, enters in: up starts a thing
Naked as needs be—"What, you rogue, 'tis you?
Back,—how can I have taken a farthing yet?
Mercy on me, poor sinner that I am!
Here's . . . why, I took you for Madonna's self
With all that sudden swirl of silk i' the place!
What may your pleasure be, my bonny dame?"
Your Excellency supplies aught left obscure?
One of those women that abound in Rome,

137| MS:of *P1868:*o' 141-43| MS:cheer,—/ Comes *P1868:*cheer,—/ Never a bottle now for friend at need,—/ Comes 145| MS:And makes <> up as to the <> do— *P1868:*Then makes <> up, sees the <> do: 146| MS:so deliberately shuts § crossed out § snaps missal § crossed out and replaced above by two words § house-book clasp, *P1868:*so, deliberately, snaps *1872:*deliberate 155| MS:stairs *P1868:*stairs, 157| MS:in the dark ajar *P1868:*i' the dark, ajar 161| MS:am, *P1868:*am! 162| MS:Here's . . why *1888:*Here's . . . why 163| MS:that silk sudden in this poor place! *P1868:*that sudden swirl of silk i' the place! 164| MS:bonny Dame?" *1868:*bonny dame?" 165| MS:Your Excellency sees what's left unsaid— *P1868:*Your Excellency supplies aught left obscure? 166| MS:women who abound in Rome *P1868:*women that abound in

Whose needs oblige them eke out one poor trade
By another vile one: her ostensible work
Was washing clothes, out in the open air
At the cistern by Citorio; her true trade—
Whispering to idlers, when they stopped and praised
The ankles she let liberally shine
In kneeling at the slab by the fountain-side,
That there was plenty more to criticize
At home, that eve, i' the house where candle blinked
Decorously above, and all was done
I' the holy fear of God and cheap beside.
Violante, now, had seen this woman wash,
Noticed and envied her propitious shape,
Tracked her home to her house-top, noted too,
And now was come to tempt her and propose
A bargain far more shameful than the first
Which trafficked her virginity away
For a melon and three pauls at twelve years old.
Five minutes' talk with this poor child of Eve,
Struck was the bargain, business at an end—
"Then, six months hence, that person whom you trust,
Comes, fetches whatsoever babe it be;
I keep the price and secret, you the babe,
Paying beside for mass to make all straight:
Meantime, I pouch the earnest-money-piece."

Down stairs again goes fumbling by the rope

Rome, 167| MS:them to eke *P1868:*them eke 168| MS:one: whose ostensible *P1868:*one: her ostensible 169| MS:clothes out *P1868:*clothes, out 170| MS:By § crossed out and replaced above by § At <> by Citorio; but was wont *P1868:*by Citorio; but true trade— *1872:*by Citorio; her true trade— 171| MS:To whisper idlers when *P1868:*Whispering to idlers *1872:*idlers, when 172| MS: ancles *1888:*ankles 173| MS:fountain-side *P1868:*fountain-side, 174| MS:criticise *1888:*criticize 175| MS:home that evening when the candle *P1868:*home, that eve, i' the house where candle 176| MS:above and *P1868:* above, and 177| MS:In *P1868:*I' 178| MS:Pompilia, now *P1868:*Violante, now 179| MS:And noticed her as of propitious *P1868:*Noticed and envied her propitious 180| MS:noted it, *P1868:*noted too, 182| MS:than that first *P1868:*than the first 185| MS:of Eve *P1868:*of Eve, 186| MS:business was at end— *P1868:*business at an end— 187-92| MS:Then <> that cousin whom you trust/ Brings it from you to me and takes the price."/ Down *P1868:*"Then <> that person whom you trust,/ Comes, fetches whatsoever babe it be;/ I keep the price and secret, you the babe,/ Paying beside for mass to make all straight:/ Meantime, I

Violante, triumphing in a flourish of fire
From her own brain, self-lit by such success,—
Gains church in time for the "*Magnificat*"
And gives forth "My reproof is taken away,
And blessed shall mankind proclaim me now,"
So that the officiating priest turns round
To see who proffers the obstreperous praise:
Then home to Pietro, the enraptured-much
But puzzled-more when told the wondrous news—
How orisons and works of charity,
(Beside that pair of pinners and a coif,
Birth-day surprise last Wednesday was five weeks)
Had borne fruit in the autumn of his life,—
They, or the Orvieto in a double dose.
Anyhow, she must keep house next six months,
Lie on the settle, avoid the three-legged stool,
And, chiefly, not be crossed in wish or whim,
And the result was like to be an heir.

Accordingly, when time was come about,
He found himself the sire indeed of this
Francesca Vittoria Pompilia and the rest
O' the names whereby he sealed her his, next day.
A crime complete in its way is here, I hope?
Lies to God, lies to man, every way lies
To nature and civility and the mode:

---

pouch the earnest-money-piece." § ¶ § Down 193| MS:Violante triumphing *P1868:*Violante, triumphing 195| MS:the "Magnificat" *P1868:*the "*Magnificat*" 196-200| MS:forth "my <> taken a way"/ <> round./ <> to Pietro—the enraptured much *P1868:*forth "My <> taken away,/ And blessed shall mankind proclaim me now,"/ <> round/ To see who proffers the obstreperous praise:/ <> to Pietro, the enraptured-much 201| MS:puzzled more <> news *P1868:*puzzled-more <> news— 202-5| MS:charity/ Had *P1868:*charity,/ (Beside that pair of pinners and a coif,/ Birth-day surprise last Wednesday was five weeks)/ Had <> the Autumn *1888:///* the autumn 207| MS:Anyhow she *P1868:*Anyhow, she 208| MS: three legged *P1868:*three-legged 209-11| MS:or will:/ § no ¶ § Accordingly when *1868:*or whim,/ And the result was like to be an heir./ § ¶ § Accordingly, when 212| MS:sire in very deed *P1868:*sire indeed of this 213| MS:Of Francesca *P1868:*Francesca 214| MS:Of <> whereby they sealed her theirs next *P1868:*O' <> whereby he sealed her his next *1872:*his, next 215| MS:hope *P1868:*hope? 216| MS:man, lies every way *P1868:*man, every way lies 217| MS:nature, civility

Flat robbery of the proper heirs thus foiled
O' the due succession,—and, what followed thence,
Robbery of God, through the confessor's ear
Debarred the most note-worthy incident
When all else done and undone twelve-month through
Was put in evidence at Easter-time.
All other peccadillos!—but this one
To the priest who comes next day to dine with us?
'Twere inexpedient; decency forbade.

Is so far clear? You know Violante now,
Compute her capability of crime
By this authentic instance? Black hard cold
Crime like a stone you kick up with your foot
I' the middle of a field?

I thought as much.
But now, a question,—how long does it lie,
The bad and barren bit of stuff you kick,
Before encroached on and encompassed round
With minute moss, weed, wild-flower—made alive
By worm, and fly, and foot of the free bird?
Your Highness,—healthy minds let bygones be,
Leave old crimes to grow young and virtuous-like
I' the sun and air; so time treats ugly deeds:
They take the natural blessing of all change.

---

and the natural law: *P1868:*nature and civility and the mode: 219| MS:Of *P1868:*O' 220| MS:Robbing from God *P1868:*Robbery of God 221| MS:Of this note-worthy incident—reserved *P1868:*Debarred the most note-worthy incident 222| MS:undone through the year *P1868:*undone twelve-month through 224| MS:peccadillos,—but *P1868:*peccadillos!—but 225| MS:the Priest *P1868:* the priest 226| MS:inexpedient: decency *P1868:*inexpedient; decency 226-27| MS:§ no ¶ § *P1868:*§ ¶ § 227| MS:know the couple now, *P1868:*know Violante now, 228| MS:Compute their capability *P1868:*Compute her capability 229| MS:instance? Black, hard, cold *P1868:*instance? Black hard cold 230| MS: Even as a stone *P1868:*Crime like a stone 231| MS:In < > field. § no ¶ § I *P1868:*I' < > field? § ¶ § I 233| MS:That bad *P1868:*The bad 234| MS: encompassed quite *P1868:*encompassed round 236| MS:worm and fly and *P1868:*worm, and fly, and 237| MS:be— *P1868:*be, 238| MS:virtuouslike *P1868:*virtuous-like 239| MS:In < > air: so < > deed— *P1868:*I' < > air; so < >

There was the joy o' the husband silly-sooth,
The softening of the wife's old wicked heart,
Virtues to right and left, profusely paid
If so they might compensate the saved sin.
And then the sudden existence, dewy-dear,
O' the rose above the dungheap, the pure child
As good as new created, since withdrawn
From the horror of the pre-appointed lot
With the unknown father and the mother known
Too well,—some fourteen years of squalid youth,
And then libertinage, disease, the grave—
Hell in life here, hereafter life in hell:
Look at that horror and this soft repose!
Why, moralist, the sin has saved a soul!
Then, even the palpable grievance to the heirs—
'Faith, this was no frank setting hand to throat
And robbing a man, but . . . Excellency, by your leave,
How did you get that marvel of a gem,
The sapphire with the Graces grand and Greek?
The story is, stooping to pick a stone
From the pathway through a vineyard—no-man's-land—
To pelt a sparrow with, you chanced on this:
Why now, do those five clowns o' the family
O' the vinedresser digest their porridge worse
That not one keeps it in his goatskin pouch
To do flint's-service with the tinder-box?
Don't cheat me, don't cheat you, don't cheat a friend,
But are you so hard on who jostles just

---

deeds: 241| MS:of *P1868:*o' 243| MS:To right and left, virtues profusely *P1868:*Virtues to right and left, profusely 244| MS:the one saved *P1868:*the saved 246| MS:Of *P1868:*O' 247| MS:as if § crossed out and replaced above by one word § new created—since *P1868:*as new created, since 250| MS:well,—the fourteen <> of wretched youth,— *P1868:*well,—some fourteen <> of squalid youth, 251| MS:libertinage and leprosy, *P1868:*libertinage, disease, the grave— 252| MS:Death in <> here,—hereafter <> hell— *P1868:*Hell in <> here, hereafter <> hell: 253| MS:§ crowded between lines 252-54 § Look, at <> repose— *P1868:*Look at <> repose! 255| MS:Then even *P1868:*Then, even 256| MS:Why, this *P1868:*'Faith, this 257| MS:but . . Excellency *1888:*but . . . Excellency 258| MS:gem *P1868:*gem, 259| MS:the god's head grand *P1868:*the Graces grand 261| MS:§ crowded between lines 260-62 § vineyard not your own *1868:*vineyard—no-man's-land— 263| MS:Why, now <> of *P1868:* Why now <> o' 264| MS:Of <> their supper the worse *P1868:*O' <> their porridge worse 266| MS:flint's service *P1868:*flint's-service 267–69| MS:you,

A stranger with no natural sort of claim
To the havings and the holdings (here's the point)
Unless by misadventure, and defect
Of that which ought to be—nay, which there's none
Would dare so much as wish to profit by—
Since who dares put in just so many words
"May Pietro fail to have a child, please God!
So shall his house and goods belong to me,
The sooner that his heart will pine betimes"?
Well then, God doesn't please, nor heart shall pine!
Because he has a child at last, you see,
Or selfsame thing as though a child it were,
He thinks, whose sole concern it is to think:
If he accepts it why should you demur?

Moreover, say that certain sin there seem,
The proper process of unsinning sin
Is to begin well-doing somehow else.
Pietro,—remember, with no sin at all
I' the substitution,—why, this gift of God
Flung in his lap from over Paradise
Steadied him in a moment, set him straight
On the good path he had been straying from.
Henceforward no more wilfulness and waste,
Cuppings, carousings,—these a sponge wiped out.

---

don't cheat our friends—/ But strangers, with no natural claim at all *P1868:*you, don't cheat a friend!/ But are you so hard on who jostles just/ A stranger with no natural sort of claim *1888:*friend DC,BrU:friend, *1889:*friend,
270| MS:holdings of Pietro—here's the point— *P1868:*holdings (here's the point)
271| MS:misadventure—the defect of that *P1868:*misadventure—and defect
272| MS:Which < > be—which there's no worthy man *P1868:*Of that which < > be—nay, which there's none 274| MS:dares say in *P1868:*dares put in
275| MS:"May this man fail < > God,— *P1868:*"May Pietro fail < > God!
276| MS:me— *P1868:*me, 277| MS:pine away?" *P1868:*pine betimes?" *1888:*betimes"? 278| MS:Well, then, God don't please—nor his heart shall break, *P1868:*Well then < > shall pine! *1888:*then,God doesn't please, nor heart
280| MS:The selfsame < > as if a < > were *P1868:*Or selfsame < > as though a < > were, 281| MS:thinks—whose < > think— *P1868:*thinks, whose < > think:
282-83| MS:§ no ¶ § *P1868:*§ ¶ § 283| MS:there was, *P1868:*there seem,
285| MS:else *P1868:*else. 286| MS:For Pietro *P1868:*Pietrô 287| MS:In *P1868:*I' 288| MS:over Paradise wall *P1868:*over Paradise
289| MS:Sobered him *P1868:*Steadied him 290| MS:In the *P1868:*On the
292| MS:carousals < > out: *P1868:*carousings < > out.

All sort of self-denial was easy now
For the child's sake, the chatelaine to be,
Who must want much and might want who knows what?
And so, the debts were paid, habits reformed,
Expense curtailed, the dowry set to grow.
As for the wife,—I said, hers the whole sin:
So, hers the exemplary penance. 'Twas a text
Whereon folk preached and praised, the district through:
"Oh, make us happy and you make us good!
It all comes of God giving her a child:
Such graces follow God's best earthly gift!"

Here you put by my guard, pass to my heart
By the home-thrust—"There's a lie at base of all."
Why, thou exact Prince, is it a pearl or no,
Yon globe upon the Principessa's neck?
That great round glory of pellucid stuff,
A fish secreted round a grain of grit!
Do you call it worthless for the worthless core?
(She doesn't, who well knows what she changed for it.)
So, to our brace of burgesses again!
You see so far i' the story, who was right,
Who wrong, who neither, don't you? What, you don't?
Eh? Well, admit there's somewhat dark i' the case,
Let's on—the rest shall clear, I promise you.
Leap over a dozen years: you find, these past,
An old good easy creditable sire,

294| MS:be: *P1868:*be, 295| MS:might want Heaven knows what. *P1868:*might want who knows what? 296| MS:so the *CP1868:*so, the 298| MS:And for <> said: hers <> sin, *P1868:*As for <> said, hers <> sin: 299| MS:Her's the <> penance: 'twas *P1868:*So, hers the <> penance. 'Twas 300| MS:Whereon they preached and praised the <> through. *P1868:*Whereon folk preached and praised, the <> through: 302| MS:of God's *P1868:*of God 303-4| MS:§ no ¶ § *P1868:*§ ¶ § 305| MS:home thrust *P1868:*home-thrust 306| MS:exact sir, is <> no *P1868:*exact Prince, is <> no, 307| MS:neck— *P1868:*neck? 308| MS:stuff *P1868:*stuff, 309| MS:The fish <> grit— *P1868:*A fish <> grit! 311| MS:§ crowded on bottom of page § don't *1868:*it!) *1888:*doesn't <> it.) 312-13| MS:So excellency, to <> burgesses./ Surely the bitterness of death was past,/ <> in the story who *P1868:*So, to <> burgesses again!/ <> i' the story, who 315| MS:in the case *P1868:*i' the case, 316| MS:rest is clear, I'll promise *P1868:*rest shall clear, I promise 317| MS:find *P1868:*find, these passed, *1888:*past, 318| MS:creditable man, *P1868:*creditable

A careful housewife's beaming bustling face,
Both wrapped up in the love of their one child,
The strange tall pale beautiful creature grown
Lily-like out o' the cleft i' the sun-smit rock
To bow its white miraculous birth of buds
I' the way of wandering Joseph and his spouse,—
So painters fancy: here it was a fact.
And this their lily,—could they but transplant
And set in vase to stand by Solomon's porch
'Twixt lion and lion!—this Pompilia of theirs,
Could they see worthily married, well bestowed,
In house and home! And why despair of this
With Rome to choose from, save the topmost rank?
Themselves would help the choice with heart and soul,
Throw their late savings in a common heap
To go with the dowry, and be followed in time
By the heritage legitimately hers:
And when such paragon was found and fixed,
Why, they might chant their "*Nunc dimittis*" straight.

Indeed the prize was simply full to a fault,
Exorbitant for the suitor they should seek,
And social class should choose among, these cits.
Yet there's a latitude: exceptional white
Amid the general brown o' the species, lurks

---

sire, 319| MS:beaming happy face, *P1868:*beaming bustling face, 320| MS:child *P1868:*child, 322| MS:of <> in <> sunsmit *P1868:*o' <> i' <> sun-smit 324| MS:In <> spouse: *P1868:*I' <> spouse,— 325| MS:fancy,—here <> fact— *P1868:*fancy:here <> fact. 326| MS:lily,—oh, could *P1868:*lily,—could 327| MS:stand in Solomon's *P1868:*stand by Solomon's 328| MS:Twixt lion and lion! In prose, this <> theirs *P1868:*'Twixt lion and lion!—this <> theirs, 329| MS:bestowed *1872:*bestowed, 330| MS:home—and *P1868:*home! And 331| MS:from save <> rank *P1868:*from, save <> rank? 332| MS:Since they would *P1868:*Themselves would 333| MS:Throwing their savings into a *P1868:*Throw their late savings in a 334| MS:and that to be *P1868:*Should go <> dowry, to be *1888:*To go <> dowry, and be 335-37| MS:hers,—/ <> their "Nunc Dimittas" straight. *P1868:*hers:/ And when such paragon was found and fixed/ <> their "*Nunc dimittas*" straight. *CP1868:dimittis* 337-38| MS:§ no ¶ § *P1868:*§ ¶ § 338| *P1868:*fault: *1872:*fault, 340| MS:Too good for the proper class to choose among. *P1868:*And social class <> among, these cits. *1888:*class should choose 341| MS:latitude,—exceptional *CP1868:*latitude: exceptional 342| MS:of the

A burgess nearly an aristocrat,
Legitimately in reach: look out for him!
What banker, merchant, has seen better days,
What second-rate painter a-pushing up,
Poet a-slipping down, shall bid the best
For this young beauty with the thumping purse?
Alack, were it but one of such as these
So like the real thing that they pass for it,
All had gone well! Unluckily, poor souls,
It proved to be the impossible thing itself,
Truth and not sham: hence ruin to them all.

For, Guido Franceschini was the head
Of an old family in Arezzo, old
To that degree they could afford be poor
Better than most: the case is common too.
Out of the vast door 'scutcheoned overhead,
Creeps out a serving-man on Saturdays
To cater for the week,—turns up anon
I' the market, chaffering for the lamb's least leg,
Or the quarter-fowl, less entrails, claws and comb:
Then back again with prize,—a liver begged
Into the bargain, gizzard overlooked.
He's mincing these to give the beans a taste,
When, at your knock, he leaves the simmering soup,

---

burgess soul, *P1868:*o' the species, lurks 343| MS:nearly like an aristocrat— *P1868:*nearly an aristocrat, 344| MS:him:*P1868:*him! 345-47| MS:merchant, painter a-pushing up/ Poet *P1868:*merchant, has seen better days,/ What second-rate painter a-pushing up,/ Poet 349| MS:Alack, had it been but *1872:*Alack, were it but 350| MS:thing it might pass *P1868:*thing they may pass *1888:*thing that they pass 351| MS:well: but unlucky fate would have *P1868:*well! Unluckily fate must needs *1872:*well! Unluckily, poor souls, 352| MS:It should prove to <> itself: *P1868:*It proved to <> itself; *1888:*itself, 353| MS:The real noble and not the sham—hence *P1868:*The truth and not the sham: hence *1888:*Truth and not sham 354| MS:Count Guido *CP1868:*For, Guido 357| MS:common there. *P1868:*common too. 358| MS:overhead *CP1868:*overhead, 361| MS:In the market chaffering <> leg *P1868:*I' the market, chaffering <> leg, 362| MS:quarter fowl *P1868:*quarter-fowl *1888:*comb DC,BrU:comb: *1889:*comb: 363| MS:back with his prize again,—a liver thrown *P1868:*back again with prize,—a liver begged 364| MS:bargain, a gizzard overlooked,— *P1868:*bargain, gizzard *1872:*overlooked. 365| MS:He's cooking these to give the soup a *P1868:*He's mincing these to give the beans a 366| MS:simmering mess

Waits on the curious stranger-visitant,
Napkin in half-wiped hand, to show the rooms,
Point pictures out have hung their hundred years,
"Priceless," he tells you,—puts in his place at once
The man of money: yes, you're banker-king
Or merchant-kaiser, wallow in your wealth
While patron, the house-master, can't afford
To stop our ceiling-hole that rain so rots:
But he's the man of mark, and there's his shield,
And yonder's the famed Rafael, first in kind,
The painter painted for his grandfather,
And you have paid to see: "Good morning, Sir!"
Such is the law of compensation. Still
The poverty was getting nigh acute;
There gaped so many noble mouths to feed,
Beans must suffice unflavoured of the fowl.
The mother,—hers would be a spun-out life
I' the nature of things; the sisters had done well
And married men of reasonable rank:
But that sort of illumination stops,
Throws back no heat upon the parent-hearth.
The family instinct felt out for its fire
To the Church,—the Church traditionally helps
A second son: and such was Paolo,

---

*P1868:*simmering soup, 368| MS:halfwiped hand to <> rooms— *P1868:*half-wiped hand, to <> rooms, 369| MS:years *P1868:*years,
370| MS:"Priceless" he <> in your place *P1868:*"Priceless," he <> in his place
371| MS:money—yes <> banker this *P1868:*money: yes <> banker-king
372| MS:Merchant the other, and you roll in wealth *P1868:*Or merchant-kaiser, wallow in your wealth 373| MS:While the patron, the house master can't *P1868:* While patron, the house-master, can't 374| MS:stop yon cieling-hole the rains have worn— *P1868:*stop our ceiling-hole that rain so rots— *1872:*rots:
376| MS:famed Raffael, first in its kind, *P1868:*famed Rafael <> in kind,
377| MS:grandfather— *1872:*grandfather, 378| MS:You have paid a paul to see: good *P1868:*see: "Good *1872:*And you have paid to *1888:*morning, Sir! DC,BrU: morning, Sir!" *1889:*morning, Sir!" 379| MS:compensation. Here *1888:* compensation. Still 380| MS:getting too acute; *1888:*getting nigh acute;
381| MS:There were so *P1868:*There gaped so 382| MS:fowl: *P1868:*fowl.
383| MS:The Lady mother <> a long life *P1868:*The mother <> a spun-out life
384| MS:In <> things: the <> well, *P1868:*I' <> things; the <> well
385| MS:rank— *P1868:*rank: 386| MS:stops— *P1868:*stops, 387| MS: parent-house: *P1868:*parent-hearth. 389| MS:helps. *P1868:*helps
390| MS:The second son accordingly, Paolo, *P1868:*A second son: and such was Paolo,

Established here at Rome these thirty years,
Who played the regular game,—priest and Abate,
Made friends, owned house and land, became of use
To a personage: his course lay clear enough.
The youngest caught the sympathetic flame,
And, though unfledged wings kept him still i' the cage,
Yet he shot up to be a Canon, so
Clung to the higher perch and crowed in hope.
Even our Guido, eldest brother, went
As far i' the way o' the Church as safety seemed,
He being Head o' the House, ordained to wive,—
So, could but dally with an Order or two
And testify good-will i' the cause: he clipped
His top-hair and thus far affected Christ.
But main promotion must fall otherwise,
Though still from the side o' the Church: and here was he
At Rome, since first youth, worn threadbare of soul
By forty-six years' rubbing on hard life,
Getting fast tired o' the game whose word is—"Wait!"
When one day,—he too having his Cardinal
To serve in some ambiguous sort, as serve
To draw the coach the plumes o' the horses' heads,—
The Cardinal saw fit to dispense with him,
Ride with one plume the less; and off it dropped.

Guido thus left,—with a youth spent in vain

392| MS:Played the whole regular < > abate, *P1868:*Who played the regular < > Abate, 394| MS:personage, his course was clear *P1868:*personage: his course lay clear 395| MS:flame *P1868:*flame, 396| MS:And though his clipt wings < > still at home, *P1868:*And, though unfledged wings < > still i' the cage, 397| MS:a Canon, and so *P1868:*a Canon, so 398| MS:Amid the poverty held on in *P1868:*Clung to the higher perch and crowed in 399| MS:our Guido, as the eldest *P1868:*our Guido, eldest 400| MS:in < > of < > safety was— *P1868:*i' < > o' < > safety seemed, 401| MS:of < > wive, *P1868:*o' < > wive,— 402| MS:So could < > an order *P1868:*So, could < > an Order 403| MS:good will in the cause—he clipt *P1868:*good-will i' the cause: he *1888:*clipped 404| MS:and so far < > Christ— *P1868:*and thus far < > Christ. 406| MS:of *P1868:*o' 407| MS:soul, *P1868:*soul 408| MS:forty six years *P1868:* forty-six years' 409| MS:of *P1868:*o' 410| MS:day—he *P1868:*day,—he 411| MS:sort—as *P1868:*sort, as 412| MS:on < > head— *P1868:*o' < > heads,— 413| MS:with his help, *P1868:*with him, 414| MS:Go with < > less,—so off *P1868:*Ride with < > less; and off 414-15| MS:§ no ¶ § *P1868:*§ ¶ §

And not a penny in purse to show for it,—
Advised with Paolo, bent no doubt in chafe
The black brows somewhat formidably, growled
"Where is the good I came to get at Rome?
Where the repayment of the servitude
To a purple popinjay, whose feet I kiss,
Knowing his father wiped the shoes of mine?"

"Patience," pats Paolo the recalcitrant—
"You have not had, so far, the proper luck,
Nor do my gains suffice to keep us both:
A modest competency is mine, not more.
You are the Count however, yours the style,
Heirdom and state,—you can't expect all good.
Had I, now, held your hand of cards . . . well, well—
What's yet unplayed, I'll look at, by your leave,
Over your shoulder,—I who made my game,
Let's see, if I can't help to handle yours.
Fie on you, all the Honours in your fist,
Countship, Househeadship,—how have you misdealt!
Why, in the first place, these will marry a man!
Notum tonsoribus! To the Tonsor then!
Come, clear your looks, and choose your freshest suit,

415| MS:with his youth *P1868:*with a youth 416-18| MS:Without a penny,—advised with Paolo, bent/ <> formidably the while,— *P1868:*And not a penny in purse to show for it,/ Advised with Paolo, bent no doubt in chafe/ <> while. *1872://* <> formidably, growled *1888:*it,— 419| MS:was <> Rome, *P1868:*is <> Rome? 420| MS:the pay of the ten years' servitude *P1868:*the repayment of the servitude 421| MS:whose shoes I wipe, *P1868:*whose feet I kiss, 422| MS: father blacked the *P1868:*father wiped the 422-23| MS:§ no ¶ § *P1868:*§ ¶ § *1888:*§ no ¶; paragraph restored. See Editorial Notes. § 423| MS:"Patience," tries Paolo with the *P1868:*"Patience," pats Paolo the 424| MS:You <> far, a luck like mine, *P1868:*"You <> far, the proper luck, 426| MS:I have a modest competency—not *P1868:*A modest competency is mine, not 427| MS:the Count moreover, have the *P1868:*the Count however, yours the 428| MS:Heirship and all,—you *P1868:*Heirdom and state,—you 429| MS:cards . . well, well. *P1868:*well, well— *1888:*cards . . . well, well— 430| MS:unplayed . . I'll *P1868:*unplayed, I'll 431| MS:shoulder,—I have made *P1868:*shoulder,—I who made 432-34| MS:yours./ <> how shall we deal with these? *P1868:*yours./ Fie on you, all the Honours in your fist,/ <> how have you misdealt! 435| MS:place, they will *1872:*place, these will 436| MS:Notum tonsoribus! To the Tonsor's *P1868:Notum Tonsoribus!* To the Tonsor 437| MS:looks, choose

And, after function's done with, down we go
To the woman-dealer in perukes, a wench
I and some others settled in the shop
At Place Colonna: she's an oracle. Hmm!
'Dear, 'tis my brother: brother, 'tis my dear.
Dear, give us counsel! Whom do you suggest
As properest party in the quarter round
For the Count here?—he is minded to take wife,
And further tells me he intends to slip
Twenty zecchines under the bottom-scalp
Of his old wig when he sends it to revive
For the wedding: and I add a trifle too.
You know what personage I'm potent with.' "
And so plumped out Pompilia's name the first.
She told them of the household and its ways,
The easy husband and the shrewder wife
In Via Vittoria,—how the tall young girl,
With hair black as yon patch and eyes as big
As yon pomander to make freckles fly,
Would have so much for certain, and so much more
In likelihood,—why, it suited, slipped as smooth
As the Pope's pantoufle does on the Pope's foot.
"I'll to the husband!" Guido ups and cries.
"Ay, so you'd play your last court-card, no doubt!"
Puts Paolo in with a groan—"Only, you see,
'Tis I, this time, that supervise your lead.

---

you your *P1868:*looks, and choose your 438| MS:And after *P1868:*And, after 439| MS:woman dealer *P1868:*woman-dealer 441| MS:In Place <> she's our oracle. *P1868:*At Place <> she's an oracle. Hmm! 442| MS:"Dear, 'tis my Brother: Brother <> Dear: *P1868:*'Dear, 'tis my brother: brother <> dear. 443| MS:counsel:whom *P1868:*counsel! Whom 444|. MS:round, *1888:*round 445| MS:here, who is <> wife *1868:*here?—he is <> wife, 447| MS:zecchines into the *P1868:*zecchines under the 448| MS:send you it *P1868:*send it 449| MS:wedding, and I'll <> too— *P1868:*wedding: and I *CP1868:*too. 450| MS:with." *P1868:*with.' " 451| MS:first: *P1868:*first. 452| MS:told him of *P1868:*told them of 454| MS:girl *P1868:*girl, 455-57| MS:yon wig and twice as thick/ Would *P1868:*yon patch and eyes as big/ As yon pomander to make freckles fly,/ Would 458| MS:slipt *1888:*slipped 459| MS:pantoufle goes on *P1868:*pantoufle does on 460| MS:"I'll go to the Husband," Guido <> cries— *P1868:*"I'll to the husband!" Guido <> cries. 461| MS:doubt,— *P1868:*doubt!" 463| MS:that have a care of the game. *P1868:*that supervise your

Priests play with women, maids, wives, mothers—why?
These play with men and take them off our hands.
Did I come, counsel with some cut-beard gruff
Or rather this sleek young-old barberess?
Go, brother, stand you rapt in the ante-room
Of Her Efficacity my Cardinal
For an hour,—he likes to have lord-suitors lounge,—
While I betake myself to the grey mare,
The better horse,—how wise the people's word!—
And wait on Madam Violante."

Said and done.

He was at Via Vittoria in three skips:
Proposed at once to fill up the one want
O' the burgess-family which, wealthy enough,
And comfortable to heart's desire, yet crouched
Outside a gate to heaven,—locked, bolted, barred,
Whereof Count Guido had a key he kept
Under his pillow, but Pompilia's hand
Might slide behind his neck and pilfer thence.
The key was fairy; its mere mention made
Violante feel the thing shoot one sharp ray
That reached the womanly heart: so—"I assent!
Yours be Pompilia, hers and ours that key

lead. 464| MS:Priests deal with <> mothers,—for why? *P1868:*Priests play with <> mothers,—why? *1872:*mothers—why? 465| MS:These deal with *P1868:*These play with 467| MS:rather with this <> young barberess? *P1868:*rather this <> young-old barberess? 468| MS:anteroom *P1868:*ante-room 469| MS:Of the efficacious man my *P1868:*Of Her Efficacity my 470| MS:have Count-suitors *P1868:*have lord-suitors 471| MS:myself, as the proverb bids, § last four words crossed out and replaced above by four words § to the grey mare, *P1868:*myself to 472| MS:To the grey mare, that's also the better horse § line crossed out and replaced above by § That's the better horse,—who wise the peoples' word!— *P1868:*The better horse,—how wise the people's 473| MS:on Madam Violante." § no ¶ § Said and done: *P1868:*on Madam Violante." § ¶ § Said and done. 474| MS:He § in margin § Was *P1868:*He was 476| MS:Of <> enough *P1868:*O' <> enough, 477| MS:yet sate *P1868:*yet crouched
480| MS:pillow—and which Pompilia's *P1868:*pillow, but Pompilia's
482| MS:fairy, mention of it, made *1888:*fairy; its mere mention made
483| MS:Violante see the same shoot *P1868:*Violante feel the thing shoot
484| MS:the heart of the woman: "I assent— *P1868:*o' the woman. "I assent: *1888:* the womanly heart: so—"I assent! 485| MS:be Pompila; hers *P1868:*be Pompilia,

To all the glories of the greater life!
There's Pietro to convince: leave that to me!"

Then was the matter broached to Pietro; then
Did Pietro make demand and get response
That in the Countship was a truth, but in
The counting up of the Count's cash, a lie.
He thereupon stroked grave his chin, looked great,
Declined the honour. Then the wife wiped tear,
Winked with the other eye turned Paolo-ward,
Whispered Pompilia, stole to church at eve,
Found Guido there and got the marriage done,
And finally begged pardon at the feet
Of her dear lord and master. Whereupon
Quoth Pietro—"Let us make the best of things!"
"I knew your love would license us," quoth she:
Quoth Paolo once more, "Mothers, wives and maids,
These be the tools wherewith priests manage men."

Now, here take breath and ask,—which bird o' the brace
Decoyed the other into clapnet? Who
Was fool, who knave? Neither and both, perchance.
There was a bargain mentally proposed
On each side, straight and plain and fair enough;
Mind knew its own mind: but when mind must speak,
The bargain have expression in plain terms,
There came the blunder incident to words,

---

hers 486| MS:life,— *P1868:*life! 487-88| MS:§ no ¶ § *P1868:*§ ¶ § 491| MS:lie: *1872:*lie. 492| MS:stroked down his *P1868:*stroked grave his 493| MS:the honor: then < > wiped one *P1868:*the honour. Then < > one— *1872:*wiped tear, 494| MS:eye, went out with Paolo, *P1868:*eye turned Paolo-ward, 496| MS:done *P1868:*done, 497| MS:And bitterly begged *P1868:*And finally begged 498| MS:master:whereupon *P1868:*master. Whereupon 499| MS:Says Pietro *P1868:*Quoth Pietro 500| MS:licence *1888:*license 501| MS:once again "Women-maids, wives and mothers, *P1868:*once more, "Mothers, wives and maids, 502| MS:wherewith we manage *P1868:*wherewith priests manage 502-3| MS:§ no ¶ § *P1868:*§ ¶ § 503| MS:of *P1868:*o' 505| MS:both, I say. *P1868:*both, perchance. 507| MS:On both sides < > enough: *P1868:*On each side < > enough; 509| MS:terms *P1868:*terms, 510| MS:There was confusion incident

And in the clumsy process, fair turned foul.
The straight backbone-thought of the crooked speech
Were just—"I Guido truck my name and rank
For so much money and youth and female charms."—
"We Pietro and Violante give our child
And wealth to you for a rise i' the world thereby."
Such naked truth while chambered in the brain
Shocks nowise: walk it forth by way of tongue,—
Out on the cynical unseemliness!
Hence was the need, on either side, of a lie
To serve as decent wrappage: so, Guido gives
Money for money,—and they, bride for groom,
Having, he, not a doit, they, not a child
Honestly theirs, but this poor waif and stray.
According to the words, each cheated each;
But in the inexpressive barter of thoughts,
Each did give and did take the thing designed,
The rank on this side and the cash on that—
Attained the object of the traffic, so.
The way of the world, the daily bargain struck
In the first market! Why sells Jack his ware?
"For the sake of serving an old customer."

---

*P1868:*was the blunder incident *1888:*There came the 512| MS:backbone of the crooked fact were just *P1868:*backbone-thought of the crooked speech 513| MS:"I, Guido, truck <> and social power *P1868:*Were just—"I Guido truck <> and rank 514| MS:money, and youth and handsomeness—" *P1868:*money and youth and female charms."— *1872:*charms.— § emended to § charms."— § see Editorial Notes § 515| MS:"We, Pietro *P1868:*"We Pietro *1888:*'We § emended to § "We § see Editorial Notes § 516| MS:in <> thereby—" *P1868:*i' <> thereby." *1872:*thereby. *1888:*thereby." 517| MS:The naked thought in the chamber of the *P1868:*Such naked truth while chambered in the 518| MS:of the tongue,— *P1868:*of tongue,— 520| MS:need on <> side of *P1868:*need, on <> side, of 521| MS:serve § followed by illegible erasure § as decent § inserted above § wrappage: and Guido *P1868:*wrappage: so, Guido 522| MS:money,— they, good name for name, *P1868:*money,—and they, bride for groom, 523| MS:he—not a doit *P1868:*he, not a doit 525| MS:words each <> each, *P1868:*words, each <> each; 526| MS:of mind *P1868:*of thoughts, 527| MS:designed— *P1868:*designed, 528| MS:the money on *P1868:*the cash on 529| MS:traffic, I say. *P1868:*traffic, so. 530| MS:world:that's just the bargain *P1868:*world, the daily bargain 531| MS:market—why sells the one his ware *P1868:*market! Why sells Jack his ware? 532| MS:customer—"

Why does Jill buy it? "Simply not to break
A custom, pass the old stall the first time."
Why, you know where the gist is of the exchange:
Each sees a profit, throws the fine words in.
Don't be too hard o' the pair! Had each pretence
Been simultaneously discovered, stript
From off the body o' the transaction, just
As when a cook (will Excellency forgive?)
Strips away those long rough superfluous legs
From either side the crayfish, leaving folk
A meal all meat henceforth, no garnishry,
(With your respect, Prince!)—balance had been kept,
No party blamed the other,—so, starting fair,
All subsequent fence of wrong returned by wrong
I' the matrimonial thrust and parry, at least
Had followed on equal terms. But, as it chanced,
One party had the advantage, saw the cheat
Of the other first and kept its own concealed:
And the luck o' the first discovery fell, beside,
To the least adroit and self-possessed o' the pair.
'Twas foolish Pietro and his wife saw first

---

*P1868:*customer." 533| MS:does the other buy it? "Not to *P1868:*does Jill buy it? "Simply not to 534| MS:stall this first *P1868:*stall the first 535| MS:gist of the bargain is— *P1868:*gist is of the exchange: 536| MS:sees his profit and throws *P1868:*sees a profit, throws 537| MS:on the parties. Had both § crossed out and replaced above by § each pretence *P1868:*o' the pair! Had
538| MS:simultaneously renounced § crossed out and replaced above by § discovered, stripped off *P1868:*stripped *1888:*stript 539-46| MS:The body of the transaction like garnish of legs/ From the meat and truth of the crayfish, on both sides/ At one and the same time,—balance had been kept,/ And neither blamed the other,—so, starting fair,/ All *P1868:*From off the body o' the transaction, just/ As when a cook . . will Excellency forgive?/ Strips away those long loose superfluous legs/ From either side the crayfish, leaving folk/ A meal all meat henceforth, no garnishry,/ (With your respect, Prince!)—balance <> / No party blamed <> / All *1872:*/ <> cook (will <> forgive?)/ <> long superfluous *1888:*// <> long rough superfluous
546| MS:by wrong— *P1868:*by wrong 547| MS:In *P1868:*I' 548| MS:Had been on <> terms: but *P1868:*Had followed on <> terms. But 549| MS:One had *P1868:*One party had 550| MS:other and <> concealed. *P1868:*other first and <> concealed: 551| MS:of <> besides, *P1868:*o' <> beside,
552| MS:of *P1868:*o' 553| MS:'Twas the foolish burgess couple that saw

The nobleman was penniless, and screamed
"We are cheated!"

Such unprofitable noise
Angers at all times: but when those who plague,
Do it from inside your own house and home,
Gnats which yourself have closed the curtain round,
Noise goes too near the brain and makes you mad.
The gnats say, Guido used the candle-flame
Unfairly,—worsened that first bad of his,
By practising all kinds of cruelty
To oust them and suppress the wail and whine,—
That speedily he so scared and bullied them,
Fain were they, long before five months had passed,
To beg him grant, from what was once their wealth,
Just so much as would help them back to Rome
Where, when they finished paying the last doit
O' the dowry, they might beg from door to door.
So say the Comparini—as if it came
Of pure resentment for this worse than bad,
That then Violante, feeling conscience prick,
Confessed her substitution of the child
Whence all the harm fell,—and that Pietro first
Bethought him of advantage to himself

P1868:'Twas foolish Pietro and his wife saw 554| MS:The man though noble was *P1868:*The nobleman was 555| MS:cheated!" § no ¶ § This unprofitable *P1868:*cheated!" § ¶ § Such unprofitable 556| MS:times—but <> who scream *P1868:*times: but <> who plague, 557| MS:inside of your house *P1868:*inside your own house 558| MS:Gnats you yourself <> curtains *P1868:*Gnats which yourself <> curtain 559| MS:It goes to near *P1868:*Noise goes too near 560| MS:say that he used the candle flame *P1868:*say, Guido used the candle-flame 561| MS:his *P1868:*his, 562| MS:By practise of all kinds *P1868:*kind *1888:*By practising all kinds 563| MS:suppress their wail *P1868:*suppress the wail 564| MS:That he speedily so <> them *P1868:*That speedily he so <> them, 565| MS:That they were fain before five months were out, *P1868:*Fain were they, long before *1888:*months had passed, 566| MS:grant from <> their all *P1868:* grant, from <> their wealth, 568| MS:they had finished *1888:*they finished 569| MS:Of *P1868:*O' 570| MS:the Comparini—and that it was *P1868:*the Comparini—as if it were *1888:*it came 571| MS:In pure <> bad *P1868:*bad, *1888:*Of pure 572| MS:That Violante, feeling first her conscience *P1868:*That then Violante, feeling conscience 573| MS:Confessed the substitution *P1868:* Confessed her substitution 574| MS:harm came,—and Pietro thereupon *P1868:* and that Pietro first DC,BrU:harm fell,—and *1889:*harm fell,—and 575| MS:

I' the deed, as part revenge, part remedy
For all miscalculation in the pact.

On the other hand "Not so!" Guido retorts—
"I am the wronged, solely, from first to last,
Who gave the dignity I engaged to give,
Which was, is, cannot but continue gain.
My being poor was a bye-circumstance,
Miscalculated piece of untowardness,
Might end to-morrow did heaven's windows ope,
Or uncle die and leave me his estate.
You should have put up with the minor flaw,
Getting the main prize of the jewel. If wealth,
Not rank, had been prime object in your thoughts,
Why not have taken the butcher's son, the boy
O' the baker or candlestick-maker? In all the rest,
It was yourselves broke compact and played false,
And made a life in common impossible.
Show me the stipulation of our bond
That you should make your profit of being inside
My house, to hustle and edge me out o' the same,
First make a laughing-stock of mine and me,
Then round us in the ears from morn to night
(Because we show wry faces at your mirth)

---

himself— *P1868:*himself 576| MS:Not only the revenge, but remedy *P1868:*I' the act as part revenge, part remedy *CP1868:*the deed, as 577-78| MS:pact,/ And getting quit of the bond which pressed too much./ § no ¶ § On *P1868:*pact./ § ¶ § On 578| MS:retorts *P1868:*retorts— 579| MS:last *P1868:*last, 580| MS:I gave *P1868:*Who gave 581| MS:That was <> gain *P1868:*Which was <> gain. 582| MS:bye-circumstance— *P1868:*bye-circumstance, 583| MS:An uncalculated <> untowardness *P1868:*Miscalculated <> untowardness, 584| MS:Which might end to-morrow should heaven's <> ope *P1868:*Might end to-morrow did heaven's <> ope, 585| MS:My uncle *P1868:*Or uncle 586| MS:flaw *P1868:*flaw, 587| MS:jewel, if wealth *P1868:*jewel. If wealth, 588| MS:rank had <> thoughts *P1868:*rank, had <> thoughts, 589| MS:the Butcher's <> the son *P1868:*the butcher's <> the boy 590| MS:Of the Baker and candlestick maker <> rest *P1868:*O' the baker or candlestick-maker *CP1868:*rest, 591| MS:'Twas yourselves broke the compact <> false *P1868:*It was yourselves broke compact <> false, 592-94| MS:By making the stipulated provisions null,/ The projected life in common impossible:/ It was scarce part of the original pact/ That *P1868:*And made a life in common impossible./ Show me the stipulation of our bond/ That 595| MS:house to <> of it: *P1868:*house, to <> o' the same, 596| MS:laughing stock *P1868:*laughingstock *CP1868:*laughing-stock 598| MS:Because we made

That you are robbed, starved, beaten and what not!
You fled a hell of your own lighting-up,
Pay for your own miscalculation too:
You thought nobility, gained at any price,
Would suit and satisfy,—find the mistake,
And now retaliate, not on yourselves, but me.
And how? By telling me, i' the face of the world,
I it is have been cheated all this while,
Abominably and irreparably,—my name
Given to a cur-cast mongrel, a drab's brat,
A beggar's bye-blow,—thus depriving me
Of what yourselves allege the whole and sole
Aim on my part i' the marriage,—money to-wit.
This thrust I have to parry by a guard
Which leaves me open to a counter-thrust
On the other side,—no way but there's a pass
Clean through me. If I prove, as I hope to do,
There's not one truth in this your odious tale
O' the buying, selling, substituting—prove
Your daughter was and is your daughter,—well,
And her dowry hers and therefore mine,—what then?
Why, where's the appropriate punishment for this
Enormous lie hatched for mere malice' sake
To ruin me? Is that a wrong or no?
And if I try revenge for remedy,

---

wry <> mirth, *P1868:*(Because we show wry <> mirth) 599| MS:you were robbed <> not. *P1868:*you are robbed <> not! 600| MS:lighting-up;— *P1868:*lighting-up, 601| MS:miscalculation, too— *P1868:*miscalculation too: 602| MS:nobility gained <> price *P1868:*nobility, gained <> price, 603| MS: satisfy,—found your mistake,— *P1868:*satisfy,—find the mistake, 604| MS: retaliate not on yourselves but *P1868:*retaliate, not on yourselves, but 605| MS: in *P1868:*i' 606| MS:That I it is who have <> all the while, *P1868:*I it is have <> all the while, 608| MS:cur-cast creature, a <> brat *P1868:*cur-cast mongrel, a <> brat, 610| MS:allege is the *P1868:*allege the 611| MS:in the marriage; the money to-wit: *P1868:*i' the marriage,—money to-wit. 613| MS:counterthrust *P1868:*counter-thrust 617| MS:Of the buying and selling and substituting and the rest, *P1868:*O' the buying, selling, substituting—prove 618| MS:That you *P1868:*Your 620| MS:Why what do you deserve for the hatching this *P1868:*Why, where's the appropriate punishment for this 621| MS: lie merely for malice' *P1868:*lie hatched for mere malice' 623| MS:try a remedy for the same *P1868:*try revenge for remedy, 624| MS:enough? *P1868:*enough?"

Can I well make it strong and bitter enough?"

I anticipate however—only ask,
Which of the two here sinned most? A nice point!
Which brownness is least black,—decide who can,
Wager-by-battle-of-cheating! What do you say,
Highness? Suppose, your Excellency, we leave
The question at this stage, proceed to the next,
Both parties step out, fight their prize upon,
In the eye o' the world?
They brandish law 'gainst law;
The grinding of such blades, each parry of each,
Throws terrible sparks off, over and above the thrusts,
And makes more sinister the fight, to the eye,
Than the very wounds that follow. Beside the tale
Which the Comparini have to re-assert,
They needs must write, print, publish all abroad
The straitnesses of Guido's household life—
The petty nothings we bear privately
But break down under when fools flock to jeer.
What is it all to the facts o' the couple's case,
How helps it prove Pompilia not their child,
If Guido's mother, brother, kith and kin
Fare ill, lie hard, lack clothes, lack fire, lack food?
That's one more wrong than needs.

On the other hand,
Guido,—whose cue is to dispute the truth
O' the tale, reject the shame it throws on him,—

624-25| MS:§ no ¶ § *P1868:*§ ¶ § 625| MS:however—all I should say is this: *P1868:*however—only ask, 626| MS:two cheats sinned *P1868:*two here sinned 627| MS:decide you § crossed out and replaced above by § who can, 628| MS:This wager *P1868:*Wager 630| MS:next. *P1868:*next, 630-31| MS:§ ¶ § *P1868:* § no ¶ § 631| MS:out then to fight <> prize *P1868:*out, fight <> prize upon, 632| MS:of the world—take weapons, law 'gainst *P1868:*o' the world? § ¶ § They brandish law 'gainst 633| MS:blades, each upon each, *P1868:*blades, each parry of each, 634| MS:thrusts— *P1868:*thrusts, 636| MS:that happen. Beside *P1868:*that follow. Beside 637| MS:reassert, *P1868:*re-assert, 640| MS: nothings men bear *P1868:*nothings we bear 641| MS:But go mad if they come to be made known. *P1868:*But break down under when fools flock around. *1872:*flock to jeer. 642| MS:of <> case *P1868:*o' <> case, 643| MS:Who come to prove *P1868:*How helps it prove 644| MS:That Guido's <> brother, and himself *P1868:*If Guido's <> brother, kith and kin 646| MS:There's one <> than should be: § no ¶ § on *P1868:*That's one <> than needs. § ¶ § On 647| MS:Guido, whose *P1868:*Guido,—whose 648| MS:Of the tale, resist the

He may retaliate, fight his foe in turn
And welcome, we allow. Ay, but he can't!
He's at home, only acts by proxy here:
Law may meet law,—but all the gibes and jeers,
The superfluity of naughtiness,
Those libels on his House,—how reach at them?
Two hateful faces, grinning all a-glow,
Not only make parade of spoil they filched,
But foul him from the height of a tower, you see.
Unluckily temptation is at hand—
To take revenge on a trifle overlooked,
A pet lamb they have left in reach outside,
Whose first bleat, when he plucks the wool away,
Will strike the grinners grave: his wife remains
Who, four months earlier, some thirteen years old,
Never a mile away from mother's house
And petted to the height of her desire,
Was told one morning that her fate had come,
She must be married—just as, a month before,
Her mother told her she must comb her hair
And twist her curls into one knot behind.
These fools forgot their pet lamb, fed with flowers,
Then 'ticed as usual by the bit of cake

<> him, *P1868:*O' the tale, reject the <> him,— 649| MS:retaliate, plague his foes *P1868:*retaliate, fight his foe 650| MS:allow: ay <> can't— *P1868:*allow. Ay <> can't! 651| MS:here, *P1868:*here: 652-54| MS:Law meets the law,—but the <> jeers, you see,/ The libels <> house <> those *P1868:*Law may meet law,—but all the <> jeers,/ The superfluity of naughtiness,/ Those libels <> House <> them? 655-57| MS:§ line 655 crowded between lines 654-57 § aglow,/ Who spit at him <> tower, I ask? *P1868:*a-glow,/ Not only make parade of spoil they filched,/ But foul him <> tower, you see. 658| MS:Unluckily a temptation <> hand, *P1868:*Unluckily temptation <> hand— 660| MS:left outside the door, *P1868:*left in reach outside, 661| MS:bleat when <> away *P1868:*bleat, when <> away, 662-63| MS:grave and spoil their sport./ His wife remains,—plague her and he plagues them—/ The little wife, the poor Pompilia thing/ Who four <> earlier, being thirteen *P1868:*grave: his wife remains/ Who, four <> earlier, some thirteen 664| MS:from the mother's *P1868:*from mother's 666| MS:her time was come, *P1868:*her fate was *1888:*fate had come, 667| MS:be wed § crossed out § married—just as a <> before *P1868:*as, a <> before, 668| MS: mother had told *P1868:*mother told 669| MS:behind— *P1868:*behind. 670| MS:As I said, the pet <> fed since a year with flowers, *P1868:*These fools forgot their pet <> fed with flowers, 671| MS:Then led as *P1868:*Then 'ticed as <>

Out of the bower into the butchery.
Plague her, he plagues them threefold: but how plague?
The world may have its word to say to that:
You can't do some things with impunity.
What remains . . . well, it is an ugly thought . . .
But that he drive herself to plague herself—
Herself disgrace herself and so disgrace
Who seek to disgrace Guido?

There's the clue
To what else seems gratuitously vile,
If, as is said, from this time forth the rack
Was tried upon Pompilia: 'twas to wrench
Her limbs into exposure that brings shame.
The aim o' the cruelty being so crueller still,
That cruelty almost grows compassion's self
Could one attribute it to mere return
O' the parents' outrage, wrong avenging wrong.
They see in this a deeper deadlier aim,
Not to vex just a body they held dear,
But blacken too a soul they boasted white,
And show the world their saint in a lover's arms,
No matter how driven thither,—so they say.

On the other hand, so much is easily said,
And Guido lacks not an apologist.

---

cake, DC,BrU:cake *1889:*cake 672-75| MS:By the old garden-door into the butcher's pen:/ Here was she, scared, staring at the four walls,—/ Ill-treat her,—he ill-treats them,—but how ill-treat?/ The world, you know, has its < > that—/ You *P1868:*Out of the bower into the butchery./ Plague her, he plagues them threefold: but how plague?/ The world may have its < > that:/ You 676| MS:remains . . well < > thought . . *1888:*remains . . . well < > thought . . . 677| MS:that you drive her to ill-treat herself— *P1868:*that he drive herself to plague herself— 678| MS:so—disgrace them *P1868:*so disgrace 679| MS:disgrace Guido? § no ¶ § There you have the *P1868:*disgrace Guido? § ¶ § There's the 681| MS:time the extremest screw *P1868:*time forth the rack 682| MS:Was put upon *P1868:*Was tried upon 683| MS:into the exposure *P1868:*into exposure 684| MS:of < > still *P1868:*o' < > still, 685| MS:That it would almost grow compassion itself *P1868:*That cruelty almost grows compassion's self 687-90| MS:Of < > wrong revenging wrong—/ That simply the trying to vex a body they held dear,/ That to blacken a < > white— *P1868:*O' < > wrong avenging wrong./ They see in this a deeper deadlier aim,/ Not to vex just a < > / But blacken too a < > white, 691| MS:show their saint to the world in *P1868:*show the world their saint in 692-93| MS:§ no ¶ § *P1868:*§ ¶ § 694| MS:And Guido's friends are ready in reply.

The pair had nobody but themselves to blame,
Being selfish beasts throughout, no less, no more:
—Cared for themselves, their supposed good, nought else,
And brought about the marriage; good proved bad,
As little they cared for her its victim—nay,
Meant she should stay behind and take the chance,
If haply they might wriggle themselves free.
They baited their own hook to catch a fish
With this poor worm, failed o' the prize, and then
Sought how to unbait tackle, let worm float
Or sink, amuse the monster while they 'scaped.
Under the best stars Hymen brings above,
Had all been honesty on either side,
A common sincere effort to good end,
Still, this would prove a difficult problem, Prince!
—Given, a fair wife, aged thirteen years,
A husband poor, care-bitten, sorrow-sunk,
Little, long-nosed, bush-bearded, lantern-jawed,
Forty-six years old,—place the two grown one,
She, cut off sheer from every natural aid,
In a strange town with no familiar face—

---

*P1868:*And Guido lacks not an apologist. 695| MS:The Couple had *P1868:*The pair had 696| MS:throughout, no more, no less. *P1868:*throughout, no less, no more: 697| MS:They thought of themselves *P1868:*—Cared for themselves 698| MS:In bringing about the marriage,—that § crossed out and replaced above by § which, turning ill, *P1868:*And brought about the marriage; good proved bad, 699| MS:Just as little they thought about the victim—her *P1868:*As little they cared for her its victim—nay, 700| MS:She meant should stay and < > chance of the scrape *P1868:*Meant she should stay behind and < > chance, 701| MS:happly < > themselves thence. *P1868:*haply < > themselves free. 702| MS:catch the fish *P1868:*catch a fish 703| MS:worm,—failed of their prize,—and *P1868:*worm, failed o' the prize, and 704-7| MS:unbait their tackle, let the worm float or sink./ Under the best circumstances they could have hoped,/ Had *P1868:*unbait tackle, let worm float/ Or sink, amuse the monster while they 'scaped./ Under the best stars Hymen brings above,/ Had 707| MS:been honest and plain on *P1868:*been honesty on 708| MS:With a < > to carry out the plan,— *P1868:*A < > to good end, 709| MS:would have proved < > problem to solve *P1868:*would prove < > problem, Prince! 710| MS:—Given—a pure beautiful girl, of thirteen years § last three words inserted above and followed by / indicating end of line § —And a husband poor, harrassed with many cares, *P1868:*—Given, a fair wife, aged thirteen years,/ A husband poor, care-bitten, sorrow-sunk, 712| MS:long nosed, lantern-jawed, black-bush-bearded, *P1868:*long-nosed, bush-bearded, lantern-jawed, 713-15| MS:Forty-six-years old,—she with none of her natural helps,/ < > town without a familiar *P1868:*Forty-six-years full,—place

He, in his own parade-ground or retreat
If need were, free from challenge, much less check
To an irritated, disappointed will—
How evolve happiness from such a match?
'Twere hard to serve up a congenial dish
Out of these ill-agreeing morsels, Duke,
By the best exercise of the cook's craft,
Best interspersion of spice, salt and sweet!
But let two ghastly scullions concoct mess
With brimstone, pitch, vitriol and devil's-dung—
Throw in abuse o' the man, his body and soul,
Kith, kin and generation, shake all slab
At Rome, Arezzo, for the world to nose,
Then end by publishing, for fiend's arch-prank,
That, over and above sauce to the meat's self,
Why, even the meat, bedevilled thus in dish,
Was never a pheasant but a carrion-crow—
Prince, what will then the natural loathing be?
What wonder if this?—the compound plague o' the pair
Pricked Guido,—not to take the course they hoped,
That is, submit him to their statement's truth,

---

the two grown one,/ She, cut off sheer from every natural aid,/ <> town with no familiar *1872:*Forty-six-years old,—place *1888:*Forty-six years 716-18| MS:He in his own place and free from all the checks/ To *P1868:*He, in his own parade-ground or retreat/ As need were, free from challenge, much less check/ To *1888:*If need 718| MS:an irritable, disappointed *P1868:*an irritated, disappointed 719| MS: How to make happiness come from *P1868:*How evolve happiness from 720| 1889:Twere § see Editorial Notes § 721| MS:morsels and meats *P1868:*morsels, Duke, 723| MS:spice and salt and sweet. *P1868:*spice, salt and sweet! 724| MS:ghastly cooks concoct the mess *P1868:*ghastly scullions concoct mess 725| MS:devil's dung— *P1868:*devil's-dung—
726| MS:of *P1868:*o' 727| MS:generation, shake up the pan *P1868:*shake all slab § see Editorial Notes § 728| MS:At Rome, at Arezzo, for all the <> to smell. *P1868:*At Rome, Arezzo, for the <> to nose, 729| MS:And end all by revealing your arch-feat and cheat *P1868:*Then end by publishing, for fiend's arch-prank, 730-32| MS:That over and above the sauce <> meat itself/ The bestiality that all recognize as enough,/ Why even the meat thus bedevilled in his dish,/ <> carrion crow! *P1868:*That, over and above sauce to the meat's self,/ Why <> meat bedevilled thus in dish,/ <> carrion crow— *CP1868:*/ Why, even the meat, bedevilled <> / <> carrion-crow— 733| MS:Why, what will the <> loathing grow to then *P1868:*Prince, what will then the <> loathing be? 734| MS:if to this, that the <> plague *P1868:*if this?—the <> plague o' the pair 736| MS:is, submitting to the statements' truth *P1868:*is, submit him to their statement's truth,

Accept its obvious promise of relief,
And thrust them out of doors the girl again
Since the girl's dowry would not enter there,
—Quit of the one if baulked of the other: no!
Rather did rage and hate so work in him,
Their product proved the horrible conceit
That he should plot and plan and bring to pass
His wife might, of her own free will and deed,
Relieve him of her presence, get her gone,
And yet leave all the dowry safe behind,
Confirmed his own henceforward past dispute,
While blotting out, as by a belch of hell,
Their triumph in her misery and death.

You see, the man was Aretine, had touch
O' the subtle air that breeds the subtle wit;
Was noble too, of old blood thrice-refined
That shrinks from clownish coarseness in disgust:
Allow that such an one may take revenge,
You don't expect he'll catch up stone and fling,
Or try cross-buttock, or whirl quarter-staff?
Instead of the honest drubbing clowns bestow,

737| MS:To take the obvious relief it left in his way, *P1868:*Accept its obvious promise of relief, 738| MS:of his doors *P1868:*of doors 739| MS:And bid them take her, dowry and all—himself *P1868:*Since the girl's dowry would not enter there, 740-43| MS:Quit < > other: and so/ Consummate their triumph?—No, it rather pricked/ In the working of rage, hate, disappointment, thus—/ < > should so contrive as bring *P1868:*—Quit < > other: no!/ Rather did rage and hate so work in him,/ Their product proved the horrible conceit/ < > should plot and plan and bring 744| MS:How his wife should, of *P1868:*His wife might, of 745| MS:presence and rid his house, *P1868:*presence, get her gone, 748| MS:Along with unimaginable disgrace *P1868:*While blotting out, as by a belch of hell,
749-50| MS:§ 750 comes at top of page but apparently no ¶ intended § *P1868:*§ ¶ §
750| MS:was an Aretine, *P1868:*was Aretine, had touch 751| MS:Of < > wit, *P1868:*O' < > wit; 752| MS:He was < > too, of the old refined blood *P1868:*Was < > too, of the old blood thrice-refined *CP1868:*of old
753| MS:That has the clownish *P1868:*That shrinks from clownish
755| MS:stones and throw, *P1868:*stone and fling, 756| MS:Nor try cross-buttock nor whirl quarter staff? *P1868:*Or try cross-buttock, Or whirl quarter-staff? *CP1868:*cross-buttock, or 757| MS:drubbing a clown bestows

When out of temper at the dinner spoilt,
On meddling mother-in-law and tiresome wife,—
Substitute for the clown a nobleman,
And you have Guido, practising, 'tis said,
Immitigably from the very first,
The finer vengeance: this, they say, the fact
O' the famous letter shows—the writing traced
At Guido's instance by the timid wife
Over the pencilled words himself writ first—
Wherein she, who could neither write nor read,
Was made unblushingly declare a tale
To the brother, the Abate then in Rome,
How her putative parents had impressed,
On their departure, their enjoinment; bade
"We being safely arrived here, follow, you!
Poison your husband, rob, set fire to all,
And then by means o' the gallant you procure
With ease, by helpful eye and ready tongue,
Some brave youth ready to dare, do and die,
You shall run off and merrily reach Rome
Where we may live like flies in honey-pot:"—
Such being exact the programme of the course
Imputed her as carried to effect.

They also say,—to keep her straight therein,

---

*P1868:*drubbing clowns bestow, 758-60| MS:temper and his dinner <> / Substitute the same spirit in another form— *P1868:*temper at the dinner <> / On meddling mother-in-law and tiresome wife,—/ Substitute for the clown a nobleman, 761| MS:have him planning and practicing, as they say, *P1868:*have Guido,—practicing, 'tis said, *CP1868:*have Guido, practicing 762| MS:Unmitigably *1872:*Immitigably 763| MS:This finer *P1868:*The finer 764| MS:Of *P1868:*O' 765| MS:On Guido's compulsion by *P1868:*At Guido's instance by 766| MS:first *CP1868:*first— 767| MS:And set before her who <> read. *P1868:*Wherein she, who <> read, 768| MS:Wherein she was made <> declare *P1868:*Was made <> declare a tale 770| MS:impressed *P1868:*impressed, 771| MS:departure their enjoinment thus. *P1868:*departure, their enjoinment; bade 772| MS:arrived, follow you us, *P1868:*arrived here, follow, you! 773| MS:rob and fire the house, *P1868:*rob, set fire to all, 774| MS:of the lover you shall procure *P1868:*o' the gallant you procure 776| MS:Some brisk youth <> dare and do *P1868:*The brave youth <> dare, do and *1888:*Some brave 777| MS:shall elope and merrily run to Rome *P1868:*shall run off and merrily reach Rome 778| MS:Where we'll all live <> in a honey-pot:" *P1868:*Where we may live <> in honey-pot:"— 779| MS:being the exact programme *P1868:*being exact the programme 780| MS:Imputed to her as carried into effect:—

All sort of torture was piled, pain on pain,
On either side Pompilia's path of life,
Built round about and over against by fear,
Circumvallated month by month, and week
By week, and day by day, and hour by hour,
Close, closer and yet closer still with pain,
No outlet from the encroaching pain save just
Where stood one saviour like a piece of heaven,
Hell's arms would strain round but for this blue gap.
She, they say further, first tried every chink,
Every imaginable break i' the fire,
As way of escape: ran to the Commissary,
Who bade her not malign his friend her spouse;
Flung herself thrice at the Archbishop's feet,
Where three times the Archbishop let her lie,
Spend her whole sorrow and sob full heart forth,
And then took up the slight load from the ground
And bore it back for husband to chastise,—
Mildly of course,—but natural right is right.
So went she slipping ever yet catching at help,
Missing the high till come to lowest and last,

---

*P1868:*Imputed her as carried to effect. 780-81| MS:§ no ¶ § *P1868:*§ ¶ § 781| MS:say that to <> straight thereto, *P1868:*say,—to <> straight therein, 782-84| MS:was steadily increased,/ <> fear *P1868:*was piled, pain on pain,/ On either side Pompilia's path of life,/ <> fear, 785| MS:by month and week by week *P1868:*by month, and week 786| MS:And day by <> by hour, close, closer *P1868:*By week, and day by <> by hour, 787| MS:And closer still with pain, fire here, fire there, *P1868:*Close, closer and yet closer still with pain, 788| MS:encroaching fire save one *P1868:*encroaching pain save just 789| MS:Whereat stood—Caponsacchi: just there,—life, *P1868:*Where stood one saviour like a piece of heaven, 790| MS:Heaven: hell's arms straining round with this gap left: *P1868:*Hell's arms would strain round but for this blue gap. 791| MS:For, they say further, she tried *P1868:*She, they say further, first tried 792| MS:in the ring, *P1868:*i' the fire, 793-95| MS:escape: she rushed into the street,/ Ran to the Commissary and Governor,/ Who *P1868:*escape: ran to the Commissary,/ Who 794-95| MS:spouse;/ Tried three times what the Church could do to help,/ <> herself at <> feet in prayer *P1868:*spouse;/ <> herself thrice at <> feet, 796| MS:And three <> lie *P1868:*Where three <> lie, 797| MS:Tell her <> sob her full heart out *P1868:*Spend her <> sob full heart forth, 799| MS:And brought her back for the husband *P1868:*And bore it back for husband 800| MS:but according to his natural right. *P1868:*but natural right is right. 801| MS:ever, yet *P1868:*ever yet 802| MS:Failing the <> till she came to the

To-wit a certain friar of mean degree,
Who heard her story in confession, wept,
Crossed himself, showed the man within the monk.
"Then, will you save me, you the one i' the world?
I cannot even write my woes, nor put
My prayer for help in words a friend may read,—
I no more own a coin than have an hour
Free of observance,—I was watched to church,
Am watched now, shall be watched back presently,—
How buy the skill of scribe i' the market-place?
Pray you, write down and send whatever I say
O' the need I have my parents take me hence!"
The good man rubbed his eyes and could not choose—
Let her dictate her letter in such a sense
That parents, to save breaking down a wall,
Might lift her over: she went back, heaven in heart.
Then the good man took counsel of his couch,
Woke and thought twice, the second thought the best:
"Here am I, foolish body that I be,
Caught all but pushing, teaching, who but I,
My betters their plain duty,—what, I dare
Help a case the Archbishop would not help,
Mend matters, peradventure, God loves mar?
What hath the married life but strifes and plagues
For proper dispensation? So a fool

---

lowest *P1868:*Missing the <> till come to lowest 803| MS:No more than a certain monk of *P1868:*certain friar of *1872:*To-wit a 804| MS:Who had heard <> confession and wept, *P1868:*Who heard <> confession, wept, 805| MS:within the priest. *P1868:*within the monk. 806| MS:in *P1868:*i' 807| MS:my wrongs, nor *P1868:*my woes, nor 808| MS:might *P1868:*may 809| MS:I do not own a coin, could I find an *P1868:*I no more own a coin than have an 810| MS:to this place *P1868:*to church, 812| MS:To buy <> of a scribe in the market place. *P1868:*How buy <> of scribe i' the market-place? 813| MS:Will you write *P1868:*Pray you, write 814| MS:Of <> parents should get me hence?" *P1868:*O' <> parents take me hence!" 817| MS:That her parents to save her breaking <> wall *P1868:*That parents, to save breaking <> wall, 818| MS:in her heart. *1888:*in heart. 819| MS:man went home, took counsel of sleep, *P1868:*man took counsel of his couch, 821| MS:am, *P1868:*be, 822| MS:pushing in, teaching *P1868:*pushing, teaching 823| MS:their duty,—what am I daring to do? *P1868:*their plain duty,—what, I dare 824| MS:Just help *P1868:*Help 825| MS:Mend a matter, peradventure, God has marred— *P1868:*Mend matters, peradventure, God loves mar? 826| MS:plagues, *CP1868:*plagues 827| MS:The natural dispensation *P1868:*For proper

Once touched the ark,—poor Uzzah that I am!
Oh married ones, much rather should I bid,
In patience all of ye possess your souls!
This life is brief and troubles die with it:
Where were the prick to soar up homeward else?"
So saying, he burnt the letter he had writ,
Said *Ave* for her intention, in its place,
Took snuff and comfort, and had done with all.
Then the grim arms stretched yet a little more
And each touched each, all but one streak i' the midst,
Whereat stood Caponsacchi, who cried, "This way,
Out by me! Hesitate one moment more
And the fire shuts out me and shuts in you!
Here my hand holds you life out!" Whereupon
She clasped the hand, which closed on hers and drew
Pompilia out o' the circle now complete.
Whose fault or shame but Guido's?—ask her friends.

But then this is the wife's—Pompilia's tale—
Eve's . . . no, not Eve's, since Eve, to speak the truth,
Was hardly fallen (our candour might pronounce)
When simply saying in her own defence

---

dispensation 828| MS:ark,—oh, Hophni that *P1868:*ark,—poor Hophni that *1888:*poor Uzzah that 829| MS:Oh, married <> I say, *P1868:*Oh married <> I bid, 832| MS:up heavenward else?" *P1868:*up homeward else?"
833| MS:saying he burnt *P1868:*saying, he burnt
834| MS:Said a prayer for her intention in *P1868:*Said *Ave* for her intention, in
835| MS:Took a reflection, and <> with it all. *P1868:*Took snuff and comfort, and <> with all. 837| MS:And touched, all but one narrow space in *P1868:*And each touched each, all but one streak i' 838| MS:Wherein stood Caponsacchi who cried "This *P1868:*Whereat stood Caponsacchi, who cried, "This 839| MS:By me! But hesitate *P1868:*Out by me! Hesitate 840| MS:the grim fire shuts me out and you in *P1868:*the fire shuts out me and shuts in you! 841| MS:holds out life to you. Whereat *P1868:*holds you life out!" Whereupon 842| MS:She touched his hand <> hers, and *P1868:*She clasped the hand <> hers and 843| MS:Her out of the circle which shut behind her back. *P1868:*Pompilia out o' the circle now complete. 844| MS:ask his friends *P1868:*ask her friends. 845| MS:the woman's tale—the wife's— *P1868:*the wife's—Pompilia's tale— 846| MS:Eve's . . no, not Eve's since <> truth *P1868:*not Eve's, since <> truth, *1888:*Eve's . . . no 847-48| MS:fallen (one well nigh might <> / So much of paradisal nature did she show/ When *P1868:*fallen (our candour might <> / <> nature, Eve's, / When

"The serpent tempted me and I did eat."
So much of paradisal nature, Eve's!
Her daughters ever since prefer to urge
"Adam so starved me I was fain accept
The apple any serpent pushed my way."
What an elaborate theory have we here,
Ingeniously nursed up, pretentiously
Brought forth, pushed forward amid trumpet-blast,
To account for the thawing of an icicle,
Show us there needed Ætna vomit flame
Ere run the crystal into dew-drops! Else,
How, unless hell broke loose to cause the step,
How could a married lady go astray?
Bless the fools! And 'tis just this way they are blessed,
And the world wags still,—because fools are sure
—Oh, not of my wife nor your daughter! No!
But of their own: the case is altered quite.
Look now,—last week, the lady we all love,—
Daughter o' the couple we all venerate,
Wife of the husband we all cap before,
Mother o' the babes we all breathe blessings on,—
Was caught in converse with a negro page.
Hell thawed that icicle, else "Why was it—
Why?" asked and echoed the fools. "Because, you fools,—"

---

*1872:*pronounce)/ When 849-51| MS:eat."/ Her *1872:*eat."/ So much of paradisal nature, Eve's!/ Her 852| MS:fain to bite *P1868:*fain accept 854| MS:here *P1868:*here, 855-57| MS:How ingeniously <> pretentiously brought forth,/ To *P1868:*Ingeniously <> pretentiously/ Brought forth, pushed forward amid trumpet-blast/ To *CP1868:*/ <> trumpet-blast, 858| MS:Showing how there needed Aetna to vomit *P1868:*Show us there <> Aetna vomit 859| MS:To run the chrystal <> dew-drops: else, *P1868:*Ere run <> dew-drops! Else, *1872:*crystal 861| MS:lady e'er go wrong? *P1868:*lady go astray? 862| MS:blessed: *P1868:* blessed, 863| MS:world goes round,—because good men feel sure *P1868:*world wags still,—because fools are sure 864| MS:Oh <> wife, sister, daughter *P1868:*wife nor your daughter *CP1868:*—Oh 866| MS:week was the <> all know,— *P1868:*week, the <> all love,— 867| MS:§ crowded between lines 866-68 § of the saintly pair that we *P1868:*o' the couple we 868| MS:the perfect husband we all prize *P1868:*the husband we all cap before, 869| MS:of *P1868:* o' 870| MS:Caught in the act of shame with a Negro Page: *P1868:*Was caught in converse with a negro page. 872| MS:you fools,— *P1868:*you fools,—"

So did the dame's self answer, she who could,
With that fine candour only forthcoming
When 'tis no odds whether withheld or no—
"Because my husband was the saint you say,
And,—with that childish goodness, absurd faith,
Stupid self-satisfaction, you so praise,—
Saint to you, insupportable to me.
Had he,—instead of calling me fine names,
Lucretia and Susanna and so forth,
And curtaining Correggio carefully
Lest I be taught that Leda had two legs,—
—But once never so little tweaked my nose
For peeping through my fan at Carnival,
Confessing thereby 'I have no easy task—
I need use all my powers to hold you mine,
And then,—why 'tis so doubtful if they serve,
That—take this, as an earnest of despair!"
Why, we were quits: I had wiped the harm away,
Thought 'The man fears me!' and foregone revenge."
We must not want all this elaborate work
To solve the problem why young Fancy-and-flesh
Slips from the dull side of a spouse in years,

873| MS:could— *P1868:*could, 875| MS:no matter whether it be witheld *P1868:*no odds whether withheld 876| MS:say *P1868:*say, 877| MS:And with < > goodness and absurd faith *P1868:*And, with < > goodness, absurd faith, *CP1868:*And,—with 878-79| MS:And stupid self-satisfaction,—therefore insupportable. *P1868:*Stupid self-satisfaction, you so praise,/ Saint to you, insupportable to me. *CP1868:*praise,— 880-85| MS:he, instead < > names/ But once spat never so little in my face/ For peeping out of my fan at carnival-time, *P1868:* he,—instead < > names,/ Lucretia and Susanna and so forth,/ And curtaining Corregio carefully/ Lest I be taught that Leda had two legs,—/—But once never so little tweaked my nose/ For peeping through my fan at Carnival, 886| MS: thereby—"I have *P1868:*thereby 'I have 887| MS:hold this wife, § last two words crossed out and replaced above by two words § you mine, 888| MS:tis < > if my strength will serve *P1868:*'tis < > if they serve, 889| MS:as the expression of my despair!" *P1868:*as an earnest of despair!' 890-92| MS:quits—I had foregone revenge,"/ No, we *P1868:*had wiped the harm away,/ Thought 'The man fears me!' and foregone revenge." / We *1872:*quits: I 893| MS:young flesh-and-fancy *P1868:* young fancy-and-flesh *1872:*young Fancy-and-flesh 894| MS:years *P1868:*years,

Betakes it to the breast of Brisk-and-bold
Whose love-scrapes furnish talk for all the town!

Accordingly one word on the other side
Tips over the piled-up fabric of a tale.
Guido says—that is, always, his friends say—
It is unlikely, from the wickedness,
That any man treat any woman so.
The letter in question was her very own,
Unprompted and unaided: she could write—
As able to write as ready to sin, or free,
When there was danger, to deny both facts.
He bids you mark, herself from first to last
Attributes all the so-styled torture just
To jealousy,—jealousy of whom but just
This very Caponsacchi! How suits here
This with the other alleged motive, Prince?
Would Guido make a terror of the man
He meant should tempt the woman, as they charge?
Do you fright your hare that you may catch your hare?

895| MS:And betakes itself to <> of a brisk young man *P1868:*Betakes it to <> of brisk-and-bold *1872:*of Brisk-and-bold 896| MS:§ no ¶ § *P1868:*§ ¶ § *1888:* § no ¶; paragraph restored; see Editorial Notes § 897| MS:Accordingly Guido's word, on <> side, *P1868:*Accordingly, one word on <> side *1872:*Accordingly one 898| MS:piled up *P1868:*piled-up 899| MS:He says <> say for him— *P1868:*Guido says <> say— 900| MS:"The tale is unlikely from its excessive wickedness, *P1868:*It is <> from the wickedness, DC,BrU:unlikely, from *1889:*unlikely, from 901| MS:man should treat any woman thus." *P1868:*man treat any woman so. 902| MS:He says—"The <> her own: *P1868:*The <> her very own, 903| MS:unaided—she *P1868:*unaided:she 904| MS:write, as <> sin, as free *P1868:*write as <> sin, or free, 905| MS:To deny both when 'twas useful so to do. *P1868:*When there was danger, to deny both facts.
906| MS:They point to the fact—herself *P1868:*He bids you mark, herself
907| MS:Attributes the so-styled cruelty to herself *P1868:*so-styled torture just *CP1868:*Attributes all the 908| MS:jealousy,—and that, jealousy of just *P1868:*jealousy,—jealousy of whom but just 909| MS:very Caponsacchi: how does that suit *CP1868:*very Caponsacchi! How suits here 910-13| MS:With the alleged motive of all the cruelty/ To drive her precisely into the arms of the same?/ Do you hunt § crossed out and replaced above by § fright your hare because you have caught § last two words crossed out and replaced above by two words § would catch your *P1868:*This with the other alleged motive, Prince?/ Would Guido make a terror of the man/ He meant should tempt the woman, as they charge?/ Do you fright your

Consider too, the charge was made and met
At the proper time and place where proofs were plain—
Heard patiently and disposed of thoroughly
By the highest powers, possessors of most light,
The Governor for the law, and the Archbishop
For the gospel: which acknowledged primacies,
'Tis impudently pleaded, he could warp
Into a tacit partnership with crime—
He being the while, believe their own account,
Impotent, penniless and miserable!
He further asks—Duke, note the knotty point!—
How he,—concede him skill to play such part
And drive his wife into a gallant's arms,—
Could bring the gallant to play his part too
And stand with arms so opportunely wide?
How bring this Caponsacchi,—with whom, friends
And foes alike agree, throughout his life
He never interchanged a civil word
Nor lifted courteous cap to—him how bend
To such observancy of beck and call,
—To undertake this strange and perilous feat

---

hare that you may catch your 914| MS:They say moreover that the case against him was made and met. *P1868:*Consider too, the charge was made and met 915| MS:where the proofs *P1868:*where proofs 917| MS:powers and possessors <> light *P1868:*powers, possessors <> light, 918| MS:The Governor, for the law, if you like and *P1868:*law, and *1888:*The Governor for 919| MS:gospel,—these two acknowledged judges in chief *P1868:*gospel: which acknowledged primacies, 920| MS:It is impudently pretended he had the power to warp *P1868:*'Tis impudently pleaded, he could warp 921| MS:partnership in crime— *P1868:*partnership with crime— 922| MS:being, according to their *P1868:*being the while, believe their 923| MS:miserable. *P1868:*miserable! 924| MS:They further ask—and this is a knotty point— *P1868:*He further asks—Duke, note the knotty point!— 925| MS:he,—with every power to play this part *P1868:*he,—concede him skill to play such part 926| MS:arms— *CP1868:*arms,— 927| MS:part as well *P1868:*part too 928| MS:with them open to her so opportunely *P1868:*with arms so opportunely wide? 929| MS:How get this <> whom,—friends, foes *P1868:*How bring this <> whom, friends 930| MS:Alike agree in assuring, in all his *P1868:*And foes alike agree, throughout his life 931| MS:never had interchanged *P1868:*never interchanged 932-34| MS:lifted a courteous cap to him,—to answer his ends,/ And undertake *P1868:*lifted courteous cap to—how bend him,/ To such observancy of beck and call,/—To undertake *1888:*to—him how bend

For the good of Guido, using, as the lure,
Pompilia whom, himself and she avouch,
He had nor spoken with nor seen, indeed,
Beyond sight in a public theatre,
When she wrote letters (she that could not write!)
The importunate shamelessly-protested love
Which brought him, though reluctant, to her feet,
And forced on him the plunge which, howsoe'er
She might swim up i' the whirl, must bury him
Under abysmal black: a priest contrive
No better, no amour to be hushed up,
But open flight and noon-day infamy?
Try and concoct defence for such revolt!
Take the wife's tale as true, say she was wronged,—
Pray, in what rubric of the breviary
Do you find it registered—the part of a priest
Is—that to right wrongs from the church he skip,
Go journeying with a woman that's a wife,
And be pursued, o'ertaken and captured . . . how?
In a lay-dress, playing the kind sentinel

935-41| MS:the sake of a woman whom—himself and she/ Aver alike—he had never spoken to/ Or seen, beyond once in a public place,/ Before she wrote him (she that could not write!)/ The importunate shameless letters full of love/ Which <> him though reluctant to her feet *P1868:*the good of Guido, using, as the lure,/ Pompilia whom, himself and she avouch,/—He had nor spoken with nor seen, indeed,/ Beyond sight in a public theater,/ When she wrote letters (she that could not write!)/ The importunate shamelessly-protested love/ Which <> him, though reluctant, to her feet, *CP1868://* He 942| MS:forced him take the step which *P1868:*forced on him the plunge which 943-46| MS:The event might profit her must ruin him—/ No pardonable amour to be hushed up/ But an open flight must brand him ever more *P1868:*She might swim up i' the whirl, must bury him/ Under abysmal black: a priest contrive/ No mitigable amour <> up,/ But open flight and noon-day infamy? *1872://* No better, no amour 947| MS:The priest, the celibate, the castaway? *P1868:*Try and concoct defence for such revolt! 948| MS:wife's story as true—say <> wronged, *P1868:*wife's tale as true, say <> wronged,— 950| MS:it set down as the *P1868:*it registered the *1888:*it registered—the 951| MS:That <> wrongs he skip from the church bounds, *P1868:*church-door, *1888:*Is—that <> wrongs from the church he skip, 952-53| MS:Take journeyings of indefinite length alone,/ He a young man, with a young lovely wife,/ And be at last o'ertaken and found . . how? *P1868:*Go journeying with a woman that's a wife,/ And be pursued o'ertaken and captured . . . how? *CP1868:*/ <> pursued, o'ertaken *1888:*/<> captured . . . how? 954| MS:lay-dress, sentinel at the lone inn-door

Where the wife sleeps (says he who best should know)
And sleeping, sleepless, both have spent the night!
Could no one else be found to serve at need—
No woman—or if man, no safer sort
Than this not well-reputed turbulence?

Then, look into his own account o' the case!
He, being the stranger and astonished one,
Yet received protestations of her love
From lady neither known nor cared about:
Love, so protested, bred in him disgust
After the wonder,—or incredulity,
Such impudence seeming impossible.
But, soon assured such impudence might be,
When he had seen with his own eyes at last
Letters thrown down to him i' the very street
From behind lattice where the lady lurked,
And read their passionate summons to her side—
Why then, a thousand thoughts swarmed up and in,—
How he had seen her once, a moment's space,
Observed she was both young and beautiful,
Heard everywhere report she suffered much

---

*P1868:*lay-dress, playing the sentinel *1872:*the kind sentinel 955| MS:sleeps, says <> know, *P1868:*sleeps (says <> know) 956| MS:sleeping or sleepless, both have past the night. *P1868:*sleeping, sleepless, both have spent the *CP1868:*night! 957| MS:serve in this sort— *P1868:*serve at need— 958| MS:safer man *P1868:*safer sort 959| MS:well-reputed turbulent priest? *P1868:*well-reputed turbulence? 959-60| MS:§ no ¶ § *P1868:*§ ¶ § 960| MS:of the case— *P1868:*o' the case! 961| MS:He says that being the stranger I have said *P1868:*He, being the stranger and astonished one, 962| MS:He received letter after letter of love *P1868:*Yet received protestations of her love 963| MS:From the lady he neither knew nor <> about— *P1868:*From lady neither known nor <> about: 964| MS:Which thus beginning bred disgust in him *P1868:*Love, so protested, bred in him disgust 965| MS:incredulity rather, *P1868:*incredulity, 966| MS:impossible *P1868:*impossible. 967| MS:But when assured <> be— *P1868:*But, soon assured <> be, 968| MS:When had seen with own *P1868:*When he had seen with his own 969| MS:in the public street *P1868:*i' the very street 970| MS:behind the lattice <> lurked *P1868:*behind lattice <> lurked, 972| MS:thoughts came in his head— *P1868:*thoughts swarmed up and in,— 973| MS:That he <> once for a *P1868:*How he <> once, a 974| MS:Observed that she was young and beautiful—*CP1868:*Observed she was so young and beautiful, *1872:*was both young 975| MS:That man reported she was

From a jealous husband thrice her age,—in short
There flashed the propriety, expediency
Of treating, trying might they come to terms,
—At all events, granting the interview
Prayed for, one so adapted to assist
Decision as to whether he advance,
Stand or retire, in his benevolent mood!
Therefore the interview befell at length;
And at this one and only interview,
He saw the sole and single course to take—
Bade her dispose of him, head, heart and hand,
Did her behest and braved the consequence,
Not for the natural end, the love of man
For woman whether love be virtue or vice,
But, please you, altogether for pity's sake—
Pity of innocence and helplessness!
And how did he assure himself of both?
Had he been the house-inmate, visitor,
Eye-witness of the described martyrdom,
So, competent to pronounce its remedy
Ere rush on such extreme and desperate course—

---

suffering much *P1868:*Heard everywhere report she suffered much 977| MS:He saw the propriety and expediency *P1868:*There flashed the propriety, expediency 978| MS:treating and seeing if they might come *P1868:*treating, trying might they come 980| MS:So flatteringly prayed for,—which might help *P1868:*Prayed for, and so adapted to assist *1872:*for, one so 981| MS:he should go on, *P1868:*he advance, 982| MS:Or stop short, or turn back, in his benevolent course *P1868:*Stand or retire, in his benevolent mood. *1872:*mood! 983| MS:So did the interview take place, says he— *P1868:*Therefore the interview befell at length *CP1868:*length; 985| MS:saw to his satisfaction the course *P1868:*saw the sole and single course 986| MS:him and all his powers *P1868:*him, head, heart and hand, 987| MS:braved all consequence *P1868:*braved the consequence, 988| MS:of a man *P1868:*of man 989| MS:For a woman whether it be right or wrong, *P1868:*For woman whether love be virtue or vice, 991| MS:Pity for her misery and *P1868:*Pity of innocence and 992| MS:of the facts? *P1868:*of both? 993| MS:the house's inmate, a visitor *P1868:*the house-inmate, visitor, 994| MS:And eye-witness *P1868:*Eye-witness 995| MS:pronounce on the remedy *P1868:*pronounce its remedy 996| MS:Before taking such <> desperate step *P1868:*Ere rush on such <> desperate course, *1872:*course—

Involving such enormity of harm,
Moreover, to the husband judged thus, doomed
And damned without a word in his defence?
Not he! the truth was felt by instinct here,
—Process which saves a world of trouble and time.
There's the priest's story: what do you say to it,
Trying its truth by your own instinct too,
Since that's to be the expeditious mode?
"And now, do hear my version," Guido cries:
"I accept argument and inference both.
It would indeed have been miraculous
Had such a confidency sprung to birth
With no more fanning from acquaintanceship
Than here avowed by my wife and this priest.
Only, it did not: you must substitute
The old stale unromantic way of fault,
The commonplace adventure, mere intrigue
In prose form with the unpoetic tricks,
Cheatings and lies: they used the hackney chair
Satan jaunts forth with, shabby and serviceable,
No gilded gimcrack-novelty from below,

997-1000| MS:such wrong moreover to the husband he judged/ Without having let him say a word in his own defence!/ But no,—he felt the truth by instinct, he says— *P1868:*such enormity of harm,/ Moreover, to the husband judged thus, doomed/ And damned without a word in his defence?/ But no,—the truth was felt by instinct here! *1872:/// * Not he! the < > here, 1001| MS:A process < > of time and trouble, *P1868:*—Process < > of trouble and time, *1872:*time. 1002| MS:And that's his story < > to its air, *P1868:*And there's his < > to it, *1872:*There's the priest's story 1003-5| MS:Trying it by your own instinct also, since that is to be the mode?/ "And < > version and be fair," *P1868:*Trying its truth by < > instinct too,/ Since that's to be the expeditious mode?/ "And < > version," Guido cries: 1006| MS:Cried Guido: "Yes, friends, I agree with you: *P1868:*"I accept argument and inference both. 1008| MS:confidence sprung into birth *P1868:*confidency sprung to birth 1010| MS:Than is avowed < > and her friend the priest: *P1868:*Than were avowed < > and this priest. 1012| MS:The old and unromantic way of crime— *P1868:*The old stale unromantic way of fault, 1013| MS:adventure, the intrigue *P1868:*adventure, mere intrigue 1014| MS:In the old form < > tricks *1868:*In the prose form < > tricks, *1872:*In prose 1015| MS:Cheating and lies,—they used the old hackney *P1868:*Cheatings and lies: they used the hackney 1016| MS:That the devil plies with, the shabby old useful thing, *P1868:*Satan jaunts forth with, shabby and serviceable, 1017| MS:gilded splendid novelty from hell *P1868:*gilded jimcrack novelty from below, *CP1868:*jimcrack-novelty *1888:*

To bowl you along thither, swift and sure.
That same officious go-between, the wench
Who gave and took the letters of the two,
Now offers self and service back to me:
Bears testimony to visits night by night
When all was safe, the husband far and away,—
To many a timely slipping out at large
By light o' the morning-star, ere he should wake.
And when the fugitives were found at last,
Why, with them were found also, to belie
What protest they might make of innocence,
All documents yet wanting, if need were,
To establish guilt in them, disgrace in me—
The chronicle o' the converse from its rise
To culmination in this outrage: read!
Letters from wife to priest, from priest to wife,—
Here they are, read and say where they chime in
With the other tale, superlative purity
O' the pair of saints! I stand or fall by these."

But then on the other side again,—how say
The pair of saints? That not one word is theirs—

---

gimcrack-novelty 1018| MS:bowl you § inserted above line § along by a new swift sure strange coach. *P1868:*along thither, swift and sure. 1019| MS:the woman *P1868:*the wench 1020| MS:That gave <> letters between the *P1868:*letters of the *1888:*Who gave 1021| MS:She offers her services now to me, you must know: *P1868:*Now offers self and service back to me: 1023| MS:When the way was safe and the husband out and *P1868:*When all was safe, the husband far and 1024| MS:And to the timely slippings out in the large § apparently written over now illegible word § *P1868:*To many a timely slipping out at large 1025| MS:of <> should be back. *P1868:*o' <> should wake. 1026| MS:were caught at last *P1868:*were found at last, 1028| MS:The protest that they made of *P1868:*What protest they might make of 1029-31| MS:All the documents wanting to establish disgrace,/ The chronicle of the connexion from *P1868:*All documents yet wanting, if need were,/ To establish guilt in them, disgrace in me—/ The chronicle o' the converse from 1032| MS:To its culmination in outrageous guilt: *P1868:*To culmination in this outrage: read! 1033| MS:from the wife to the priest, from the priest to the wife,— *P1868:*from wife to priest, from priest to wife,— 1034| MS:read them and <> they fit in *P1868:*read and <> they chime in 1035| MS:To the <> tale of the superlative *P1868:*With the <> tale, superlative 1036| MS:On either side! I rest my case thereon." *P1868:*O' the pair of saints! I stand or fall by these." 1037| MS:how reply *P1868:*how say 1038| MS:That priest and wife? That

No syllable o' the batch or writ or sent
Or yet received by either of the two.
"Found," says the priest, "because he needed them,
Failing all other proofs, to prove our fault:
So, here they are, just as is natural.
Oh yes—we had our missives, each of us!
Not these, but to the full as vile, no doubt:
Hers as from me,—she could not read, so burnt,—
Mine as from her,—I burnt because I read.
Who forged and found them? *Cui profuerint!*"
(I take the phrase out of your Highness' mouth.)
"He who would gain by her fault and my fall,
The trickster, schemer and pretender—he
Whose whole career was lie entailing lie
Sought to be sealed truth by the worst lie last!"

Guido rejoins—"Did the other end o' the tale
Match this beginning! 'Tis alleged I prove

---

*P1868:*The pair of saints? That 1039| MS:No letter of the batch was ever written or *P1868:*No syllable o' the batch writ or *CP1868:*batch or writ 1040| MS:Or received at all by <> the pair *P1868:*Or yet received by <> the two. 1041| MS: "Forged," says <> because you needed *P1868:*"Found," says <> because he needed 1042| MS:prove your case: *P1868:*prove our fault: *1888:*§ punctuation at end of line decayed; emended to § fault: § see Editorial Notes § 1043| MS:So here *P1868:*So, here 1044| MS:us— *P1868:*us! 1046| MS:She as § inserted above line § from me,—which she *P1868:*Hers as from me,—she 1047| MS:I as from her,—which I <> read: *P1868:*Mine as from her,—I <> read. 1048| MS:and sent these? *Cui profuerint—*" *P1868:*and found them? *Cui profuerint*!" 1049| MS: mouth.) *P1868:*mouth) § emended to § mouth.) § See Editorial Notes § 1050| MS:He *P1868:*"He 1051| MS:The ignoble trickster <> pretender *P1868:*The trickster <> pretender—he 1052| MS:was one whole falsification of facts *P1868:*was lie entailing lie 1053-54| MS:Which thus he eventually sought to seal/ By a general slaughter and smothering up of truth./ Guido rejoins—"Try the other <> of *P1868:*Sought to be sealed truth by the worst lie last!" § ¶ § Guido rejoins—"Did the other <> o' 1055| MS:See how the two ends suit: I am, you allege, *P1868:*Match this beginning! 'Tis alleged I prove

A murderer at the end, a man of force
Prompt, indiscriminate, effectual: good!
Then what need all this trifling woman's-work,
Letters and embassies and weak intrigue,
When will and power were mine to end at once
Safely and surely? Murder had come first
Not last with such a man, assure yourselves!
The silent *acquetta*, stilling at command—
A drop a day i' the wine or soup, the dose,—
The shattering beam that breaks above the bed
And beats out brains, with nobody to blame
Except the wormy age which eats even oak,—
Nay, the staunch steel or trusty cord,—who cares
I' the blind old palace, a pitfall at each step,
With none to see, much more to interpose
O' the two, three, creeping house-dog-servant-things
Born mine and bred mine? Had I willed gross death,
I had found nearer paths to thrust him prey
Than this that goes meandering here and there
Through half the world and calls down in its course
Notice and noise,—hate, vengeance, should it fail,
Derision and contempt though it succeed!
Moreover, what o' the future son and heir?
The unborn babe about to be called mine,—

1056| MS:end,—a < > force, *P1868:*end, a < > force 1058| MS:need of all < > woman's-work *P1868:*need all < > woman's-work, 1059| MS:At letters < > intrigue *P1868:*Letters < > intrigue, 1060| MS:When the will < > were in me to *P1868:*When will < > were mine to 1061-63| MS:first not last:/ The silent acquetta, killing at *P1868:*first/ Not last with such a man, assure yourselves!/ The silent *acquetta*, stilling at 1064| MS:in < > soup, enough— *P1868:*i' < > soup, the dose,— 1065| MS:that drops in the corridor *P1868:*that breaks above the bed 1066| MS:And crushes life out; with *P1868:*And beats out brains, with 1067| MS: the worms and age that eats even oak *P1868:*the wormy age which eats even oak,— 1068| MS:the sure steel < > cord, who cares? *P1868:*the staunch steel < > cord,—who cares 1069| MS:In < > pitfall on each hand, *P1868:*I' < > pitfall at each step, 1070| MS:more try to prevent *P1868:*more to interpose 1071| MS:Of the two or three *P1868:*O' the two, three 1072| MS:mine,—had I willed her death *P1868:* mine?—had I willed gross death, *1888:*mine? Had 1073| MS:There had been nearer ways with the wife thereto *P1868:*I had found nearer paths to thrust him prey 1075| MS:calls unnecessarily down *P1868:*calls down in its course 1076-78| MS: Scorn, hatred, jeers and derision, even though it succeed!/ < > what do you say to my son and heir *P1868:*Notice and noise,—hate, vengeance, should it fail,/ Derision and contempt though it succeed!/ < > what o' the future son and heir? 1079| MS:The

What end in heaping all this shame on him,
Were I indifferent to my own black share?
Would I have tried these crookednesses, say,
Willing and able to effect the straight?"

"Ay, would you!"—one may hear the priest retort,
"Being as you are, i' the stock, a man of guile,
And ruffianism but an added graft.
You, a born coward, try a coward's arms,
Trick and chicane,—and only when these fail
Does violence follow, and like fox you bite
Caught out in stealing. Also, the disgrace
You hardly shrunk at, wholly shrivelled her:
You plunged her thin white delicate hand i' the flame
Along with your coarse horny brutish fist,
Held them a second there, then drew out both
—Yours roughed a little, hers ruined through and through.
Your hurt would heal forthwith at ointment's touch—
Namely, succession to the inheritance
Which bolder crime had lost you: let things change,
The birth o' the boy warrant the bolder crime,
Why, murder was determined, dared and done.

---

babe about to be born to me,—what end *P1868:*The unborn babe about to be called mine,— 1080| MS:In piling all this useless shame on him *P1868:*What end in heaping all this shame on him, 1081| MS:share. *P1868:*share? 1082| MS: crooknesses I say *P1868:*crookednesses, say, 1083| MS:able, as you say, to manage the *P1868:*able to effect the 1083-84| MS:§ no ¶ § *P1868:*§ ¶ § 1084| MS:you!" The Priest and the wife may be supposed to retort *P1868:*you!"—one may hear the priest retort, 1085| MS:in <> guile *P1868:*i' <> guile, 1086| MS:And the ruffianism of you but <> graft: *P1868:*And ruffianism but <> graft. 1087| MS:a coward's ways *CP1868:*a coward's arms, 1088| MS:Trick, like, chicane *P1868:*Trick and chicane 1089| MS:violence come, and like the fox *P1868:*violence follow, and like fox 1091| MS:Which hardly hurt you wholly <> her— *P1868:*You hardly shrunk at, wholly *CP1868:*her: 1092| MS:her wan-white <> hand, as it were, *P1868:*her thin white <> hand i' the flame 1093| MS:horny fist in the flame, *P1868:*horny brutish fist, 1095| MS:—Yours singed a little but hers <> through— *P1868:*Yours roughed a little, hers <> through. 1096| MS:Yours, too, would <> at an ointment's touch *P1868:*Your hurt would <> at ointment's touch— 1097| MS:To-wit, the succession *P1868:* Namely, succession 1098-1100| MS:Which the bolder way had lost you—tried at last/ Because the birth of the boy changed things at once/ Saved you from what had been loss before—that known/ Why *P1868:*Which bolder crime had lost you: let

For me," the priest proceeds with his reply,
"The look o' the thing, the chances of mistake,
All were against me,—that, I knew the first:
But, knowing also what my duty was,
I did it: I must look to men more skilled
In reading hearts than ever was the world."

Highness, decide! Pronounce, Her Excellency!
Or . . . even leave this argument in doubt,
Account it a fit matter, taken up
With all its faces, manifold enough,
To ponder on—what fronts us, the next stage,
Next legal process? Guido, in pursuit,
Coming up with the fugitives at the inn,
Caused both to be arrested then and there
And sent to Rome for judgment on the case—
Thither, with all his armoury of proofs,
Betook himself: 'tis there we'll meet him now,
Waiting the further issue.
                                        Here you smile
"And never let him henceforth dare to plead,—
Of all pleas and excuses in the world
For any deed hereafter to be done,—

---

things change,/ The birth o' the boy warrant the bolder crime,/ Why 1101| MS: me," the priest goes on with his reply *P1868:*me," the priest proceeds with his reply, 1102| MS:of *P1868:*o' 1103| MS:that I knew from the first *P1868:*that, I knew the first: 1105| MS:must trust to men well-skilled *P1868:*must look to men more skilled 1106| MS:In the heart: and, missing their verdict, wait for God's." *P1868:* In reading hearts than ever was the world." 1106-7| MS:§ no ¶ § *P1868:*§ ¶ § 1107| MS:Who shall decide? How says your Excellency? *P1868:*Highness, decide! Pronounce, Her Excellency! 1108| MS:Let's even <> this other stage in doubt *P1868:*Or . . . even <> this argument in doubt, 1109-11| MS:Call it a fit matter, taken up with all its faces,/ To put upon—what we find as the next stage— *P1868:* Account it a fit matter, taken up/ With all its faces, manifold enough,/ <> what fronts us, the next stage, *1872:*// To ponder on—what 1112| MS:process,—to-wit, when Guido *P1868:*process!—Guido *1872:*process? Guido 1113-14| MS: fugitives in the morn at the Inn/ And finding them as was said, contented himself/ With causing both *P1868:*fugitives at the inn,/ Caused both 1116-17| MS: Whither, with <> proofs/ Witnesses and those documents aforesaid/ He betook himself,—and where we meet *P1868:*Thither, with <> / Betook himself, and there we'll meet *1872:*/ <> himself: 'tis there *1888:*proofs, 1118| MS:issue. § no ¶ § Here some hoot *P1868:*issue. § ¶ § Here some smile *1872:*issue. § ¶ § Here you smile 1119| MS:plead *P1868:*plead,— 1120-22| MS:all imaginable excuses <> / His

His irrepressible wrath at honour's wound!
Passion and madness irrepressible?
Why, Count and cavalier, the husband comes
And catches foe i' the very act of shame!
There's man to man,—nature must have her way,—
We look he should have cleared things on the spot.
Yes, then, indeed—even tho' it prove he erred—
Though the ambiguous first appearance, mount
Of solid injury, melt soon to mist,
Still,—had he slain the lover and the wife—
Or, since she was a woman and his wife,
Slain him, but stript her naked to the skin
Or at best left no more of an attire
Than patch sufficient to pin paper to,
Some one love-letter, infamy and all,
As passport to the Paphos fit for such,
Safe-conduct to her natural home the stews,—
Good! One had recognized the power o' the pulse.
But when he stands, the stock-fish,—sticks to law—
Offers the hole in his heart, all fresh and warm,
For scrivener's pen to poke and play about—
Can stand, can stare, can tell his beads perhaps,
Oh, let us hear no syllable o' the rage!

<> wound, *P1868:*all pleas and excuses <> / For any deed hereafter to be done,—/ His <> wound! 1123| MS:The passion and the madness: "irrepressible?" *P1868:*Passion and madness irrepressible? 1124| MS:The Count and Cavalier *P1868:*Why, Count and cavalier *1888:*§ line indented; emended to remove indentation; see Editorial Notes § 1125| MS:catches his foe in <> shame: *P1868:*catches foe i' *1872:*shame! 1127| MS:have slain him on *P1868:* have cleared things on 1128| MS:it should prove *P1868:*it prove 1129| MS: That the <> appearance of things *P1868:*Though the <> appearance, mount 1130| MS:Admitted of being cleared up afterward,— *P1868:*Of solid injury, melt soon to mist, 1131| MS:Then,—had *P1868:*Still,—had 1133| MS:Not slain her, but *P1868:*Slain him, but 1134| MS:left her no more of her chemise *P1868:*left no more of an attire 1135| MS:Than a strip sufficient to pin a paper to *P1868:* Than patch sufficient to pin paper to, 1136| MS:Those letters with their infamy, to wit,— *P1868:*Some one love-letter, infamy and all, 1137| MS:the innermost shrine of shame— *P1868:*the Paphos fit for such, 1138| MS:And so sent her to her parents, or the *P1868:*Safe-conduct to her natural home the 1139| MS:the right of the blood. *P1868:*the power o' the pulse. 1140| MS:stockfish,—calls in law— *P1868:*stock-fish,—sticks to law— 1141| MS:heart all-freshly made *P1868:* heart, all fresh and warm, 1142| MS:To a scrivener's <> and turn about— *P1868:*For a scrivener's <> and play about— 1143| MS:Can wait, can breathe, and tell *P1868:*Can stand, can stare, can tell 1144| MS:of *P1868:*o'

Such rage were a convenient afterthought
For one who would have shown his teeth belike,
Exhibited unbridled rage enough,
Had but the priest been found, as was to hope,
In serge, not silk, with crucifix, not sword:
Whereas the grey innocuous grub, of yore,
Had hatched a hornet, tickle to the touch,
The priest was metamorphosed into knight.
And even the timid wife, whose cue was—shriek,
Bury her brow beneath his trampling foot,—
She too sprang at him like a pythoness:
So, gulp down rage, passion must be postponed,
Calm be the word! Well, our word is—we brand
This part o' the business, howsoever the rest
Befall."
                    "Nay," interpose as prompt his friends—
"This is the world's way! So you adjudge reward
To the forbearance and legality
Yourselves begin by inculcating—ay,
Exacting from us all with knife at throat!
This one wrong more you add to wrong's amount,—
You publish all, with the kind comment here,

1145| MS:Rage and madness are a <> afterthought. *P1868:*Such rage were a <> afterthought 1146| MS:The fact is, he would <> teeth forthwith, *P1868:*For one who would <> teeth belike, 1147| MS:rage with full effect, *P1868:*rage enough, 1148| MS:to be hoped, *P1868:*to hope, 1149| MS:In a serge corselet, armed with a crucifix; *P1868:*In serge, not silk, with crucifix, not sword: 1150| MS:grub that was *P1868:*grub, of yore, 1151| MS:hornet not to be lightly touched. *P1868:*hornet, tickle to the touch, 1152-53| MS:into a knight/ Down to the sword he showed all will to use:/ <> was to shriek *P1868:*into knight./ <> was—shriek, 1154| MS:And roll her naked breasts beneath his foot,— *P1868:* Bury her brow beneath his trampling foot,— 1155-56| MS:a lioness/ And was choaked off by the guards with pains enough:/ So the programme broke down; rage must *P1868:*a pythoness:/ So, gulp down rage, passion must 1157| MS: Calmness!—was the word. We begin by branding here *P1868:*Calm be the word! Well, our word is—we brand 1158| MS:of the business, however he deserve for the rest!" *P1868:*o' the business, howsoever the rest 1159| MS:"Nay<>prompt the friends of him— *P1868:*Befall." "Nay <> prompt his friends— *CP1868:*Befall." § ¶ § "Nay 1160| MS:way—so *P1868:*way! So 1161| MS:For the very forbearance and rational calm of a man *P1868:*To the forbearance and legality 1162-64| MS:inculcating and demanding./ The one <> to any wrong— *P1868:* inculcating—ay,/ Exacting from us all with knife at throat!/ This one <> to wrong's amount,— 1165| MS:That you publish with all this compassionate scorn,

'Its victim was too cowardly for revenge.' "
Make it your own case,—you who stand apart!
The husband wakes one morn from heavy sleep,
With a taste of poppy in his mouth,—rubs eyes,
Finds his wife flown, his strong box ransacked too,
Follows as he best can, overtakes i' the end.
You bid him use his privilege: well, it seems
He's scarce cool-blooded enough for the right move—
Does not shoot when the game were sure, but stands
Bewildered at the critical minute,—since
He has the first flash of the fact alone
To judge from, act with, not the steady lights
Of after-knowledge,—yours who stand at ease
To try conclusions: he's in smother and smoke,
You outside, with explosion at an end:
The sulphur may be lightning or a squib—
He'll know in a minute, but till then, he doubts.
Back from what you know to what he knew not!
Hear the priest's lofty "I am innocent,"
The wife's as resolute "You are guilty!" Come!
Are you not staggered?—pause, and you lose the move!
Nought left you but a low appeal to law,
"Coward" tied to your tail for compliment!
Another consideration: have it your way!

---

*P1868:*You publish all, with the kind comment here, 1166| MS:"Its <> revenge." *P1868:*'Its <> revenge.' " 1167| MS:Be just and calm here—you <> apart,— *P1868:*Make it your own case,—you <> apart! 1168| MS:from a heavy *P1868:* from heavy 1169| MS:poppies <> rubs his eyes *P1868:*poppy <> rubs eyes, 1171| MS:can, and overtakes her thus: *P1868:*can, overtakes i' the end. 1173| MS: He's not cool-blooded *P1868:*He's scarce cool-blooded 1174| MS:sure to fall— *P1868:*sure, but stands 1175| MS:Stands bewildered <> minute: beside, *P1868:* Bewildered <> minute,—since 1176| MS:first face of *P1868:*first flash of 1177| MS:from and act upon, not the lights which came *P1868:*act with, not the steady lights *CP1868:*from, act 1178| MS:By after-knowledge *P1868:*Of after-knowledge 1179| MS:in the smother *P1868:*in smother 1180| MS:We outside, and the explosion's *P1868:*You outside, with explosion 1181| MS:be hell-fire or a mere squib— *P1868:*be lightning or a squib— 1182| MS:He will know <> but, till that minute, he *P1868:*He'll know <> but, till then he *CP1868:*but till then, he 1183| MS:Go back <> not— *P1868:*Back <> not! 1184| MS: The priest is affirming "I am innocent" *P1868:*Hear the priest's lofty "I am innocent," 1185| MS:The wife shrieking "You it is are guilty here" *P1868:*The wife's as resolute "You are guilty!" Come! 1186-89| MS:staggered like him,— § altered to § him?—pause,—lose <> / Another <> your own way, Highness! *P1868:*

Admit the worst: his courage failed the Count,
He's cowardly like the best o' the burgesses
He's grown incorporate with,—a very cur,
Kick him from out your circle by all means!
Why, trundled down this reputable stair,
Still, the Church-door lies wide to take him in,
And the Court-porch also: in he sneaks to each,—
"Yes, I have lost my honour and my wife,
And, being moreover an ignoble hound,
I dare not jeopardize my life for them!"
Religion and Law lean forward from their chairs,
"Well done, thou good and faithful servant!" Ay,
Not only applaud him that he scorned the world,
But punish should he dare do otherwise.
If the case be clear or turbid,—you must say!

Thus, anyhow, it mounted to the stage
In the law-courts,—let's see clearly from this point!—
Where the priest tells his story true or false,
And the wife her story, and the husband his,
All with result as happy as before.
The courts would nor condemn nor yet acquit

---

staggered?—pause, and you lose <> / Nought left you but a low appeal to law,/ "Coward" tied to your tail for compliment!/ Another <> your way! 1190| MS: the man: *P1868:*the Count, 1191-93| MS:the burgesses he's incorporate with,—/ <> means— *P1868:*the best o' the burgesses/ He's grown incorporate with,—a very cur,/ Kick <> means! 1194| MS:trundle down these respectable stairs, as he does, *P1868:*trundled down this reputable stair, 1195| MS:the church-doors lie wide <> in *P1868:*the Church-door lies wide *CP1868:*in, 1196| MS:the law-courts' also <> to either,— *P1868:*the Court porch also <> to each,— *CP1868:* the Court-porch 1197| MS:lost my wife, and my honor thereby, *P1868:*lost my honour and my wife, 1198| MS:But, being an utterly ignoble soul, *P1868:*And, being moreover an ignoble hound, 1199| MS:I would not peril my life to recover these,—" *P1868:*I dare not jeopardize my life for them!" 1200| MS:Why, Religion <> chairs *P1868:*Religion <> chairs, 1202| MS:him for doing as he has done, *P1868:*him that he scorned the world, 1203| MS:But would punish him should *P1868:*But punish should 1204| MS:There, sirs,—if the case is clear, or not clear,—you must say— *P1868:*If the case be clear or turbid,—you must say! 1204-5| MS:§ no ¶ § *P1868:*§ ¶ § 1205| MS:Thus anyhow it mounted up to *CP1868:*Thus, anyhow, it mounted to 1206| MS:the Law Courts,—let's go on clearly <> point, at least: *P1868:*the law-courts,—let's see clearly <> point!— 1207| MS:the Priest <> story or true *P1868:*the priest <> story true 1208| MS: the Husband *P1868:*the husband 1209| MS:With result just as satisfactory as *P1868:*All with result as happy as 1210| MS:The Court would neither condemn

This, that or the other, in so distinct a sense
As end the strife to either's absolute loss:
Pronounced, in place of something definite,
"Each of the parties, whether goat or sheep
I' the main, has wool to show and hair to hide.
Each has brought somehow trouble, is somehow cause
Of pains enough,—even though no worse were proved.
Here is a husband, cannot rule his wife
Without provoking her to scream and scratch
And scour the fields,—causelessly, it may be:
Here is that wife,—who makes her sex our plague,
Wedlock, our bugbear,—perhaps with cause enough:
And here is the truant priest o' the trio, worst
Or best—each quality being conceivable.
Let us impose a little mulct on each.
We punish youth in state of pupilage
Who talk at hours when youth is bound to sleep,
Whether the prattle turn upon Saint Rose
Or Donna Olimpia of the Vatican:
'Tis talk, talked wisely or unwisely talked,
I' the dormitory where to talk at all,
Transgresses, and is mulct: as here we mean.

---

*P1868:*The courts would nor condemn 1211| MS:other in <> a way *P1868:* other, in <> a sense 1212| MS:the dispute to someone's absolute *P1868:*the strife to either's absolute 1213| MS:No: they said, in the place *P1868:*So said, in place *CP1868:*Pronounced, in 1214| MS:of these parties, whether right or wrong, *P1868:*of the parties, whether goat or sheep 1215| MS:In <> has white to show and black to hide *P1868:*I' <> has wool to show and hair to hide. 1216| MS:has given somehow trouble and been the cause *P1868:*has brought somehow trouble, is somehow cause 1217| MS:Of scandal enough <> worse be proved. *P1868:*Of pains enough <> worse were proved. 1218| MS:husband who cannot manage his *P1868:*husband, cannot rule his 1221| MS:that runaway wife,—who shames her sex, *P1868:*that wife,—who makes her sex our plague, 1222| MS: Makes marriage impossible,—yet perhaps <> enough *P1868:*Wedlock, our bugbear, —perhaps <> enough: 1223| MS:priest, worst case of all *P1868:*priest o' the trio, worst 1224| MS:best—since good ends are conceivable here too: *P1868:*best—each quality being conceivable. 1225| MS:Now, we propose a <> mulct for each: *P1868:*Let us impose a <> mulct on each. 1226-28| MS:punish pupils who talk when they should sleep,/ <> prattle be of Saint Rose of Lima *P1868:*punish youth in state of pupilage/ Who talk at hours when youth is bound to sleep,/ <> prattle turn upon Saint Rose 1229| MS:the Vatican *P1868:*the Vatican: 1230| MS:talk, whether unwisely or wisely talked, *P1868:*talk, talked wisely or unwisely talked, 1231| MS:In <> where should be no talk *P1868:*I' <> where to talk at all, 1232| MS:So is punished: thus we mean to punish now. *P1868:*Transgresses, and is

For the wife,—let her betake herself, for rest,
After her run, to a House of Convertites—
Keep there, as good as real imprisonment:
Being sick and tired, she will recover so.
For the priest, spritely strayer out of bounds,
Who made Arezzo hot to hold him,—Rome
Profits by his withdrawal from the scene.
Let him be relegate to Civita,
Circumscribed by its bounds till matters mend:
There he at least lies out o' the way of harm
From foes—perhaps from the too friendly fair.
And finally for the husband, whose rash rule
Has but itself to blame for this ado,—
If he be vexed that, in our judgments dealt,
He fails obtain what he accounts his right,
Let him go comforted with the thought, no less,
That, turn each sentence howsoever he may,
There's satisfaction to extract therefrom.
For, does he wish his wife proved innocent?
Well, she's not guilty, he may safely urge,
Has missed the stripes dishonest wives endure—
This being a fatherly pat o' the cheek, no more.

---

mulct: as here we mean. 1233| MS:herself for *P1868:*herself, for 1234| MS: of Convertites *P1868:*of Convertites— 1235| MS:And keep < > imprisonment— *P1868:*Keep < > imprisonment: 1236| MS:Which, being < > will find easy to bear. *P1868:*Being < > will recover so. 1237| MS:priest, the sprightly *P1868:* priest, sprightly 1238| MS:Who has made Arezzo too hot < > him,—what *P1868:*Who made Arezzo hot < > him,—Rome 1239| MS:So fit as brief withdrawal < > scene? *P1868:*Profits by his withdrawal < > scene. 1240| MS: relegated to Civita *P1868:*relegate to Civita, 1241| MS:bounds a year or so, *P1868:*bounds till matters mend: 1242| MS:Where he will at least be out of *P1868:*There he at least lies out o' 1243| MS:perhaps temptation from < > fair: *P1868:*perhaps from < > fair. 1244| MS:husband—whose unwise rule *P1868:* husband, whose rash rule 1245| MS:Has itself < > for causing this ado, *P1868:*Has but itself < > for this ado,— 1246| MS:he is vexed that in these judgments of ours *P1868:*he be vexed that, in our judgments dealt, 1247| MS:He does not obtain exactly his full will, *P1868:*He fails obtain what he accounts his right, 1248| MS:Yet let *P1868:*Let 1249| MS:sentence whichsoever way he will, *P1868:* sentence howsoever he may, 1250| MS:There's a sort of satisfaction < > therefrom: *P1868:*There's satisfaction < > therefrom. 1252| MS:not criminated, he may safely say, *P1868:*not guilty, he may safely urge, 1253| MS:the scourge dishonest < > obtain— *P1868:*the stripes dishonest < > endure— 1254| MS:on < > more: *P1868:*o' < > more. 1255| MS:her proved guilty? Well, were *P1868:*

Does he wish her guilty? Were she otherwise
Would she be locked up, set to say her prayers,
Prevented intercourse with the outside world,
And that suspected priest in banishment,
Whose portion is a further help i' the case?
Oh, ay, you all of you want the other thing,
The extreme of law, some verdict neat, complete,—
Either, the whole o' the dowry in your poke
With full release from the false wife, to boot,
And heading, hanging for the priest, beside—
Or, contrary, claim freedom for the wife,
Repayment of each penny paid her spouse,
Amends for the past, release for the future! Such
Is wisdom to the children of this world;
But we've no mind, we children of the light,
To miss the advantage of the golden mean,
And push things to the steel point." Thus the courts.

Is it settled so far? Settled or disturbed,
Console yourselves: 'tis like . . . an instance, now!
You've seen the puppets, of Place Navona, play,—
Punch and his mate,—how threats pass, blows are dealt,
And a crisis comes: the crowd or clap or hiss

---

her guilty? Were 1257-59| MS:the suspected man—/ Whose <> in *P1868:*the outside world,/ And that suspected priest in banishment/ Whose <> i' *CP1868:*/ < >banishment, 1260| MS:thing *P1868:*thing, 1261| MS:some judgment neat *P1868:*some verdict neat 1262| MS:of the dowry assured to you *P1868:*o' the dowry in your poke 1263| MS:With a full <> the detested wife, *P1868:*With full <> the false wife, to boot, 1264| MS:heading or hanging for the obnoxious priest— *P1868:*heading, hanging for the priest, beside— 1265| MS:Of, on the other hand, full liberty again, *P1868:*Or, contrary, claim freedom for the wife, 1266| MS:With restitution of dowry falsely obtained, *P1868:*Repayment of each penny paid her spouse, 1267-71| MS:And punishment for all cruelty in the past,/ With release from fear in the future! But we've no mind/ To forego the advantages of sobriety/ And push things to extremes thus. Judged the Case!" *P1868:*Amends for the past, release for the future! Such/ Is wisdom to the children of this world;/ But we've no mind, we children of the light,/ To miss the advantage of the golden mean,/ And push things to the steel point." Thus the courts. 1271-72| MS:§ no ¶ § *P1868:*§ ¶ § 1272| MS:far? Well, settled or not, *P1868:*far? Settled or disturbed, 1273| MS:yourselves: it is like a common case— *P1868:*yourselves: 'tis like . . an instance, now! *1888:*like . . . an 1274| MS:the puppet-show at Piazza Navona, *P1868:*the puppets, of Place Navona, play,— 1275| MS:his wife,—how *P1868:* his mate,—how 1276| MS:crowd cry victory *P1868:*crowd or clap or hiss

Accordingly as disposed for man or wife—
When down the actors duck awhile perdue,
Donning what novel rag-and-feather trim
Best suits the next adventure, new effect:
And,—by the time the mob is on the move,
With something like a judgment *pro* and *con*,—
There's a whistle, up again the actors pop
In t'other tatter with fresh-tinseled staves,
To re-engage in one last worst fight more
Shall show, what you thought tragedy was farce.
Note, that the climax and the crown of things
Invariably is, the devil appears himself,
Armed and accoutred, horns and hoofs and tail!
Just so, nor otherwise it proved—you'll see:
Move to the murder, never mind the rest!

Guido, at such a general duck-down,
I' the breathing-space,—of wife to convent here,
Priest to his relegation, and himself
To Arezzo,—had resigned his part perforce
To brother Abate, who bustled, did his best,

1277| MS:According as they are disposed for this side or that— *P1868:*Accordingly as disposed for man or wife— 1278| MS:duck, are awhile below *P1868:*duck awhile perdue, 1279| MS:Donning the novel rag and feather costume *P1868:*Donning what novel rag-and-feather trim 1280| MS:In private for the next adventure wholly new, *P1868:*Best suits the next adventure, new effect: 1281| MS:And, by < > is preparing to move away, *P1868:*And,—by < > is on the move, 1283| MS: whistle and up the < > pop again *P1868:*whistle, up again the < > pop 1284| MS:In the t'other < > with the novel arms *P1868:*In t'other < > with fresh tinseled staves, *CP1868:*fresh-tinseled 1285-87| MS:in a fight shall eclipse the first./ Note < > climax, last appearance of all *P1868:*in one last worst fight more/ Shall show, what you thought tragedy was farce./ Note < > climax and the crown of things 1288| MS:Is invariably the Devil himself, complete *P1868:*Invariably is, the devil appears himself, 1289-91| MS:Horns, hoofs and tail; nor otherwise proved it here—/ Let's move to that and never < > rest. *P1868:*Armed and accoutred, horns and hoofs and tail!/ Just so, nor otherwise it proved—you'll see:/ Move to the murder, never < > rest! 1292| MS:Well Guido, at this general ducking down *P1868:*Guido, at such a general duck-down, 1293| MS:In the breathing-while,—of the wife to her convent *P1868:*I' the breathing-space,—of wife to convent 1294| MS:The priest to his place of relegation, himself *P1868:*Priest to his relegation, and himself 1295| MS:To his house at Arezzo,—had given his place perforce *P1868:*To Arezzo,—had resigned his part perforce 1296| MS:To his brother the Abate, who bustled and did his best *P1868:*To brother Abate, who bustled, did his

Retrieved things somewhat, managed the three suits—
Since, it should seem, there were three suits-at-law
Behoved him look to, still, lest bad grow worse:
First civil suit,—the one the parents brought,
Impugning the legitimacy of his wife,
Affirming thence the nullity of her rights:
This was before the Rota,—Molinès,
That's judge there, made that notable decree
Which partly leaned to Guido, as I said,—
But Pietro had appealed against the same
To the very court will judge what we judge now—
Tommati and his fellows,—Suit the first.
Next civil suit,—demand on the wife's part
Of separation from the husband's bed
On plea of cruelty and risk to life—
Claims restitution of the dowry paid,
Immunity from paying any more:
This second, the Vicegerent has to judge.
Third and last suit,—this time, a criminal one,—
Answer to, and protection from, both these,—
Guido's complaint of guilt against his wife

---

best, 1297| MS:To retrieve matters somewhat by managing the suits— *P1868:* Retrieved things somewhat, managed the three suits— 1298| MS:were still three *P1868:*were three 1299| MS:him attend to, lest bad grow far worse: *P1868:*him look to, still, lest bad grow worse: 1300| MS:First Civil Suit,—the one that Pietro brought, *P1868:*First civil suit,—the one the parents brought, 1301| MS:of the girl *P1868:*of his wife, 1302| MS:And affirming <> her dowry: *P1868:* Affirming <> her rights: 1303-5| MS:the Rota,—its judge, Molines,/ Partially decided for Guido at first, as *P1868:*the Rota,—MolineOs,/ That's judge there, made that notable decree/ Which partly leaned to Guido, as 1306| MS:the decision *P1868:*the same 1307| MS:very tribunal which will judge him now, *P1868:*very court will judge what we judge now— 1308| MS:Whereof Tomati is judge,—this is Suit the First. *P1868:*Tommati and his fellows,—Suit the first. 1309| MS:Next Civil Suit,—a demand on Pompilia's part *P1868:*Next civil suit,—demand on the wife's part 1310| MS:For separation from the marital bed *P1868:*Of separation from the husband's bed 1311| MS:of the cruelty and danger of life— *P1868:*of cruelty and risk to life— 1312| MS:Claiming restitution also of <> paid *P1868:* Claims restitution of <> paid, 1313| MS:And immunity from keeping the other engagements— *P1868:*Immunity from paying any more: 1314| MS:This—before the Tribunal of the Vice gerent: *P1868:*This second, the Vicegerent has to judge. 1316| MS:The answer to and <> from both of these,— *P1868:*Answer to, and <> from, both these,— 1317| MS:Guido's own charge of adultery against *P1868:*

In the Tribunal of the Governor,
Venturini, also judge of the present cause.
Three suits of all importance plaguing him,
Beside a little private enterprise
Of Guido's,—essay at a shorter cut.
For Paolo, knowing the right way at Rome,
Had, even while superintending these three suits
I' the regular way, each at its proper court,
Ingeniously made interest with the Pope
To set such tedious regular forms aside,
And, acting the supreme and ultimate judge,
Declare for the husband and against the wife.
Well, at such crisis and extreme of straits,—
The man at bay, buffeted in this wise,—
Happened the strangest accident of all.
"Then," sigh friends, "the last feather broke his back,
Made him forget all possible remedies
Save one—he rushed to, as the sole relief
From horror and the abominable thing."
"Or rather," laugh foes, "then did there befall
The luckiest of conceivable events,
Most pregnant with impunity for him,

Guido's complaint of guilt against 1318| MS:the Governor *P1868:*the Governor, 1319| MS:Venturini who will judge the <> cause:— *P1868:*Venturini, also judge of the <> cause. 1320| MS:§ crowded between lines 1319-21 § him *P1868:*him, 1322| MS:Of Guido's own,—an essay <> cut,— *P1868:*Of Guido's,—essay <> cut. 1323| MS:the proper way *P1868:*the right way 1324| MS:Had ingeniously, even <> superintending the other suits *P1868:*Had, even <> superintending these three suits 1325| MS:In <> way at the proper courts of law, *P1868:*I' <> way, each at its proper court, 1326| MS:Made interest and appealed to the Pope himself *P1868:*Ingeniously made interest with the Pope 1327| MS:set those tedious *P1868:*set such tedious 1328| MS:acting as the *P1868:*acting the 1329| MS: Declare the wife guilty and give the husband his desire. *P1868:*Declare for the husband and against the wife. 1330-33| MS:extreme strait as this,/ "Then" say his friends "the <> back *P1868:*extreme of straits,/ The man at bay, buffeted in this wise,/ Happened the strangest accident of all./ "Then," sigh friends, "the <> back, *1888:* straits,—/ <> wise,— 1334| MS:And made *P1868:*Made 1335| MS:one—which he <> to, since his sole *P1868:*one—he <> to, as the sole 1336| MS: From the horror of the abominable accident." *P1868:*From horror and the abominable thing." 1337| MS:rather" say his foes "then did befall *P1868:*rather" laugh foes, "then did there befall *CP1868:*rather," laugh 1338| MS:of imaginable events *P1868:*of conceivable events, 1339| MS:with all good effects for *P1868:*with impunity for 1340| MS:Which turned <> attacks on himself, *P1868:*Which

Which henceforth turned the flank of all attack,
And bade him do his wickedest and worst."
—The wife's withdrawal from the Convertites,
Visit to the villa where her parents lived,
And birth there of his babe. Divergence here!
I simply take the facts, ask what they show.

First comes this thunderclap of a surprise:
Then follow all the signs and silences
Premonitory of earthquake. Paolo first
Vanished, was swept off somewhere, lost to Rome:
(Wells dry up, while the sky is sunny and blue.)
Then Guido girds himself for enterprise,
Hies to Vittiano, counsels with his steward,
Comes to terms with four peasants young and bold,
And starts for Rome the Holy, reaches her
At very holiest, for 'tis Christmas Eve,
And makes straight for the Abate's dried-up font,
The lodge where Paolo ceased to work the pipes.
And then, rest taken, observation made
And plan completed, all in a grim week,
The five proceed in a body, reach the place,

---

henceforth turned <> attack, 1341| MS:Dispensed with all preservatives and defences now." *P1868:*And bade him do his wickedest and worst." 1342-44| MS: The withdrawal from the Convent to the Villa/ And the birth of his son and heir: now, here as before, *P1868:*—The wife's withdrawal from the Convertites,/ Visit to the villa where her parents lived,/ And birth there of his babe. Divergence here! 1345| MS: facts and ask *P1868:*facts, ask 1345-46| MS:§ no ¶ § *P1868:*§ ¶ § 1346| MS: of complete surprise: *P1868:*of a surprise: 1347| MS:the regular signs *P1868:* the signs 1348| MS:earthquake: Paolo was first to vanish *P1868:*earthquake. Paolo first 1349| MS:Was swept off like a bird and lost to the Roman sky: *P1868:*Vanished, was swept off somewhere, lost to Rome: 1350| MS:(So § word and parenthesis added in margin § Wells <> blue:) *P1868:*(Wells <> blue.) 1351| MS:And a fortnight ago only, when Guido heard that news, *P1868:*Then Guido girds himself for enterprise, 1352| MS:He goes to his Villa, consults there with *P1868:*Hies to Vittiano, counsels with 1353| MS:peasants trusty young *P1868:*peasants young 1354| MS:the Holy, and reaches *P1868:*the Holy, reaches 1355| MS:At her very <> 'twas *P1868:*At very <> 'tis 1356| MS:make <> the dried basin aforesaid *P1868:*makes <> the Abate's dried-up font, 1357| MS:The Villa where Paolo had ceased *P1868:*The lodge where Paolo ceased 1358| MS:taken and preparations made, *P1868:*taken, observation *CP1868:*made 1359| MS:And the observations completed in a week, *P1868:*And plan completed, all in a grim week, 1360| MS:five in a body proceeded, reached the villa, *P1868:*five

—Pietro's, at the Paolina, silent, lone,
And stupefied by the propitious snow.
'Tis one i' the evening: knock: a voice "Who's there?"
"Friends with a letter from the priest your friend."
At the door, straight smiles old Violante's self.
She falls,—her son-in-law stabs through and through,
Reaches through her at Pietro—"With your son
This is the way to settle suits, good sire!"
He bellows "Mercy for heaven, not for earth!
Leave to confess and save my sinful soul,
Then do your pleasure on the body of me!"
—"Nay, father, soul with body must take its chance!"
He presently got his portion and lay still.
And last, Pompilia rushes here and there
Like a dove among the lightnings in her brake,
Falls also: Guido's, this last husband's-act.
He lifts her by the long dishevelled hair,
Holds her away at arm's length with one hand,
While the other tries if life come from the mouth—
Looks out his whole heart's hate on the shut eyes,
Draws a deep satisfied breath, "So—dead at last!"

---

proceed in a body, reach the place, 1361-63| MS:(The other, Pietro's, by Santa Paolina) the silent and propitious:/ At one in the evening: knocked *P1868:*—Pietro's, by Paolina, silent, lone,/ And stupified by the propitious snow,—/ At <> knock *1872:*—Pietro's, at the Paolina <> / <> snow./ 'Tis one i' 1364| MS:the Canon your *P1868:*the priest your 1365| MS:The door opens and there smiles <> self, *P1868:*At the door smiles <> self. *CP1868:*door, straight smiles 1366| MS:stabs her through and through *P1868:*stabs through and through, 1367-69| MS:And arrives at <> "With us two, good sire!"/ He <> heaven though not *P1868:*Reaches thro' her at <> "With your son/ This is the way to settle suits, good sire!"/ He <> heaven, not *1888:*through 1371| MS:Then have your pleasure with the *P1868:*Then do your pleasure on the 1372| MS:"Nay *P1868:*—"Nay 1374| MS:last Pompilia—rushing *P1868:*Pompilia rushes *CP1868:*last, Pompilia 1375| MS:brake— *P1868:*brake DC,BrU:brake, *1889:*brake, 1376| MS:Fell also: Guido did this <> husband's act *P1868:*Falls also: Guido's, this <> act. *CP1868:*husband's-act. 1377| MS:lifted <> the length of dishevelled *P1868:*lifts <> the long dishevelled 1378| MS:Held her from him at armslength, with *P1868:*Holds her away at arms' length with *1888:*arm's 1379| MS:tried if breath came *P1868:*tries if life come 1380| MS:Looked *P1868:*Looks 1381| MS:Drew <> breath "She is dead

Throws down the burden on dead Pietro's knees,
And ends all with "Let us away, my boys!"

And, as they left by one door, in at the other
Tumbled the neighbours—for the shrieks had pierced
To the mill and the grange, this cottage and that shed.
Soon followed the Public Force; pursuit began
Though Guido had the start and chose the road:
So, that same night was he, with the other four,
Overtaken near Baccano,—where they sank
By the way-side, in some shelter meant for beasts,
And now lay heaped together, nuzzling swine,
Each wrapped in bloody cloak, each grasping still
His unwiped weapon, sleeping all the same
The sleep o' the just,—a journey of twenty miles
Brought just and unjust to a level, you see.
The only one i' the world that suffered aught
By the whole night's toil and trouble, flight and chase,
Was just the officer who took them, Head
O' the Public Force,—Patrizj, zealous soul,
Who, having but duty to sustain weak flesh,
Got heated, caught a fever and so died:

---

*P1868:*Draws < > breath, "So—dead 1382| MS:Threw < > burthen *P1868:*Throws *1888:*burden 1383| MS:ended < > us be off, my *P1868:*ends < > us away, my 1383-84| MS:§ no ¶ § *P1868:*§ ¶ § 1384| MS:And as *CP1868:*And, as 1387| MS:the Officers and pursuit *P1868:*the Public Force; pursuit 1388| MS:had gotten the start and chosen *P1868:*had the start and chose 1389| MS:So that *P1868:*So, that 1390| MS:Overtaken as they lay tired out with the road *P1868:*Overtaken near Baccano,—where they sank 1391| MS:At the Inn at Baccano,—they had really reached so far,— *P1868:*By the way-side, in some shelter meant for beasts, 1392| MS:now were heaped in the straw, huddled like swine, *P1868:*now lay heaped together, huddled swine, *CP1868:*together, nuzzling swine, 1393| MS:in his bloody *P1868:*in bloody 1394| MS:sleeping one and all *P1868:*sleeping all the same 1395| MS:of the just man,—a < > of thirty miles *P1868:*o' the just, —a < > of twenty miles 1396| MS:Bringing < > see— *P1868:*see. *1872:*Brought 1397-1401| MS:in < > suffered by the exertion/ Being the Officer < > them, one Patrizj,/ Who had nothing but his sense of duty to sustain him *P1868:*i' < > suffered aught/ By the whole night's toil and trouble, flight and chase,/ Was just the officer < > them, Head/ O' the Public Force,—Patrizj, zealous soul,/ Who, having duty to sustain the flesh, *1888:*//// < > having but duty to sustain weak flesh, 1402| MS:So got

A warning to the over-vigilant,
—Virtue in a chafe should change her linen quick,
Lest pleurisy get start of providence.
(That's for the Cardinal, and told, I think!)

Well, they bring back the company to Rome.
Says Guido, "By your leave, I fain would ask
How you found out 'twas I who did the deed?
What put you on my trace, a foreigner,
Supposed in Arezzo,—and assuredly safe
Except for an oversight: who told you, pray?"
"Why, naturally your wife!" Down Guido drops
O' the horse he rode,—they have to steady and stay,
At either side the brute that bore him bound,
So strange it seemed his wife should live and speak!
She had prayed—at least so people tell you now—
For but one thing to the Virgin for herself,
Not simply,—as did Pietro 'mid the stabs,—
Time to confess and get her own soul saved
But time to make the truth apparent, truth
For God's sake, lest men should believe a lie:
Which seems to have been about the single prayer
She ever put up, that was granted her.

<> and died forthwith, *P1868:*Got <> and so died: 1403-7| MS:to over vigilant officers./ Well <> back Guido and his friends to Rome, *P1868:*to the over-vigilant,/ —Virtue in a chafe should change her linen quick,/ Lest pleurisy get start of providence./ (That's for the Cardinal, and told, I think!) § ¶ § Well <> back the company to Rome. 1408| MS:Says Guido "By <> would know *P1868:*Says Guido, "By <> would ask 1409-10| MS:deed/ You altogether mistake,—but of that, presently!/ What gave you the notion 'twas I, a *P1868:*deed?/ What put you on my trace, a 1411| MS:Supposed to be in <> and who had been there *P1868:* Supposed in <> and assuredly safe 1412| MS:for a blunder: who was it told you, pray!"— *P1868:*for an oversight: who told you, pray?" 1414-16| MS:On the horse,—they <> steady him on either side,/ So <> seemed the wife should be living yet; *P1868:*O' the horse he rode,—they <> steady and stay,/ At either side the brute that bore him, bound,/ So <> seemed his wife should live and speak! DC,BrU:/ <> him bound, *1889:*/ <> him bound, 1418-20| MS:the Virgin—not simply, as Pietro did,/ Time <> saved— *P1868:*the Virgin for herself,/ Not simply, as did Pietro 'mid the stabs,—/ Time <> saved— DC:/ <> simply,—as <> / <> saved BrU:/ <> stab,/ <> saved *1889:*/ <> simply,—as <> stabs,—/ <> saved 1421| MS:apparent to all, *CP1868:*apparent, truth 1422| MS:sake, whereof truth the splendor is: *P1868:*sake, lest men should believe a lie: 1423| MS:And it seems *P1868:*Which seems 1424| MS:was ever granted her: *P1868:*was granted her.

With this hope in her head, of telling truth,—
Being familiarized with pain, beside,—
She bore the stabbing to a certain pitch
Without a useless cry, was flung for dead
On Pietro's lap, and so attained her point.
Her friends subjoin this—have I done with them?—
And cite the miracle of continued life
(She was not dead when I arrived just now)
As attestation to her probity.

Does it strike your Excellency? Why, your Highness,
The self-command and even the final prayer,
Our candour must acknowledge explicable
As easily by the consciousness of guilt.
So, when they add that her confession runs
She was of wifehood one white innocence
In thought, word, act, from first of her short life
To last of it; praying, i' the face of death,
That God forgive her other sins—not this,
She is charged with and must die for, that she failed
Anyway to her husband: while thereon

1425| MS:telling the truth, *CP1868:*telling truth,— 1426| MS:Being moreover familiarized with pain, *P1868:*Being familiarized with pain, beside, *CP1868:*beside,— 1427| MS:stabbing up to *P1868:*stabbing to 1428| MS:cry, so was *P1868:*cry, was 1429| MS:As I say, on her father's lap, attained *P1868:*On Pietro's lap, and so attained 1430| MS:friends say all this <> done it justice? *P1868:*friends subjoin this <> done with them?— 1431| MS:And say the last miracle of her continued *P1868:*And cite the miracle of continued life— *CP1868:*life 1432| MS:(And she <> arrived at this house) *P1868:*(She <> arrived just now) 1433| MS:Is an attestation to her innocence. *P1868:*As attestation to her probity. 1433-34| MS:§ no ¶ § *P1868:*§ ¶ § 1434| MS:your Excellency so? Why, to be candid, your *P1868:*your Excellency? Why, your 1435-38| MS:The great self-possession and even prayer are explainable/ As easily by the consciousness of her guilt/ And fear of the punishment infallibly her due./ So when <> that all her confession is *P1868:*The self-command and even the final prayer,/ Our candour must acknowledge explainable/ As <> of guilt./ So, when that her confession runs *1872:*/ <> acknowledge explicable 1439| MS:That she was absolutely innocent *P1868:*She was of wifehood one white innocence 1440| MS:act; from the first *P1868:*act, from first 1441| MS:To the end of it; saying, in *P1868:*To last of it; praying, i' 1442| MS:"May God forgive my many sins—not this *P1868:*That God forgive her other sins—not this, 1443| MS:I am charged with and have to die for, that I failed *P1868:*She is charged with and must die for, that she failed 1444| MS:to my husband: failure was none." *P1868:*to her husband: while thereon

Comments the old Religious—"So much good,
Patience beneath enormity of ill,
I hear to my confusion, woe is me,
Sinner that I stand, shamed in the walk and gait
I have practised and grown old in, by a child!"—
Guido's friends shrug the shoulder, "Just this same
Prodigious absolute calm in the last hour
Confirms us,—being the natural result
Of a life which proves consistent to the close.
Having braved heaven and deceived earth throughout,
She braves still and deceives still, gains thereby
Two ends, she prizes beyond earth or heaven:
First sets her lover free, imperilled sore
By the new turn things take: he answers yet
For the part he played: they have summoned him indeed:
The past ripped up, he may be punished still:
What better way of saving him than this?
Then,—thus she dies revenged to the uttermost
On Guido, drags him with her in the dark,
The lower still the better, do you doubt?
Thus, two ways, does she love her love to the end,
And hate her hate,—death, hell is no such price
To pay for these,—lovers and haters hold."

1445| MS:And comments *P1868:*Comments 1446| MS:Patience, beneath <> of wrong, *P1868:*Patience beneath <> of ill, 1448| MS:that I am, shamed in the very walk *P1868:*that I stand, shamed in the walk and gait 1449| MS:child!" *P1868:*child!"— 1450| MS:friends say to it all "Just what you say, *P1868:*friends shrug the shoulder, "Just this same 1451| MS:Of this prodigious calm *P1868:*Prodigious absolute calm 1452| MS:us,—is the natural consequence *P1868:*us,—being the natural result 1453| MS:proves all of a piece to the end. *P1868:*proves consistent to *CP1868:*the close. 1454| MS:braved Heaven <> throughout *P1868:*braved heaven <> throughout, 1455-57| MS:She will brave and deceive even now, and gain two ends/ First set <> free, in imminent peril *P1868:*She braves still and deceives still, gains thereby/ Two ends, she prizes beyond earth or heaven:/ First sets <> free, imperilled sore 1458| MS:things have taken, to answer *P1868:*things take: he answers 1459| MS:have sent for him of course, *P1868:*have summoned him indeed: 1460| MS:The Past will be ripped <> punished yet: *P1868:*The past ripped <> punished still: 1461| MS:And what <> this of hers? *P1868:*What <> this? 1462| MS:thus also is she revenged *P1868:*thus she dies revenged 1463-65| MS:On her husband, drags him down to the grave with her./ Thus two ways does *P1868:*On Guido, drags him with her in the dark,/ The lower still the better, do you doubt?/ Thus, two ways, does 1466-68| MS:death is <> price to pay for these./ But <> another supposition, you see: *P1868:*death, hell is <> price/ To pay for these,—lovers and haters hold."/ But <>

But there's another parry for the thrust.
"Confession," cry folks—"a confession, think!
Confession of the moribund is true!"
Which of them, my wise friends? This public one,
Or the private other we shall never know?
The private may contain,—your casuists teach,—
The acknowledgment of, and the penitence for,
That other public one, so people say.
However it be,—we trench on delicate ground,
Her Eminence is peeping o'er the cards,—
Can one find nothing in behalf of this
Catastrophe? Deaf folks accuse the dumb!
You criticize the drunken reel, fool's speech,
Maniacal gesture of the man,—we grant!
But who poured poison in his cup, we ask?
Recall the list of his excessive wrongs,
First cheated in his wife, robbed by her kin,
Rendered anon the laughing-stock o' the world
By the story, true or false, of his wife's birth,—
The last seal publicly apposed to shame

---

another parry for the thrust. 1469-71| MS:"The confession," cry people,—"A confession is true!"/ Which, my friends?—The <> one,—as this is— *P1868:*"Confession," cry folks—"a confession, think!/ Confession of the moribund is true!"/ Which of them, my wise friends? This <> one, 1472| MS:private one which we may never hear of? *P1868:*private other we shall never know? 1473| MS:contain,—as we have experience every day,— *P1868:*contain,—your casuists teach,— 1474-76| MS:of and penitence for the other—/ But however that be,—for we *P1868:*of, and the penitence for,/ That other public one, so people say—/ However it be,—we *CP1868:*/ <> say. 1477| MS:And his Eminence <> o'er his cards,— *P1868:*Her Eminence <> o'er the cards,— 1478| MS:Can his friends say nothing <> this last *P1868:*Can one say nothing <> this *CP1868:* one find nothing 1479| MS:Of Guido's acts? Oh, they are by no means dumb! *P1868:*Catastrophe? Deaf folks accuse the dumb! 1480-82| MS: reel, mad gesture of the man,/Who poured the poison into his *P1868:*reel, fool's-speech,/ Maniacal gesture of the man,—we grant!/ But who poured poison in his *1888:*fool's speech, 1483| MS:Remember the *P1868:*Recall the 1484| MS:robbed of her dowry next, *P1868:*robbed by her kin, 1485| MS: laughing stock of *P1868:*laughing-stock o' 1487| MS:publicly set to his infamy

By the open flight of wife and priest,—why, Sirs,
Step out of Rome a furlong, would you know
What anotherguess tribunal than ours here,
Mere worldly Court without the help of grace,
Thinks of just that one incident o' the flight?
Guido preferred the same complaint before
The court at Arezzo, bar of the Granduke,—
In virtue of it being Tuscany
Where the offence had rise and flight began,—
Self-same complaint he made in the sequel here
Where the offence grew to the full, the flight
Ended: offence and flight, one fact judged twice
By two distinct tribunals,—what result?
There was a sentence passed at the same time
By Arezzo and confirmed by the Granduke,
Which nothing baulks of swift and sure effect
But absence of the guilty, (flight to Rome
Frees them from Tuscan jurisdiction now)
—Condemns the wife to the opprobrious doom
Of all whom law just lets escape from death.
The Stinche, House of Punishment, for life,—
That's what the wife deserves in Tuscany:
Here, she deserves—remitting with a smile

---

*P1868:*publicly apposed to shame 1488-91| MS: of his wife with a Priest,—why, sirs,/ Would you know what another sort of Tribunal than ours/ A worldly one without <> grace *P1868:*of wife and priest,—why, Sirs,/ Step out of Rome a furlong, would you know/ What anotherguess tribunal than ours here,/ Mere worldly Court without <> grace, 1492| MS:of *P1868:*o' 1493-1500| MS:Guido made the <> before the court at Arezzo/ In <> being there that the flight began,/ That he made before the court at Rome, since at Rome/ It was that the flight had its end: one fact, judged twice/ By <> Tribunals,—and what's the result? *P1868:*Guido preferred the <> before/ The court at Arezzo, bar of the Granduke,—/ In <> being Tuscany/ Where the offence had rise and flight began,—/ Self-same complaint he made in the sequel here/ Where the offence grew to the full, the flight/ Ended: offence and flight, one fact judged twice/ By <> tribunals,—what result? 1501-3| MS:time/ Which was only hindered from being carried into effect *P1868:*time/ By Arezzo and confirmed by the Granduke,/ Which nothing baulks of swift and sure effect 1504| MS:By the absence <> guilty,—the flight *P1868:*But absence <> guilty, (flight 1505| MS:Having freed them § inserted above § from the Tuscan jurisdiction of course. *P1868:*Frees them from Tuscan jurisdiction now) 1506| MS:There,—she was condemned to the opprobrious fate *P1868:*—Condemns the wife to the opprobrious doom 1507| MS:whom the Law <> death *P1868:*whom law <> death. 1508-10| MS:Condemned to the House of Punishment, the Stinche, for life./ Here, the self-same fact is found just to deserve—a visit *P1868:*The Stinche, House of

To her father's house, main object of the flight!
The thief presented with the thing he steals!

At this discrepancy of judgments—mad,
The man took on himself the office, judged;
And the only argument against the use
O' the law he thus took into his own hands
Is . . . what, I ask you?—that, revenging wrong,
He did not revenge sooner, kill at first
Whom he killed last! That is the final charge.
Sooner? What's soon or late i' the case?—ask we.
A wound i' the flesh no doubt wants prompt redress;
It smarts a little to-day, well in a week,
Forgotten in a month; or never, or now, revenge!
But a wound to the soul? That rankles worse and worse.
Shall I comfort you, explaining—"Not this once
But now it may be some five hundred times
I called you ruffian, pandar, liar and rogue:
The injury must be less by lapse of time"?
The wrong is a wrong, one and immortal too,
And that you bore it those five hundred times,
Let it rankle unrevenged five hundred years,
Is just five hundred wrongs the more and worse!

Punishment, for life,—/ That's what the wife deserves in Tuscany:/ Here, she deserves—remitting with a smile 1511| MS:house, the object of the very flight, *P1868:*house, main object of the flight! 1512| MS:thief is presented *P1868:*thief presented 1512-13| MS:§ no ¶ § *P1868:*§ ¶ § 1513| MS:For madness at <> judgments *P1868:*At <> judgments—mad, 1514| MS:office of judge, *P1868:*office, judged; 1516| MS:Of *P1868:*O' 1517| MS:Is . . what <> you? that, in taking his revenge, *P1868:*you?—that, revenging wrong, *1888:*Is . . . what 1518| MS:not take it sooner *P1868:*not revenge sooner 1519| MS:last: that really is the charge. *P1868:*last! That is the final charge. 1520| MS:"Sooner <> late?" the friends enquire *P1868:*Sooner <> late i' the case?—ask we. 1521| MS:A natural wound in the flesh wants soon redress; *P1868:*A wound i' the flesh no doubt, wants prompt redress: *CP1868:*doubt wants 1522| MS:smarts less day by day, is well *P1868:*smarts a little to-day, well 1523| MS:month; revenge that now or never? *P1868:*month; or never, or now, revenge! 1524| MS:the honor—that grows worse and worse, *P1868:*the soul? That rankles worse and worse. 1525| MS:comfort a man by saying—"Not once only *P1868:*comfort you, explaining—"Not this once 1527| MS:Have I *P1868:*I 1528| MS:The pain must sure be less by the time that's past; § altered to § ?" *P1868:*The injury must be less by lapse of time?" § emended to § time"? § see Editorial Notes § 1530| MS:that he has borne it *P1868:*that you bore it 1531| MS:Or let it go unrevenged *P1868:*Let it rankle unrevenged 1532| MS:wrongs more and so much worse: *P1868:*wrongs the more

Men, plagued this fashion, get to explode this way,
If left no other.

"But we left this man
Many another way, and there's his fault,"
'Tis answered—"He himself preferred our arm
O' the law to fight his battle with. No doubt
We did not open him an armoury
To pick and choose from, use, and then reject.
He tries one weapon and fails,—he tries the next
And next: he flourishes wit and common sense,
They fail him,—he plies logic doughtily,
It fails him too,—thereon, discovers last
He has been blind to the combustibles—
That all the while he is a-glow with ire,
Boiling with irrepressible rage, and so
May try explosives and discard cold steel,—
So hires assassins, plots, plans, executes!
Is this the honest self-forgetting rage
We are called to pardon? Does the furious bull
Pick out four help-mates from the grazing herd

---

and worse! 1533| MS:Men, tried this *P1868:*Men, plagued this
1534-38| MS:If you leave them no other." "We left this man so many others,"/ It is <> arms:/ But we <> open to him a whole armoury of such *P1868:*If left no other. § ¶ § "But we left this man/ Many another way, and there's his fault,"/ 'Tis <> arm/ O' the law to fight his battle with. No doubt/ We <> open him an armoury
1539| MS:from, and then reject after all: *P1868:*from, use, and then reject.
1540| MS:one piece and fails,—then tries *P1868:*one weapon and fails,—he tries
1541| MS:And the next: he tries his wit *P1868:*And next: he flourishes wit
1542| MS:him,—then he tries the regular law, *P1868:*him,—he plies logic doughtily,
1543| MS:That fails him too,—and then he discovers *P1868:*It fails him too,—thereon, discovers 1544| MS:That he has been overlooking another way still, *P1868:*He has been blind to the combustibles— 1545| MS:he has been mad with ire *P1868:*he is a-glow with ire, 1546| MS:Overboiling with *P1868:*Boiling with
1547| MS:May use that weapon and discard the rest. *P1868:*May try explosives and discard cold steel,— 1548| MS:So he hires <> plots, plans, executes— *P1868:*So hire <> plot, plan, execute! *1888:*hires <> plots, plans, executes!
1551| MS:four companions from *P1868:*four help mates from *1872:*help-mates

And journey with them over hill and dale
Till he find his enemy?"

What rejoinder? save
That friends accept our bull-similitude.
Bull-like,—the indiscriminate slaughter, rude
And reckless aggravation of revenge,
Were all i' the way o' the brute who never once
Ceases, amid all provocation more,
To bear in mind the first tormentor, first
Giver o' the wound that goaded him to fight:
And, though a dozen follow and reinforce
The aggressor, wound in front and wound in flank,
Continues undisturbedly pursuit,
And only after prostrating his prize
Turns on the pettier, makes a general prey.
So Guido rushed against Violante, first
Author of all his wrongs, *fons et origo*
Malorum—drops first, deluge since,—which done,
He finished with the rest. Do you blame a bull?

In truth you look as puzzled as ere I preached!

1553| MS:his foe? "No," is returned to this— *P1868:*his enemy?" § ¶ § What rejoinder? save 1554| MS:He was far more like a bull than that—he acted *P1868:*That friends accept our bull-similitude. 1555| MS:Bull-like: the very indiscriminate slaughter, *P1868:*Bull-like,—the indiscriminate slaughter, rude 1556| MS:The useless aggravation of the deed, *P1868:*And reckless aggravation of revenge, 1557-60| MS:in <> of the creature who never ceases/ To remember the first aggressor, first giver of the wound, *P1868:*i' <> o' the brute who never once/ Ceases, amid all provocation more,/ To bear in mind the first tormentor, first/ Giver o' the wound that goaded him to fight: 1561-63| MS:reinforce him,/ He continues undisturbedly the pursuit, *P1868:*reinforce/ The aggressor, wound in front and wound in flank,/ Continues undisturbedly pursuit, 1564| MS:prostrating him and ending him *P1868:*reinforce/ The aggressor, wound in front and wound in flank,/ Continues undisturbedly pursuit, 1564| MS:prostrating him and ending him *P1868:*prostrating his prize 1565| MS:Does he turn on the others and make a general slaughter. *P1868:*Turns on the pettier, makes a general prey.
1566| MS:So did Guido go against Violante first *P1868:*So Guido rushed against Violante, first 1567-69| MS:The author <> *fons et origo malorum* § last four words apparently underlined in revision since ink is different §/ Then, increasingly drunk, finished with the rest as you know. *P1868:*Author <> *origo/ Malorum*—increasingly drunk,—which justice done,/ He finished with the rest. Do you blame a bull? *1872:/ Malorum*—drops first, deluge since,—which done,/ He
1570| MS:puzzled as when you began! *P1868:*puzzled as ere I preached!

How is that? There are difficulties perhaps
On any supposition, and either side.
Each party wants too much, claims sympathy
For its object of compassion, more than just.
Cry the wife's friends, "O the enormous crime
Caused by no provocation in the world!"
"Was not the wife a little weak?"—inquire—
"Punished extravagantly, if you please,
But meriting a little punishment?
One treated inconsiderately, say,
Rather than one deserving not at all
Treatment and discipline o' the harsher sort?"
No, they must have her purity itself,
Quite angel,—and her parents angels too
Of an aged sort, immaculate, word and deed:
At all events, so seeming, till the fiend,
Even Guido, by his folly, forced from them
The untoward avowal of the trick o' the birth,
Which otherwise were safe and secret now.
Why, here you have the awfulest of crimes
For nothing! Hell broke loose on a butterfly!
A dragon born of rose-dew and the moon!

1571-75| MS:difficulties on any supposition perhaps./ Each < > much for its object of compassion:/ Say the < > friends, here was this enormous *P1868:*difficulties perhaps/ On any supposition, and either side./ Each < > much, claims sympathy/ For its object of compassion, more than just./ Cry the < > friends, "O the enormous
1576| MS:Committed without any the least provocation < > world: *P1868:*Caused by no provocation < > world!" 1577-82| MS:Was the wife not a < > weak? punished overmuch if you please/ But a little deserving punishment? Treated inconsiderately/ Rather than one requiring no treatment at all of the harsh sort? *P1868:*Was not the wife a < > weak?"—inquire—/ Punished extravagantly, if you please,/ But meriting a little punishment?/ One treated inconsiderately, say,/ Rather than one deserving not at all/ Treatment and discipline o' the harsher sort?" 1583| MS:Oh, no—they < > her pure, purity itself— *P1868:*No—they < > her purity itself, *CP1868:*No, they
1584| MS:An angel < > parents are angels *P1868:*Quite angel < > parents angels
1585| MS:sort, harmless in word and deed, *P1868:*sort, immaculate, word *1872:*deed:
1586-89| MS:events, seeming so, till Guido's own folly/ Forced from them the single untoward avowal/ Of what would otherwise have been secret for ever. *P1868:*events, so seeming till the fiend,/ Even Guido, by his folly, forced from them/ The untoward avowal of the trick o' the birth,/ Would otherwise be safe and secret now. *1872:*/// Which otherwise were safe 1590-92| MS:have then the < > crimes—for nothing!/ A dragon is born out of roses, dew and the moon! *P1868:*have the < > crimes/ For nothing! Hell broke loose on a butterfly!/ A dragon born of rose-dew and the moon!

Yet here is the monster! Why he's a mere man—
Born, bred and brought up in the usual way.
His mother loves him, still his brothers stick
To the good fellow of the boyish games;
The Governor of his town knows and approves,
The Archbishop of the place knows and assists:
Here he has Cardinal This to vouch for the past,
Cardinal That to trust for the future,—match
And marriage were a Cardinal's making,—in short,
What if a tragedy be acted here
Impossible for malice to improve,
And innocent Guido with his innocent four
Be added, all five, to the guilty three,
That we of these last days be edified
With one full taste o' the justice of the world?

The long and the short is, truth seems what I show:—
Undoubtedly no pains ought to be spared
To give the mob an inkling of our lights.
It seems unduly harsh to put the man
To the torture, as I hear the court intends,
Though readiest way of twisting out the truth;

1593| MS:the dragon, look at him! Why, he's *P1868:*the monster! Why *1872:*Why he's 1595-97| MS:him, his brothers stick to him yet,/ The *P1868:*him, still his brothers stick/ To the good fellow of the boyish games;/ The 1598| MS:of the same knows and assists, *P1868:*of the place, knows and assists: *1868:*place knows 1599| MS:Here in Rome, he has Cardinal this to *P1868:*Here he has Cardinal This to 1600| MS:Cardinal the other to be ready to trust the future, *P1868:*Cardinal That to trust for the future,—match 1601| MS:This marriage was *P1868:*And marriage were 1602| MS:tragedy have been acted all this while *P1868:*tragedy be acted here 1603| MS:Impossible to be improved upon *P1868:*Impossible for malice to improve, 1604-5| MS:his innocent friends/ (Over-zealous only in behalf of the innocent)/ Be <> the victims three *P1868:*his innocent four/ Be <> the guilty three, 1606-8| MS:That you may be edified with the justice of the world?/ He will in that case have been wronged indeed./ § no ¶ § <> and short is, the truth is hard to understand— *P1868:*That we of these last days be edified/ With one full taste o' the justice of the world?/ § ¶ § <> and the short is, truth is what I show:— *1888:*// <> truth seems what 1609-13| MS:And undoubted <> spared:/ It seems hard to <> man to the torture, for instance,/ The readiest way of getting us out the truth: *P1868:*Undoubtedly <> spared/ To give the mob an inkling of our lights./ It seems unduly harsh to <> man/ To the torture, as I hear the court intends,/ Though readiest way of twisting out

He is noble, and he may be innocent.
On the other hand, if they exempt the man
(As it is also said they hesitate
On the fair ground, presumptive guilt is weak
I' the case of nobility and privilege),—
What crime that ever was, ever will be,
Deserves the torture? Then abolish it!
You see the reduction *ad absurdum*, Sirs?

Her Excellency must pronounce, in fine!
What, she prefers going and joining play?
Her Highness finds it late, intends retire?
I am of their mind: only, all this talk talked,
'Twas not for nothing that we talked, I hope?
Both know as much about it, now, at least,
As all Rome: no particular thanks, I beg!
(You'll see, I have not so advanced myself,
After my teaching the two idiots here!)

---

the truth; 1614| MS:and may be innocent: and yet *P1868:*and he may be *1872:*innocent. 1615| MS:hand if they do not put him to the torture *P1868:*hand, if they exempt the man 1616| MS:is said they hesitate to do *P1868:*is also said they hesitate 1617-19| MS:the ground that the presumptive guilt is not strong enough)/ What <> was or ever will be *P1868:*is weak/ I' the case of nobility and privilege),—/ What <> was, ever will be, *CP1868:*the fair ground, presumptive 1620-22| MS:Will deserve it? As well abolish it altogether./ § line 1622 comes at top of page but no ¶ indicated § Your Excellency must pronounce—I have spoken for that: *P1868:*Deserve the torture? Then abolish it!/ You see the reduction *ad absurdum*, Sirs?/ § ¶ § Her Excellency must pronounce, in fine! 1623| MS:What, you prefer going and joining the cardplayers? *P1868:*What, she prefers going and joining play? 1624| MS:And your Highness <> late and intends to retire? *P1868:*Her Highness <> late, intends retire? 1625| MS:of your mind—only, after all this talk, *P1868:*of their mind: only, all this talk, talked, *1888:*talk talked, 1626| MS:It was <> that I have spoken, I hope! *P1868:*'Twas <> that we talked, I hope? 1627| MS:Now you both <> it, at *P1868:*Both know <> it, now, at 1629-30| MS:§ omitted § *P1868:*(You'll see, I have not so advanced myself,/ After my teaching the two idiots here!)

Editorial Notes

THE RING AND THE BOOK, Books 1-4

Emendations to the Text

The following emendations have been made to the 1888-89 text:
1. *The Ring and the Book*

1. 52: In 1888 and 1889 the apostrophe is missing, though the space for it remains. The MS-1872 reading has been restored.
1.57: All editions omit a comma after *porphyry*, thus restricting the adjectives *Polished and rough* in the next line to *porphyry*. The sense of line 57 seems to require the application of the adjectives to the whole list of stone samples; therefore the MS comma after *porphyry* has been restored.
1.1140: The line, which came at the top of the page in 1888 and 1889, was for no apparent reason indented in that edition. The indentation has been removed to conform to MS-1872.
1.1166: The line, which comes at the top of the page in 1888 and 1889, was for no apparent reason indented in that edition. The indentation has been removed to conform to MS-1872.
1.1182: The 1888-89 edition lacks an exclamation point after *faithful*, although the space for it remains. The MS-1872 reading is restored.
1.1298: The colon at the end of this line did not print in most copies of 1888-89. Its presence can be detected in the large paper copies of the first impression. In the trade copies of the first impression and in the second impression (1889) only the upper point of the colon appears.
1.1358: The MS-1872 reading *now shrouds, now shows* was changed to *now shrouds nor shows* in 1888-89, thus eliminating the clearly intended opposition between *shrouds* and *shows*. The earlier reading is restored.

2. *Half-Rome*

2.230: Browning's script characteristically separates parts of compound words. Although in the MS the space between parts of a single word is usually distinctly narrower than the space between words, the difference between one word and two can be deceiving. Here the narrow spacing in the MS, the rhythm of the line, standard spelling, and Browning's consistent use of this compound in other instances, argue that one word rather than two is correct despite the reading of 1868-1889. The 1889 text is emended to conform to MS.

2.1144: The sense of the passage makes the verb *were* conditional, and requires that the line be an introductory adverbial clause, not the end of a sentence. The 1889 period is emended to a comma to conform to MS-1872.

3. *The Other Half-Rome*

3.238: The 1888-89 edition reads *surmount*; the MS-1872 reading *surmounts* is restored to maintain agreement with the verb subject *sliver.*

4. *Tertium Quid*

4.514-15: Quotation marks in MS and 1868 make clear that these two lines belong to different speakers. The punctuation is incorrect or missing in 1872-1889. The 1888-89 text has been emended to restore the MS -1868 punctuation.

4.720 and 4.727: The apostrophe at the beginning of line 720 is clearly printed in 1888 and faintly visible in some copies of 1889. The comma after *generation* in line 727 is faintly printed in 1888 and missing from 1889. These are type failures and thus printing them is not, strictly speaking, emendation.

4.1042: Because of faulty type the punctuation after *fault* is imperfect in all copies collated of 1888 and 1889. The colon has been restored to conform to MS-1872.

4.1049: The line, in parentheses, is a full sentence, preceded and followed by full sentences. The MS period after *mouth*, missing in 1868-1889, has been restored.

4.1124: The line, which comes at the top of the page in 1888-89, was for no apparent reason indented in that edition. The indentation has been removed to conform to MS-1872.

4.1528: When B altered the punctuation at the end of this line in MS, he misplaced the question mark. We have placed the question mark outside the quotation marks since the entire sentence, not the quoted passage, is interrogative.

B indicated divisions in discourse by line spacing rather than by indentation. During the printing history of *The Ring and the Book* paragraph divisions were occasionally lost when they happened to occur between pages. We have restored all of B's paragraphs. These form a separate class of emendations to the 1888-89 text. Paragraphing is restored at:
1.29-30
1.237-38
1.1153-54
2.340-41
2.1525-26
3.468-69
3.835-36
3.1369-70
3.1457-58
4.69-70
4.422-23
4.896-97

Notes frequently cross-referenced

The Old Yellow Book: *Sources* and 1.32n.
Italian currency: 1.65n.
Holy orders: 1.260-62n.
Cencini: 1.268n.
Innocent XII: 1.298n.
Jansenism: 1.303-13n.
Molinism: 1.303-13n.
Caponsacchi's order: 1.379n.
Houses of the Comparini: 1.389n.
Arezzo: 1.491n.
Castelnuovo: 1.502n.
The Franceschini family: 1.547n.; 2.289n., 769n., 4.384n.
Myth and day of St. George: 1.579n.
Torture: 1.971-72n.
San Lorenzo Church (Rome): 2.6n.
Philosophic sin: 2.176-77n.
Jubilee: 2.532n.
Ages of the Comparini: 2.571n.
Pompilia's literacy: 2.1145n.
Civita Vecchia: 2.1171n.

Detail of map of Italy dated 1701, showing Tuscany, the southern and western boundaries of the States of the Church, the principal post roads, and places mentioned in *The Ring and the Book*. Published by permission of the British

Chronology of Important Events, including Legal Processes, in The Ring and the Book *and* The Old Yellow Book

16 July 1680	Pompilia was born to a needy woman in Rome and in an elaborate deception was represented as the newborn offspring of 47-year-old Violante Comparini, wife of Pietro Comparini, of Rome.
June 1693	Count Guido Franceschini of Arezzo initiated negotiations with the Comparini through a hairdresser for marriage to Pompilia. Guido's age is not given in OYB; he was actually 36 at this time, but B made him 46.
6 Sept. 1693	The real date of the marriage, which B placed in December (see 3.449 and n.) The marriage took place in Rome, according to B secretly and without Pietro's consent, but there is no assurance of this in the records.
30 Nov. 1693	Pompilia and the Comparini arrived in Arezzo to live with Guido, his mother, and a brother. The Comparini soon found that their confidence in Guido's wealth had been abused. In disappointment they returned to Rome after three months in Arezzo.
March 1694	The Comparini returned to their house in Rome. Violante confessed her deception in the birth of Pompilia and brought suit that summer to invalidate Guido's claim to the illegitimate Pompilia's dowry. Guido countersued, appeals were made, and the question of the dowry was still in litigation at the time of the murders.
23 April-12 Oct. 1697	B changed the date of Pompilia's and Caponsacchi's flight from Arezzo to Rome from 28 April to 23 April, St. George's Day (see 1.579n.). At this time Pompilia was one month pregnant. The fugitives spent the night at an inn in Castelnuovo, where Guido caught up with them and had them arrested. He prosecuted them for flight and adultery both in Rome (that summer) and in Arezzo (the following in autumn). The decision of the Roman court was relegation (exile) for Caponsacchi to Civita Vecchia for three years, and temporary restraint for Pompilia at the convent Le Scalette. (Through an apparent confusion, B placed her in the Monastery of the Convertites. See 2.1189-90n.) The Arezzo sentence was more severe: life imprisonment for Pompilia.

	However, she was no longer under Tuscan jurisdiction (see *Sources* and map). Pompilia stayed about three weeks at Le Scalette, until 12 October, after which she gave her bond to remain *domus pro carcere* (under house arrest) at her parents' home. That same autumn Pompilia sued for legal separation from Guido, a suit which was not decided at the time of the murders.
18 Dec. 1697	Pompilia's child Gaetano was born at the Comparini's house.
24 Dec. 1697	Guido and four hired assassins left Arezzo for Rome, where they spied on the Comparini household for a week before the attack.
2 Jan. 1698	Pietro and Violante Comparini were killed at their house and Pompilia, with twenty-two knife wounds, was left for dead. She survived for four days, however, and was able to give the information leading to Guido's arrest before he could escape the States of the Church for the relative safety of Tuscany and its separate jurisdiction (see *Sources* and map).
Late Jan.-Feb.	Trial of Guido and his accomplices for murder.
18 Feb. 1698	All the accused were found guilty and sentenced to death. Guido's case was appealed to the Pope, who denied the appeal 20 Feb.
22 Feb. 1698	Guido was beheaded and his accomplices hanged in a public execution in the Piazza del Popolo.
May 1698	A decision was made in favor of Pompilia in a suit brought by the Convent of the Convertites for Pompilia's property, a claim based on this convent's right to the estate of any loose woman who died within the city. In effect, the judgment cleared Pompilia's name and saved her estate for her heir.

Sources

The Old Yellow Book The chief source for *The Ring and the Book* was a volume found by B in an open market in Florence in June 1860, among a miscellany of second-hand goods. The dramatic discovery and its sequence are preserved in the poem (1.37-82). The value of the book to B was from the beginning both real and talismanic. Its very touch felt "medicinable," "restorative," comparable to Elijah raising the dead (1.750-769); B tosses it in the air, half exuberantly, half as if to snatch it back again from careless fate. B enlarges upon the "predestination" and sheer accident of his find, but he had, in addition to grace and luck, a practiced eye for objects of esthetic or antiquarian value in the flea markets of the day. Ten years earlier, for example, Elizabeth had reported, "he covered himself with glory by discovering and seizing on (in a corn shop a mile from Florence) five pictures among heaps of trash; and one of the best judges in Florence (Mr. Kirkup) throws out such names for them as Cimabue, Ghirlandaio, Giottini. . . " (*Letters of EBB*, I, 448; letter dated May 4, [1850]).

B considered the literary worth of OYB self-evident, and apparently between 1860 and 1864, he offered the subject to a number of people, including Miss Ogle the novelist, W.C. Cartwright the historian, even Anthony Trollope and Alfred Tennyson. The 266p. volume is composed of 22 documents bound together. It concerns the trial in 1698 of Count Guido Franceschini, who, with four hired confederates, stood accused of the murder of his estranged wife Pompilia and her adoptive parents Pietro and Violante Comparini. Of the 266 pages, including title page, 235 pages are printed, 14 are in manuscript, and 17 are blank. 191 pages are in Latin and 91 are in Italian. A full technical description of OYB is given below, but it may be generalized here that even the physical format of the book supports what must have been B's immediate sense of his find: that the grip of human passion and circumstance is beyond human law to grasp or resolve, and beyond the grave in its reach.

The unity of the narrative contrasts with the separate and self-contained documents which tell and retell the story. These self-contained sections, in a sense, reflect the complex social and legal structures of the period. Italy in the seventeenth century was divided into several separate states, which included the Papal State of Rome and the various city states to the N and S (see map). Within the Papal States the Catholic Church had civil as well as ecclesiastic jurisdiction, while in the states to the N (Tuscany, Venice, Milan, etc.) and S (Naples, Sicily, Sardinia) the judicial systems were independent from the church. The two chief governing bodies in the Papal State were the Sacred Roman Rota, or Supreme Court, whose ecclesiastic jurisdiction extended throughout the Catholic world but whose civil jurisdiction even within the Papal State was almost exclusively appellate, and the Reverend Apostolic Chamber, headed by the Governor of Rome, whose jurisdiction was both civil and criminal. It was before the latter court that Guido Fransceschini was tried.

According to the practice of the time, the case was argued not orally between the opposing parties in open court, but in a series of printed documents summarizing and weighing evidence, applicable laws, and precedents. Both defense and prosecution were assigned lawyers by the court. Guido's lawyers were Arcangeli and Spreti, whose positions were formally designated Advocate of the Poor and Procurator of the Poor; Pompilia's lawyers were Bottini and Gambi, Advocate and Procurator of the Fisc (office of the Treasury). These titles and distinctions seem to have had little real significance, except that the Advocate and Procurator of the Poor always spoke for the defense and took precedence in the order of the trial over the lawyers for the prosecution, the Advocate and Procurator of the Fisc. All arguments composed by the two sides were printed by the official papal press and presented to the court. Fourteen of these documents (six for the prosecution, five for the defense, three summaries of related suits and matters involving the litigants) are the legal kernel of the OYB. They are written in late Church Latin, and bear the imprint of the papal press, *Typis Rev. Cam. Apos.* (In the Type of the Reverend Apostolic Chamber).

In addition to the printed legal pamphlets in Latin there are eight other documents in the OYB: two anonymous printed pamphlets in Italian, one summarizing the case from a view favoring Guido, and a similar one favoring Pompilia, both pamphlets apparently being intended for the public; three letters in Italian addressed to the probable compiler of the book, a lawyer in Florence named Cencini; and three court records of judgments of cases related to the murder trial (an abduction suit and a property suit). These latter judgments are the first and last entries in the OYB, and both concern Pompilia. The judgment in the abduction case finds her guilty of complicity with her abductor-rescuer Caponsacchi; the last judgment, in the property suit, clears her name of suspicion of promiscuity. These initial and final judgments are a kind of frame symbolically forecasting the poem's compass of guilt and innocence.

The anonymous pamphlets in the popular tongue, which B drew upon in Books 2 and 3 (*Half-Rome* and *The Other Half-Rome*), are themselves a comment upon the society of the time. In seventeenth-century Rome the more sensational sort of news was published and circulated by *ad hoc* methods, since the daily newspapers were published by the Church and were mainly concerned with ecclesiastical matters. That there was an eager market for scandal, particularly when an execution was in prospect, is attested by the records: at the five-fold execution of Guido and his accomplices, special stands were constructed to hold the 40,000 spectators, and tickets for window viewing went for high prices. One foreign nobleman rented an apartment for three months in order to secure his afternoon's seats. The anonymous pamphlets in the OYB were thus probably a response to popular demand. They may have been written by lawyers involved in the case and been intended to sway popular opinion in support of one or the other side.

The documents in the OYB seem to be a virtually complete record of the trial. One of the letters bound into the volume mentions a missing argument by the prosecution, which may concern the confederates (Gest, 35). As for the sources used in the trial itself, it is possible that the full testimonies of witnesses briefly quoted by the lawyers, and in particular Guido's deposition, may yet be discovered.

As any reader of *The Ring and the Book* is aware, B regarded the OYB as much more than a source. He claimed to have read it closely eight times through, and he repeatedly urges that the poem is meant to be a realization and a recreation of the characters and events in the OYB, not a merely fanciful reconstruction. Yet any careful reader is also aware of numerous divergences of fact, emphasis, and motive between book and poem. It is safe to assume that B was conscious of these discrepancies, at least in the main, and intended his recreation to be consistent.

The OYB was presented after B's death to the library of Balliol College, Oxford, by Pen Browning. Its vellum binding is in reasonably good condition. The cover measures 26cm × 19.5cm, and the book when compressed is about 2cm thick. On the spine is written in a medium brown ink by a seventeenth-century hand, probably the same one as that of the title page, "Romana Homicid. / an / Maritus / possit / occidere / Vxorem / Adulteram" (a Roman [case] of Homicide concerning whether a Husband may kill an Adulterous Wife).

In the upper half of the inside front cover is pasted a rectangular piece of paper measuring about 2.5cm × 2.2cm with the overlapping initials AV (AV), about 1.5cm high, written on it in ink. This label may have been originally affixed to the lower portion of the spine, where there is some evidence of pasting, and may have served as a classification mark signifying "Vxor Adultera" (Adulterous Wife). In the lower half of the inside front cover is pasted a rectangular piece of paper, 12.4cm × 10.75cm, on which is represented a blazon suspended by a bowed ribbon. B describes the coat of arms closely, using the appropriate heraldic terminology, in 12.818-20: "Shield, Azure, on a Triple Mountain, Or, / A Palm-tree, Proper, whereunto is tied / A Greyhound, Rampant, striving in the slips. . . " (see n.). The coat of arms has been sketched in pencil and filled in with water colors. In the upper righthand corner B has written in ink, "(From Seymour Kirkup, Florence)." In the lower lefthand corner, presumably in Kirkup's hand, is written "Arme Franceschini / Famiglia Aretina" and in the lower righthand corner, "Da un MS Priorista / Aretino esistente presso / la famiglia Albergotti / Arezzo Luglio 1868" (from a manuscript record of leading Aretine families preserved by the Albergotti family Arezzo July 1868.)

On the flyleaf B has written his signature, "Robert Browning.", in ink, and under it the words ἐμοὶ μεν ὧν Μοῖσα καρτερώτατον βέλος ἀλκᾷ τρέφει ("For me the Muse in her strength is preparing her mightiest arrow" [Pindar, *Olympian Odes* 1.111-12]). The title page, reproduced at the front of this volume, is written in a neat, open, sloped, non-cursive seventeenth-century Italian hand. It reads, "Posizione / Di tutta La Causa Criminale / Contro / Guido Franceschini Nobile / Aretino, e suoi Sicarij stati / fatti morire in Roma il di 22. / Feb. 1698. / Il primo con la decollazione gl'altri / quattro di Forca quando / Romana Homicidiorum / Disputatur an et quando Maritus / possit occidere Vxorem / Adulteram / absque incursu poene Ordinariae." The translation runs, "A Setting-forth / of the entire Criminal Case / Against / Guido Franceschini Nobleman / of Arezzo, and his hired Assassins / who were put to death in Rome 22 / February 1698. / The first by beheading the other / four by the Gallows / Roman Murder Case / Disputing if and when a Husband / may kill an Adulterous Wife / without incurring the Ordinary penalty." For B's translation see 1.119-29. There follows a table of contents, headed "Indice," covering both sides of a leaf. This is in the same hand, but in a Roman commercial style. The next two leaves contain, in the same hand and style, the report by Joseph Vesinius of Pompilia's earlier conviction. All printed pages in the book are 24.7 cm × 18.4 cm, each hand-numbered in ink at the upper righthand corner.

The order in which the pamphlets are arranged does not always accord with the order of the Index. The following divergences exist: 1) the 17th item (Spreti's argument for Guido) is cited 21st (last) in the Index; 2) the 18th and 19th items (the three letters) are cited 19th and 20th in the Index; 3) the 10th item (Lamparelli's argument) is cited 18th in the Index; and 4) The 21st (last) item in the book (Instrument restoring Pompilia's fame) is cited 17th in the Index.

Bound as the 18th and 19th items are three letters to Francesco Cencini, a Florentine lawyer who probably was the compiler of the Book, all dated 22 February 1698, the day of the executions. The first letter, from Arcangeli, is 26.6 cm × 20 cm, covering one side of a leaf. For binding it is folded down the center and bound horizontally. The sheet which served as its envelope is bound in following the next two letters and shows folds for posting, the impression of a seal, and the color of the wax.

The other two letters are to Cencini from two Roman lawyers not involved in the case, Gasparo del Torto and Carlo Antonio Ugolinucci. They are on paper 19.75 cm × 13.3 cm. Each of the two letters is written on the recto and verso of a separate sheet of paper, folded to make two leaves and fit inside one another. The final page of the gathering comprising these two letters—which were evidently sent together—bears the direction to Cencini and the mark of the seal.

Throughout the book there are underlinings and brief marginal annotations in several different hands. Many show a legal interest, as they mark legal citations, identify persons, define and qualify familial relationships, and call attention to the penalty for killing an adulterous wife. One final notation, "Beatrice Cenci," is in an apparently nineteenth-century hand (not B's), a hand found nowhere else in the book.

The Secondary Source In addition to the anonymous pamphlets in the vernacular, another sort of anonymous contemporary account of celebrated historical incidents was also common in seventeenth-century Italy. This kind of anonymous pamphlet was written in a consciously literary, often florid and moralistic style, probably by clerics, who may or may not have had first-hand knowledge of their subjects. At least two of these accounts concerning the Franceschini trial are known to exist, each in several copied and somewhat altered versions. B knew and used one of these (see below, *Composition*), and it is consequently referred to as the Secondary Source. The other, commonly called the post-Browning pamphlet, was discovered in 1900. The Secondary Source appears to have been written from a more ready access to the facts of the case than the post-Browning pamphlet, although what B consulted in 1862 was probably not the original. Beatrice Corrigan has traced no less than six versions of the Secondary Source (including one she discovered in 1940 which she conjectures may be the original), and three versions of the post-Browning pamphlet. This type of literary-cautionary anonymous pamphlet was usually reproduced in MS form, a practice which may account for variations in different examples. The location of B's copy of the Secondary Source is not known, although an Italian transcription was printed from B's copy in *Miscellanies of the Philobiblion Society*, 12 (1868-69).

Composition

The Ring and the Book was written over a period of four years, from October 1864 to October 1868, but according to B the real inception of the work dated from the day he acquired the OYB in June, 1860, a genesis confirmed in at least one other account. Rudolph Lehmann recollects B's having said (at an unspecified date), "When I first read the book, my plan was at once settled. I went for a walk, gathered twelve pebbles from the road, and put them at equal distances on the parapet that bordered it. These represented the twelve chapters into which the poem is divided and I adhered to that arrangement to the last" (*An Artist's Reminiscences* [London, 1894], 224). Lehmann has been thought unreliable because B's comment is undated and apparently recollected long after it was made. Another second-hand account which also claims B's authority dates the conception of the twelve-book form closer to the actual writing of the poem. In a diary entry of March 1868, a few months before the poem was to be published, W. M. Rossetti records after a visit from B that the poet said he "laid out the full plan of the twelve cantos" during a stay in August near Bayonne, where he was vividly impressed by the mountain pass called the Pas de Roland, after the myth of its creation by an epic kick of the hero advancing before Charlemagne's forces—*pas* signifying here both *passage* and *footstep*. The conception of the poem, according to Rossetti's version, was a similar coup and the design was carried out in sequence, "not some of the later parts before the earlier" (*Rossetti Papers, 1862 to 1870* [London, 1903], 224).

The years between the finding of the OYB and the writing of the poem were for B costly and fruitful. On 29 June 1861, a year after the discovery of the book, EBB died in Florence. The Bs had spent the preceding winter in Rome, where according to EBB's correspondence, B did little writing. Surprisingly, considering B's enthusiasm for his project and the customary fullness of EBB's record of her husband's work, there is no mention of either the discovery of the OYB or B's plans for it. It is possible that EBB's strong distaste for the subject may have led B to put it aside for a time; according to B, writing at a much later date to Julia Wedgwood, EBB found the content of the OYB so sordid that she refused even to examine it (*Robert Browning and Julia Wedgwood: A Broken Friendship as revealed in their letters*, ed. Richard Curle [London, 1937], 168 [January 21, 1869]). After EBB's death B and his twelve-year-old son Pen returned to London to live, and now the project began to gather force. In September 1862 B wrote to Isa Blagden from Brittany requesting her assistance in acquiring from a mutual friend in Florence a pamphlet relating to the murder trial (*Dearest Isa: Robert Browning's Letters to Isabella Blagden*, ed. Edward C. McAleer [Austin, Texas, 1951], 124). The pamphlet was waiting for B when he returned to London in October. This Secondary Source proved useful, especially in details it provided about the execution. Two years later when the poem was in fact begun, *Dramatis Personae* (1864) was enjoying immediate popular and critical success, marking a peak of reputation and reception unknown to B before that time and perhaps helping to launch and sustain his great work.

The next known step toward the making of the poem was B's letter of October 1864 to Frederic Leighton in Rome (Orr, *Life*, 273), requesting descriptive particulars about the Church of San Lorenzo in Lucina, the church identified in the Secondary Source as the location of Pompilia's marriage and exhibition in death. The certificate of her baptism there is bound into the OYB. B may have been struck by the function of the church as a witness to the various milestones (birth, marriage, death) of Pompilia's short life, and perhaps was further intrigued by the notion of events brought full circle once again in his own discovery and resurrection of the story outside another San Lorenzo church, in Florence, and in another century.

However fixed B's early conception of the twelve-book form remained, it is likely that the length of the poem, over 20,000 lines, far exceeded his initial intention. In that same October 1864 B wrote to Isa Blagden that he expected to finish his "Italian murder thing" by summer (*Dearest Isa: Robert Browning's Letters to Isabella Blagden*, ed. Edward McAleer [Austin, Texas, 1951], 196). By July 1865 he had written 8,400 lines. By November 1865, just over a year since beginning, the count had reached 15,000 lines. Apparently only a thousand lines were added during the next year and a half, but between 1865 and 1867 Robert Browning Senior died in Paris and Sarianna Browning came to live with her brother and his son; B broke with his publishers Chapman and Hall and moved to Smith,Elder; and B tutored his son Pen lengthily but unsuccessfully for matriculation at Balliol. But between 23 April and 17 May 1867 B wrote 2,000 lines, and between May and October 1868, some 3,000 more, to finish the poem. As late as 30 July 1868 B was still undecided on a title, but favored "The Franceschini" over "The Book and the Ring," which he thought "too pretty-fairy-story like" (British Library MS, letter to G.M. Smith; see *Text*). B's choice of "The Ring and the Book" conceivably followed the realization that the initials of that title were also his own. He had written to EBB as early as 1845 that he had always wanted to create "R.B. a poem" (RB-EBB, ed. Kintner, I, 17 [February 11, 1845]).

Text and Publication

The manuscript of *The Ring and the Book* is in the Department of Manuscripts of the British Library. It is in two green leather-bound volumes, each containing six books. The height of the manuscript pages is 26.2 cm; the width approximately 20 cm. The lined pages are written in ink on one side only, with the exception of the last eight lines of Book 3, which are on the back of sheet 172. In some of the books, B has placed page numbers on alternate sheets; the British Library staff has numbered the sheets consecutively, rectos only. B was numbering pages separately in each book, but the British Library staff has numbered the sheets consecutively through volume one and, beginning again, through volume two. B's page numbers have been crossed out and re-numbered in places. There are names in pencil notation, apparently type-setters' marks, in the top left corners of some of the pages. Four letters are mounted in volume one, all from B to G.M. Smith. They are dated July 30, 1868; New Year's Day '69; February 11, 1869; and September 8, 1875.

The Ring and the Book was published in four monthly volumes: on 21 November and 26 December 1868, and on 30 January and 27 February 1869. There were two further editions of *The Ring and the Book* in B's lifetime: 1872 (four volumes); 1888-89 (three volumes, 8-10 of the collected works). Further primary materials are proof sheets of the 1868-69 and 1872 editions with corrections in B's hand, which are in the Beinecke Library at Yale. The manuscript corrections to the Beinecke 1872 proof sheets do not correspond to the published 1872 edition, except for a very few corrections of obvious misprints which may have been made by printers. These proof sheets seem to have been used later to make corrections for the 1888-89 edition, where many of the corrections do appear, although many others were apparently never printed. For this reason we list no CP1872 variants.

Corrections appearing in the 1868-69 proofs are entered as CP1868 and CP1869. In the proof sheets of Volume 1 (Books 1-3) there are sixteen pages, comprising two gatherings, which vary from the 1868 edition but which are identical with 1872 proof sheets. These pages (Book 2.411-1024) were apparently substituted for missing pages in the 1868 set by whoever assembled the Beinecke proofs. There are therefore no P1868 readings for these lines in the variant listings. In the 1872 proofs all of Volume 2 (Books 4-6) is missing, and there are therefore no P1872 entries for these books.

In the corrected proof for 1868-69 there are irregularly spaced listings of forthcoming corrections at the tops of some pages, usually those containing a correction. There is a handwritten table of contents for Volume 1 (Books 1-3), and on the title page of that volume the word "Revises" is written. Volume 2 (Books 4-6) is page proof with a handwritten table of contents. Volume 3 (Books 7-9) is galley, as is Volume 4 (Books 10-12) up to 11.2415, then page proof from 11.2388 to the end of Book 11. Book 12 is page proof.

The Dykes Campbell and Brown University lists also contain variants for *The Ring and the Book.*

Book 1, The Ring and the Book

1-24] *Ring . . . fume* The town of *Chiusi* was the capital of the ancient country in W central Italy called *Etruria*, which gave its name to the Etruscan period in art (c. 700-200 B.C.) and to the area of Italy called Tuscany. The highly developed civilization of the Etruscans included an elaborate burial cult, which has in turn led researchers back to a vivid understanding of Etruscan life. Etruscan peoples built necropolises (cities of the dead), in which underground rooms were furnished and decorated with possessions of the dead, especially jewelry and other art work. In the early nineteenth century relics from such tombs were discovered on hillsides outside Chiusi, and subsequently the tombs themselves were explored. Intricacy of technique was characteristic of Etruscan art in general. Gold ornaments were richly embellished by means of granulation and filigree techniques, a lost art by which very tiny beads of gold, and fine braided or shaped wire, were soldered to a gold surface in an intricate design. In some pieces it was later found that over centuries of burial the action of salts in the earth had leached away the alloy metal of the solder (copper, or copper and silver) at the surface level, causing an effect known as "enrichment." The famous *Castellani* firm of Roman jewellers, founded in 1814, through diligent search discovered in a remote Umbrian village craftsmen who still practiced some of the Etruscan processes. These masters and others instructed by them succeeded in imitating Etruscan originals in very pure gold, and there was a vogue among Victorians for Etruscan pieces and other classical jewelry. The surface "enrichment" effect, also called "coloring," was achieved by dipping the article into an acid solution which removed surface alloy. It has been recently discovered that the *ring* B refers to was one given to him by Isa Blagden, probably in 1858, a Castellani ring with the words *Vis Mea* (My Strength) on an oval bezel ornamented on each side by a ribbed design. This ring is in the Balliol college library. A ring of EBB's formerly identified as the ring of the poem was not a Castellani ring. Her ring was stolen from the Balliol library in 1971. See A.N. Kincaid, "The Ring and the Scholars," *BIS* 8 (1980) 151-60.
22] *repristination* A coinage of B's, meaning a return to an earlier, purer state.
27] *Gold . . . evermore* "As it was in the beginning, is now, and ever shall be; world without end. Amen." B paraphrases the closing phrase of the traditional "Gloria Patri" in the *Book of Common Prayer*, in preparation for the analogy he will develop between truth and gold.

32] *this . . . Book* The Old Yellow Book which B found in the Florentine stall was a collection of 22 documents, 4 handwritten and 18 in print, in Latin and Italian, the whole amounting to 266 pages and comprising records of the trial of Guido Franceschini for murder, summaries of related trials and materials, 3 letters, and title page and contents. See *Sources.*

32] *I toss* See 1.66n.

35] *Secreted* A pun conveying the senses of both *secret* and *secrete.* As George Wasserman notes, the imagery here may be related to "oozings from the mine," 1.10 ("The Meaning of Browning's Ring-Figure," *MLN* 76 [1961], 220-26).

41] *fierce* Probably a reference to a brisk wind (see 1.66-68 and n.).

42-50] *Square . . . Medici* The square is named San Lorenzo after the church on its W side. Baccio Bandinelli's (1493-1560) statue of Giovanni delle Bande Nere, 1498-1526 (John of the Black Bands, military leader and member of the powerful Medici family) stands between the church, where the Medici are buried, and the Palazzo Medici-Riccardi, which was originally their palace. San Lorenzo (in Lucina) was also the name of the church in Rome where Pompilia was baptized and married, and where her body and the bodies of the Comparini were laid out. B does not stress the circumstantial circularity of the settings of his poem, but like the poem they reflect the cyclic interplay of past and present.

50] *knaves* In the archaic sense of servants, mercenaries.

51] *re-venders* Another coinage serving a double purpose. The OYB is not only revender's ware, it is also very much a revenge tragedy. The book and its history reflect the scenic contrast here, in which second hand dealers (no longer knavish revengers) on the palace steps illustrate the petty "ravage" of a less "high-blooded" age than the Medici's.

57] *jet, breccia, porphyry* Respectively, a black mineral that takes a high polish; a type of marble that appears to be formed of rock fragments cemented together; a purplish rock formation containing crystals.

60] *wreck* First used in the nineteenth century for an object in a state of ruin.

64] *scagliola* An inlaid, patterned marble or stone floor. In 1848 the Bs discovered the arms of the Guidi family in scagliola on their bedroom floor when old carpeting was removed.

65] *two crazie* The crazia was a Tuscan coin. Before the unification of Italy in the 1870's, coins of different governments were used throughout the country. Two crazie were worth about 1½ pence in the money of B's time.

66-68] *a conch . . . Sienese* The painter and engraver Luigi Ademollo (1764-1849), identified 1.364. Prints of the artist's work are held down here by a conch shell; later, 1.366, by a stone. B's fancy seems taken by the image of the prints "sowing" (1.67) or "snowing" (1.366) the Square, and he seems to risk that danger himself by tossing the precious book in the air (1.32, 83).

71-73] *Lionard . . . Louvre* Mona Lisa, La Gioconda (or Joconde), by Leonardo da Vinci, was indeed stolen from the Louvre, but not until 1911; the claim made here refers to a popular rumor of long standing that the whereabouts of the original Mona Lisa were unknown and that the Louvre possessed only a copy made by a contemporary of da Vinci's.

76] *Spicilegium* Anthology.

77] *Frail . . . Dumas* The prose romance *La Dame aux Camelias* by Alexandre Dumas, fils, appeared in 1852 and was still at the height of its popularity in 1860, when B discovered the OYB. B and his wife had seen Dumas' dramatized version in Paris in the first year of its production, as EBB reported in a letter of 12 April, 1852:

> What do you think I did the other night? Went to the Vaudeville to see the 'Dame aux Camelias' on about the fifteenth night of the representation. I disagree with the common outcry about its immorality. According to my view, it is moral and human. But I never will to to see it again, for it almost broke my heart and split my head. . . . Even Robert, who gives himself out for blasé on dramatic matters, couldn't keep the tears from rolling down his cheeks (*Letters of EBB*, 2, 117).

78] *Vulgarized Horace* The Latin poet's work in Italian for school use.

82] "*Stall!*" Probably short for stall-man, stall-keeper.

90-93] *Lorenzo . . . statue* See 1.42n.

100] *plait* Braided straw for hats.

102] *festas* Holy festival or feast days.

107] *None . . . prize* The line sounds ironic after the detailed observation of the preceding 13 lines. Yet B's walk—like the journey related in the book he is reading—has a tone of purpose, risk, and destiny which both absorbs and informs details observed in passing, from the "perilous" path through straw-work, "tribes" of tongs, and "skeleton" bedsteads to the "black" and "cold" of the "first stone-slab" of the staircase: all suggestive of a pilgrimage, in ordinary and familiar circumstances, through trial toward death.

108-109] *title-page . . . index, on* B is not saying that he has read the entire book, merely the title page and index, which in the original are sequential.

110] *Strozzi . . . Bridge* The Palazzo Strozzi, the column in the Piazza Santa Trinita, and the Bridge of Santa Trinità are all landmarks on B's route from San Lorenzo Square to his home.

112] *Casa Guidi . . . Church* Casa Guidi, the chief residence of the Bs from shortly after their arrival in Florence (1847) until EBB's death (1861), is across the Arno from the center of Florence, adjacent to the Church of San Felice, and obliquely across from the Pitti Palace. The Bs occupied the second floor seven-room suite in the Casa Guidi, which was built in the fourteenth century for the powerful Guidi family. The building is strikingly wedge-shaped, with a façade part brown stucco and part rough stone.

117] *Print . . . rest* An inexact description. Only the title page and index, the copy of the Arezzo sentence, and the three letters are handwritten.

118] *"Romana Homicidiorum"* Literally, a Roman case (*causa* is understood) of murders.

124] *heading . . . ranks* Guido, being of noble blood, was beheaded; his four accomplices were hanged. Capital punishment, originally and literally loss of the head, was reserved for offenders of noble rank as a symbolic divesture of privilege with life; "common" criminals were hanged.

129] *Word for word* Some of this translation is loose rather than literal; see *Sources.*

133-35] *Latin . . . streaks* See *Sources* for full description of the OYB. The arguments of the lawyers are written in colloquial medieval Latin but the testimony of witnesses is in vernacular Italian.

133] *cramp* i.e., cramped, difficult. The syntax of sentences in the OYB is often involved and the references to civil law are profuse and technical. Gest surmises that the arguments were dictated and printed with little revision, probably the same day.

142] *Primary lawyer-pleadings* There were two stages in the legal arguments, separated by the infliction of torture on three of the defendants near the end of January. Three pleadings by Arcangeli and Spreti for Guido and his confederates, and four by Bottini and Gambi for Pompilia, occupy the first stage.

146] *Apostolic Chamber's type* Legal documents were printed by the Papal press and carried its imprint. See *Sources* for the circumstances of this practice.

149-55] *Rome's . . . courts* The Governor of Rome, who at the time of the OYB was named Pallavicino, presided over the Reverend Apostolic Chamber, the court having both civil and criminal jurisdiction in the Curia Romana. The Governor's deputy, Marco Antonio Venturini, in fact presided over Guido's trial.

152] *no judgment-bar* In Roman courts there was no physical confrontation between lawyers or between lawyers and witnesses. All arguments were conducted in writing. See *Sources.*

160] *advocate of each* Each side had in fact two lawyers, an advocate concerned especially with the law, and a procurator concerned with the facts of a case, although in practice the distinction was not strictly observed. Pompilia's lawyers (the prosecution) were Bottini and Gambi, respectively the Advocate and Procurator of the Fisc (from the same root as *fiscal;* these lawyers represented the Office of the Treasury). Guido's lawyers (the defense) were Spreti and Arcangeli, the Advocate and Procurator of the Poor.
162] *Fisc began* B errs; unlike English trial procedure, Roman practice granted to the defense the privilege of speaking first. In Books 8 and 9 the sequence is correct.
163] *in print* See 1.152n.
166] *qualities of bad* Aggravating circumstances. Actually six, not five, are treated at length in Book 8.
168] *cockatrice* Legendary creature which could kill by look or breath. It had the head, crest, wings and feet of a cock, and the tail of a serpent. It is sometimes identified with the basilisk. Caponsacchi, imagining a meeting in hell between Judas and Guido, says "The cockatrice is with the basilisk" (6.192)—implying that there is little to choose between the two monsters.
174-76] *Patron . . . better* In fact counsel for both sides was customarily appointed without cost to them by the court. The intimation that Arcangeli and Spreti are inferior lawyers conflicts with many indications in the OYB of their mastery of detail, pertinence and succinctness in the presentation of argument, and general professionalism. In the poem B virtually caricatures Arcangeli as a gross, flattering, grandiloquent, familial, and continually distracted *bon vivant* who in the deepest sense misrepresents Pompilia's character as well as her situation. Spreti is referred to by Bottini as "mannikin and dandiprat" (12.434), an ambitious, foppish show-off.
192] *To . . . else* Uzzah was struck dead for reaching out to steady the Ark of God containing the ten commandments, as it shook on Nachon's threshing floor (2 Sam. 6:6-7). Guido's defense represents the fidelity of wives as basic to the stability of society's ark, and suggests that the murders were Guido's impulsive but well-intentioned corrective gesture toward the spirit of the law. Cf. 1.329 and n. for another interpretation of an unsanctioned touch of a religious object by Guido.
212-13] *firebrand . . . cornfield* Samson, in reprisal against his Philistine father-in-law, caught 300 foxes, tied them in pairs together by their tails with a torch between, and turned them loose in the Philistine wheat-fields ripe for harvest (Judg. 16:4-5). *Corn* is the English term for wheat.

215-33] *Authority . . . friend* These references, all contained in the OYB, offer more "authority and precedent for putting wives to death" than for "letting wives live," and they range over more offenses than adultery. *Solon* (c. 640-559 B.C.) was an Athenian legislator who was known as an economic and constitutional reformer, and who in fact repealed or modified most of the Draconian code then in effect, which punished almost every offense by death. Solon is cited in the first pamphlet in the OYB by Guido's defense (Arcangeli) as "wisest of legislators," and is said to sanction the murder of adulterous wives by enraged husbands. But according to Plutarch (*Lives*, Solon, 23) and Aeschines (*Speech against Timarchus*, 183), Solon's penalties of fines or death were specifically directed against rapists and adulterous men, though a woman found guilty of adultery was forbidden to wear ornaments or to go to public sacrifices—the equivalent, apparently, of loss of citizenship—and she could be made the victim of any abuse or disgrace short of death or mutilation. The Roman code, which Plutarch says originated with *Romulus*, punished adultery severely. Under the Byzantine Emperor *Justinian* (483-565) a commission of jurists was appointed to collate the laws; the fifty books of extracts from their collation, the Pandects, were still the basis for legal decisions at the end of the seventeenth century. There were numerous glosses on the Pandects. *Bartolus* was a fourteenth-century lawyer whose commentaries were considered authoritative, and *Baldus* was a celebrated pupil of his. The Cornelian law, or *Lex Cornelia de Sicariis*, on poisoners and murderers (81 B.C.), the Pompeian law, or *Lex Pompeia*, on parricides (c. 55 B.C.), and the Julian law, or *Lex Julia* on adultery (17 B.C.), are named for their authors or promoters, and are all decisions included in the Pandects. (The adjectival proper names are feminine to accord with the feminine gender of *Lex*, law, in Latin.) *Lex Cornelia de Sicariis* decrees death for homicides. *Lex Pompeia* punished parricide (a term applied to causing the death of any near relative) by death. The ancient form of this law dictated also the means of death, indicating thereby the special abhorrence associated with this type of crime:

> The criminal is sewn up in a sack with a dog, a cock, a viper, and an ape, and in this dismal prison is thrown into the sea or a river, according to the nature of the locality, in order that even before death he may begin to be deprived of the enjoyment of the elements, the air being denied him while alive, and interment in the earth when dead (quoted in Gest, 647).

The *Lex Julia* punished adulterers with death. *Solomon* (Prov. 6:32-35) and *Paul* (Rom. 7:2-3) agree in forbidding adultery, although it is of course Paul who confirms Solomon. The "nice decision" of *Dolabella*,

Roman proconsul (c. 70-43 B.C.) who was lenient toward a woman who killed her husband and son in revenge for their murder of her son by a former marriage, is recounted in 8.904-939. *Theodoric*, King of the Eastern Goths, conquered Italy in 493. The "pregnant instance" of one of his decrees cites animals' defense of their mates as proof that the love of honor is a natural law. The decision is described in 8.474-79. The Roman author *Aelian*'s *On Animals* (written c. 200 A.D., in Greek) is a collection, divided into 17 books, of moralizing anecdotes about animals. A number of selections depict the virtuous qualities of elephants, variously illustrating their valor, loyalty, continence, and hatred of evil. In the example B cites, an elephant discovered the wife of his trainer in the act of adultery and drove his tusks through her and her lover (11. 15).

238] *brangled* Disputed angrily, an archaic term close in meaning to *wrangle*.

252] *priest* See 1.257n.

254-56] *epistles . . . advocate* Among the three letters to himself which Cencini bound into the OYB (see *Sources*), the one from Guido's lawyer Arcangeli informing Cencini of the failure of Guido's appeal follows Spreti's printed plea for Guido.

257] *clerkly privilege* Ecclesiastics were granted immunity from civil prosecution.

259] *chrism* A consecrated oil used for sacramental annointments.

260-62] *presbyter . . . Sacerdos* There were four minor orders (porters, readers, exorcists, acolytes), and three holy or major orders. The New Testament, supplemented by Church tradition, decreed three orders of Christian ministry: Bishops, Presbyters (priests), and Deacons. With some variation over the centuries, these three are the major orders. Those who receive any major order in the Roman Catholic Church are bound to celibacy, whereas holders of minor orders are not. B's list here is both inconsistent and redundant. *Subdiaconus* (subdeacon) and *presbyter* or *sacerdos* (which both mean priest) would have been major orders, but *Primae tonsurae* (of the first tonsure) is not an order at all; it is a designation given to boy clerks. It is not clear in the records which of the minor orders Guido had taken, but it cannot have been any of those named.

267] *resumes . . . orator* The word *Resumes* here apparently means "makes a résumé," because the reference is not to the letter from Arcangeli mentioned at 1.254 above, as *resumes* appears to suggest, but to the third letter, from a lawyer not involved in the case named Ugolinucci, who says that "Guido's good friends began to breathe again" when the appeal was made on the basis of his clerical privilege. Like the others, Ugolinucci's letter was written on the evening of the execution and

summarizes the course of the trial for his colleague in Florence, Cencini.
268] *a friend* Francesco Cencini, a lawyer in Florence and friend of the Franceschini family, to whom the documents comprising the OYB were sent; see *Sources*.
280] *Ghetto* The term *Ghetto* was first applied to the quarter of Venice to which Jews were restricted in the sixteenth century. In seventeenth-century Rome, Jews were subject to strict laws and often to cruel harassment.
281] *Emperor's Envoy* Martinez, the Ambassador from Austria, the center of the Holy Roman Empire (*Christendom*, 1.283), ruled by the Hapsburgs. See 12.94-99, where he is referred to with similar irony as "the Caesarian Minister."
283] *civility* Social order.
293] *Herodotus* Greek historian (c. 484-425 B.C.) who moralized upon the fall through vanity and ambition of such powerful rulers as Croesus, Xerxes, and Polycrates.
296-98] *Pope's . . . Naples* Pope Innocent XII officiated in the years 1691-1700. He was interested in church reform and tolerant of controversy, critical of the sale of church appointments, and known for his accessibility to the poor. In reality he was 83 at the time of the trial. B's portrayal of Innocent XII in Book 10 is both historically accurate in the main and fully individualized, the roles of "great guardian of the fold" (1.642) and of Antonio Pignatelli of Naples having equal force in his search for the truth, as B suggests here. See Cook, Appendix VII, and his Introduction to Book 10.
303-13] *Jansenists . . . Molinists* Cornelius Jansen (1585-1638), Bishop of Ypres, and his followers questioned both free will and priestly mediation as ways to salvation, believing that divine guidance and grace flowed directly between God and the spiritually receptive individual. Miguel de Molinos (1627-96) taught Quietism, his own doctrine and method, to a large following, especially in Rome and Naples. The guiding principle of Quietism is that the individual soul, in a state of contemplative passivity, is immediately receptive to God, and does not need mediation of God's grace through priest and sacrament. The affinities between Jansenism and Molinism are obvious, but the similarity for B's purposes was probably that both sects were initially treated sympathetically by Pope Innocent XI and later denounced by him. Innocent XII, the pope of *The Ring and the Book*, took office in 1691, three years after Molinos had been condemned for heresy by the Inquisition.

Molinos was already famous as a spiritual director in his native Spain before he came to Rome, where his *Spiritual Guide* was published in 1675. Immensely popular and influential, the *Guide* went through 20 editions in most major European languages in the next five years. But in 1687, as a result of pressure exerted on Pope Innocent XI by Louis XIV through his ambassador in Rome, Cardinal d'Estrées, Molinos' teachings were declared heretical and he was sentenced to life imprisonment. He died in prison in December 1697, one year before the winter of the murders.

In *The Ring and the Book* the terms *Molinism* and *Molinist* are used frequently but loosely to signify religious heresy, and by extension, any immoral act or belief. The only monologists who refer favorably to Molinism are the Pope and Caponsacchi; the only one who does not refer to it at all is the aloof and condescending Tertium Quid; the one who refers to it most often is Guido—eight times in all, out of a total of 35 in the poem. For Guido and for most of the other characters, *Molinism* is a scapegoat word, a fashionable and convenient label of disapproval. For B the associations of the term were historically useful, lending authenticity to his rendering of the period and more generally reflecting the pervasive presence of the Church in the most everyday affairs of the time. For none of these purposes, B's or his characters', was a very exact understanding of Molinism necessary, nor does the poem show, in any obvious way, that B did possess such an understanding.

Yet the real issues of Molinism, especially the radical attitudes toward sin which it suggested, are close to the poem's central involvement with the permutations of point of view upon the forms and modes of truth, and the emphasis that B gives to Molinism reflects his own predisposition toward private rather than institutional faith. For information on Molinism B would have had to have read beyond the OYB, where Molinism appears only once, in a casual reference (like most of those in the poem) in one of the anonymous pamphlets.

Molinos' thought has roots in both oriental and western mysticism, and indeed a contemporary intellectual claimed to have found "almost all the doctrines of the condemned priest" in the works of St. Theresa (John Bigelow, *Molinos the Quietist* [New York 1882], 10n.). Molinos taught that the ultimate exercise of individual will was the extinction of will and the "annihilation" of self. This state, called "the interior way," was achieved by disciplined meditation, then contemplation, in which the subject communed immediately with God, without external assistance or sign. Variously called "prayer of quietude," "fixed contemplation," "the state of indifference," "mystic death," "holy idleness," this exalted state rendered the communicant neither aware of, resistant to, nor capable of, sin, even though he might appear to sin. Molinos argued that such apparently sinful acts were the work of the sense alone without assent of the superior soul, which was united with God. Both Molinos' methods and his reasoning thus depreciate, even negate, the rule of moral law, priest, sacrament, and church.

Molinos' thought and its reception differ in several significant respects from his predecessors' teachings; most obviously, perhaps, in that unlike St. Theresa he was not canonized for his mystical insights, and just as importantly, in the reasons he was regarded as a dangerous example rather than an inspirational one. The experiences and practices he described were, almost by definition, available to ordinary Christians and were not confined to saints or persons of exceptional religious experience. The interior way was open without instruction to a Pompilia, to whom, in the Pope's words, "It was not given . . . to know much, / Speak much, to write a book, to move mankind," but who was no "less pre-eminent angel" for all that (10.1015-17, 1008). William Coyle, in "Molinos: 'The Subject of the Day' in *The Ring and the Book*" (*PMLA* 67 [1952], 308-14), and Helen Loschky in "Free Will Versus Determinism in *The Ring and the Book*" (*VP* 6 [1968], 333-52) discuss the relevance of Molinos and his doctrine to B's poem.

304] *frowsy tune* See 2.175-77n.

306] *clown-like* The word *clown* here has the archaic sense of an uneducated rustic.

310] *spoil* In two senses: to "strip" (now rare), and to "plunder." In 1.314 the Pope is said to peel off Nepotism, or in other words to spoil the spoils of office.

313] *world . . . thus* The word *hate* has the Biblical sense here. "Because ye are not of the world, but I have chosen you out of the world, therefore the world hateth you" (John 15:19).

315, 319] *Nepotism . . . nephews* Nepotism is, literally, favoritism to nephews; by extension, patronage in general. Innocent's tolerance of Molinism for the religious idealism it represented was complemented by his opposition to abuses of power within the church, abuses which often took the form of preferment of relatives or friends to sinecures such as Guido himself seems to have held. The needs of the poor replaced kinship in the concern of the Pope.

316] *Halt . . . blind* Jesus' parable of the rich man who sent his servant out to invite the poor to supper because his friends had put other obligations before his invitation, signifies that Jesus' followers should put him before all other things. "Then the master of the house being angry said to his servant, . . . bring in hither the poor, and the maimed, and the halt, and the blind" (Luke 14:21).

317] *fat things* Rich food. "And in this mountain shall the Lord of hosts make unto all people a feast of fat things" (Isa. 25:6).

318] *gather . . . feast* After the miracle of the loaves and the fishes, Jesus "said unto his disciples, Gather up the fragments that remain, that nothing be lost" (John 6:12).
320] *five carlines* See l.65n. A carlino was a Neopolitan coin worth about four pence in the currency of B's time.
327-28] *tonsured . . . sole* The shaved crown of the head, and sandals, were among the outward signs of Roman Catholic clerics.
329-31] *Instead . . . robe* A reference to the famous story of the woman who had an issue of blood and was healed by touching the hem of Christ's robe in the midst of a crowd (Luke 8:43-44).
337-38] *Cut . . . Hang* See l.124 n.
341] *chirograph* Handwriting.
346-54] *bridge-foot . . . Square* The Castel St. Angelo, originally the early Roman emperor Hadrian's tomb, is on the other side of the Tiber from old Rome, across the Ponte St. Angelo (Hadrian's Pons Aelius). B's emphasis on the difference between the Castel Angelo and "the city's newer gayer end" is his interpolation, although it is true that the executions took place in the Piazza del Popolo. The fact that the date was Saturday of the first week of Lent may have had a bearing on the choice of location. Executions which happened to fall in the Carnival week preceding Lent were customarily held in the Piazza del Popolo because of its commodious size, and were often the occasion of great festivity, the scaffold being decorated and the executioner and his assistant costumed as clowns. Several features of B's descriptions of the "newer gayer end" of the city are anachronisms: the *Pincian gardens* and B's *fountains* are actually of seventeenth-century design, although there was another fountain at the foot of the obelisk on the S side. The *obelisk*, taken from Egypt by Augustus Caesar, was first erected in 10 B.C. and was moved to the Piazza in 1589. The Church of Santa Maria del Popolo, built in 1480, is adjacent to the Porta del Popolo or the North Gate of Rome, built in 1562. The church has a steep flight of steps in front, which would have served many spectators as a vantage from which to view the executions. The Piazza del Popolo was in general less fashionable than B suggests, being truly a place of the people, especially travelers and vendors.
364-66] *Ademollo's . . . stone* See l.65, 66, 68 and nn.
378] *Canon* Caponsacchi was a canon of Santa Maria della Pieve Church in Arezzo (*Pieve* means parish). Canon is a title given to a clergyman who is a member of the staff of a cathedral or collegiate church.
379] *The priest* B consistently calls Caponsacchi a priest, although he was not one and is not called a priest in the OYB. He was a subdeacon, the lowest of the major orders.

388] *known name* i.e., Caponsacchi's.
389] *lone villa* B assumed from his reading of the OYB that the Comparini had two houses, one of which was in the more secluded suburbs of Rome. He was led to this conclusion because in the OYB there are apparently two locations given for the Comparini's house or houses, the Strada Vittoria and the Via Paolina. B interpreted the reference to the Via Paulina as being to the Pauline district in the suburbs of Rome. Sir Frederick Treves discovered, however, that the references were to the same house, which was near the corner of the two streets, one of which had changed names by B's time (Treves, 101).
391] *an angel-guest* "Be not forgetful to entertain strangers: for thereby some have entertained angels unawares" (Heb. 13:2).
400] *Gaetano* See *Chronology*.
405] *British . . . not* There is evidence to show that, even as B composed *The Ring and the Book*, his reputation and popularity were rising. His new volume of poems, *Dramatis Personae* (1864), was well enough received to go into a second edition; the *Selections* of his poetry, prepared by Forster and Cornwall and published in December 1862, had caused reviewers and other critics to take fresh interest in his poetry; and the editions of his *Poetical Works* in 1863 and 1865 further assisted the rise of his reputation. For a judicious estimate of B's British reputation in the early 1860's see C.C. Watkins, "Browning's 'Fame Within These Four Years' " *MLR* 53 (1958), 492-500. B's *Men and Women* volumes (1855) had, however, with few exceptions, been treated cavalierly by reviewers; and he remembered vividly the harsher earlier treatment of his *Sordello* (1840). His books sold far less well than Tennyson's even as late as 1881.
408] *Truth must prevail* This English proverbial expression is drawn from the Latin translation—*magna est veritas et praevalet*—of 1 Esd. 4:51, which reads "Great is truth and mighty above all things."
413] *Decads* Decades.
426] *Diario* Daily newspaper.
426] *quotha* Archaic dialect form for *quoth he*, used especially when the quotation is made scornfully (*OED*).
427-28] *French . . . nation* The French occupied Rome 1849-70. B's reference to destroying records expresses a widespread Italian dislike of the French.
428] *rap-and-rending* The phrase *rap and rend* is idiomatic for *seize*.
429] *gird* Gibe.
430] *Temporality* The power of the church in secular matters was under debate at the time B was writing *The Ring and the Book*, and was finally revoked by the Vatican Council of 1870.
432-33] *the world . . . devil* "From all the deceits of the world, the

flesh, and the devil, Good Lord, deliver us" ("Litany," *Book of Common Prayer*).
437-41] *Mend . . . Wiseman* The doggerel punning and self-interest of the Church's voice here are an indication that B's poem is by no means "clean for the church." Henry Edward *Manning* (1808-92) and John Henry *Newman* (1801-90), both converts from Anglicanism, were received into the Catholic church in 1851 and 1845 respectively. At the time B was writing, Nicholas Patrick Stephen *Wiseman* was the only one of the three churchmen who had been named cardinal (in 1850); Manning and Newman were made cardinals in 1875 and 1879. In the early 1860's Manning was provost of the Westminster Metropolitan Chapter; Newman was writing his *Apologia pro Vita Sua* (1864), and Wiseman was serving as the first Archbishop of Westminster.
453] *lingot* Ingot.
460] *Thridded . . . fast* The word *Thridded* (an archaic form of *threaded*) and *thrown* both mean "twisted into thread"; the usage here is figurative for the rings threaded and fastened by a javelin.
461] *djereed* A wooden spear about five feet long, and the Arabian or Turkish equestrian game in which it is thrown through rings.
467-69] *agate . . . mirror* The mantelpiece and over it the mirror, with its carved gilt frame, are depicted as B describes them in the painting "Salon at Casa Guidi" by George Mignaty, except that in the painting the 4 ft. 8 in. high mirror does not reach to the ceiling; over it is hung an altar piece by Ghirlandaio.
476-79] *Felice . . . nights* Music from San Felice church was apparently a familiar accompaniment to life at Casa Guidi at all seasons. Hawthorne described hearing the chants from the balcony overlooking the church during a visit to the Bs in the winter of 1857, and repeated B's comment that "this was the first church where an oratorio had ever been performed" (*The French and Italian Notebooks, The Centenary Edition of the Works of Nathaniel Hawthorne*, Vol. 14 [Columbus, 1980], 300).
484] *gold . . . Rhodes* Both the riches and the craftsmen of Rhodes were legendary, and the reference here may be to both. As the myth is retold in Pindar's Seventh *Olympian Ode,* Hercules' son Tlepolemos was counseled by the oracle at Delphi to sail to "a pasture ringed with sea, where sometime the great king of the gods rained on the city golden snow" (1.34). A translation by B of a portion of Pindar's poem was found after his death in a letter (see *New Poems*, 40).
489-90] *datura . . . lampfly* Datura, a plant of the poisonous nightshade family, has large white blooms like lilies. The datura on the Bs' balcony were small trees. The lamp-fly (firefly) is the subject of the verbs *waxed* and *waned.*
491-95] *Over . . . Arezzo* At first glance the lines seem to mean that

the poet looked N toward Rome, which is an impossibility. But a map shows that outside the Porta Romana, which was at the end of the Via Romana, about a quarter of a mile (a bowshot) from the Casa Guidi, the old Roman Road did turn N for a short distance (*away* may be taken in the sense of "a way") to cross the Arno and follow the river's course toward Arezzo. Arezzo is a town about 56 mi. SE of Florence, 154 mi. N of Rome, in the Apennine chain of mountains running N and S through Italy. Arezzo (*the man's town*) was the home of the Franceschini family.

502] *Castelnuovo* A small town 15 mi. N of Rome. It was to an inn here that Guido pursued Pompilia and Caponsacchi.

515] *Deep . . . deep* Ps. 42:7. The Biblical context of the phrase is the thirst of the soul for God.

536-37] *"Now . . . peace* Paraphrase of the *Nunc Dimittis.* Simeon's words upon beholding Jesus, as he had been promised by the Holy Ghost, were "Lord, now lettest thou thy servant depart in peace, according to thy word: For mine eyes have seen thy salvation" (Luke 2:29-30).

538] *star . . . fen* Fog o' the fen is the phosphorescence of rotting wood in a swamp; it was believed to carry disease.

547] *Abate . . . Girolamo* Older brothers of Guido, both ecclesiastics. Paolo was a churchman in Rome; Girolamo was, like Caponsacchi, a canon of the Pieve Church in Arezzo (see 1.378n.) *Abate* was, in the seventeenth century, an honorific title signifying Reverend.

548] *pest* Pestilence.

561] *Prince . . . Air.* A designation, in Eph. 2:2, for Satan, here applied to Guido. In St. Paul's time evil spirits, of which Satan was supreme, were thought to inhabit the air between earth and heaven.

564-82] *satyr-family . . . Saved* Francesco-Maria Guazzo in *Compendium Maleficorum* (Milan, 1608) lists the eleven steps in the profession of witchcraft, the eighth of which reads: "They take this oath to the Demon standing in a circle described upon the ground, perchance because a circle is the Symbol of Divinity, and the earth God's footstool and thus he assuredly wishes them to believe that he is the lord of Heaven and earth" (Translated and quoted by Montague Summers, *The History of Witchcraft and Demonology* [London, 1969], 85). The initiation ceremony culminated in a sexual act performed between the initiate and, supposedly, an "incubus" or "succubus," an evil spirit who for the occasion assumed the form of a man or woman, or, sometimes, of an animal. Frequently, an incubus appeared to a woman in the shape of a buck goat. B's *satyr-family* extends and adapts the beast figure in the ceremony. The fire and the pot, to which B refers, apparently did not appear within the circle, but they were familiar objects to all gatherings of witches. In the pot was brewed a stew compounded of noxious ingredients, of which the initiates drank or with which their bodies were rubbed in a perverse kind of baptism. Whether Pompilia is unwilling initiate or unholy sacrifice here is perhaps deliberately ambiguous, but the intrusion and superimposition of the St. George myth on the rituals of witchcraft help to illuminate the perverse parallels between religious ritual and demonic rite. The *grey mother* is Donna Beatrice, Guido's mother.

566] *mopping and mowing* Making faces. Cf. Edgar's reference to the female fiend Flibbertigibbet in *King Lear* 4.1.61.

579] *St. George* St. George was a Christian martyr of the early fourth century. History offers few facts about St. George, but legend portrays him as a Christian knight who rescued a maiden dressed as a bride, about to be offered in sacrifice to a dragon. St. George first tamed the dragon and later killed it upon the promise of the threatened city to believe in Christ and to be baptized. The legend first appears in the thirteenth-century *Legenda Aurea* (*Golden Legend*), a popular manual of the lives of the saints, and may originate from an early association of the myth of Perseus with St. George; tradition held that St. George came from, and was buried in, Lydda, where Perseus slew a sea monster and rescued the virgin Andromeda. In 1347 Edward III founded the Order of the Garter and declared St. George the patron saint of England. The arms of St. George are a red cross on a white ground, and he is often represented wearing armor bearing this sign. Popular festivals linked him with the coming of spring, his feast day being 23 April. Caponsacchi is frequently associated with St. George in B's poem, and B in fact altered his MS to make St. George's day the date of Pompilia's flight with Caponsacchi instead of 29 April. In the MS, 6.1094 reads, "That being the last Monday in the month"; in the first edition the line reads, "This being last Monday in the month but one." There are numerous other references to Caponsacchi as a St. George figure throughout the poem. There was a St. George by Vasari over the altar in the Pieve Church in Arezzo (Caponsacchi's church), and a copy of Caravaggio's Andromeda hung over the young B's desk. DeVane explores the historical backgrounds of both myths and their correspondences with those personal qualities in B which were dramatized in his elopement with Elizabeth, in "The Virgin and the Dragon," *Yale Review* 37 (1947), 33-46.

587-88] *messenger . . . life* The word *angel* derives from a Greek word meaning messenger. The "dusk misfeatured messenger" who interrupts both B's vision and the journey is undoubtedly Guido in a role both literal and figurative.

591-94] *Prince . . . cage* See 1.561n.

598] *solitary villa* See 1.389n.

617] *Gabriel . . . gate* Gabriel was the keeper of the Gates of Paradise and therefore the protector of Adam and Eve. The name Lucifer, here signifying Satan, is not used in the Bible to refer to Satan; it derives from the references to Satan's fall in terms of a falling star, Rev. 9:1 and Luke 10:18, and was applied to Satan by St. Jerome, and by poets.
632-34] *Tophet . . . judgment* The word *Tophet* originally meant a place for burning. It was an actual location in the Valley of Gehenna where rebellious Jews made propitiative burnt offerings of their children to appease the wrath of Moloch. The practice was condemned by all prophets and eventually given up. Tophet became a dumping ground where refuse was burned. The writer or writers of the book of Enoch, a non-canonical document of the first and second century B.C., anticipating a terrestrial eschatology and final judgment, turns it into a place of punishment, a fiery pit into which the wicked would be hurled. In the New Testament, Tophet is divorced from its terrestrial topography and transferred to the world beyond as a place of fire for the everlasting punishment of the wicked. B's image of Guido hanging in suspense over the flames while he awaits judgment derives less from history than from folk lore.
637-38] *primal . . . lie* Here *primal* has the sense of initial; *primal curse* is that sin from which all others spring, and the sin is to usurp God's powers through not loving His truth, as "the world come to judgment" does here. According to the description of the day of judgment in 2 Thess. the punishment of those who make lies is that they shall be condemned to believe, or love, lies: "God shall send them strong delusion" (2 Thess. 2:3, 4, 11; see also Rev. 22:14-15).
641] *fell* Hide.
642] *great guardian* Pope Innocent XII. See 1.298n.
643] *the crook* The crozier or shepherd's crook is the symbol of the office of bishop.
646-48] In language and in imagery this description of Hell is close to Rev. 9:1-2.
664] *entablature* The parts of a classical column above the shaft.
670] *abacus* Square at the top of a column's capital. See also 1.671 where B plays on the sense of *abacus* as *counter*.
672] *style* Pillar.
678] *favoured* Embellished.
683] *crease* The letters and some of the pamphlets in OYB were folded for mailing.
689] *Who bound* Cencini. See 1.268n.
696] *malleolable* The word has been the subject of much speculation. Did B really intend to write *malleable*? If not, and the 1868, 1872, and 1888-1889 editions represent B's intentions, what does the word mean?

Malleolable is an apparent coinage, for which Cook offers the following explanation: "Malleus = 'hammer', malleolus = 'little hammer'; 'malleolable' . . . is therefore more suitable here than the usual 'malleable', the workmanship of the poet's fancy being delicate like that required in fashioning an Etruscan ring" (Cook, 19).

702-3] *"In. . . lisp* The lines may be a glancing reference to the lisping Friar in the Prologue of Chaucer's *Canterbury Tales* and his sweet sounding *In principio* (lines 254, 264). B's conflation of the beginning of a child's primer, the first verse of the book of Genesis, and the opening of a great early English poem is probably intentional as he prepares to launch his own poetic credo in the next lines.

722-52] B's terminology in these lines invokes a body of occult theory which was the object of wide speculation in the nineteenth century. According to the teaching of Franz Mesmer (1734-1815), the human body was a microcosm of the design of the universe and was both influenced by the planets and, through animal magnetism, capable of exerting influence on other bodies and objects. Mesmer assigned mystical and curative powers to mummified animal matter as well as to certain objects, and he exercised these powers through mesmerism, a process akin to hypnotism. Mesmer and his followers held that the hypnotist is a repository and conductor of a "universal magnetic fluid" radiated by all material objects. Certain movements ("passes") of the hands supposedly transmit this insubstantial force (later called "odyl") to a subject, thus making control of the subject possible. EBB was a believer in mesmerism, and B probably learned most of what he knew about it from her, although, as with spiritualism, he appears to have been at once curious and skeptical. *Mage, adepts*—magician, experts, with the connotation of medieval pseudo-science.

729-30] *lamp . . . earth* "He shall order the lamps upon the pure candlestick before the lord continually" (Lev. 24:4).

733] *galvanism* The spasmodic jerks which can be produced in a recently dead organism by the application of electric current.

747] *Smoking flax* "A bruised reed shall he not break, and the smoking flax shall he not quench" (Isa. 42:3; Matt. 12:20). The "smoking flax" is the smoldering wick of a lamp (see l.730-31); the figure is that of Jesus, sent to be a light to the Gentiles.

752-64] *Faust's . . . opened* Faust was a German magician, alchemist, and astrologer (c. 1480-1538), who in medieval legend sold his soul to the devil in return for knowledge and power. In Christopher Marlowe's *Dr. Faustus* (5.1) Mephistophilis raised Helen of Troy from the dead at Faust's request. But Elisha returned a dead child to actual life, not merely to the magical semblance of life. The miracle is recounted in 2 Kings 4:29, 31-45.

766] *medicinable* Restorative. B's description of the book's effect makes himself appear not only a medium but also an object of the revivifying and galvanizing power the preceding lines describe. B may intend a slanting reference to the "healing" leaves of the tree of life in Rev. 22:2.
767] *In London . . . erst* Four years intervened between the finding of the OYB in Florence, probably June 1860, and the commencement of the poem after EBB's death and B's return to London.
769] *lifts . . . hair* Perhaps a reference to *galvinism* 1.733, which can be literally hair-raising.
772] *Count. . . Aretine* Citizen of Arezzo. B here begins a list of the central characters in his poem and a summary of the plot.
774-76] *beak-nosed . . . old* The physical description corresponds to that given in B's secondary source, but according to the records at Arezzo, Guido was only 40 at the time of the trial.
785] *nobler birth* The second anonymous pamphlet, which is directed against Guido, says that of eight ranks in Arezzo, Guido's nobility was of the second degree (next to highest), which it was. B has Caponsacchi claim (6.223) that he is a nobleman of the primary degree. After Guido's death his sister acquired for the family a certificate of the first order of nobility.
787] *a Christmas night* 2 January, the ninth night of the Christmas season.
792] *style* Title.
810] *stark* Rigid in death.
810] *worm of hell* In Teutonic and Norse legend as well as in *Beowulf* *worm* is a designation of dragons and great serpents.
823-24] *milk . . . meat* Paul compared those who were not yet spiritually mature to "babes in Christ. I have fed you with milk, and not with meat: for hitherto ye were not able to bear it" (1 Cor. 3:1-2).
839-874] Summary of Book 2, "Half-Rome."
860] *Æacus* In Greek mythology, one of three judges of the shades in the underworld. In life he had been a righteous king of the island of Aegina.
866-67] *Lorenzo . . . Corso side* The church of San Lorenzo in Lucina is slightly off the W side of the Corso, the main thoroughfare in Rome. It is mentioned in Pompilia's baptismal certificate in the OYB, and in the Secondary Source (see *Sources*) as the scene of her marriage and of the exhibition of the bodies (see also 2.6n.).
868] *Fiano . . . Ruspoli* The palaces are on either side of the entrance from the Corso to the small Piazza in Lucina in front of Lorenzo Church.
875-901] Summary of Book 3, "The Other Half-Rome."

889] *Barberini . . . Capucins* The church of the Capucins is just off the Piazza Barberini. It is famous for its bone sculptures fashioned from monks' skeletons. The Piazza Barberini is a large market place some distance E of the Corso. It is named for the family whose palace is on one side of the square and whose arms ornament the fountain at the center.
891-94] *plated . . . caritellas* The Triton fountain dominating the Piazza Barberini is a figure of the sea god sounding his horn. Triton had the head and shoulders of a man and the body of a fish; *plated* means covered with scales. The statue is by Giovanni Lorenzo Bernini, sculptor and architect (1598-1680), who also designed the Barberini palace on one side of the square. *Caritellas* is probably a misspelling for *cartellas,* insignia or signs; the arms of the Barberini family are mounted on each side of the fountain between the four dolphins supporting the statue.
902-934] Summary of Book 4, "Tertium Quid."
908] *tertium quid* In logic and argumentation, a third "what" or third essence, left over to be accounted for after two other comparatively clear things have been distinguished.
921] *musk* Perfume.
922-23] *solitaire . . . back* There was a vogue in the early eighteenth century for confining the back hair of men's wigs in a black silk bag with ribbon drawstrings. The arrangement of the drawstrings was called the *solitaire*: they were drawn around the neck to the front and fastened with a pin or bow to a frilled shirt front.
926] *saloon* Salon
927] *girandole* Branched candlestick, especially one projecting from a wall. The word was also applied to fireworks, which the multiplied reflected lights might well suggest.
931] *observance* Courteous attention, as contrasted to the mob's avid *approbation* 1.928.
935-1007] Summary of Book 5, "Count Guido Franceschini."
944] *Tommati, Venturini* Marco Antonio Venturini, as Vice-Governor of Rome, was the presiding judge at Guido's trial. B adds two other judges to the board before which Guido sat. Dominicus Tomati (or Thomatus in the OYB) was actually the judge in the action for annulment of the dowry brought earlier by Pietro Comparini (see *Chronology*).
954-55] *pour . . . Job* Satan pours his blame on Job in the sense that he uses his mischief-making powers to cause the guiltless Job suffering, just as the Comparini made Guido pay for their offense.
971-72] *Cord . . . facetiously* The torture of the Vigil, which in the early fifteenth century was the privation of sleep for forty hours, later in the century became combined with the more painful torture of the cord, a procedure consisting of stripping the victim naked, seating him on a

bench elevated from the floor with his hands tied behind him by a cord attached to a pulley overhead, and then either jerking his arms up and down or actually hoisting the sufferer's weight by the cord, for a period of five to ten hours. The tortures of the vigil and the cord became synonymous, although B seems to think the term *vigil* is used euphemistically, *facetiously*. B has Guido complain at length of being tortured, but it is uncertain whether he was in fact tortured between the two parts of the trial, or whether he confessed under threat of torture (see Cook, 297, and Gest, 97).

980] *pinching . . . pulling* Hot pincers to tear flesh, thumbscrews to apply unbearable pressure, or the rack to stretch and dislocate human limbs, were methods of torture fitting this description.

984] *recusants* Non-conformists in religious matters.

985-1001] *Religion overlooked* The use of torture as a means of judicial proceeding was widespread throughout Europe in the 15th century and later as a consequence of the power of the Inquisition. But even during the Inquisition victims were tortured by civil, not ecclesiastical, courts, although ecclesiastics could be present as witnesses. By the end of the 18th century the practice of torture was legally abolished almost everywhere, apparently as much from general revulsion of feeling as from civil or religious authority.

1008-1067] Summary of Book 6, "Giuseppe Caponsacchi."

1017] *Cupid* Winged Eros of myth, not the infant of Baroque art.

1020] *consecrative work* A reference to the rite of ordination by which one is set apart as a minister of the church.

1031] *relegation,—exile* Caponsacchi was banished to Civita Vecchia (see 2.1171 and n.) for three years for the abduction of Pompilia. *Relegation* is the term applied to punishment by exile.

1044] *Tommati, Venturini* See 1.944n.

1055] *eight months since* Since May 1697, the date of the suit by Guido in Rome against Pompilia and Caponsacchi for flight and adultery.

1068-96] Summary of Book 7, "Pompilia."

1073] *hireling . . . alien* "But he that is an hireling, and not the shepherd, . . . seeth the wolf coming, and leaveth the sheep, and fleeth" (John 10:12-13). The reference suggests a contrast between the good shepherd-Pope (1.642) and the self-interested ministrations and curiosity of those around Pompilia's bed. The testimony of a number of these is included in the OYB.

1077] *good house* B set Pompilia's death at St. Anna's hospital, though she in fact died at her parents' house. See 3.4-5n.

1111] *pen . . . tongue* See *Sources* for the way in which Roman trials were conducted.

1116-56] Summary of Book 8, "Dominus Hyacinthus de Archangelis."
1120] *Don . . . Arcangeli* See *Sources* for the function of the Procurator of the Poor.
1131] *efficacious personage* Cardinal. As Cook points out (67), *efficacious* was a word B characteristically associated with cardinals.
1139] *buckle* The metaphor is another reminder of Arcangeli's girth, which is as difficult to compass or restrain as his various obligations are to reconcile in one "bond."
1145] *levigate* To reduce to powder in order to analyze.
1147] *inchoates* Begins.
1149] *Ovidian . . . crank* Ovid (Publius Ovidius Naso, 43 B.C.-A.D. 17) was a Roman poet noted for vivacity of expression and vividness of imagery. Marcus Tullius Cicero (106-43 B.C.) was a Roman statesman and orator known for rhetorical elegance. The juxtaposition conveys that Arcangeli was master of a full range of effects. *Crank* as defined by Johnson included the example from Milton's "L'Allegro," "quips and cranks and wanton wiles." Johnson defines *crank* as a "conceit formed by twisting . . . the form or meaning of a word."
1153] *first speech* See l.162n.
1157-1211] Summary of Book 9, "Juris Doctor Johannes-Baptista Bottinius."
1157] *clap* "To do anything with a sudden hasty motion, or unexpectedly" (Johnson's *Dictionary*).
1164-66] *Giovambattista . . . persecutor* The function of prosecutor was customarily taken by the office of the Fisc, which was represented in Guido's trial by Bottini and Gambi; in the later trial concerning the claim of the Convertites to Pompilia's property (See *Chronology*)—in which the dead Pompilia was the defendant—Gambi alone represented the Fisc. The latter trial was, however, decided in Pompilia's favor.
1182] *"Well . . . faithful!"* The judgment delivered by the Lord to the servants who invested and increased his goods in the parable of the talents (Matt.25:21). Here Caution quotes Scripture to her own purpose in B's fable illustrating Bottini's unlikely "composite" of traits and functions. Having lured the unsuspecting bark by a false light, Caution (Bottini in the role of protector) turns wrecker (the Fisc as Prosecutor in the case against Pompilia brought by the Convertites).
1193] *scrannel* Meagre, grating. The earliest recorded use is Milton's in "Lycidas." " . . . their lean and flashy songs / Grate on their scrannel pipes of wretched straw" (lines 123-24).
1199] *Forum . . . Hill* The Forum in Rome, and Mars Hill, or Areopagus, in Athens, were famous for the debate and oratory which took place there.

1201-2] *Clavecinist . . . trill* Player of a keyboard instrument, a clavichord or a harpsichord. Early keyboard instruments had no sustaining pedals and the melodic lines of pieces written for them were often elaborately ornamented and figured rather than held. B was himself an accomplished pianist.
1204-1206] *rondo . . . Haendel* The most common use of the term *suite* applies to a set of four or five formally contrasting pieces, a form especially important in the Baroque period. Each piece had the title and character of an earlier dance form, but none was as a rule designated rondo. The rondeau, a form marked by a recurrent refrain, was popular with seventeenth-century clavecinists, and it was later developed into the rondo movement of the classical sonata. Another kind of suite, to which a rondeau might belong, was a lengthy series of loosely related pieces which were not necessarily intended to be played consecutively or on the same program; this kind of suite was popular with the French clavecinists. Arcangelo *Corelli* (1653-1715) and Georg Friedrich *Haendel* (1685-1759) were composers and performers of solo and ensemble music, both vocal and instrumental. Handel (the more customary English spelling) did come to Rome and did know Corelli there, but not until 1706.
1212-63] Summary of Book 10, "The Pope."
1222] *what . . . drop* The ancient Greek practice of dropping a black ball into an urn to express a negative vote passed into proverbial usage.
1231] *lathen* Made of lath, a crude, thin strip of wood.
1242] *huge tome* A manuscript history of the popes. See 10.1-23.
1244] *stands. . . stead* Does daily service.
1264-1321] Summary of Book 11, "Guido."
1265-66] *Satan's . . . life* After God destroyed the sons of Job, and Job did not curse God, Satan argued to God that a man can bear any trial except threat to his own life (Job 2:4). The sense of the passage seems to be that Guido, having accepted death, no longer seeks to prolong life by lies.
1271] *rivelled* Shrivelled (archaic).
1276] *New . . . Angelo* B's designation yokes under one name two prisons in the same vicinity. The Torre di Nona, just S of Castle Angelo, was a tower in the Roman city wall used as a papal prison since 1410. Eight years before Guido's arrest it was torn down and replaced by the New Prison in the Via Giulia, not far away.
1284-85] *Cardinal . . . Abate* Accaioli and Panciatichi, both members of old Florentine families and of the Confraternita della Misericordia (see l.1303n.). Accaioli is called *Cavaliere* (noble) by the author of the "Description of the death of Guido Franceschini" included in the doc-

uments discovered by Beatrice Corrigan; she thinks that the author was a member of the fraternity (Corrigan, xix, 93).

1296-97] *enemy . . . up* "When the enemy shall come in like a flood, the Spirit of the Lord shall lift up a standard against him" (Isa. 59:19).

1303] *Brotherhood of Death* The Confraternita della Misericordia, founded in Florence possibly as early as 1240, was a voluntary brotherhood not connected with a church, its members selected from all ranks of life. In addition to their robes they wore black hoods with eye slits, perhaps to preserve anonymity. In one description of Guido's last hours, it is recounted that Guido recognized a patron among the brotherhood and had a private conversation with him (Corrigan, 97). The fraternity were committed to the care of prisoners in their last hours and especially to obtaining and hearing confession. They accompanied the condemned to the scaffold, holding aloft a tall, narrow black standard worked with a cross and a skull and bones, and a bronze crucifix. In the course of the procession they chanted psalms and accepted contributions for masses later said for the souls of the dead.

1311-12] *"Out . . . profound* The phrase *De Profundis* (Out of the deep) are the first two words of Ps. 130:1 in Latin. B's lines employ two English versions (*deeps, profound*) of the Latin, which is part of the Roman Catholic burial service.

1317] *longest way* Treves has retraced this route and describes it in detail (138-44). It took Treves thirty-five minutes to accomplish the walk, and he estimates one hour (2:00-3:00 p.m.) for the condemned men in their separate carts, the crowd of the curious, and the Brotherhood of Mercy to cover the distance.

1320] *Mannaia* Literally, blade; refers to the Italian guillotine.

1322-1408] In place of a preview of Book 12 ("The Book and the Ring"), the final lines of Book 1 fall into three parts: a transition from the world of the poem back to the poet's present (1.1322-29), a reflection on the changing seasons as a figure for the mutability and ambiguity of human affairs (1.1340-70), and a famous set piece of invocation and dedication to EBB (1.1381-1408). The transitional first part treats the imaginative journey which has just been summarized in Book 1 as a kind of heavenly pilgrimage, from which B now guides the traveler back to the earthly present. Coming as it does after the image of Guido facing the crown of his efforts atop the raised scaffold, the reader's return to *mother-earth* has an ironic quality of reprieve (1.1319-21, 1327).

1328-1330] *fat . . . wine* "Therefore God give thee of the dew of heaven, and the fatness of the earth, and plenty of corn and wine" (Gen. 27:28). These are the words of Isaac's blessing to Esau masquerading as Jacob. B seems to reverse the context of the allusion, saying that after unfolding his drama, he will bless and undeceive his audience by returning them to familiar reality.

1331] *Much . . . fleece* The language, the idea of spared life, and the panoramic point of view recall the end of the book of Jonah. "And should not I spare Ninevah, that great city, wherein are more than sixscore thousand persons that cannot discern between their right hand and their left hand, and also much cattle?" (Jon. 4:11). *many-folded*: manifold.

1334] *wistful . . . eye* The eagle is traditionally considered to have keen and unfaltering vision and is also associated with courage, honor, immortality, and other idealized qualities. Cf. Milton's "Methinks I see her as an eagle . . . kindling her undazzled eyes at the full midday beam" (*Aeropagitica*), and Shakespeare's "A lover's eyes will gaze an eagle blind" (*Love's Labors Lost* 4.3.331). The eagle has a scaly, "horny" eyelid.

1338-39] *heaven. . . beanstalk-rungs* The lines seem to merge the Biblical Jacob, who dreamed of a ladder reaching to heaven (Gen. 28:12) and the Jack of folktale.

1343] *House of Fame* Chaucer's House of Fame contained stories painted on its walls; the poet was brought there in a dream, by an eagle.

1354] *Red. . . white* The predominant colors of the seasons. White seems here to represent both winter and eternity, death and transformation: colors merge into white, as do facts into truth, life into spirit. Color is a unifying thread in these somewhat digressive and ambiguous final three sections of the Book. Green may be taken as the color of the first section, with its emphasis on growth and spring, furrow and sward. Red, blue, and white are to be important in the final invocation, where they are translated into the colors of earth and heaven: the *red-ripe of the heart* (1388), and the *holier blue* (1386), *blanched blue* (1390), *whiteness* (1407) and *wanness* (1408), of the *realms of help*.

1359] *glass . . . a-top* A reference to an "electric egg," a device in which an electric current was discharged in a partial vacuum, so that as the glass vessel was progressively exhausted the pattern and shades of color of the charge shifted and changed.

1369] *Guy Faux* The instigator of the Gunpowder Plot (1605) against King James I and the Parliament of England.

1373-74] *Perchance . . . ran* "The Lord answered me, and said, write the vision, and make it plain upon tables, that he may run that readeth it" (Hab. 2:2). B plays upon the Biblical quotation with reference both to the obscurity of his early reputation, and to his reputation for obscurity. He changes the reader who runs—the messenger of the vision in the original—to a runner who wishes also to read. B thus adapts the quota-

tion to declare his intention to aim for lucidity and ready understanding in his present poem, then burlesques the quotation in an image of his audience fleeing from his earlier work (*erst*, formerly).
1382] *posy* An archaic variation of *poesy*, a brief motto or dedication inscribed in a ring.
1383-1408] *O Lyric. . . fall* EBB is here given a composite identity and several distinct powers. The lines have invited much speculation. Perhaps, having been B's muse and inspiration in the poem (his alloy-fancy), EBB is to return to act as the agency restoring the original purity (truth) of the ring-poem, this time by releasing the poet's fancy. Reference to the alloy metaphor is left implicit in these final lines, but note that *alloy*, if written as a posy inscribed in a ring—that is, circularly—will also read *loyal*: B's memory of his wife, dead thirteen years at the time of his writing these lines, is still an inspiration. Yet EBB's own feelings about the subject of *The Ring and the Book* were, according to B, strongly negative (see *Composition*).

Book 2, Half-Rome

6] *Lorenzo in Lucina* A church in the heart of Rome, just off the Corso, where the bodies of the Comparini and Pompilia were exposed. St. Lawrence (d. 258) was one of the most famous martyrs of the early church, and this San Lorenzo is not the oldest one in Rome—hence the attributive *in Lucina* (a street intersecting the Corso about midway).
8] *Corso* A main Roman street running N and S, the old Roman Via Flaminia, which took its name *Corso* from its use as a race course in Carnival time. The Piazza del Popolo is at the old N end of the Corso and the Forum is at the S end.
12, 18] *transept . . . apse . . . chancel* In a cruciform church the transept is an aisle crossing the main aisle or nave at right angles. The apse is a vaulted recess behind the chancel, which is the section of the church where the altar is; the chancel is customarily separated or enclosed, and elevated, from the rest of the church.
14] *today's . . . swine* "Neither cast ye your pearls before swine, lest they trample them under their feet, and turn again and rend you" (Matt. 7:6). Half-Rome's allusion is probably called up by the milling crowd and the mutilated bodies, but *swine* refers here to the clergy; Half-Rome is characteristically less concerned with exactness than with effect.
16] *right man* Explained in the last ten lines of this book of the poem.
28] *Honoris causa* In the cause, or objective, of honor.

31] *fray* Assault, attack. Facial mutilation is an ancient form of punishment for adultery, and the OYB says Guido confessed to ordering his wife's face disfigured.
40] *use* Usually are.
47] *nave* Central section of the church extending from the entrance to the chancel or apse.
54] *string of names* Francesca Camilla Vittoria Angela Pompilia Comparini. In reality Francesca was the name Pompilia was familiarly called by, although Francesca Pompilia is the form appearing in the records.
66] *this . . . knife* See 2.146 and n. Apparently the murder weapon was displayed at the foot of the corpses (2.144).
69] *clandestinely* The degree of secrecy connected with the wedding is controversial. The banns and wedding were duly published and witnessed, but the anonymous pamphleteers say that Pietro did not give his consent.
74-76] *Ply . . . submissiveness* The lines play on *trade* both as *exchange* and as *vocation.* Feminine inconsistency and pretence, the speaker implies, is the *sex's trick* and the stock-in-trade of a wife. *Worry* has the sense of "nagging", in contrast to *qualms*, "a fit or sudden access of some quality" (*OED*); i.e. quietness. The lines reveal Half-Rome's own distracted state and mistrust of women generally.
83] *Master Guido Reni* A painter (1575-1642) with whose version of the crucifixion B was familiar. When he wrote to Frederick Leighton 17 Oct. 1864 for particulars of the interior of the church, B noted the painting and its position above the altar (Orr, *Life* 273).
94] *porphyry* A marble-like, purplish-red rock containing crystals, often used in church decoration.
114] *Barbers. . . sings* "Omnibus et lippis notum et tonsoribus": "Known to every blear-eyed man and barber" (Horace, *Satires* 1.7.3). Barber shops and apothecaries are proverbial centers of gossip, and a hairdresser was in fact the agency of Violante's introduction to Guido. Half-Rome's superiority to cheap gossip-mongers is a trifle misplaced, in the light of his ensuing inquiries to Luca Cini and Curate Carlo (apparently imaginary characters).
124] *seals up the sum* Ezek. 28:12.
125] *Molinos* See 1.303n.
126] *Antichrist . . . near* "And as ye have heard that antichrist shall come, even now are there many antichrists; whereby we know that it is the last time" (1 John 2:18). According to early Hebrew legend, Antichrist, or the Man of Sin, would appear at the end of time. Some Christians held that the second coming of Christ would be preceded by

the coming of Antichrist, basing their belief on 2 Thess. 2:1-12, and Rev. 13. In the history of the church the term has served loosely to label any event or person or belief felt to be an enemy of Christ, as Luca Cini in his free allusions to scripture illustrates here.

127] *May . . . peace* Simeon's words upon beholding the infant Jesus (Luke 2:29-30; see 1.536-37n.).

146] *Triangular . . . Genoese* B found in his secondary source that Guido's knife was *alla Genovese*, "in the Genoese style," the blade triangular and edged with hooked notches designed to catch in withdrawal.

153-55] *Cardinal . . . once* Guido's older brother Paolo's patron Cardinal Lauria had lent his support to the marriage, but had died two months after it; Guido's patron was Cardinal Nerli, but for reasons unexplained in the OYB but perhaps connected with Innocent XII's discouragement of nepotism (see 1.315n.), Guido was no longer in his service.

158] *Curate* The title originally meant "holder of a cure," or spiritual guardianship of the souls in a parish, but came to mean assistant to a clergyman.

163] *she . . . crime* In her confession Pompilia in fact maintained her innocence.

166-68] *Lucifer . . . fall.* See Gen. 3:1-7.

174-75] *tares . . . wheat* "The Kingdom of heaven is likened unto a man which sowed good seed in his field: But while men slept, his enemy came and sowed tares among the wheat, and went his way. But when the blade was sprung up . . . then appeared the tares also" (Matt. 13:24-25).

176-77] *abominable . . . sin* The *philosophic sin* was an idea and a term introduced in 1686 by the Jesuits, presumably "the abominable sect" which Carlo offhandedly dismisses. There was no connection between the philosophic sin and Molinism other than contemporaneity, and the fact that both Jesuits and Jansenists, who were bitter theological disputants, are separately linked with Molinism (see 1.303 and n.) underscores the looseness and vagueness with which these controversial labels were applied.

The philosophic sin was first proposed for the annual theological debate at the college of Jesuits at Dijon by Francois Musnier, a professor whose name has survived almost entirely by favor of Jansenist attacks on what was apparently intended as a scholarly exercise for students. The philosophic sin rests on the theological distinction between natural and divine law, and raises the question whether a sinner who is conscious only of violating his rational nature (viewed by orthodox Catholic thought as a reflection of God's intellect and plan) is indeed guilty of sin in the theological sense, or only in a "philosophical" sense. As intro-

duced by Musnier, the philosophic sin was a hypothesis intended as a subject for metaphysical argument but not as a possible case in fact. The philosophic sin, and the sin which seemed possible in the passive Quietist state Molinos described, are not the same, one being a sin of ignorance of God, the other being a result of perfect union with God and a consequent extinction of the will to resist worldly temptation. The philosophic sin was condemned in 1690, but without either Musnier or the Jesuits being named in connection with it. In the interim, however, the somewhat artificial and manufactured controversy achieved such notoriety that street ditties about it were chanted to popular tunes; cf. 1.303-304 ". . . Molinists / 'Gainst whom the cry went, like a frowsy tune" (Hugues Beylard, "Le Péché Philosophique," *Nouvelle Revue Philosophique* 62 [1935], 592-616, 673-98).
178] *Cardinal . . . same* B does not identify the Cardinal nor is there external evidence to suggest who he might have been. Whoever he was, it is quite likely that he or any ambitious cardinal serving during the controversy over the philosophic sin might have written his contribution to it; many did.
187] *Ruspoli* The palace by which one passes going from the Piazza San Lorenzo to the Corso; Half-Rome and his listener are presumably moving back into the main thoroughfare of the Corso. The line has a symbolic ring after the image of the murder plot as a maze; Half-Rome has his own direct route to the solution of the tragedy, a solution contrary to that of the cousin of 2.189 (see last 10 lines of Book 2).
191] *handsel* Literally hand-gift, handshake; thus, earnest-money, first step in a bargain.
192-93] *gay / And galliard* The adjectives are almost synonymous. Besides lively, *galliard* can also mean a brisk dance for two people.
201-206] *one . . . district* The Via Vittoria connects the Corso and the Via del Babuino (the former Strada Paolini; see 1.389n.). The Comparini's dwelling was near the intersection of the Via Babuino (Paolina) and the Via Vittoria.
202] *aspectable* Attractive
210] *usufruct* Literally, the fruit of use (of property belonging to another); interest, from a trust fund, for example.
211] *determine* Terminate.
221-22] *spite . . . manifest* Perhaps an allusion to Abraham's wife Sarah, who was 90 when Isaac was conceived (Gen. 18), and to Elizabeth, mother of John the Baptist, who was also "well stricken in years" (Luke 1:5-25).
229] *fiddle-pin's end* A fiddle pin is a tuning peg. The exclamation here seems compounded of *fiddlesticks, not worth a pin,* and *fig's end*—all signifying trivial or nonsensical (Altick).

251] *after-wit* "The contrivance of expedients, after the occasion of using them is past" (Johnson's *Dictionary*).
251-52] *lest . . . hers* The reference is to Genesis 3, and in particular to verse 16, "and he shall rule over thee."
254] *stump* The leafless stalk of a cabbage.
255-56] *Pietro's . . . care* The decline in Pietro's fortunes was due not to negligence on his part but to the re-funding by Pope Innocent XI in 1685 of certain bonds at reduced interest. A contemporary observer maintained that many were ruined by the re-funding (Bishop Burnet, *Travels through France, Italy, Germany and Switzerland* [1685-6], [London 1750], 179).
289] *younger poorer brother* The records examined by Corrigan show that there were four Franceschini brothers, among whom Guido was the second youngest. Paolo, the first born, was seven years older than Guido; Girolomo was four years older. Antonio Maria, the youngest, is not mentioned in the OYB. It seems probable that B made Guido the eldest for two reasons, as an intensification of his desire for an heir to perpetuate the family name, and as an excuse for his not having taken major orders, which would have required celibacy.
290] *regular priest* See 1.260-62n. and 1.549n.
292] *Galilean pool* The Sea of Galilee is a lake in Israel through which the River Jordan flows. It is rich in Christian associations, hence its use here as a figure for the church.
294] *dab-chick* Familiar name for the Little Grebe, a diving bird which does not have webbed feet and which has almost no tail.
295] *fond* Silly.
302] *thirty years* Paolo, not Guido, had spent thirty years in Rome. B misread a passage in the First Anonymous Pamphlet (OYB, Everyman, 151). We do not know exactly when Guido went to Rome, but it was after his father died in 1681.
306] *concurrence* Competition.
316] *trimmed . . . loins* "Let your loins be girded about, and your lights burning" (Luke 12:35) in readiness for the second coming. Guido's retreat is in a different spirit.
331-36] *Donna Beatrice . . . Girolamo* Guido's mother, Donna Beatrice, lived with Girolamo in the family home in Arezzo. She is first mentioned in 1.565; see 1.564-82n.
337] *callow* Bare, bald. Callow birds are not yet feathered.
346] *threatened fate* See 2.261.
355] *one blind eve* B, following his secondary source, put the marriage in December. It was really in September, as Treves discovered by consulting the San Lorenzo Church Register, and it took place in the morning (OYB, Everyman, 218).

358] *priest-confederate* Pompilia says the attendant priest was Paolo (8.43); the church register says he was the Curate of the parish, one Ignatius Bonechi. By ascribing this role to Paolo B emphasizes his confederacy in the deception.
374] *count the cost* "For which of you, intending to build a tower, sitteth not down first, and counteth the cost" (Luke 14:28).
385] *devoir* Homage, respect.
389] *lots . . . lap* "The lot is cast into the lap" (Prov. 16:33).
410] *purple flushing him* A pun on the two senses of *flush* as "well supplied with money," and "to color." Cardinals rank with princes of the royal blood, and although they wore red customarily, they did wear purple, the royal color, on occasion.
412] *moiety* Part, share.
418-20] *Pietro . . . land* "And take your father, and your households, and come unto me; and I will give you the good of the land of Egypt, and ye shall eat the fat of the land" (Gen. 45:18).
424] *Solomon . . . all* "Thou hast ravished my heart with one of thine eyes" (Song of Sol. 4:9).
438] *Plutus . . . whim* According to Greek mythology, Plutus, the god of riches, was blinded by Zeus in order that his gifts might be freely distributed and not determined by merit or need.
442] *minister* Administer.
443] *qualmish* Feverish, sick.
443-44] *Stay . . . flagons* "Stay me with flagons, comfort me with apples" (Song of Sol. 2:5).
446] *Lust . . . eye* "For all that is in the world, the lust of the flesh, and the lust of the eyes, . . . is not of the father, but is of the world" (John 2:16).
453-54] *walk . . . spirit* "I shall go softly all my years in the bitterness of my soul" (Isa. 38:15).
470] *verjuice* The sour juice of green or unripe grapes or other fruit.
483] *Tommaso's death* In 1681.
484] *doited* Old and feeble.
486] *novercal* Stepmotherly.
487] *Girolamo* See 2.289n.
489] *mumps* Sulks.
496] *malapert . . . complaisant* Impudent . . . flirtatious. B found the hint of Girolamo's "dishonorable advances" to Pompilia in the forged letter to Paolo, where they are represented as part of the slander concocted by the Comparini after they returned to Rome (see 2.678n.).
509] *goody . . . sib* Terms literally indicating some degree of kinship or friendship, but used loosely by B to suggest curious prattling women.

521] *signorial* Anglicization of *seigneurial*, pertaining to a feudal lord, or landed gentry.
526] *bride . . . quietness* Possibly an echo of Keats' "still unravished bride of quietness" ("Ode on a Grecian Urn" l.1).
531] *Her . . . return* B took this version of Violante's confession from the Secondary Source, which was mistaken, according to Violante's deposition found among the Cortona records. After detailing the circumstances of the feigned birth, Violante says that she informed Pietro of the deception in Arezzo, and that he forgave her but did not speak to her for several days (Corrigan, 36). The confession thus may well have been decisive in determining the Comparini's departure at the end of March; the facts could hardly have been made known while they were still under Guido's roof.
532] *Jubilee* The Holy Year celebrated by the Catholic Church derived from the Hebrew year of Jubilee: "And ye shall hallow the fiftieth year, and . . . it shall be a jubilee unto you (Lev. 25:10). In Jubilee sins could be absolved and vows commuted with exceptional leniency. Boniface VIII held the first Catholic jubilee in 1300, and decreed that there be one every 100 years. The interval was subsequently altered to 50, 33, and 25 years; in addition a time of jubilee could be declared to commemorate some special occasion. The Jubilee Year declared on 3 Dec. 1693 was for the purpose of bringing peace among Christian people through divine aid.
536] *Short shrift* A brief time allowed a condemned man for confession and absolution before his execution. B here uses the term to suggest a hasty confession.
539] *commuted* Exchanged a heavier punishment or fine for an easier one. Usually a fine, sentence, or penance is spoken of as commuted, not the offense itself, as here.
543] *compound for* Come to terms over.
547] *changeling . . . grace* One child substituted for another would be pardonable. The puzzling distinction between a substitute child and a faked birth may have reference to the fact that the practice of substituting one baby for another at birth was apparently by no means unknown in the period. There was even a legal term for this class of crime, *partus suppositus*, and it appears frequently in the OYB (Gest, 401).
554] *Catch . . . kennel* Salvage from the gutter (*kennel* is a later form of *cannel*, channel or canal).
556] *professed . . . trade* Practiced as a vocation the harlot's business.
558] *Communis meretrix* Common prostitute. Corrigan discovered that Pompilia's mother was actually a recent widow from a small village, but B did not know this (Corrigan, 38).

567-68] *crown . . . shape* "A virtuous woman is a crown to her husband" (Prov. 12:4).
571] *fifty years* Violante was actually 48, Pietro 51, in the year of Pompilia's birth, according to the Second Anonymous Pamphlet and the San Lorenzo register.
599] *colourable* Plausible.
604-607] *Erase . . . palace* Half-Rome's alliterative flight in defense of Guido recalls the rustics' version of *Pyramus and Thisbe* in *A Midsummer Night's Dream*: "Whereat with blade, with bloody blameful blade / He bravely broached his boiling bloody breast" (5.1.146-47).
607] *Peter and Paul* Perhaps an allusion to the ancient proverbial expression "to rob Peter to pay Paul": i.e., to weigh the dowry against the shameful birth would be to take away with one hand what was offered by the other.
627] *lazar-badge* A badge worn by a person with a severe or loathsome disease to warn others away.
652] *slanders* The OYB supports Half-Rome's allegation that Pietro had printed and circulated "mordant writings" against Guido both in Rome and in Arezzo.
667] *six . . . mouths* The Comparini's three, her own, Girolamo's, and Guido's.
678] *she wrote* This letter to Paolo recounting the Comparini's suggestions to Pompilia about ruining Guido is dated 14 June 1694 (two months after the Comparini left Arezzo), and Pompilia later testified that at this time she could neither read nor write. According to Pompilia, Guido wrote the letter and made her trace his writing. When the letter was used in evidence by Paolo (who by a "mandate of procuration" dated 7 Oct. 1694 was Guido's legal representative at Rome) in the suit for nullification of the dowry contract, it became public property (see 2.717). The letter is reproduced in OYB, Everyman, 56-57.
684] *qualified* Described.
687] *Quiet as Carmel* Mount Carmel (near modern Haifa) is the site of an ancient monastery in which monks lived lives of silence, seclusion, and extreme austerity. An associate order of nuns, The Order of Our Lady of Mount Carmel, was founded c. 1154. The figure suggests utter quiet and peace. It may further associate Pompilia with the Virgin Mary. The Carmelites wore white robes, were especially dedicated to the service of the Blessed Virgin and the Holy Child, and were among the first theologians to advance the doctrine of the Immaculate Conception. The flower which grows abundantly in the plain of Sharon just S of Mt. Carmel and is referred to in the Bible as the lily is actually the red Palestinian anemone.

706] *posset-cup* A soothing or medicinal drink made of hot milk curdled with ale or wine, often flavored with sugar and spices.
720-49] *cause. . . hour* In the summer of 1694 Pietro brought suit to recover Pompilia's dowry. The suit was denied in spite of the testimony of six witnesses to Pompilia's illegitimacy, and Pietro's appeal of his case was still undecided at the time of the murders.
769] *four times* B consistently added ten years to Guido's age, making him 46 rather than his actual 36 at this period. Pompilia was 13.
778] *portly make* A goodly port, handsome bearing.
779] *tonsure* See 1.327-28n.
784] *saint . . . household* Here and in 2.786 Half-Rome uses ironic parallels to imply Caponsacchi's hypocrisy. According to St. Paul's organization of the early church, a local church was made up of bishops, deacons, and saints, the latter being simply members, believers. In Phillippians 4.22 St. Paul refers to "saints that are of Caesar's household," meaning Christians employed in the Roman administration. Half-Rome misinterprets or deliberately perverts the Biblical "saints of Caesar's household," implying that Caesar's "saints" are worldly and therefore fitter companions for the cavalier Caponsacchi than the more spiritual followers of St. Paul.
786] *Apollos . . . Apollo* Here the contrast is between a Christian and a pagan god. *Apollos* was an early Christian leader, a contemporary and friend of St. Paul (1 Cor. 3:4-6). *Apollo*, a paragon of manly beauty and the Greek god of archery, music, and poetry, slew the sacred python at Delphi. B also suggests here a perverse misuse of the St. George, and the Perseus-Andromeda legends: this speaker has turned Pompilia from a beseiged maiden into a snake or dragon. Far from being a threatened innocent, she "writhes transfixed" under Caponsacchi's power.
787] *spires* Coils, with paradoxical overtones of hopes, aspirations.
793] *comfits* Bonbons. *Comfit* in Italian is *confetto*, pl. *confetti*. Throwing confetti was a custom of carnival time in Italy. It was actually Canon Conti, brother-in-law of Guido's married sister, who threw the comfits (OYB, Everyman, 91-92).
794] *Carnival* Usually, the week before Lent, a traditional time of celebration and license before the time of fast and abstinence.
806] *day-book* Account book.
808] *villa* Guido's vineyards at Vittiano, about 9 mi. from Arezzo on the road to Perugia, are also mentioned in the OYB. Three other farms are listed in the description of Guido's holdings found by Corrigan (9-10).
813] *grange* Farm building.
814] *outhouse* Detached outbuilding.

816] *Mum. . . there* Both *mum* and *budget* suggest close-keeping; a budget was originally a pouch or wallet. *Mumbudget* means "be silent," and may be from an old children's game requiring silence. B may have had in mind here the lines in *Merry Wives of Windsor* in which another would-be clandestine lover (Slender) describes the same signal. *Horn madness* (2.824) strengthens the possible association; cuckoldry jokes are central to *MWW* (5.2.5).

817] *musk* A pun. Musk is a heavy perfume used by gentlemen of elegance, and also the term for the scent of the trail of a hunted prey, especially a deer.

824] *horn-madness* Jealousy, fear of cuckoldry; see 2.816n. above.

831] *brush* Tail of a fox.

836-38] *eclipse . . . system* An eclipse was considered to portend general ill fortune. Guido portrays his world as a solar system intruded upon by an alien body.

844] *larum* Alarm (archaic poetic usage).

851] *litanies* Ceremonial prayers, involving antiphonal exchange between leader and congregation.

866-67] *Governor . . . Archbishop* See 3.965 and n.

879] *cap . . . fit* Cap and bells suggests a jester's costume, the appropriate (fit) garb for a laughable cuckold.

882] *After the cuckoo* Both after the cuckoo's own rising, which is early, and after its visit; the cuckoo lays its eggs in other birds' nests, from which habit the epithet *cuckold* originated.

885] *poppy-milk* Laudanum, the tincture of opium.

886] *scritoire* Writing desk.

888] *money . . . wings* "For riches certainly make themselves wings" (Prov. 23:5).

895] *fifteen years* Pompilia would in fact be seventeen the coming July.

900] *waif . . . stray* A legal expression referring to property which falls to the lord of the manor if it is unclaimed within a certain fixed period.

901] *Spoiled the Philistine* "For the Lord will spoil the Philistines" (Jer. 47:4).

926] *Guillichini* A relative of Guido's who, Pompilia said, was originally to have accompanied her in her escape but was prevented by illness.

931] *milk-swollen poppy-heads* An allusion both to the red hats of the higher clergy and to the source of laudanum. The milk of the poppy is its narcotic juice, which gives the likeness a very literal appropriateness to Guido's case. But milk can also mean to extract undue benefit, as the lines suggest that titled nobility do from church positions.

941] *Money . . . go* Proverbial expression meaning money makes anything possible.
948-51] *Perugia . . . Foligno* In his dramatic recreation Half-Rome errs both in geography and in timetable. Camoscia is only 17 mi. from Arezzo, and presumably the fugitives were well past there when Guido woke at noon. Neither does the road from Perugia to Rome pass through Chiusi (see map). This error may be intentional on B's part; Half-Rome betrays himself more than once as not over-scrupulous about details.
958] *Castelnuovo* See 1.502n. and map.
959] *Osteria* Hostel, inn.
991] *flung . . . far* As a sub-deacon, Caponsacchi was allowed to wear secular costume for an occasion such as a journey.
993] *over . . . boots* The expression has both literal and figurative application here. As a proverb meaning the same as "the die was cast," its first known appearance is a jest in *Two Gentlemen of Verona*, where Shakespeare has one young lover say that Leander "was more than over shoes in love" and the other answer, " 'Tis true, for you are over boots in love, / And yet you never swam the Hellespont" (1.1.24-26). But here the *perfect cavalier* doubtless had indeed discarded his clerical buckled shoes (2.984) for boots.
995-98] *Helen . . . Paris* The elopement of Paris, son of the king of Troy, and Helen, wife of the King of Sparta, caused the Trojan war.
1010] *priests . . . priest* The priest has a right to be tried in an ecclesiastical court.
1014] *Commissary* The title can mean governor (4.793); here it may mean simply officer of rank. The records differ (Hodell, 312, n. 226).
1022] *as . . . truth* Possibly from Ps. 45:3-4, "Gird thy sword upon thy thigh . . . And in thy majesty ride prosperously, because of truth . . . and thy right hand shall teach thee terrible things." See also 1.408 and n.
1023] *sword* It is not certain from the OYB that it was Guido's sword which Pompilia drew; it may have been Caponsacchi's. Perhaps B chose this version of the incident for the symbolic association of the sword with truth ("useless" to Guido) and simply remained consistent with it. Note that Caponsacchi is not "disarmed" of a sword, but merely of his hands. In the MS, B had Pompilia snatch Caponsacchi's sword; the change underscores both Guido's duplicity and his unmanliness.
1030] *pinked* Stabbed superficially. B also puns on pink as a color.
1036] *sbirri* Police.
1040] *lead a measure* To dance, especially a slow, stately dance.
1043] *poke* Colloquial term for bag or pocket. Doubtless also a bawdy pun.

1047] *nose . . . length* An Italian proverb signifying disappointed plans or expectations; much the same as the English "to put someone's nose out of joint."
1062] *regale* A choice article of entertainment or refreshment.
1070] *proemium* Prologue.
1073] *cross himself* In recognition of finished business, as a priest makes the sign of the cross at the end of a service.
1092-93] *charity . . . all* "Charity . . . believeth all things" (1 Cor. 13:4-7).
1094] *natural law* In 1 Corinthians 13 Paul emphasizes the superiority of charity (love) over other virtues, but assuming that the relationship was merely lust, Half-Rome puts a hypocritical defense in Pompilia's mouth: God creates nature, nature obeys God's laws, hence in following natural inclinations she follows the will of God.
1095] *cloak for sin* "If I had not come and spoken unto them, they had not had sin: but now they have no cloak for their sin" (John 15:22). Jesus makes ignorance rather than pretence the "cloak."
1100] *thought . . . deed* See *Book of Common Prayer,* "Confession."
1105-6] *Difficult . . . patron-saint* The name *Joseph* is *Giuseppe* (Caponsacchi's given name) in Italian. The reference here may be to Joseph's questioning the virgin birth of Jesus (Matt. 1:18-20).
1111] *faculty and fleshliness* Ability and desire.
1118] *repugns* Finds repugnant.
1121] *both in a tale* That is, both agreeing in their story, and tale-telling (casting blame on a third party—Guido).
1128] *pearls to swine* Matt. 7:6. See 2.14n.
1132] *fardel* Bundle.
1137] *fox . . . stench* The proverb "The fox is the finder" means that the one pretending to discover a fault is actually the one guilty of it.
1145] *she . . penned* It is not clear from the records when Pompilia learned to write. B accepts her contention that she could not have written the letter to Paolo or the love letters. In the records Pompilia contends that it was before she left Arezzo but after the alleged correspondence with Caponsacchi that she learned to write. The love letters were therefore forgeries, according to both Pompilia and Caponsacchi. For a fuller discussion of Pompilia's literacy see Cook, Appendix IV, 285.
1150] *apage* "Get thee hence," Jesus' answer to Satan after the temptation on the mountain (Matt. 4:10).
1157] *films* Fine threads; web.
1159] *Gordian through* It was said that whoever undid the knot tied by Gordius, King of Phrygia, would rule over the East. Alexander the Great

answered the challenge by cutting the knot through with his sword. "Cutting the Gordian knot" signifies decisive action, but the reference here to conquering law is sarcastic.

1171] *Civita* Civita Vecchia, a seaport 35 mi. NW of Rome.

1178] *Easter eves* Spring evenings during the Easter season, the forty days between Easter Sunday and the Ascension.

1189-90] *Convertites . . . remade* Pompilia was actually sent to a nunery called Le Scalette, in the Via Lungara, although the nunnery of Santa Maria Maddalena delle Convertite, in the Corso, later laid claim to her property as that of a loose woman. B thought that Pompilia was sent to the Convertites. The identification of the sinful woman who washed Jesus' feet with her tears (Luke 7:37-38) as the Mary Magdalene "out of whom went seven devils" (Luke 8:2) is traditional but possibly mistaken. The name *Magdalen* is popularly synonymous with prostitute.

1192] *patiently . . . soul* "In your patience possess ye your souls" was Jesus' counsel to the disciples when they should meet with adversity and persecution (Luke 21:19).

1209] *plait* Fold, pleat.

1212-13] *As Ovid . . . Pontus* Ovid (see 1.1149) was exiled to Tomis on the Black Sea (originally called Pontus Euximus), ostensibly because of the immorality of his *Ars Amatoria*, but really—according to literary and popular tradition—because of complicity in Caesar's daughter's adultery. Unlike Caponsacchi's relegation, Ovid's exile was for life, and the conditions of the place were harsh and uncivilized, as well as remote.

1231] *Penitents* Those undergoing sacramental penance. See 2.1189-90n.

1235] *Pontifex Maximus* High priest in pre-Christian Rome, who flogged any Vestal Virgin who neglected her duties.

1240-41] *old . . . Fiesole* A reference to Caponsacchi's forebear and a reminder of his ancient heritage. The name Caponsacchi means "head in the sack." Caponsacchi later makes reference to "Capo-in-Sacco our progenitor" (6.228-338), and Dante mentions this same Caponsacco (*Paradiso* 16:121-22). The family lived first at Fiesole, an ancient town near Florence which was conquered and despoiled by Florence in 1125, and later in Florence.

1242] *firk* Attack by blow or thrust.

1246-47] *sixth . . . seventh* "Thou shalt not kill. Thou shalt not commit adultery" (Ex. 20:13-14). Guido had not broken the sixth, whether or not Pompilia had broken the seventh.

1260] *alembic* A simple apparatus for making distillations.

1261] *Canidian* The real Canida had spurned the love of the Roman poet Horace and in reprisal he made her into a symbol of malice and evil in his *Satires* and *Epodes.*
1278] *bed and board* The marriage state.
1281] *charge* A pun indicating *accusation*, and *explosive device.*
1285] *engine* Half-Rome is referring to a kind of powerful crossbow that was wound up by a crank on the side. Several of these are in the Armory of the Tower of London.
1297] *contorts his tail* A scorpion's sting is at the end of a jointed tail.
1333] *Domus pro carcere* Literally, a house for a prison; a condition corresponding to our "house arrest."
1356] *blind mute villa* See 1.389n.
1367-68] *One . . . quintessence* Toads were popularly held to be full of poison. The *master-squeeze* which gave *birth* to *hell's quintessence* in the gradual poisoning of Guido's mind is a curious parody of the actual birth (2.1374) of Pompilia's son.
1388] *clown* Ignorant rustic
1389] *clodpole* Blockhead (from clodpoll, lumphead).
1390-91] *law . . . out* When the Pharisees wished Jesus to rebuke a multitude of his disciples for loudly rejoicing in him, Jesus answered, "if these should hold their peace, the stones would immediately cry out" (Luke 19:40).
1401-2] *strong . . . false* "And for this cause God shall send them strong delusion that they should believe a lie" (2 Thess. 2:11). See 1.637-38n.
1403-4] *And . . . God* "For it is written, Vengence is mine, I will repay, saith the Lord" (Rom. 12:19).
1422] *"Giuseppe Caponsacchi!"* Pompilia's lawyer Bottini says that in order to gain entry Guido pretended to be delivering a letter from Caponsacchi (OYB, Everyman, 191-92).
1435] *Viper-like* Folklore holds that snakes can re-form themselves after being hacked apart and, if mortally wounded, will not die till sunset (2.1440).
1444] *saloon* Hall or reception room.
1454] *New Prison* The Carceri Nuovo was located in the Via Giulia near the site of the old prison at Tor di Nonna in the city wall, which was destroyed ten years before Guido's arrest. Following the OYB B has Half-Rome say—correctly—that Guido was taken to the New Prison. In Book 5, however, Guido speaks of being transferred to the New Prison from the Tor di Nonna.
1463] *civility* Civilization.

1466] *Astræa's* Greek goddess of justice, the last one of the gods to leave the world at the end of the mythical golden age.
1468] *"the . . . die"* "The adulterer and the adulteress shall surely be put to death" (Lev. 20:10).
1474] *a natural* An idiot.
1477] *male-Grissel . . . Job* Griselda is a character in Boccaccio's *Decameron* and in Chaucer's *Clerk's Tale* who, like Job, is made to suffer to test exemplary virtue.
1485] *Rolando-stroke* The great warrior Roland, nephew of Charlemagne, possessed an unbreakable sword called Durandal (there are variations of the name).
1530-31] *rod . . . brine* "To have rods in pickle" is to have punishment in store. Birch rods were kept in brine to keep them flexible.
1533] *jackanapes* Impertinent fellow.
1536] *cousin* cf. 2.930.

Book 3, The Other Half-Rome

4-5] *white . . . body* Misled by a reference in the OYB to Pompilia's confessor Fra Celestino (3.18) as being "of St. Anna," B placed Pompilia's death in a hospital of that name (3.37). But Pompilia was in fact never moved from her parents' home, where she was attacked.
16] *blue* Symbolic color of the Blessed Virgin Mary.
18] *Augustinian Brother* Fra Celestino, Pompilia's confessor. The Augustinian Brotherhood was originally the fourth of the Mendicant Orders or Begging Friars. In the OYB Fra Celestino designates himself "barefooted Augustinian."
30] *Care . . . concerns* Pompilia made a will in her son's favor on her deathbed. She had earlier taken precautions to protect him from his father.
34] *Molinists* See 1.303n.
35] *lazar-house* A hospital. A lazar was a poor person with a severe disease of any sort, not necessarily specifically leprosy (from which *lazar* derives).
37] *Saint Anna's* See 3.4-5.
39] *wicket* A small door within a larger one.
41] *men of art* Physicians.
42-44] *lawyers . . . witness* There is no record of this in the OYB.

51] *Mona Baldi* A fictitious character whose name was suggested by Maddalena Baldi Albergotti, mentioned in the OYB as a former employer of a maid in the Franceschini household who gave testimony.
58-59] *Cavalier . . . Maratta* Carlo Maratta was a painter (1625-1713) whose reputation was high during his lifetime but declined sharply after his death. He painted so many portraits of the Virgin that he was nicknamed Carlo della Madonna. *Cavalier* can mean one who dedicates his service to a married lady. This association of Pompilia with the Virgin is one of many.
62] *figuring* Sketching.
74] *Via Vittoria* See 1.389n.
75] *parterre* Flower garden with paths between the beds.
95] *Antichrist* See 2.126n.
96-97] *Philosophic . . . sect* See 2.175n. This unidentified character moralizes in the same righteous and misguided vein as Curate Carlo, mistakenly linking Molinism and the philosophic sin.
103-4] *whistle . . . church* The allusions in these lines are compressed and elliptical. In loose paraphrase lines 95-104 might read, "The permissive license of the Molinist doctrine of Philosophic Sin is at the root of all this recent trouble." "No, original sin, as the Jesuits have long recognized, accounts for it!" It was a superstition popular among sailors that whistling at sea would raise a wind or even a storm. Through perversion of the original superstition, "whistling to the wind" has come to signify effort to no purpose. B seems here to adapt the expression yet again to mean effort to a purpose already manifest; there was a strong prevailing wind in the piazza outside Gesu Church, the principal church of the Roman Jesuits (Cook, 56). The Jesuits, like the Augustinians, believed in original sin and the natural depravity of man, and were anti-Molinist.
118] *Triton's trump* Other Half-Rome's monologue is delivered in the Piazza Barberini, at the center of which is the Triton fountain by Bernini. See 1.889-94n.
126] *mean . . . mix* The golden mean of moderation in all things was highly valued by the ancients. See the *aurea mediocritas* of Horace (*Odes* 2.10.5).
154] *One flesh* The Bible says, "and they shall be one flesh," with no mention of a child (Gen. 2:24).
170] *Eve . . . taste* See Gen. 3:6.
174-76] *mill-stone . . . grist* The sense of these lines is confusing, and seems dictated rather by alliteration than by the mill figure of 165-68. *Quartz from the quarry* may mean a millstone fresh from the source; quartz was an important mineral in the composition of millstones. *Go*

bring grist glances at the expression "to bring grist to the grindstone," to occasion profit.

180] *Jubilee* See 2.532n.

191] *Who . . . whit* Jesus' denunciation of the hypocrisy of the Pharisees, "Ye blind guides, which strain at a gnat, and swallow a camel" (Matt. 23:24), has passed into proverbial usage.

192-93] *far-over-fifty . . . sixty-and-under* See 2.571n.

207] *double death* Death both in the physical and in the spiritual sense. An infant who died before baptism was thought to be barred from heaven through original sin.

211] *old Tiber* The river which flows through Rome toward the Mediterranean.

222] *inconscious* Now rare for *unconscious.*

234] *slipt* The small branch taken from a tree for rooting or grafting is called a slip. The preservation of a graft from one of the trees of Eden appears in several legends. The apochryphal book of Enoch prophesies that the Tree of Life "shall be transplanted to the holy place, to the temple of the Lord" in the New Jerusalem (1 Enoch 25:4-5). According to another legend, the archangel Michael instructed Eve to plant a branch from the Tree of Knowledge on Adam's grave. Solomon transplanted the tree from Adam's grave to the garden of his temple (George Ferguson, *Signs and Symbols in Christian Art* [Oxford, 1959], 21).

235] *tongue-leaved . . . tree* The image has a medieval, allegorical tone, but may be simply Browningized scripture. In the garden of Eden the tree of knowledge was one of many that were "good for food, and . . . pleasant to the eyes" (Gen. 3:6).

243] *coping-stone* Both literally and figuratively. The coping-stone is the top, often decorative, edge of a wall; thus the finishing touch.

250] *one . . . priest* Only in the post-B pamphlet was Paolo said to be the instigator of the marriage; in the anonymous pamphlets and the Secondary Source it is the Comparini or Guido who initiate negotiations.

253] *younger brother* See 2.289n.

257] *A cardinal* See 2.153n.

282] *red cloth* A reference to Paolo's hopes for a cardinalate.

302] *one . . . plough* "No man, having put his hand to the plough, and looking back, is fit for the kingdom of God" (Luke 9:62).

309-311] *wild villa . . . Vittiano* See 2.808n. Vittiano is a village 9 mi. S of Arezzo.

316] *cicala* Cicada.

329] *happy . . . dole* A proverbial expression. *Dole* puns on both "portion" and "sorrow."

335-36] *sprinkle . . . sparrow-hawk* The proverbial advice to children about catching birds by sprinkling salt on their tails is made more improbable still by identifying the bird as the legendary phoenix, the only one of its kind. Searching for a phoenix, the symbol of resurrection, Guido, left to his own devices, was as likely to secure a sparrow hawk, a bird of prey.
338] *lured . . . looking-glass* Larks were a table delicacy. The looking-glass probably also conveys the vanity and social climbing motives of Rome's marriageable daughters, who, Paolo suggests, were as comon as larks. Hunters commonly attracted larks and other small birds by tying an owl to a pole and placing a mirror on the ground beneath. The curiosity of larks is strong, and the combined flutter and glitter of the device drew them in numbers, to be shot (W.W. Story, *Roba di Roma* [Boston, 1887], 448).
340-42] *cuckoo . . . brood* The cuckoo is famous for its unusual way of raising its young. Cuckoos make no nest and do not brood. They leave their eggs in the nests of other birds, and leave to them the task of hatching and rearing their offspring. They shame the brood not only by being different, but also by destroying the other young birds in the nest.
343] *eagles* Perhaps a reference to the Roman eagle, the symbol carried on the Roman military standard.
352] *pant* Pulsate.
359] *rutilant* Glowing.
361] *spiritualty* Clergy.
363] *tenement* Abode, without pejorative connotations.
368] *fillet virginal* Possibly a reference to the head-band or chaplet of flowers with which the heads of sacrificial victims were adorned in antiquity.
375] *purple gleam* A reference to Paolo's hopes of being "raised to the purple"; i.e., created a cardinal. A cardinal's robes and insignia are in fact red; the association of high rank with the color purple dates from ancient Greek and Roman times (see 2.410n.).
384-85] *Hesperian . . . Hercules* One of the labors of Hercules was to steal some of the golden apples guarded by the Hesperides (three sisters) and a dragon. *Hesperian* means *western*, and the Hesperian Gardens are often represented in myth and poetry as a paradise located W of the Straits of Gibraltar and variously called the Blessed Isles, the Happy Isles, the Fortunate Islands.
391-93] *Square . . . Boat-Fountain* The fountain called La Barcaccia, by Bernini, is a stone boat forming a basin for a fountain in the middle, with spouts around the sides. It is located at the bottom of the

Spanish steps leading from the Square of Spain (Piazza di Spagna) and within walking distance of the Comparini's house on the Via Babuino (or Paolina; see 1.389n.). The *six steps* refer to the distance across the Via Babuino.

401] *cross i' the poke* Money in the purse. The cross on one side of an English coin in Elizabethan times led to the popular usage of the word *cross* for money generally.

402] *All . . . rapacity* An ironic parody of 1 Cor. 13:13, "And now abideth faith, hope, charity."

403-4] *Humours. . . head* According to the ancients, an excess of any one of the four humors (phlegm, blood, choler, black bile) caused an unbalanced or ill nature. Other Half-Rome seems to contrast Guido's excesses with the "just degree" (3.125) and composure of the moderate Comparini. Pietro's informants liken Guido's state of mind and fortune to a festering boil (*imposthume*). *Humours* also suggests willful moods and *head* refers both to the boil and to Guido's misfortunes having come to a head or crisis.

405] *rankly-salted soil* Another pun. Jesus called his disciples "the salt of the earth" (Matt. 5:13). But in this case the disciples have become so numerous with the ranking nobility of Italy that the soil has become rankly salted and therefore barren for Guido. There is a further reference to the drawing of boils by applying salt packs to them.

405] *cardinal* See 2.153n.

410-12 ff.] *town . . . mouse* Guido's retreat from Rome apparently reminded B of the fable of the city mouse and the country mouse, in which the country mouse, having visited the city, realizes that he is better off at home.

413] *pricked for* Decided for

419] *snuffed* Sniffed out, and extinguished.

422] *burgesses* Citizens of a borough who hold full municipal rights.

439] *Danae . . . dreams* Because of a prophecy that her son would kill her father, Danae, daugher of the king of Argos, was locked up to prevent her from marrying. But Zeus visited her in a shower of gold and begot Perseus, who later killed his grandfather, fulfilling the prophecy. Violante of course has not renounced her gold dreams, and the comparison to Danae portends some of the irony of subsequent events: she, too, through her misguided efforts brings about her own doom.

442-43] *fairly . . . integrity* "Till I die I will not remove mine integrity from me" (Job 27:5,6). "I put on righteousness, and it clothed me" (Job 29:14).

449] *December day* According to the San Lorenzo Church register

Pompilia was married on 6 September. She returned home with her parents for three months; they all went to Arezzo 30 November 1693 (Corrigan, p. xxvi). B found the December date in the Secondary Source.
455] *perhaps . . . Paolo.* See 2.358n.
456] *clandestinely* See 2.370n.
464] *chaffer* Haggle.
467] *shambles* Slaughter house. The slaughter of cattle within the city was permitted until the time of Pope Leo XII (1823-29).
477] *"a hinge"* The title cardinal comes from Latin *cardo*, hinge. A personage or thing upon which others turn or depend is a central or principal force; hence our *cardinal.*
487-88] *faith . . . mountains* "If ye have faith, and doubt not . . . ye shall say unto this mountain, Be thou removed, and be thou cast into the sea; it shall be done" (Matt. 21:21).
498] *doit* A Dutch coin; used figuratively to signify a minute amount.
502-3] *cast . . . lap* "The lot is cast into the lap" (Prov. 16:33).
505] *having and holding* Belongings and land; an ancient legal term.
508] *usufruct* See 2.210n.
511] *charge* Maintenance.
514] *orts* Table scraps.
518] *quag* Bog.
525] *graduated* Measured out.
543] *tributary* Contributive. Pietro, begging from his old friends, receives the ironical tribute "I told you so."
544] *bowels* The deepest source of humanitarian feelings, as in "bowels of compassion."
550-51] *God / Whose finger* When Aaron caused a plague of lice to descend upon Egypt, Pharaoh's magicians attempted to duplicate the miracle. When they could not, "the magicians said unto Pharaoh, This is the finger of God" (Ex. 8:17-19).
554] *Holy Year* See 2.532n.
555-57] *sin . . . supposed* There is no such categorization of sin by theologians, although sins are classified as mortal or venial, formal and material; nor is there any relationship betweeen these four classifications and B's list. B is perhaps lightly satirizing the Roman Catholic distinctions, which might appear to him legalistic. The satire encompasses also the whole concept of jubilee. B's catalogue is reminiscent of Touchstone's famous catalogue of lies, from the "Retort Courteous" to the "Lie Direct" (*As You Like It* 5.4.68-82).
564] *Saint Peter pays* That is, as patron saint of St. Peter's Basilica in the Vatican City, the seat of the popes and of the government of the Roman Catholic Church. Peter's authority is believed to derive from

Jesus' words to him, "Upon this rock I will build my church . . . and I will give unto thee the keys of the kingdom of heaven" (Matt. 16:18-19). Each pope is regarded by the Roman Catholic Church as the lineal successor to Peter's rule.

566-68] *great door . . . throne* The Porta Santa at the right of the W front of St. Peter's is kept walled up except at Jubilee time, when it is ceremonially opened by the pope. The left transept of St. Peter's contains confessionals presided over by Penitentiaries, priests who administer the sacrament of penance. The *formidable throne* is an elevated platform from which the Grand Penitentiary, usually a cardinal, dispenses absolution on high festival days and otherwise in matters of great importance.

572] *gully-hole . . . discharge* A gully-hole is a street drain or sewer opening. *Discharge* has a double sense, both effluence and forgiveness.

591] *alienate* To transfer property or ownership.

636] *cutting . . . ear* Purses were formerly carried hanging outside street garments. One punishment for thievery was to cut off the offender's ear.

638] *red-letters* Ironic reference to the special day this news will mark in Guido's calendar. Red letters are used in the Christian calendar to designate the feast days of saints and martyrs, and Pietro sees this news as devastating Guido and his hopes for gain.

644] *he carried case* The Comparini's suit to declare Pompilia illegitimate and to recover the dowry was entered in the summer of 1694.

653] *six witnesses* Fact, according to the OYB.

664] *losels* Lost persons, good-for-nothings (archaic and dialectic).

665] *leasing* Lying (archaic).

670] *changeling* See 2.547n.

679-80] *appeal . . . absolute* Uncompromising. Pietro appealed the decision, but there is no record that Guido did.

710] *excogitate* Devise.

737] *letter . . . Abate* See 2.678n.

744] *Complot* Combine in plotting some act, usually criminal (*OED*).

750-62] *This . . . cause* See 2.678n.

767] *figured* Prefigured.

783] *popinjay* Literally, parrot; figuratively, a dandy.

786] *tenebrific passage* In the double sense of dark alley, and obscure section.

793] *brass* Church vessels were commonly made of brass.

795] *lazar-house* See 2.35n.

803] *silly-sooth* Unsophisticatedly truthful, with an imputation of gullible.

834] *charactery* Writing, used in this case as the record to be read and interpreted.
840] *decent* In the archaic sense of suitable, proper.
840] *stall* A seat enclosed at back and sides, set in a row of like seats in the choir of a church for the use of the clergy.
847-48] *rusticity . . . silver-sphere* In architecture *rustic* can refer to the Tuscan order (the simplest of the five classical orders), and to a rough, unfinished type of surface. Here the term may carry these associations, as well as the more familiar sense of rural unsophistication. *Chastened* means refined, purified. In the Ptolemaic system the *silver-sphere* is the lowest of the 11 celestial spheres. It is the sphere described by the orbit of the moon and lies immediately outside the material sphere of earth, air, fire, and water.
872] *adventurous* Happening by chance.
899] *thyme* The fragrant herb *thyme* was a favorite of English poets. In mythology it was the herb of Venus and Mars (see 4.1444n.), and historically, medieval ladies gave their knights a sprig of thyme before battle, for courage and strength.
965-66] *Governor . . . Archbishop* The letters from these officials to Paolo confirming Pompilia's appeal to them are included in the OYB and are respectively dated 2 August 1694 and 15 September 1694. B calls the churchman the Archbishop, but he is referred to as the Bishop of Arezzo in the OYB.
985] *Molinists* See 1.303-13n.
987] *Guido's . . . fell* "Beware of false prophets, which come to you in sheep's clothing, but inwardly they are ravening wolves" (Matt. 7:15).
988-89] *frightened . . . Governor* In the letter mentioned above (3.965) the Governor says that he threatened the Comparini with imprisonment if they didn't stop complaining.
999] *Three times* Two times, according to Pompilia's deposition, and to the Bishop's letter.
1010] *post to pillar* The original form of the familiar expression, which comes from the old style of tennis courts. The phrase may have a double ironic force here; not only were Pompilia's frantic efforts to no purpose, as the proverb signifies, but those pillars of the community, Governor and Archbishop, proved no support to her.
1013] *simple friar* Mentioned in Pompilia's deposition as "an Augustinian Father, whom they call Romano." In her deposition Pompilia said it was fear of violence from Guido that impelled her to ask the friar's aid.
1020] *pluck . . . brand* "I have overthrown some of you . . . and ye were as a firebrand plucked out of the burning: yet have ye not returned

unto me, saith the Lord" (Amos 4:11). In the Biblical context the burning brand signifies one doomed to divine punishment.

1030] *woe . . . come* "But woe to that man by whom the offence cometh" (Matt. 18:7). Jesus warns specifically against offending "little ones which believe in me."

1047] *legend . . . patron-saint* A patron saint can have guardianship of a person born on his day or named for him, or of a place or profession. Since canonization meant recognition of divine powers shown through miracles or extraordinary virtue, most saints' legends were improbable, yet to be believed; which saint is referred to here remains open. Cf. 2.1105-1106 and n.

1050] *passenger* A passer-by, wayfarer.

1061] *April evening* B changed the date of the flight from 29 April to 23 April, St. George's day. See 1.579n.

1070] *Belongings . . . own* Pompilia was accused of taking valuables from a locked writing desk which she opened with a key taken from Guido's breeches. She maintained that what she took was her own property.

1075] *unembarrassed as a fate* Unhesitating, undeviating. A reference to the Three Fates, or Parcae, who were called cruel because in their arbitrary control over life and death they were indifferent to human desires.

1083] *convoy* Escort.

1093-95] *servant . . . woman-spy* Maria Margherita Contenti, a servant in the Franceschini household.

1103] *The woman's . . . word* The court did in fact rule that Maria's immorality disqualified her testimony.

1135] *red daybreak* Pompilia stuck to this story in spite of all evidence and testimony to the contrary that the fleeing couple arrived at the inn at sunset. B accepted the proffered explanation that in her state of extreme fatigue she was not unreasonably confused.

1158] *sword . . . felon* Although Pompilia claims that she took Guido's sword, the record itself merely says "a sword." See 2.1023n.

1181] *Confirm . . . one* There are in fact a number of discrepancies between the two stories, chiefly having to do with the passage of letters (which Pompilia denies) between them, and with the arrangements for the flight.

1220] *perfect* Complete.

1223] *guardian angel* There are numerous examples in the Bible of angels having care of the physical safety of the faithful; Jesus said of children, "in heaven their angels do always behold the face of my Father which is in heaven" (Matt. 18:10). Pompilia's fatigue and the consequent stop before reaching the safety of the separate jurisdiction of Rome, is explained here as a lapse of vigilance on the part of her guardian angel, perhaps in order once more to emphasize Guido's Satanic role.

1245] *Body . . . hell* "And fear not them which kill the body, but . . . rather fear him which is able to destroy both soul and body in hell" (Matt. 10:28).

1253] *secular costume* That Caponsacchi had discarded clerical for secular clothes was sufficient to create suspicion about his motives, a suspicion heightened by the fact that he carried a sword.

1268] *accoutred* Outfitted; used especially of military equipage.

1294-96] *restif . . . cup* Guido places himself in the dual role of merciful protector of Pompilia and of the poor man who falls victim to the rich one. "But the poor man had nothing, save one little ewe lamb, . . . it did eat of his own meat, and drank of his own cup, and lay in his bosom, and was unto him as a daughter. And there came a traveller unto the rich man, and he . . . took the poor man's lamb, and dressed it for the man that was come to him" (2 Sam. 12:3-4). *Froward*: disobedient; *restif*: stubborn.

1310] *One letter* The letter to Paolo. See 2.678n.

1316] *mouse-birth . . . revenge* Horace took his famous line, *Parturient montes, nascetur ridiculus mus* (The mountains will labor, a silly mouse will be born) from a Greek proverb (Horace, *Ars Poetica,* 139).

1326] *purple* See 3.375n.

1360] *unlidded . . . aware* "For his eyes are upon the ways of man, and he seeth all his goings" (Job 34:21). "Behold, he that keepeth Israel shall neither slumber nor sleep" (Ps. 121:4).

1377-79] *leprosy . . . purified* A figure derived from Lev. 13:45-58.

1389] *To . . . known* "Let your moderation be known unto all men" (Philippians 4:5).

1397] *stomach* To take offence, feel resentment. Obsolete (*OED*).

1403] *unshent, unshamed* Unpunished, unpenitent.

1405] *not imprisoned, Sirs* Relegation was banishment to a particular place for a specified period of time, but unlike imprisonment, did not carry loss of civil rights. Gest, however, insists that under Roman law imprisonment was not customary, and relegation as a penalty came next to loss of citizenship in severity (Gest, 68-69).

1407] *Civita* See 2.1171n.

1418] *breathed* Refreshed.

1440-43] *last . . . trice* The last story in *A.C. Mery Talys* (anonymous), printed by John Rastell in November 1526, concerned a widow who mourned her husband so sorely that she had a wooden effigy made,

with which she slept. One night an apprentice arranged to take the place of the dummy, and in the morning the widow gave her maid the effigy to make a fire to cook his breakfast. *Clerk* probably means cleric here.
1444-49] *Vulcan's . . . Mars*!" Venus was the wife of Vulcan, who because of Venus's affair with Mars came to be the patron of cuckolds. The story is told in the *Odyssey* 8.266-366. The *net* refers to the ingenious mechanism devised by Vulcan to catch the lovers in bed. The sentiment here attributed to Mercury was expressed in the original by Apollo to Mercury, who heartily agrees.
1461-62] *House . . . Pillar-like* An ironic likeness of Paolo to Samson (Judg. 16:25-30).
1468] *regular . . . incompetence* The First Anonymous Pamphlet says that the prolongation of the trial was sufficient motive for Paolo to appeal the case to the Pope.
1469] *nephews* See 1.315, 319n.
1471] *"Render . . . due*!" "Render therefore unto Caesar the things which are Caesar's; and unto God the things that are God's" (Matt. 22:23). The Pope's answer to Paolo's appeal implies the same as Jesus' answer to the scheming Pharisee: the separation of worldly and divine law.
1474] *divorce* Guido did not apparently seek divorce after the judgment of the Process of Flight (see *Chronology*).
1481] *the blow* Pompilia's baby. Perhaps a pun; the child may be a bastard, a "bye-blow," as in 4.609.
1482-83] *play . . . stage* B puns on *play*; the stage is the scaffold on which Guido will die, and *mannaia* is the Italian guillotine.
1485] *Months* Pompilia was actually at La Scalette for only two or three weeks.
1492] *doit by doit* See 3.498n.
1501] *Pauline way* See 1.389n.
1508] *Domus pro carcere* See 2.1333n.
1512] *He authorized* Guido's lawyers denied this.
1533-34] *"I . . . Paulo* There is no record of this letter, although Paolo did leave Rome at this time.
1535] *winch . . . hate* "he treadeth the winepress of the fierceness and wrath of Almighty God" (Rev. 19:15).
1539] *heir's birth* Perhaps a pun on *hair's breadth.*
1545-46] *her . . . his* Presumably Guido postponed the murder until the birth of the baby out of this motive.
1560] *done . . . undone* Echoing the "General Confession" of the *Book of Common Prayer*: "We have left undone those things which we ought to have done. . . . "

1569-70] *spark . . . soul* "And the Lord God formed man of the dust of the ground, and breathed into his nostrils the breath of life; and man became a living soul" (Gen. 2:7).
1576] *Christmas-Eve* Pompilia's son was born on Wednesday, 18 Dec. 1897, and Guido and his accomplices arrived in Rome on Tuesday, 24 Dec.
1577-78] *vacancy . . . Paolo* Paolo's villa was two mi. N of Rome by the Ponte Milvio.
1580] *whole week* The murders took place on 2 Jan. 1898. There is no satisfactory explanation of this delay, after Guido's initial haste to leave Arezzo.
1585] *"Good . . . man"* Luke 2:14.
1587] *finger-wise* A literal translation of the French *à tâtons* and Italian *tastone*, both idioms meaning carefully, tentatively.
1589] *lone . . . villa* See 1.389n.
1616] *confess myself* To die unshriven, without confession and absolution, was to deny the soul entry into heaven.
1621] *ticket* The pass to obtain horses and to cross the Tuscan frontier. Lacking this the murderers could not leave by the main road.
1626] *Baccano* The fugitives actually went as far as Merluccia, which is about 15 mi. from Rome and 2Î mi. short of Baccano. Merluccia is on a direct route to Arezzo, but the road was not in good condition.
1628] *grange* Farm. The murderers were in fact arrested at an inn.
1661] *three in play* The countersuit against the Comparini on the issue of the dowry, Pompilia's suit for divorce, and a suit against Pompilia on the issue of the flight.

Book 4, Tertium Quid

Tertium Quid Literally, a third thing; in logic, that which is not accounted for by either or both of the major arguments in an analysis. Tertium Quid's testimony, avoiding as it does extremes on either side of the case, fits this description. The title, with its suggestion of anonymity, also fits the character, who has no real title himself and who is acutely conscious of being on the one hand superior to "reasonless unreasoning Rome" and on the other subordinate to his chosen audience, which includes a Cardinal and a Marquis.
10] *brabble* "Discordant babble" (*OED*).
15-16] *machine . . . descend* A reference to the expression *deus ex machina* (god from a machine), which was the practice in ancient Greek

theatre of lowering a divinity by means of a crane onto the stage to resolve complications which seemed beyond solution by natural or human means. There may be an ironic side reference here to law's final resort to that other decisive "engine," the guillotine *mannaia.*

23] *three years ago* When Pietro entered the first suit in the summer of 1694 for the recovery of the dowry.

26] *tort, retort* Claim of a breach of legal right anwered by an accusation of like injury.

28] *deed of death* In the double sense of decisive legal disposition, and active move in a game of words.

31] *'Trecentos . . . appelle!'* The lines are from Horace, *Satires* 1.5.12-13; they dramatize the confusion and noise as a crowd of people (among them Horace and servants) press on board a canal boat at a stop along its way. In the original, *Huc appelle!* (Put in here!) is the first of the three cries, which are spoken by different people on shore or in the boat. "Put in here!" call the people on shore. "You're taking in three hundred: hey, that's enough now!" protest those on board.

42] *Eusebius* Ecclesiastical historian, c. 264-349, given credit for scrupulous documentation.

42] *fig's end* The word *fig* is commonly used for something trifling or worthless; a *fig's end* suggests value still more diminished.

44-46] *leash . . . Spreti* A leash of animals was generally a set of three. The distinction between Arcangeli and Spreti, respectively the Procurator and Advocate of the Poor, was merely nominal. Theoretically, a Procurator was concerned more with the facts of a case, an Advocate with the law, but in practice the division of labor does not seem to have applied. B's distinction between the bark of one lawyer and the bite of the other may concern the jealousy felt by the other lawyers toward the more youthful, up-and-coming Spreti (as B represents him).

47] *Fisc . . . Fisc* See 1.160n.

54] *basset-table* A table designed for the game of basset, which resembles faro and involves betting on cards against a banker.

55] *Her Eminence* The word *eminenza* (eminence) is a feminine noun in Italian. Tertium Quid translates the Cardinal's title *Sua Eminenza* with scrupulous literalness, but in effect his scrupulosity, like his vaunted objectivity, is an absurd affectation.

65] *burgess-life* See 3.422n.

75] *fifty and over* See 2.571n.

87] *cresset, mudlarks* Mudlarks are urchins, gutter-children. A cresset is an iron vessel in which grease was burned for light.

97] *Pietro . . . debt* According to witnesses in the records Pietro was short of money both in 1680 and in 1693, the years of Pompilia's birth and of her marriage (see 2.255n.). But Pietro's will, made in 1695, shows him to be very well off at that time.

111] *"poor . . . ones"* There were throughout Italy provision for the assistance of *poveri vergognosi*, "shame-faced poor"; poor people who were of good birth or who had lost their money.

114-15] *meat . . . providence* "Who provideth for the raven his food? when his young ones cry unto God, they wander for lack of meat" (Job 38:41).

134-35] *tenure . . . commissum* The term *fides commissum* means "entrusted to faith." In Roman law the phrase refers to a transfer of goods or money by a legatee to a third person, according to a will.

143] *frittered* Shredded.

146] *house-book* Household account book.

147] *vespers* Evening prayers.

147] *missal* Book containing the service of the mass. Violante's missal is an absurd cover-up for her errand; there is no reason to take a missal to vespers, let alone to the house of ill-repute to which she is going.

148] *proper* In the archaic sense of "belonging to the particular parish."

170] *Citorio* The Piazza di Monte Citorio is slightly S of San Lorenzo Church and, like the church, on the W side of the Corso.

179] *propitious shape* Violante was actually put in touch with Pompilia's mother through a midwife (Corrigan, 27). In any case the woman's shape was hardly "propitious" yet, although there is some disagreement among the narrators of *The Ring and the Book* as to Pompilia's mother's degree of pregnancy: Half-Rome says the meeting was "eight months before" the child's birth (2.565), but Tertium Quid says the child was to be born "six months hence" from the meeting (4.187).

184] *three pauls* A sum equal to about fifteen pence in the money of B's time. See 1.320n.

195-99] *"Magnificat" . . . praise* "Thus hath the lord dealt with me . . . to take away my reproach among men" were the words of Elizabeth when she conceived John the Baptist (Luke 1:25). The Magnificat refers to Mary's words, "My soul doth magnify the Lord . . . for, behold, from henceforth all generations shall call me blessed" (Luke 1:46, 48). The Magnificat is part of the service of Vespers. Violante's obstreperous praise is a conflation of the two songs.

202] *orisons* Prayers.

203] *pair . . . coif* A tight fitting cap with two large side flaps.

206] *Orvieto* A white wine named for the town near which it is made.

213-14] *rest . . . day* The custom was to baptize an infant within 48 hours after birth; Pompilia was, according to records, born on 17 July and baptized 23 July. She had five given names, of which Pompilia was the last (see 7.5-7 and 2.54n).

217] *nature . . . mode* Nature, law, and custom: a full catalogue.

241] *silly-sooth* Unsuspecting.

244] *saved sin* A kind of pun. The sin is unsaved, unpurged, but it is saved up, hoarded, and weighed against the many "virtues" which might serve to equal penance.

259] *Graces . . . Greek* The three Greek sister goddesses who governed pleasure, charm, and beauty. Their images often embellished vases or ornaments; thus the sapphire, a natural object, found in the dirt has been enhanced by its new setting, as Pompilia herself was.

270] *havings and holdings* See 3.505n.

306] *exact* Exacting.

322] *Lily-like . . . spouse* Strange natural phenomena in Christian folklore, such as flowers springing up in the path of Mary and Joseph on their way to Egypt, have been a favorite subject for painters of religious subjects. The Madonna lily in particular was said to be yellow until touched by the Virgin.

327-28] *Solomon's . . . lion* Solomon's throne was flanked by lions (1 Kings 10:19-20) and stood upon a "porch of judgment" (7:7). Many of the pillars in Solomon's palace were ornamented by lilies, as was the brim of his "molten sea" of brass (7:19, 22, 23, 26), but B's reference here may be to Matthew 6:28-30, "Consider the lilies of the field. . . . even Solomon in all his glory was not arrayed like one of these."

337] *"Nunc dimittis"* The opening words of the Latin version of the Song of Simeon, "Nunc dimittis servum tuum, Domine" (Lord, now lettest thou thy servant depart in peace [Luke 2:29]). The Nunc Dimittis is sung at Compline in the Roman Catholic church and the words have become proverbial for a reverent, contented leave taking. See 1.156 and 2.127 for an ironic use of the reference.

340] *cits* The abbreviation of *citizens* is contemptuous.

358] *'scutcheoned* Bearing a coat of arms.

361] *chaffering* Dickering.

376] *Rafael* That is, a painting by Rafael (Raffaello Sanzio, or Raphael), Italian painter, 1483-1520.

381] *many . . . mouths* Three; Guido's, his mother's, and his brother Girolamo's. If the youngest brother, Antonio Maria, were still at home, he would make four, but there is no mention of him in the OYB.

384] *sisters* There was actually only one sister, Porzia. She was married to a Count Conti of Arezzo, brother of the Canon Conti who first brought Caponsacchi and Pompilia together.

390] *second son* See 2.289n.

394] *a personage* Cardinal Lauria; see 2.153-55n.

395] *youngest* See 2.289n.

402] *Order or two* See 1.257n.

403-4] *clipped . . . Christ* Guido *affected* Christ by wearing the clerical tonsure, the fringe of hair left around a shaved crown of the head, symbolizing the crown of thorns worn by Christ on the way to Calvary.

408] *forty-six years'* See 2.769n.

410] *he . . . Cardinal* See 2.153-55n.

417] *chafe* Impatience.

421-22] *purple . . . mine* Cardinal Nerli was from a Tuscan family and had been Archbishop of Florence, but Guido's father, although head of an ancient and noble family, died so impoverished that his sons renounced claim to his estate in order to escape creditors (Corrigan, xxii). He probably never enjoyed the deference Guido claims for him.

429-33] *cards . . . Honours* The passage uses several technical terms from the game of whist. *Honours* are face cards, and "to make game" is to achieve a specified score.

436] *Notum . . . Tonsor* A tonsor is a barber. See 2.114n.

441] *Place Colonna* A large Piazza about midway down the Corso.

447] *Twenty zecchines* See 1.324n. A zecchine was a Venetian gold coin worth about ten shillings in the currency of B's time.

455] *patch* A small round piece of black silk or adhesive applied to the face or neck in order to heighten by contrast the fairness of a complexion.

456] *pomander* The word means "apple of amber" (ambergris); thus, perfumed ball made of or containing some medicinal substance. Pomanders were sometimes carried to ward off infection and were also sold as a panacea for complexions. *Freckle* can mean any spot or discoloration of the skin.

459] *pantoufle* Slipper.

469] *Her Efficacity* See 4.55n.

504] *clapnet* A kind of snare which can be quickly closed by pulling a string.

513] *truck* Barter.

523] *Money for money* Guido represented to Pietro that he had a fixed income, though he did not.

529] *traffic* Commerce.

565] *five months* The Comparini were at Arezzo from early December 1693 to April 1694.

582] *bye-circumstance* Incidental consideration, since what Violante chiefly bargained for was his station.

584] *heaven's . . . ope* "Bring ye all the tithes into the storehouse, . . . and prove me now herewith, saith the Lord of hosts, if I will not open you the windows of heaven, and pour you out a blessing" (Mal. 3:10).

597] *round* B seems to use the word here in a sense combining "to be round with someone," to speak without consideration for feelings; and to reiterate, as in a musical round.

609] *bye-blow* Vernacular euphemism for an illegitimate child.

631] *fight . . . upon* The word *prize* originally meant match or contest. The phrase here has the sense of our prize-fight, a confrontation for high stakes publicly enacted.

638] *write . . . publish* See 2.652n.

653] *superfluity of naughtiness* "Wherefore lay apart all filthiness and superfluity of naughtiness" (James 1:21).

663] *four . . . earlier* Seven or eight months, actually. B places the marriage in December when in fact it was in September.

706] *Hymen* Roman god of marriage and attendant of Venus, whose star is the morning star.

716] *parade-ground* Apparently in the sense of home territory, where a captive might be put on public display or parade.

723] *interspersion* Intermingling or mixture.

725] *devil's dung* A folk name for the gum-like substance asafoetida, which has a strong foul smell akin to onions and garlic.

727] *shake all slab* Mix semi-solid, with the implication of something tangible concocted from imaginary and magical ingredients.

731] *bedevilled* Spiced, and cursed.

750-51] *Aretine . . . wit* A number of famous names are associated with the town or district of Arezzo, among them the poet Petrarch, the musician and music theorist Guido d'Arezzo, the painter Michelangelo, and the art historian Giorgio Vasari. Vasari quotes Michelangelo's words to him, "Giorgio, if I have anything good in me, that comes from my birth in the pure air of your country of Arezzo" (Vasari, 4, 109).

756] *try . . . quarter-staff* To try cross-buttock was to make a wrestling move. A quarter staff was a pole tipped with iron, six to eight feet long, used as a weapon by peasants, which could be whirled about either to attack or to ward off attack.

764] *famous letter* See 2.678n.

785] *Circumvallated* Surrounded by ramparts, as for defense.

793] *Commissary* The Governor; see 3.965-66n.

795] *thrice* See 3.999n.

803] *certain friar* See 3.1013n.

828] *Uzzah* Uzzah, an ordinary man, steadied the ark containing the ten commandments when it rocked on Nachon's threshing floor, and was struck dead for touching it (2 Sam. 6:6-7). See 1.192n.

830] *In . . . souls* "In your patience possess ye your souls" was Jesus' counsel to the disciples in adversity (Luke 21:19).

831] *This . . . it* The burden of this observation derives from Job 14:1: "Man that is born of woman is of few days, and full of trouble."

834] *Ave . . . intention* Ave Maria (Hail Mary) for her sake.

849] *serpent . . . eat* Gen. 3:13.

858] *Ætna* An active volcano in Sicily.

868] *cap* To take off cap; *cap to* is regular usage when the verb is used intransitively in this sense.

870] *converse* Sexual intercourse.

881] *Lucretia and Susanna* Both were virtuous wives who were falsely accused of adultery. The story of the rape of Lucretia is told by Livy (Titus Livius) in his *History of Rome*, 1.57-58. Susanna was cleared by Daniel of two church elders' accusation of adultery; her story is told in the Book of Susannah in the Apocrypha.

882-83] *Correggio . . . Leda* Correggio was one of several Renaissance painters to depict the seduction of Leda by Zeus in the guise of a swan. The original painting has been in the Berlin Museum since the mid-eighteenth century, but there are many copies of the work. The painting (now restored) was mutilated by Duke Louis of Orleans, who found it so erotically suggestive that he slashed out the head of Leda.

885] *Carnival* See 2.794n.

898] *piled-up fabric* The word *fabric* may have two functions here, as fabrication—the one-sided argument is overturned by the opposite point of view—and as material with a nap. A stroke against the nap can change the color and appearance of a material with a pile surface, such as velvet.

931] *He . . . word* See 3.851n.

949] *rubric . . . breviary* Direction printed, usually in red, in a liturgical book, for the conduct of a Divine service.

954] *lay-dress* See 2.991n.

959] *turbulence* Disorderly character.

960-62] *his . . . love* According to his deposition in the OYB Caponsacchi did not receive any love letters from Pompilia, only letters relating to the flight.

969-71] *Letters . . . side* In the deposition these letters were said to concern the flight.

1000] *truth . . . instinct* Possibly a glance at Falstaff's famous face-saving defense after the Gadshill robbery, when he claims to have recognized Prince Hal in disguise: "Instinct is a great matter. I was now a coward upon instinct" (*1 Henry IV* 2.4.272-73).

1008] *confidency* Intimate relationship.

1015] *hackney chair* A hired chair on wheels, drawn by a bearer (here Satan). Perhaps also a pun on hackneyed behavior; Guido is saying that there was nothing original or distinctive about this affair.
1019] *go-between* See 3.1093-95n.
1046] *Hers . . . burnt* Pompilia says in her deposition in the OYB that she received no letters. In her monologue she says that Maria brought them to her (7.1139).
1048] *Cui profuerint* "To whom was the profit?" A version of *Cui bono*, a principle of the search for motive in Roman trial procedure.
1059] *embassies* Go-betweens.
1063] *silent . . . stilling* The word *acquetta* refers to *acqua tofana*, a liquid once used with frequency by Italian poisoners. *Stilling* is a pun, meaning both "distilling," and "making still, silencing."
1085-87] *Being . . . arms* The word *stock* refers both to Guido's blood line, and to the trunk of a tree; *arms* also has a double sense. (The American usage of *graft* as "bribery" is a post-B coinage and does not apply here). A coward's arms are any methods short of real weapons, and in Guido's case a coward's arms are an appeal to possession of a noble escutcheon. Guido's coat of arms was a tree with a greyhound tied to it, described and interpreted by him in 11.2154-59, where he himself says the greyhound signifies swiftness and greed.
1088] *chicane* Chicanery, legal subterfuge.
1107] *Her Excellency* See 4.55n.
1115] *And . . . Rome* According to the OYB Guido did ask that the fugitives be sent to Rome, but this is the only place in the poem where it is so represented; elsewhere it is Caponsacchi who appealed to Rome.
1137] *Paphos* The city in Cyprus where Venus, goddess of love, was worshipped. The rites were often sensual and licentious, and *Paphian* became a synonym for *prostitute*.
1138] *stews* Brothels, from the slang for public steam rooms or hot baths, which gave rise to or made excuse for immoral conduct.
1140] *stock-fish* Dried cod, "so called from its hardness" (Johnson's *Dictionary*).
1149] *serge* A durable twill fabric from which clerical garments were made.
1151] *tickle . . . touch* Sensitive; easily roused.
1169] *taste of poppy* Guido had been drugged with an opiate.
1179] *try conclusions* Propose judgments with all the evidence at hand.
1181] *squib* A harmless, sputtering firework, in contrast to *lightning*.
1201] *"Well . . . servant!"* Spoken in the parable of the talents to the servant who had invested and increased his talents (Matt. 25:21).

1214] *goat or sheep* "He shall set the sheep on his right hand, but the goats on the left" (Matt. 15:33).
1220] *scour* Range about, especially against a foe; move hastily.
1225] *mulct* Fine or penalty.
1226] *pupilage* Minority, state of being a pupil.
1228-29] *Saint . . . Olimpia* A saint and a sinner. There are more than one St. Rose, and quite a number of saints who have roses as their emblem, including the Virgin Mary. The first roses, according to medieval legend, appeared after the martyrdom of a maiden at Bethlehem; after her prayer the fire was quenched and the stake bloomed with red and white roses. Donna Olimpia Pamfili was sister-in-law to Pope Innocent X (papal reign 1644-55); she infatuated him and openly exploited him.
1234] *House of Convertites* See 2.1189-90n.
1264] *heading, hanging* See 1.124n.
1268-69] *wisdom . . . light* In the parable of the unjust steward, the steward falsifies his lord's accounts in order to ingratiate himself with the lord's debtors. "And the lord commended the unjust steward, because he had done wisely: for the children of this world are in their generation wiser than the children of light" (Luke 16:8). The parable is enigmatic, and the courts' just and equal apportionment of guilt and penalties to both sides in the abduction and dowry suits—in the name of the children of light and the golden mean—is similarly ironic.
1274] *Place Navona* The largest of Roman piazzas, a center for markets and shows.
1275-89] *Punch . . . tail* The internationally popular Punch and Judy story appeared first in Italy about 1600. In the puppet show Punch first strangles his infant, then after his wife attacks him beats her to death too. He escapes from prison and eventually triumphs in allegorical fashion over Ennui (a dog), Disease (a doctor), Death, and the Devil.
1297] *suits* See *Chronology*. Perhaps also a pun referring to "what novel rag-and-feather trim / Best suits the next adventure" (1279-80) and to "t'other tatter" (1284)—the costumes of the Punch and Judy figures.
1303-8] *Rota, Molinès . . . Tommati* The Rota was the highest ecclesiastical court. The first hearing was actually before Tommati, the appeal before Molinès (who had no connection with the Molinos of Molinism).
1314] *Vicegerent* Vicegovernor.
1315-19] *Third . . . cause* The murder case. Venturini was indeed the judge in the suit for divorce and in the murder case. But the divorce case, cited here as second, was actually the third in order of entry.
1326] *made . . . Pope* See 3.1468n.

1336] *abominable thing* God sent word to the Jews in Egypt who were burning incense to strange gods, "Oh, do not this abominable thing that I hate" (Jer. 44:4).
1339] *pregnant with impunity* A heavily ironic joke.
1348-49] *Paolo . . . Vanished* He went to Spain, finally, where he effectively turned his powers of intrigue to obtaining himself a pension.
1352] *Vittiano* See 2.808n.
1361] *Paolina* See 1.389n.
1363] *one . . . evening* Around seven o'clock, or one hour after the saying of the Angelus at the close of the day.
1375] *lightnings in her brake* Places where the light broke through a thicket. Ordinarily a brake is a refuge, but here it has become a trap.
1387] *Public Force* Police.
1390] *Baccano* See 3.1626n.
1400-1402] *Patrizj . . . died* The Captain is said in the Secondary Source to have died from being slightly wounded and much overheated in the chase.
1404] *chafe* Passion (archaic usage).
1445] *old Religious* Fra Celestino.
1470-75] *Confession . . . public one* The doctrine that *casuists teach* is "the art or science of bringing general moral principles to bear upon particular cases" (*Oxford Dictionary of the Christian Church*). The sense of *casuist* here as one who defends the divergence between individual moral decision and established practice is a perversion of the original sense of casuistry as harmony between private and public intention. Debate over competitive systems of casuistry was heated in the latter part of the seventeenth century, although the issues go back much earlier to the acceptance in the Roman Catholic Church of private penance (or *penitence*) after confession. The argument here of Pompilia's private confession and recantation of an earlier public denial of guilt would be an extreme example and an abuse of the casuist branch of moral theology.
1476] *trench on* Encroach on.
1477] *Her Eminence* See 4.55n.
1487] *apposed* Applied.
1490] *anotherguess* From *anothergates,* meaning of another kind.
1501-5] *sentence . . . jurisdiction* The Governor of Arezzo gave the opinion that Pompilia should be confined to prison for life, but since she was already in confinement in Rome the Court at Florence suspended the execution of the sentence. In any case it could not have been enforced as long as Pompilia was out of Tuscany. See *Sources* and map for jurisdiction of Italian states.

1508] *The Stinche* Prison in Florence.
1567-68] *fons . . . Malorum* Fountain and origin of the evils.
1599-1600] *Cardinal . . . future* Questionable; see 2.153n.
1621] *reduction ad absurdum* Reduction to the absurd. In logic *reductio ad absurdum* means the extension of an argument to the point where the original proposition is shown to be patently wrong. The line and the Latin tag seem to refer to Tertium Quid himself here, judging by the response of his audience.
1622-24] *Her . . . Highness* See 4.55n.